PHYSICIAN ASST. SCHOOL PROFILES

P.A. School
Admissions Data and Analysis

Rachel A. Winston, Ph.D.

ISBN 978-1946432490 (hardback); 978-1946432483 (paperback); 978-1946432506 (e-book);

LCCN: 2021924177

Lizard Publishing® 7700 Irvine Center Drive, Suite 800 Irvine, CA 92618 *www.lizard-publishing.com*

Lizard Publishing creates, designs, produces, and distributes books and resources to provide academic, admissions, and career information. Our mental process is fueled by three tenets:

- Ignite the hunger to learn and the passion to make a difference
- Illuminate the expanse of knowledge by sharing cutting edge thinking
- Innovate to create a world that makes the transition from dreams to reality

We work with academic leaders who transform the educational landscape to publish relevant content and advise students of their educational and professional options, with the aim of developing 21st-century learners and leaders. We also work with students to publish their books and present widely diverse ideas to the college/graduate school-bound community. With headquarters in Irvine, California, Lizard Publishing works virtually with authors to edit, publish, and distribute both hard copy and paperback books.

This book was published in the U.S.A. Lizard Publishing is a premium quality provider of educational reference, career guidance, and motivational publications/merchandise for global learners, educators, and stakeholders in education.

Book design by Michelle Tahan *www.michelletahan.com*

Book formatting by Obinna Chinemerem Ozuo

Book website: *www.medschoolexpert.com*

LIZARD PUBLISHING

This book is dedicated to students who seek to become patient-centered physicians and are passionately devoted to their pursuit of compassionate, ethical, and service-oriented medicine. This book was inspired by Zenobia Miro, Ida Ramezani, and Nadia Aluzri.

Working at hospitals and conducting research in neurobiochemistry at Upstate Medical School and genetics at Syracuse University, I was surrounded by pre-med hopeful students eagerly pursuing their medical career. Subsequently, I spent most of my life helping students gain admission to medical school and working with authors who wrote books on medical school admission and MCAT prep.

Surrounded by students and teaching college for thirty-five years provided a keen insight into the student pursuit. I have also completed more than a dozen degrees and certificates and know the challenge and rigor of meshing rigorous coursework with a full complement of activities. Supporting students in their quest to attend medical school further inspired me to continuously adapt to changes in medical school admissions as well as investigate the broader picture of cutting-edge medical research.

ACKNOWLEDGMENTS

There is never enough room to acknowledge every person. Many people contributed to my perspective about medicine, assisted in the development of my knowledge base, or taught me indelible lessons. In a lifetime of experiences working with students, I am wiser and more worldly.

I gratefully acknowledge Michelle Tahan, Jasmine Jhunjhnuwala, and E. Liz Kim, as well as my family, friends, colleagues, and professors. It is with profound gratitude that I mention and acknowledge the many physicians I have known.

As a faculty member in the UCLA College Counseling Certificate Program, I met numerous dedicated counselors who spend their life serving and supporting students. Meaningful contributions to the book have been made indirectly by admissions representatives, college counselors, faculty members who took a special interest in this book's success.

I would also like to thank the thousands of students I have taught, counseled, or supported in my nearly four decades of service.

Isaac Newton once said, "If I see so far, it is because I stand on the shoulders of giants."

> *"If I see so far, it is because I stand on the shoulders of giants."*
> *— Isaac Newton*

A few of those giants whose broad shoulders lifted me higher and helped teach invaluable lessons include: David Waugh, Harrison White, Dania Baseel, Hyojung Lee, Maya Abdulridha, Miriam Bargout, Casey Duan, Taya Salman, Sean Wong, Patrick Bayeh, Nayer Toma, Tarika Gujral, Ryan Johnson, and Sabrina Wang.

Finally, there would be no book on programs for physician assistants and no career college admissions counseling, without the support of Robert Helmer whose tireless efforts support me every single day.

ABOUT THE AUTHOR

Dr. Rachel A. Winston is a tireless student advocate. She has served the educational community as a university professor, college advisor, statistician, researcher, author, cryptanalyst, motivational speaker, publishing executive, and lifelong student. As one of the leading experts in college counseling and an award-winning faculty member, Dr. Winston has spent her lifetime learning, teaching, mentoring, and coaching students. Much of her counseling practice is focused on admissions to medical, dental, vet, and engineering schools.

She started college at thirteen and graduated from college programs in such widely ranging disciplines as chemistry, mathematics, computers, liberal arts, international relations, negotiation, conflict resolution, peacebuilding, business administration, higher education leadership, interpreting, college counseling, and publishing. Throughout her education, she attended Harvard, UChicago, NYU, GWU, Syracuse, Maryland, UCLA, UCI, CSUF, CSUDH, Cal Poly, ASU, Claremont Graduate University, Pepperdine, and USC among other colleges.

Her position working in Washington, D.C. on Capitol Hill and with the White House in the 1980s took her to approximately a hundred universities training campaign managers at colleges from Colorado to California, thoroughly dotting the western states. Later, she led college tours with students and their families on road trips throughout the United States. She has taught or counseled thousands of students over her career and speaks at conferences and academic programs throughout the world.

As a professor and avid writer for numerous publications, she won the 2012 McFarland Literary Achievement Award, Bletchley Park Cryptanalyst Award, and numerous other awards, including Faculty Member of the Year, Leadership Tomorrow Leader of the Year, and college service and leadership awards. While studying Human Capital at Claremont Graduate University, she was a scholarship recipient at the Drucker School of Management. She was also elected to the statewide Board of Governors for the Faculty Association for California Community Colleges, where she served on their executive committee.

She served as a faculty member for the UCLA College Counselor Certificate Program, the Director of Mathematics at Brandman University, and Embry Riddle Aeronautical University, Chapman University, Cal State Fullerton, and a handful of California Community Colleges, including Cerro Coso College where she also served as the Academic Senate President and retired in 2016. Over her career, she taught mathematics online, on television, live interactive satellite, telecourses, and in large and small lecture halls.

AUTHORS' NOTE

You are reading this book because you are considering admission to a physician assistant program. Whatever route you took to get to this point, you are in the right place. Right now, you need to gather information to make informed decisions.

While many people offer advice, suggestions differ. Friends will tell you the 'right' way or the way their neighbor was accepted. Graciously accept this anecdotal information while you commit to learning more. This opportunity to pursue medicine is your future.

Dig deeper to consider both expert and current information from counselors who have worked with hundreds of students. Changes in programs, curricula, requirements, and links happen each year.

Double-check each program's specifics yourself. This guide is current as of September 2021, with each school's profile information. However, since researching this book, changes may have taken place. There are other books about physician assistant programs written by talented and experienced counselors. We admire and cheer on their efforts.

> *"We are what we think. All that we are arises with our thoughts. With our thoughts, we make the world."*
> — *Buddha*

This set of profiles and lists is different in that it also provides and unique tidbits. We hope you find this information valuable. Your job is to begin early by assembling information for the schools you are considering. Create a road map and set yourself on a clear path.

If you see an error in this book or even a suggestion for a future edition, please write to Rachel Winston at collegeguide@yahoo.com. We will fix the entry with the next printed version. All of that said, this book was written for you in mind.

There is a wealth of information on the Internet with free downloads, FAQs, testimonials, and offers to help you with your applications. Some of these advisors are knowledgeable and could help you. Students and parents hunt around the web, searching for a tremendous number of hours to seek the information they need.

This book of profiles was designed to make your search easier. For now, though, we will assume that you are reasonably confident that you want to attend physician assistant school and are exploring this avenue as a possible way to take advantage of a program that will get you on your way toward your goal.

We assume that you are a highly academic candidate who is willing to work very hard. You may be fascinated with the human body, human physiology, or holistic health. Selflessly serving others is virtually a prerequisite for physician assistant programs. This book will help you get to your goal. Applying to physician assistant schools and writing essays for each program will require a persistent effort. Research the schools that are the best fit for your future goals.

While you might believe that physician assistant school programs are relatively similar, each program's nuances make them very different. These small differences may seem confusing. My goal with this book is to demystify this information and your application process.

CONTENTS

CHAPTER 1

INTRODUCTION TO PHYSICIAN ASSISTANT PROGRAMS

INTRODUCTION

On becoming a Physician Assistant you will enter a stable field of service with decent pay, growing opportunities, job security, and a promising future. Whether you are fascinated by the brain, lungs, heart, kidneys, skin, reproductive organs, or circulatory system, PA school covers the whole arena of human biology. In addition, PAs are experts in healthcare, patient support, and general medicine. Your comprehensive study of chemistry, biology, environmental science, psychology, and socioeconomics offers diverse skills and directions as you pursue becoming a physician assistant.

You gain specialized knowledge. With your expertise, patients rely on you for your opinion. Physicians are essential to the medical ecosystem, playing a key role in meeting with, assessing, diagnosing, and treating patients. Over the course of your studies, you will listen to lectures regarding a wide range of diseases and procedures, know cutting-edge medicines and clinical trials, and be aware of new techniques and procedures to stop the spread of diseases and improve a patient's quality of life.

With 292 PA schools, there are many schools from which you can choose. According to the Bureau of Labor Statistics, from 2020 to 2030, PA employment will increase by 31 percent. The growth is remarkable and excellent for anyone going into this field. The median wage for PAs is $115,390.[1] Therefore, due to the increasing need for PAs, it is unlikely that you will have a difficult time getting a job.

WHY CHOOSE A CAREER IN PHYSICIAN ASSISTANT?

A student recently asked me, "Why would anyone want to attend a PA school?" I think the inference was why a person would choose to attend a school to become a Physician Assistant rather than go to medical school. Especially since the acceptance rates at some schools are fairly low, why spend three years to get a master's degree when you could spend four and get an MD or DO? You will also be required to complete 2,000 hours of clinical experience.

There are many reasons. Few high school students set on a path when they leave for college to become a Physician Assistant. However, several factors may come into play during college. First, the competition for medical school (MD or DO) is tough. Second, it takes significantly longer to complete medical school through residency. Third, friends who have applied to medical school twice and have not gotten accepted weigh heavily, especially knowing that many students take gap years, complete post-bacc programs, and conduct research for a year or two before starting. Fourth, students may get a low grade in a course or two, which may have them searching for new options. Fifth, there is no MCAT, which can take significant time in preparation, though many schools require the GRE. Sixth, the realization that a career as a PA may be more rewarding for the lifestyle they seek.

Surprisingly, if difficulty to gain admission is a factor, note that the competition for entrance into Physician Assistant programs is high. For example, the following ten schools have acceptance rates of 2% to 7%. For these ten schools, you have about a one in thirty chance of admission. Certainly, there are other schools with a higher probability of admission, but these schools are some of the toughest.

Recent Acceptance Rates (2021)

1. Duke University - 2.2%
2. University of Iowa – ranked #1 among PA programs – 99% pass rate
3. Baylor College of Medicine – 2.3%
4. University of Utah – 2.3%

---

1   U.S. Bureau of Labor Statistics, "Employment Projections,"*U.S. Bureau of Labour Statistics,* 2020, https://www.bls.gov/emp/tables/occupational-projections-and-characteristics.htm

5. Emory University – 2.6%
6. George Washington University – 6%
7. University of Colorado – 2.1%
8. University of Texas Southwestern Medical Center - 4%
9. Wake Forest University - Winston Salem – 3.1%
10. Drexel University – 7%

Even so, for many students, pursuing medicine is a calling. Students feel as if they are passionately committed and want to help people through healthcare. Typically, the desire to study medicine is a combination of the love for science and a personal experience they had in life or tragic illness, pain, or death of a friend or family member. On the other hand, the student-applicant may have witnessed someone they did not know suffer from challenge with a disease, disorder, or pain. Occasionally, this event happens in childhood. While it is never too late to begin this journey, there are numerous prerequisites required and more than half know where they are headed when they begin college.

Nevertheless, while PA school is challenging and the time requirement is daunting, the profession is rewarding. You will directly impact a person's present and future, making a significant, direct impact on a family and community. From helping to bring a newborn to its first breaths to assisting in a surgical center, you will contribute to the world and become a colleague to those with similar goals and aspirations.

WHAT MAJOR SHOULD I CHOOSE?

One question students always ask is whether or not the choice of a major is more important than GPA and GRE scores. Actually, students can major in anything and attend medical school provided they complete the required courses for entrance. GPA and GRE scores are most important. I have had students get accepted to PA schools who majored in anthropology, political science, music, Spanish, and philosophy, while others major in chemistry, biology, engineering, and public health. Either way, they are in PA programs now.

The point is that if you are genuinely interested in the subject you are studying, you will be motivated to persist in the most demanding classes. When you are passionate about your classes you dive into the material with true appreciation and have numerous stories that allow you to reflect on the world and solidify your decision to serve communities, help patients and live your life as a physician assistant. Otherwise, you can get lost in the checklist approach to PA admissions – only going through the motions and not enjoying the journey along the way. Instead, know your why; take action on your how; invent your future.

Especially if you are majoring in a non-science subject, make sure that you have medical service, clinical experience, and community health experiences. You can shadow physicians and PAs. However, this passive experience, while illuminating, has little involvement. Serving as a scribe is more active while working as a medical assistant or EMT is immersive and invaluable in your preparation. International medical experiences also provide a valuable foundation.

Research aids in gaining awareness for medicine and its advances on the whole. The fine detail and continuous repetition of scientific work provide an appreciation for the field and the outcomes of science. Besides, furthering science by taking innovations one step further is beneficial to all of society. Getting published, presenting at conferences, and expanding the field are all noble goals.

One of the reasons why some students who major in a non-traditional subject have difficulties is that, with fewer science courses, a different mindset is needed to be re-oriented toward science as opposed to the orientation of, let's say, the analysis of literature.

With the ability to go back and forth between science and societal issues, medical schools get a student who can access more of the humanistic side of academia as well. Having a broader background and deeper connections to the world is invaluable for medicine. Besides, more well-rounded students with varied backgrounds add a different type of diversity to the school and contribute an engaging intellectual exchange between students.

Nearly all PA schools require a year of each of the following: Biology, General Chemistry, Organic Chemistry, Anatomy/Physiology. Most also require Biochemistry and Microbiology. Review the chart you create and work with your academic advisor to determine what classes you need and how they will fit into your college experience. In the end, your academic performance matters the most. Statistics, Psychology, Medical Terminology and other social sciences are helpful.

ADMISSION TO PHYSICIAN ASSISTANT PROGRAMS

You will need to complete the Centralized Application Service for Physician Assistants (CASPA). In this centralized application, you will add your personal information, medical experiences, college activities, transcript, personal statement, and other basic information. Supplemental essays are typically required. You may apply once per admission cycle. Some students are rejected and must apply again during the following year. If so, get cracking. There is much you can do to gain more medical experiences and improve your academic record, learning more so that you are more prepared.

Patient care experiences are essential. You will also want to gain certifications: CPR, AED, EMT, CMA, CAN, phlebotomy, etc. You want to shadow a physician or PA as well as participate in community service. You will have to write a personal statement about the direction you are pursuing and why you are intent on entering this field. GRE scores may be waived for one more year, but you will need to check each school for their requirements. I would take the test anyway. Letters of recommendation are required from medical professionals and professors to attest to your academic skills, cognitive ability, personality, and character. Finally, you will have an interview for those at the university to learn more about you, discover if you are a fit, and let you get to know a little more about them. All PA students must pass a background check and a drug screening test.

PHYSICIAN ASSISTANT SCHOOLS AND THE PANDEMIC

During the COVID-19 pandemic, life as we knew it changed. The public health crisis impacted colleges worldwide, including the way classes were taught, training for PA students, and undergraduate and graduate admissions. Admissions offices granted some flexibility to applicants throughout the process as local, state, and national requirements for masking, vaccines, distancing, and classroom access shifted with the winds.

As schools adapted, students and applicants adapted as well. Students attempted to take the GRE multiple times as test centers opened and closed. Research facilities did not allow lab assistants to work in the building, resulting in discussion-based journal clubs to suffice for laboratory experiences. Some attempted to gain work and volunteer experiences with limited success. Even getting letters of recommendation became difficult as professors refused to write letters for students they had never met in person.

Resilience cannot be understated. PA school applicants could not base their future on their past as the ground shifted underneath. With schools going test-optional, schools offering classes online, and volunteer opportunities shutting down, virtually all of the traditional requirements changed. Work experience is nearly a prerequisite to some PA schools. However, healthcare facilities had to adjust to patient needs and government regulations which often barred families of patients from entering and volunteers from assisting. Suddenly there was a 'new normal' with ever-changing rules.

Similarly, faculty needed to continue 'as usual' in transformed classroom environments that alternated from online and back to in-person as students, faculty, and staff depending upon COVID-19 results. Weekly and sometimes daily rapid COVID tests were administered. Meanwhile, classrooms filled with masked faces of socially distanced students managing their own challenges while complying with those of schools.

Admissions officers who presented at college fairs now discussed their schools virtually. Those representatives who traveled to colleges to meet with prospective students or gave tours on campus needed to find alternatives. Most interviews were conducted virtually, some with multiple interviewees in group interview days. Every participant in the PA admissions ecosystem needed to find new ways to reach out to student applicants and interview candidates.

One of the most interesting aspects taking hold at some schools was using artificial intelligence for the initial, computerized screening of applicants. In addition, a few PA schools did not meet their candidates virtually or in person, choosing students without an interview. While these changes may or may not stick, they are with us now at some schools and are likely to take root in the new normal of PA school admissions.

Pass/Fail Grades – Most PA schools accepted P/F grades for specific terms only. Check with each school.

Online Prerequisite Courses – Courses that transitioned to online during specific terms only will be counted. Otherwise, online courses may not be accepted for credit.

Standardized Tests – Some schools are test-optional, and some still require the GRE. The test does not need to be submitted with the initial application to allow students to find a convenient time to take the test.

With the uncertainty over the pandemic, admissions officers expressed concern about completing chemical laboratory classes online. Even so, many more applicants flocked to PA programs given the potential for growth in this exciting career.

PROFILES AND LISTS

The profiles and tables in this book include information available in the summer of 2021 for the fall of 2022. Outside of fee increases and new programs, changes in admission are unlikely to be significant through 2024 since many students who apply in 2024 were in college in 2020 and 2021, which the pandemic impacted coursework.

Notably, the demand for PA candidacy and the desire for students to pursue PA school varies from school to school. There are 277 programs at 292 locations in this book, which is comprehensive as of 2021. Given the number of schools and the importance of valuable information about schools, lists, and profiles, this book will prove extremely helpful to those wanting to make solid decisions.

With data about applicants, admitted students, and entering classes, along with tests, requirements, and contacts, you have the information here at your fingertips. The companion book to this profile book offers more specific information about PA school planning, GPA, eLOR, resumes, healthcare experiences, research, prerequisites, timelines, applications, essays, international programs, financial aid, and scholarships. PA school is the right place for you if you have a keen interest in anatomy and physiology, disease diagnostics, healthcare, and working directly with people.

The profiles are laid out by region with location markers in the general location of the school. Some of the PA schools are in more rural regions, while others are in cities. Wherever you work, you will find a career waiting for you when you graduate.

A FINAL NOTE

This book is a handy resource and was designed to be read in conjunction with my companion book, *Physician Assistant (PA) School: Preparation, Application, Admission*. In that book, you will find hints and information on the entire application process, as well as detailed information on alternative medical programs, what happens after the interview, and how to strengthen your application. Best wishes in your pursuit of an amazing career and your commitment to serving the healthcare needs of our society.

5
Regions

277
Programs

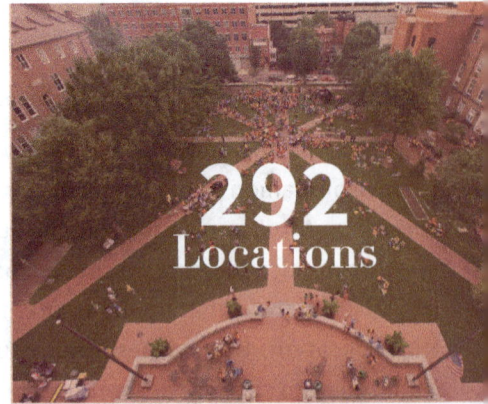

292
Locations

COLLEGE
PROFILES AND
REQUIREMENTS

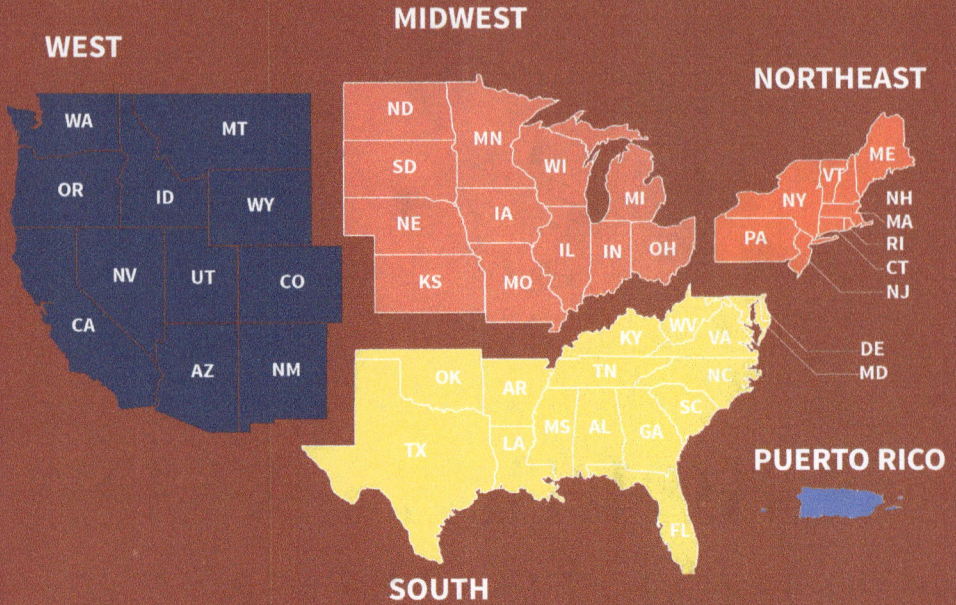

WEST

MIDWEST

NORTHEAST

PUERTO RICO

SOUTH

PA PROGRAMS BY REGION
U.S. CENSUS BUREAU CLASSIFICATIONS

REGION 1 – NORTHEAST

Connecticut, Maine, Massachusetts, New Hampshire, New Jersey, New York, Pennsylvania, Rhode Island, and Vermont

REGION 2 – MIDWEST

Illinois, Indiana, Iowa, Kansas, Michigan, Minnesota, Missouri, Nebraska, North Dakota, Ohio, South Dakota, and Wisconsin

REGION 3 – SOUTH

Alabama, Arkansas, Delaware, District of Columbia, Florida, Georgia, Kentucky, Louisiana, Maryland, Mississippi, North Carolina, Oklahoma, South Carolina, Tennessee, Texas, Virginia, and West Virginia

REGION 4 – WEST

Alaska, Arizona, California, Colorado, Hawaii, Idaho, Montana, Nevada, New Mexico, Oregon, Utah, Washington, and Wyoming

REGION 5 – U.S. TERRRITORIES

Puerto Rico

LIST OF PHYSICIAN ASSISTANT PROGRAMS

The programs listed in the following pages include physician assistant programs. This book also provides lists of MD, DO, dental, PharmD, and vet schools, since many students interested in medical school are also interested in healthcare. There are many facets of the healthcare world. One of these other areas might be a good option for you.

Physician assistant school is not for everyone.

Thus, this book aims to provide you with a more comprehensive set of lists so that you can explore your options. Keep the book handy. You may find that even after you begin college, you may find the additional programs in the back a good option for you.

Creating lists is often tedious and cumbersome. These lists were gathered to help you with this task.

These descriptions of the college programs, tuition, requirements, and deadlines are accurate as of April 2021. Requirements may have changed somewhat due to the pandemic, but all of this information is a great place to start!

Note: To simplify the text and fit information into the charts and descriptions, abbreviations were used as well as shortened sentences and acronyms.

CONNECTICUT

MAINE

MASSACHUSETTS

NEW HAMPSHIRE

NEW JERSEY

NEW YORK

PENNSYLVANIA

RHODE ISLAND

VERMONT

CHAPTER 2

REGION ONE

NORTHEAST

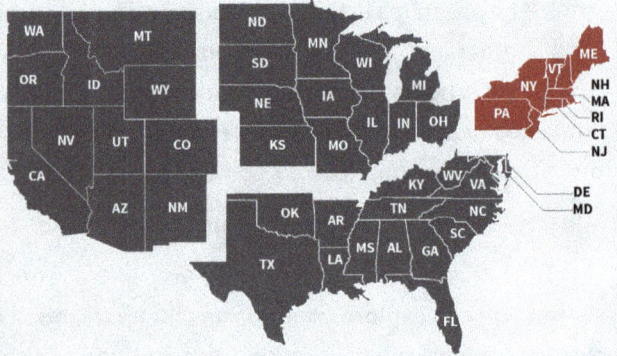

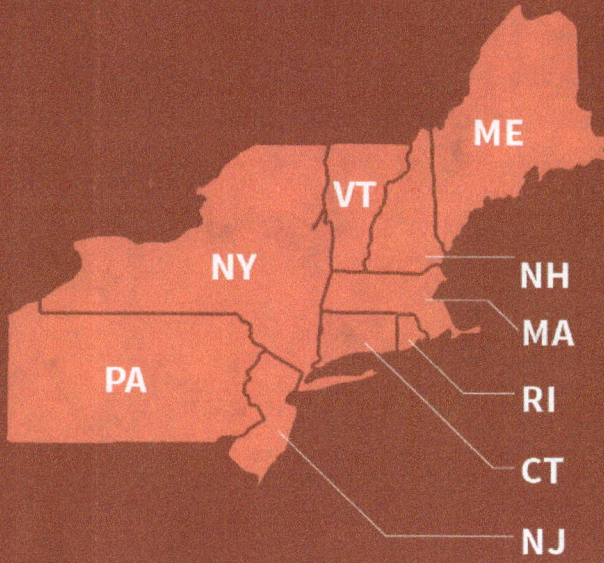

79 Programs | 9 States

1. CT - Quinnipiac University
2. CT - Sacred Heart University
3. CT - University of Bridgeport
4. CT - University of Saint Joseph
5. CT - Yale University School of Medicine
6. ME - University of New England
7. MA - Bay Path University
8. MA - Boston University School of Medicine
9. MA - Massachusetts College of Pharmacy and Health Sciences (MCPHS) - Boston
10. MA - MCPHS - Worcester
11. MA - MGH Institute of Health Professions
12. MA - Northeastern University
13. MA - Springfield College
14. MA - Tufts University
15. MA - Westfield State University
16. NH - Franklin Pierce University
17. NH - MCPHS University - Manchester
18. NJ - Kean University
19. NJ - Monmouth University
20. NJ - Rutgers University
21. NJ - Saint Elizabeth University
22. NJ - Seton Hall University
23. NJ - Thomas Jefferson University - New Jersey
24. NY - Albany Medical College
25. NY - Canisius College
26. NY - Clarkson University
27. NY - CUNY York College
28. NY - D'Youville College
29. NY - Daemen College
30. NY - Hofstra University
31. NY - Ithaca College
32. NY - Le Moyne College
33. NY - Long Island University
34. NY - Marist College
35. NY - Mercy College
36. NY - New York Institute of Technology
37. NY - Pace University - Lenox Hill Hospital
38. NY - Pace University - Pleasantville
39. NY - Rochester Institute of Technology
40. NY - St. Bonaventure University
41. NY - St. John's University
42. NY - Stony Brook University
43. NY - Stony Brook University Southampton
44. NY - SUNY Downstate Medical Center
45. NY - SUNY Upstate Medical Center
46. NY - The CUNY School of Medicine
47. NY - Touro College - Long Island
48. NY - Touro College - NUMC
49. NY - Touro College - Manhattan
50. NY - Wagner College
51. NY - Weill Cornell Graduate School of Medical Sciences
52. NY - Yeshiva University
53. PA - Arcadia University
54. PA - Chatham University
55. PA - DeSales University
56. PA - Drexel University
57. PA - Duquesne University
58. PA - Gannon University
59. PA - King's College
60. PA - Lock Haven University
61. PA - Marywood University
62. PA - Mercyhurst University
63. PA - Misericordia University
64. PA - Penn State University
65. PA - Pennsylvania College of Technology
66. PA - Philadelphia College of Osteopathic Medicine (PCOM)
67. PA - Saint Francis University
68. PA - Salus University
69. PA - Seton Hill University
70. PA - Slippery Rock University
71. PA - Temple University Lewis Katz School of Medicine
72. PA - Thiel College
73. PA - Thomas Jefferson University - Center City Campus
74. PA - Thomas Jefferson University - East Falls
75. PA - University of Pittsburgh
76. PA - University of the Sciences
77. PA - West Chester University
78. RI - Bryant University
79. RI - Johnson & Wales University

PA PROGRAMS

PA School	Ave. GPA & GRE (Verbal, Quantitative. Analy. Writing) Int'l Students: Yes/No	Admissions Statistics	Prerequisite Coursework Other than Gen Bio, Gen Chem, Human Anatomy, Human Physiology, Microbiology, Statistics, Psychology
Quinnipiac University 275 Mount Carmel Avenue, Hamden, CT 06518	3.50 (overall) 3.50 (science) GRE: Not Req. Int'l Student: Yes	Apps Received: 1,500 Interviews Offered: N/A Admission Offered: N/A Class Size: 54 Admitted Rate: 3.6%	
Sacred Heart University 5151 Park Avenue, Fairfield, CT 06825	3.0+ (overall) 3.0+ (science) GRE: Not Req. Int'l Student: No	Apps Received: N/A Interviews Offered: N/A Admission Offered: N/A Class Size: 42 Admitted Rate: N/A	OChem; Upper-level biology
University of Bridgeport 126 Park Avenue, West Hartford, CT 06117	3.0+ (overall) 3.0+ (science) GRE: Not Req. Int'l Student: No	Apps Received: N/A Interviews Offered: N/A Admission Offered: N/A Class Size: 40 Admitted Rate: N/A	English
University of Saint Joseph 1678 Asylum Avenue, West Hartford, CT 06117	3.0+ (overall) 3.0+ (science) GRE: Not Req. Int'l Student: Yes	Apps Received: N/A Interviews Offered: N/A Admission Offered: N/A Class Size: 47 Admitted Rate: N/A	
Yale University SOM 100 Church Street South, Suite A250 New Haven, CT 06519	Yale University SOM 100 Church Street South, Suite A250 New Haven, CT 06519	Yale University SOM 100 Church Street South, Suite A250 New Haven, CT 06519	Genetics; OChem or Biochemistry
University of New England 716 Stevens Avenue, Portland, ME 04103	3.55 (overall) GRE: Not Req. Int'l Student: Yes	Apps Received: N/A Interviews Offered: N/A Admission Offered: N/A Class Size: 50 Admitted Rate: N/A	English

PA School	Ave. GPA & GRE (Verbal, Quantitative, Analy. Writing) Int'l Students: Yes/No	Admissions Statistics	Prerequisite Coursework Other than Gen Bio, Gen Chem, Human Anatomy, Human Physiology, Microbiology, Statistics, Psychology
Bay Path University 1 Denslow Rd, East Longmeadow, MA 01028	3.70 (overall) 3.74 (science) GRE: Not REq. Int'l Student: Yes	Apps Received: N/A Interviews Offered: 160 Admission Offered: N/A Class Size: 30 Admitted Rate: N/A	Ethics; OChem or Biochemistry
Boston University 72 East Concord Street L 801 Boston, MA 02118	3.48 (overall) 3.40 (science) GRE: 68.2% (V) 54.8% (Q) 74.2% (A) Int'l Student: Yes	Apps Received: 2,095 Interviews Offered: 75 Admission Offered: N/A Class Size:26 Admitted Rate: 1.2%	Biochemistry; OChem; Upper-level Biology
MCPHS - Boston 179 Longwood Avenue, Boston, MA 02115	3.48 (overall) 3.40 (science) GRE: 68.2% (V) 54.8% (Q) 74.2% (A) Int'l Student: Yes	Apps Received: N/A Interviews Offered: N/A Admission Offered: N/A Class Size: 100 Admitted Rate: N/A	Upper-level Chemistry
MCPHS - Worcester 19 Foster Street, Worcester, MA 01608	3.0+ (overall) 3.2+ (science) GRE: Not Req. Int'l Student: Yes	Apps Received: N/A Interviews Offered: N/A Admission Offered: N/A Class Size: 125 Admitted Rate: N/A	Biochemistry; OChem
MGH Institute of Health Professions 36 1st Avenue, Charlestown Navy Yard, Boston, MA 02129	3.34 (overall) 3.28 (science) GRE: 58% (V) 43% (Q) 59% (A) Int'l Student: Yes	Apps Received: N/A Interviews Offered: N/A Admission Offered: N/A Class Size: 44 Admitted Rate: N/A	

NORTHEAST

PA PROGRAMS

PA School	Ave. GPA & GRE (Verbal, Quantitative, Analy. Writing) Int'l Students: Yes/No	Admissions Statistics	Prerequisite Coursework Other than Gen Bio, Gen Chem, Human Anatomy, Human Physiology, Microbiology, Statistics, Psychology
Northeastern University 202 Robinson Hall, Boston, MA 02115	3.0+ (overall) 3.0+ (science) GRE: Not Req. Int'l Student: Yes	Apps Received: 1,700 Interviews Offered: 180 Admission Offered: N/A Class Size: 52 Admitted Rate: 3.1%	
Springfield College 63 Alden Street, Springfield, MA 01109	3.50 (overall) 3.50 (science) GRE: Not Req. Int'l Student: Yes	Apps Received: 200 Interviews Offered: N/A Admission Offered: N/A Class Size: 35 Admitted Rate: 17.5%	Biochemistry; OChem; Pre-Calculus or higher level math
Tufts University SOM 136 Harrison Ave., Boston, MA 02111	3.71 (overall) 3.72 (science) GRE: N/A Int'l Student: Yes	Apps Received: N/A Interviews Offered: N/A Admission Offered: N/A Class Size: 50 Admitted Rate: N/A	
Westfield State University 577 Western Avenue, Westfield, MA 01086	3.57 (overall) GRE: Not Req. Int'l Student: Yes	Apps Received: N/A Interviews Offered: N/A Admission Offered: N/A Class Size: 30 Admitted Rate: N/A	Biochemistry; Ethics; Genetics
Franklin Pierce University 24 Airport Road, West Lebanon, NH 03784	3.0+ (overall) 3.0+ (science) GRE: Not Req. Int'l Student: Yes	Apps Received: N/A Interviews Offered: N/A Admission Offered: N/A Class Size: 24 Admitted Rate: N/A	OChem or Biochemistry
MCPHS - Manchester 1260 Elm Street, Manchester, NH 03101	3.0+ (overall) 3.2+ (science) GRE: Not Req. Int'l Student: Yes	Apps Received: N/A Interviews Offered: N/A Admission Offered: N/A Class Size: 55 Admitted Rate: N/A	Biochemistry; OChem

PA School	Ave. GPA & GRE (Verbal, Quantitative, Analy. Writing) Int'l Students: Yes/No	Admissions Statistics	Prerequisite Coursework Other than Gen Bio, Gen Chem, Human Anatomy, Human Physiology, Microbiology, Statistics, Psychology
Kean University 1000 Morris Avenue, Union , NJ 07083	3.0+ (overall) 3.0+ (science) GRE: 40%+ (V) 40%+ (Q) 40%+ (A) Int'l Student: Yes	Apps Received: N/A Interviews Offered: N/A Admission Offered: N/A Class Size: 20 Admitted Rate: N/A	Biochemistry; Medical Terminology
Monmouth University Building C, 185 State Highway 36, West Long Branch, NJ 07764	3.40 (overall) 3.60 (science) GRE: 44% (V) 36.2% (Q) 54.6% (A) Int'l Student: Yes	Apps Received: N/A Interviews Offered: N/A Admission Offered: N/A Class Size: 30 Admitted Rate: N/A	Medical Terminology
Rutgers University 675 Hoes Lane, West Piscataway, NJ 08854	3.64 (overall) 3.61 (science) GRE: Not Req. Int'l Student: Yes	Apps Received: N/A Interviews Offered: N/A Admission Offered: N/A Class Size: 50 Admitted Rate: N/A	Biochemistry; Upper-level Biology
Saint Elizabeth University 2 Convent Road, Morristown, NJ 07960	3.0+ (overall) 3.2+ (science) GRE: Not Req. Int'l Student: Yes	Apps Received: N/A Interviews Offered: N/A Admission Offered: N/A Class Size: 40 Admitted Rate: N/A	Biochemistry; English Composition; Genetics; Medical Terminology;
Seton Hall University 123 Metro Boulevard, Nutley, NJ 07110	3.2+ (overall) 3.2+ (science) GRE: N/A Int'l Student: Yes	Apps Received: N/A Interviews Offered: N/A Admission Offered: N/A Class Size: 60 Admitted Rate: N/A	Medical Terminology; OChem

NORTHEAST

PA PROGRAMS

PA School	Ave. GPA & GRE (Verbal, Quantitative, Analy. Writing) Int'l Students: Yes/No	Admissions Statistics	Prerequisite Coursework Other than Gen Bio, Gen Chem, Human Anatomy, Human Physiology, Microbiology, Statistics, Psychology
Thomas Jefferson University - NJ 443 Laurel Oak Road, Voorhees, NJ 08043	3.70 (overall) 3.60 (science) GRE: Not Req. Int'l Student: Yes	Apps Received: N/A Interviews Offered: N/A Admission Offered: N/A Class Size: 109* Admitted Rate: N/A *East Falls and NJ campus combined	English Composition; Medical Terminology
Albany Medical College 47 New Scotland Ave., Albany, New York 12208	3.67 (overall) 3.63 (science) GRE: Not Req. Int'l Student: No	Apps Received: N/A Interviews Offered: N/A Admission Offered: N/A Class Size: 42 Admitted Rate: N/A	Biochemistry or OChem; English Composition;
Canisius College 2001 Main Street, BA 202, Buffalo, NY 14208	3.0+ (overall) 3.0+ (science) GRE: Not Req. Int'l Student: Yes	Apps Received: N/A Interviews Offered: N/A Admission Offered: N/A Class Size: 30 Admitted Rate: N/A	Biochemistry; OChem; Medical Terminology
Clarkson University 8 Clarkson Avenue, Box 5882, Potsdam, NY 13699	3.25+ (overall) 3.25+ (science) GRE: 40%+ (V) 40%+ (Q) 4+ (A) Int'l Student: Yes	Apps Received: N/A Interviews Offered: N/A Admission Offered: N/A Class Size: 30 Admitted Rate: N/A	Genetics; Humanities/Social Sciences;
CUNY York College 94-20 Guy R. Brewster Boulevard, Science Building Room SC-112, Jamaica, NY 11451	3.0+ (overall) 3.0+ (science) GRE: Not Req. Int'l Student: No	Apps Received: N/A Interviews Offered: N/A Admission Offered: N/A Class Size: 30 Admitted Rate: N/A	Biochemistry
D'Youville College* 320 Porter Avenue, Buffalo, NY 14201	3.54 (overall) 3.48 (science) GRE: Not Req. Int'l Student: Yes	Apps Received: N/A Interviews Offered: N/A Admission Offered: N/A Class Size: 55 Admitted Rate: N/A	*This program is a Direct Entry PA program (4.5yr BS/PA program) intended for high school applicants.

PA School	Ave. GPA & GRE (Verbal, Quantitative, Analy. Writing) Int'l Students: Yes/No	Admissions Statistics	Prerequisite Coursework Other than Gen Bio, Gen Chem, Human Anatomy, Human Physiology, Microbiology, Statistics, Psychology
Daemen College 4380 Main Street, Amherst, NY 14226	3.5+ (overall) 3.4+ (science) GRE: Not Req. Int'l Student: Yes	Apps Received: 2,000 Interviews Offered: N/A Admission Offered: N/A Class Size: 65 Admitted Rate: 3.3%	Calculus; OChem
Hofstra University 113 Hofstra University, Hempstead, NY 11549	3.3+ (overall) 3.3+ (science) GRE: Not Req. Int'l Student: Yes	Apps Received: N/A Interviews Offered: N/A Admission Offered: N/A Class Size: 75 Admitted Rate: N/A	Biochemistry or OChem; Genetics/Cell Biology/ Upper-level Biology
Ithaca College 953 Danby Road, Ithaca, NY 14850	3.0+ (overall) 3.2+ (science) GRE: Not Req. Int'l Student: No	Apps Received: N/A Interviews Offered: N/A Admission Offered: N/A Class Size: 30 Admitted Rate: N/A (Inaugural class starts in Fall 2021)	Biochemistry; English Composition; Genetics; OChem
Le Moyne College 1419 Salt Springs Road, Syracuse, NY 13214	3.2+ (overall) 3.2+ (overall) GRE: Not Req. Int'l Student: Yes	Apps Received: N/A Interviews Offered: N/A Admission Offered: N/A Class Size: 75 Admitted Rate: N/A	Biochemistry or OChem; English Composition; Physics or Calculus; Social Science classes (2); Upper-level Biology classes (2)
Long Island University 1 University Plaza, Brooklyn, NY 11201	3.0+ (overall) 3.0+ (science) GRE: Not Req. Int'l Student: Yes	Apps Received: N/A Interviews Offered: N/A Admission Offered: N/A Class Size: 42 Admitted Rate: N/A	
Marist College 3399 North Road Rotunda, Poughkeepsie, NY 12601	3.56 (overall) 3.50 (science) GRE: Not Req. Int'l Student: Yes	Apps Received: 662 Interviews Offered: 10% - 20% Admission Offered: N/A Class Size: 48 Admitted Rate: 7.3%	Biochemistry; OChem

NORTHEAST

PA PROGRAMS

PA School	Ave. GPA & GRE (Verbal, Quantitative, Analy. Writing) Int'l Students: Yes/No	Admissions Statistics	Prerequisite Coursework Other than Gen Bio, Gen Chem, Human Anatomy, Human Physiology, Microbiology, Statistics, Psychology
Mercy College 1200 Waters Place, Bronx, NY 10461	3.0+ (overall) 3.2+ (science) GRE: Not Req. Int'l Student: Yes	Apps Received: N/A Interviews Offered: N/A Admission Offered: N/A Class Size: 65 Admitted Rate: N/A	Biochemistry; Upper-level Biology
New York Institute of Technology 352 Northern Boulevard, PO Box 8000, Old Westbury, NY 11568	3.72 (overall) 3.68 (science) GRE: Not Req. Int'l Student: Yes	Apps Received: N/A Interviews Offered: N/A Admission Offered: N/A Class Size: 56 Admitted Rate: N/A	
Pace University - Lenox Hill 163 William Street, New York, NY 10038	3.65 (overall) 3.57 (science) GRE: Not Req. Int'l Student: Yes	Apps Received: 1,105 Interviews Offered: 260 Admission Offered: N/A Class Size: 73 Admitted Rate: 6.6%	Biochemistry or OChem; Genetics
Pace University - Pleasantville 861 Bedford Road, Pleasantville, NY 10570	3.43 (overall) 3.43 (science) GRE: Not Req. Int'l Student: Yes	Apps Received: 1,912 Interviews Offered: 91 Admission Offered: N/A Class Size: 35 Admitted Rate: 1.8%	Biochemistry or OChem
Rochester Institute of Technology* 153 Lomb Memorial Drive, Rochester, NY 14623	3.0+ (overall) GRE: Not Req. Int'l Student: Yes	Apps Received: N/A Interviews Offered: N/A Admission Offered: N/A Class Size: 36 Admitted Rate: N/A	*This program is a Direct Entry PA program intended for high school applicants.
St. Bonaventure University 3261 West State Road, St. Bonaventure, NY 14778	Apps Received: N/A Interviews Offered: N/A Admission Offered: N/A Class Size: 25 Admitted Rate: N/A (Inaugural class starts in Fall 2021)	Apps Received: N/A Interviews Offered: N/A Admission Offered: N/A Class Size: 25 Admitted Rate: N/A (Inaugural class starts in Fall 2021)	Humanities/Social Sciences; Genetics

PA School	Ave. GPA & GRE (Verbal, Quantitative, Analy. Writing) Int'l Students: Yes/No	Admissions Statistics	Prerequisite Coursework Other than Gen Bio, Gen Chem, Human Anatomy, Human Physiology, Microbiology, Statistics, Psychology
St. John's University 8000 Utopia Parkway, Queens, NY 11439	3.0+ (overall) 3.0+ (science) GRE: Not Req. Int'l Student: Yes	Apps Received: N/A Interviews Offered: N/A Admission Offered: N/A Class Size: 75 Admitted Rate: N/A	Calculus or higher level math; English Composition; OChem or Biochemistry/ OChem
Stony Brook University 101 Nicolls Road, Health Science Center, Stony Brook, NY 11794	3.0+ (overall) 3.0+ (science) GRE: Not Req. Int'l Student: Yes	Apps Received: N/A Interviews Offered: N/A Admission Offered: N/A Class Size: 44 Admitted Rate: N/A	
Stony Brook University Southampton 39 Tuckahoe Road, Southampton, NY 11968	3.0+ (overall) 3.0+ (science) GRE: Not Req. Int'l Student: Yes	Apps Received: N/A Interviews Offered: N/A Admission Offered: N/A Class Size: 25 Admitted Rate: N/A	
SUNY Downstate Medical Center 450 Clarkson Avenue, Box 1222, Brooklyn, NY 11203	3.48 (overall) 3.59 (science) GRE: Not Req. Int'l Student: Yes	Apps Received: N/A Interviews Offered: N/A Admission Offered: N/A Class Size: 45 Admitted Rate: N/A	Abnormal Psychology or Life Span Psychology; English (Composition); Humanities/Social Sciences; Mathematics (not Statistics); Upper division science course
SUNY Upstate Medical Center 750 East Adams Street, Syracuse, NY 13210	3.0+ (overall) GRE: 50%+ (V) 50%+ (Q) 50%+ (A) Int'l Student: Yes	Apps Received: N/A Interviews Offered: N/A Admission Offered: N/A Class Size: 35 Admitted Rate: N/A	Biochemistry or OChem; English Composition; English Elective; Genetics; Medical Terminology; Additional behavioral or social science

NORTHEAST

PA PROGRAMS

PA School	Ave. GPA & GRE (Verbal, Quantitative, Analy. Writing) Int'l Students: Yes/No	Admissions Statistics	Prerequisite Coursework Other than Gen Bio, Gen Chem, Human Anatomy, Human Physiology, Microbiology, Statistics, Psychology
The CUNY School of Medicine 160 Convent Avenue, New York, NY 10031	3.0+ (overall) 3.0+ (science) GRE: Not Req. Int'l Student: No	Apps Received: 1,500 Interviews Offered: N/A Admission Offered: N/A Class Size: 35 Admitted Rate: 2.3%	Cell & Molecular Biology/ Genetics/Biochemistry
Touro College - Long Island* 225 Eastview Drive, Central Islip, NY 11722	3.58 (overall) 3.54 (science) GRE: Not Req. Int'l Student: Yes	Apps Received: 2,000 Interviews Offered: N/A Admission Offered: N/A Class Size: 65 Admitted Rate: 3.3%	Biochemistry or OChem; English Composition; Humanities; Pre-calculus level or above *This program is a Direct Entry PA program intended for high school applicants.
Touro College - NUMC* 2201 Hempstead Turnpike, East Meadow, NY 11554	3.58 (overall) 3.54 (science) GRE: Not Req. Int'l Student: Yes	Apps Received: 2,000 Interviews Offered: N/A Admission Offered: N/A Class Size: 32 Admitted Rate: 1.6%	Biochemistry or OChem; English Composition; Humanities; Pre-calculus level or above *This program is a Direct Entry PA program intended for high school applicants.
Touro College - Manhattan* 232 West 40th Street, New York, NY 10018	3.58 (overall) 3.55 (science) GRE: Not Req. Int'l Student: Yes	Apps Received: N/A Interviews Offered: N/A Admission Offered: N/A Class Size: 45 Admitted Rate: N/A	Biochemistry or OChem; English Composition; Humanities; Pre-calculus level or above *This program is a Direct Entry PA program intended for high school applicants.
Wagner College* One Campus Road, Staten Island, NY 10301	3.2+ (overall) 3.0+ (science) GRE: Not Req. Int'l Student: Yes	Apps Received: N/A Interviews Offered: N/A Admission Offered: N/A Class Size: 40 Admitted Rate: N/A	Biostatistics and Experimental Design; General Pathology/ Genetics; Medical Ethics or Medical Anthropology; OChem *This program is a Direct Entry PA program intended for high school applicants.

PA School	Ave. GPA & GRE (Verbal, Quantitative, Analy. Writing) Int'l Students: Yes/No	Admissions Statistics	Prerequisite Coursework Other than Gen Bio, Gen Chem, Human Anatomy, Human Physiology, Microbiology, Statistics, Psychology
Weill Cornell Graduate School of Medical Sciences 575 Lexington Avenue, New York, NY 10022	3.60 (overall) 3.60 (science) GRE: N/A Int'l Student: Yes	Apps Received: N/A Interviews Offered: N/A Admission Offered: N/A Class Size: 42 Admitted Rate: N/A	Biochemistry; English Composition
Yeshiva University 500 West 185th Street, New York, NY 10033	3.0+ (overall) 3.0+ (science) GRE: Not Req. Int'l Student: Yes	3.0+ (overall) 3.0+ (science) GRE: Not Req. Int'l Student: Yes	
Arcadia University 450 S. Easton Road, Glenside, PA 19038	3.66 (overall) GRE: N/A Int'l Student: Yes	Apps Received: 3,150 Interviews Offered: N/A Admission Offered: N/A Class Size: 56 Admitted Rate: 1.8%	OChem
Chatham University Berry Hall, Woodland Road, Pittsburgh, PA 15232	3.69 (overall) 3.64 (science) GRE: N/A Int'l Student: Yes	Apps Received: N/A Interviews Offered: N/A Admission Offered: N/A Class Size: 48 Admitted Rate: N/A	English; Medical Terminology; OChem
DeSales University 2755 Station Avenue, Center Valley, PA 18034	3.0+ (overall) 3.0+ (science) GRE: N/A Int'l Student: Yes	Apps Received: N/A Interviews Offered: N/A Admission Offered: N/A Class Size: 80 Admitted Rate: N/A	English Composition; OChem
Drexel University 1601 Cherry Street, 6th Floor, Philadelphia, PA 19102	3.63 (overall) 3.57 (science) GRE: Not Req. Int'l Student: Yes	Apps Received: 1,780 Interviews Offered: N/A Admission Offered: N/A Class Size: 77 Admitted Rate: 4.3%	Genetics; Medical Terminology

NORTHEAST

PA PROGRAMS

PA School	Ave. GPA & GRE (Verbal, Quantitative, Analy. Writing) Int'l Students: Yes/No	Admissions Statistics	Prerequisite Coursework Other than Gen Bio, Gen Chem, Human Anatomy, Human Physiology, Microbiology, Statistics, Psychology
Duquesne University* 600 Forbes Avenue, John G Rangos School of Health Sciences, Pittsburgh, PA 15282	3.0+ (overall) 3.0+ (science) GRE: N/A Int'l Student: Yes	Apps Received: N/A Interviews Offered: N/A Admission Offered: N/A Class Size: 40 Admitted Rate: N/A	*This program is a Direct Entry PA program intended for high school applicants.
Gannon University* 109 University Square, Erie, PA 16541	Medical Terminology *This program is a Direct Entry PA program intended for high school applicants.	Apps Received: N/A Interviews Offered: N/A Admission Offered: N/A Class Size: 58 Admitted Rate: N/A	Medical Terminology *This program is a Direct Entry PA program intended for high school applicants.
King's College 133 North River Street, Wilkes-Barre, PA 18711	3.2+ (overall) 3.2+ (science) GRE: Not Req. Int'l Student: Yes	Apps Received: N/A Interviews Offered: N/A Admission Offered: N/A Class Size: 75 Admitted Rate: N/A	Genetics; OChem
Lock Haven University 401 N. Fairview Street, Lock Haven, PA 17745	3.50 (overall) 3.43 (science) GRE: 308.15 (Q&V combined) 4.26 (A0 Int'l Student: Yes	Apps Received: 700 Interviews Offered: N/A Admission Offered: N/A Class Size: 72 Admitted Rate: 10.3%	Genetics
Marywood University 2300 Adams Avenue, Scranton, PA 18509	3.61 (overall) 3.54 (science) GRE: 297 (Q&V combined) Int'l Student: Yes	Apps Received: 624 Interviews Offered: 204 Admission Offered: N/A Class Size: 60 Admitted Rate: 9.6%	Immunology; OChem

PA School	Ave. GPA & GRE (Verbal, Quantitative, Analy. Writing) Int'l Students: Yes/No	Admissions Statistics	Prerequisite Coursework Other than Gen Bio, Gen Chem, Human Anatomy, Human Physiology, Microbiology, Statistics, Psychology
Mercyhurst University 501 East 38th Street, Erie, PA 16546	3.2+ (overall) 3.2+ (science) GRE: N/A Int'l Student: Yes	Apps Received: N/A Interviews Offered: N/A Admission Offered: N/A Class Size: 30 Admitted Rate: N/A	Biochemistry; Genetics; Medical Terminology
Misericordia University 301 Lake Street, Dallas, PA 18612	3.2+ (overall) 3.2+ (science) GRE: Not Req. Int'l Student: Yes	Apps Received: N/A Interviews Offered: N/A Admission Offered: N/A Class Size: 20 Admitted Rate: N/A	Biochemistry; Genetics; Medical Terminology
Penn State University 700 HMC Crescent Road, Hershey, PA 17033	3.69 (overall) 3.69 (science) GRE: 158 (V) 157 (Q) 4.3 (A) Int'l Student: Yes	Apps Received: 5,031 Interviews Offered: 88 Admission Offered: 39 Class Size: 30 Admitted Rate: 0.6%	Biochemistry or OChem; English Composition
Pennsylvania College of Technology* One College Avenue, Williamsport, PA 17701	3.5+ (overall) GRE: Not Req. Int'l Student: Yes	Apps Received: N/A Interviews Offered: N/A Admission Offered: N/A Class Size: 30 Admitted Rate: N/A	Biochemistry; Genetics; OChem; Physics *This program is a Direct Entry PA program intended for high school applicants.
PCOM 4170 City Avenue, Philadelphia, PA 19131	3.70 (overall) 3.65 (science) GRE: Not Req. Int'l Student: Yes	Apps Received: 2,693 Interviews Offered: N/A Admission Offered: 80 Class Size: 59 Admitted Rate: 2.2%	Biochemistry or OChem; Health-related science course or Physics; Math

NORTHEAST

PA PROGRAMS

PA School	Ave. GPA & GRE (Verbal, Quantitative, Analy. Writing) Int'l Students: Yes/No	Admissions Statistics	Prerequisite Coursework Other than Gen Bio, Gen Chem, Human Anatomy, Human Physiology, Microbiology, Statistics, Psychology
Saint Francis University 117 Evergreen Drive, Loretto, PA 15940	3.2+ (overall) 3.2+ (science) GRE: Not Req. Int'l Student: Yes	Apps Received: N/A Interviews Offered: N/A Admission Offered: N/A Class Size: 55 Admitted Rate: N/A	Medical Terminology
Salus University 8360 Old York Road, Elkins Park, PA 19027	3.69 (overall) 3.63 (science) GRE: 152 (V) 153 (Q) 4 (A) Int'l Student: Yes	Apps Received: 978 Interviews Offered: N/A Admission Offered: N/A Class Size: 50 Admitted Rate: 5.1%	English Composition; OChem
Seton Hill University 1 Seton Hill Drive, Greensburg, PA 15601	3.2+ (overall) 3.2+ (science) GRE: Not Req. Int'l Student: Yes	Apps Received: N/A Interviews Offered: N/A Admission Offered: N/A Class Size: 50 Admitted Rate: N/A	Medical Terminology; OChem
Slippery Rock University 105 North Hall, Slippery Rock, PA 16057	3.25+ (overall) 3.25+ (science) GRE: Not Req. Int'l Student: Yes	Apps Received: N/A Interviews Offered: N/A Admission Offered: N/A Class Size: 52 Admitted Rate: N/A	Medical Terminology; Genetics; OChem; College writing or composition; College literature
Temple University LKSOM 3500 North Broad Street, Suite 124, Philadelphia, PA 19140	3.50 (overall) 3.25 (science) GRE: Not Req. DPCE: Int'l Student: No	Apps Received: N/A Interviews Offered: N/A Admission Offered: N/A Class Size: 30 Admitted Rate: N/A	Biochemistry; Medical Terminology; OChem; Two or more from Genetics, Molecular Biology, Immunology, Microbiology, Cell Biology
Thiel College 75 College Ave., Greenville, PA 16125	3.0+ (overall) 3.0+ (science) GRE: Not Req. Int'l Student: No	Apps Received: N/A Interviews Offered: N/A Admission Offered: N/A Class Size: 40 Admitted Rate: N/A	English Composition; Medical Terminology; OChem

PA School	Ave. GPA & GRE (Verbal, Quantitative, Analy. Writing) Int'l Students: Yes/No	Admissions Statistics	Prerequisite Coursework Other than Gen Bio, Gen Chem, Human Anatomy, Human Physiology, Microbiology, Statistics, Psychology
Thomas Jefferson University - Center City 130 South 9th Street, 6th Floor, Philadelphia, PA 19107	3.40 (overall) 3.40 (science) GRE: Not Req. Int'l Student: Yes	Apps Received: N/A Interviews Offered: N/A Admission Offered: N/A Class Size: 50 Admitted Rate: N/A	English Composition; Medical Terminology
Thomas Jefferson - East Falls 201 Henry Avenue, Philadelphia, PA 19144	3.70 (overall) 3.60 (science) GRE: Not Req. Int'l Student: Yes	Apps Received: N/A Interviews Offered: N/A Admission Offered: N/A Class Size: 109* Admitted Rate: N/A *East Falls and NJ campus combined	English Composition; Medical Terminology
University of Pittsburgh 3010 William Pitt Way, Pittsburgh, PA 15238	3.67 (overall) 3.55 (science) GRE: Not Req. Int'l Student: Yes	Apps Received: N/A Interviews Offered: N/A Admission Offered: N/A Class Size: 48 Admitted Rate: N/A	English Composition; Medical Terminology
University of the Sciences 600 South 43rd Street, Philadelphia, PA 19104	3.2+ (overall) 3.2+ (science) GRE: Not Req. Int'l Student: Yes	Apps Received: N/A Interviews Offered: N/A Admission Offered: N/A Class Size: 45 Admitted Rate: N/A	Biochemistry or OChem; Medical Terminology
West Chester University 700 South High Street, West Chester, PA 19383	3.56 (overall) 3.56 (science) GRE: Not Req. Int'l Student: Yes	Apps Received: 860 Interviews Offered: N/A Admission Offered: N/A Class Size: 27 Admitted Rate: 3.1%	Biochemistry or OChem; English Composition; Ethics; Medical Terminology; Upper level Biology (Genetics preferred)

NORTHEAST

PA PROGRAMS

PA School	Ave. GPA & GRE (Verbal, Quantitative, Analy. Writing) Int'l Students: Yes/No	Admissions Statistics	Prerequisite Coursework Other than Gen Bio, Gen Chem, Human Anatomy, Human Physiology, Microbiology, Statistics, Psychology
Bryant University 1150 Douglas Pike, Smithfield, RI 02917	3.0+ (overall) 3.0+ (science) GRE: N/A Int'l Student: Yes	Apps Received: N/A Interviews Offered: N/A Admission Offered: N/A Class Size: 48 Admitted Rate: N/A	Biochemistry or OChem
Johnson & Wales University 8 Abbott Park Place, Providence, RI 02903	3.67 (overall) 3.60 (science) GRE: Not Req. Int'l Student: No	Apps Received: N/A Interviews Offered: N/A Admission Offered: N/A Class Size: 36 Admitted Rate: N/A	Genetics will be required for the 2022-23 CASPA cycle

CONNECTICUT

MAINE

MASSACHUSETTS

NEW HAMPSHIRE

NEW JERSEY

NEW YORK

PENNSYLVANIA

RHODE ISLAND

VERMONT

QUINNIPIAC UNIVERSITY

Address: 275 Mount Carmel Avenue, Hamden, CT 06518
Website: *http://www.quinnipiac.edu/gradphysicianasst*
Contact: *graduate@quinnipiac.edu*
Phone: 203-582-8672

COST OF ATTENDANCE

Tuition and Fees: $72,050
Additional Expenses: $15,120
Total: $144,100

Financial Aid: https://www.qu.edu/paying-for-college/graduate/costs-and-budgets/?tab=health-sciences

ADDITIONAL INFORMATION

Interesting tidbit: The PA program is a 27-month full-time graduate program. Due to the labor and time-intensive nature of the Physician Assistant program, students are strongly discouraged from working while enrolled in the program.

Important Updates due to COVID-19: Prerequisite labs that were changed to an online format and completed between Spring 2020-Fall 2021 as a result of the COVID-19 pandemic will be accepted.

Were tests required? No.

Are tests expected next year? No.

What international experiences are available? N/A

What dual degree options exist? BS in Health Science Studies/MHS in Physician Assistant

What service-learning opportunities exist? Urban Service Track program.

What percent of graduates place in clinical PA practice? 99% (2019)

PANCE First-Time Pass Rate: 96% (2020)

Other: Pre-PA program known as the entry-level master's physician assistant (ELMPA) program available for high school seniors.

SACRED HEART UNIVERSITY

Address: 5151 Park Avenue, Fairfield, CT 06825
Website: *https://www.sacredheart.edu/majors--programs/ physician-assistant-studies---mpas/*
Contact: *paadmissions@sacredheart.edu*
Phone: 203-371-7884

COST OF ATTENDANCE

Tuition and Fees: $50,910
Additional Expenses: N/A
Total: $50,910*

*This figure does not include cost of living or other indirect costs.

Financial Aid: https://www.sacredheart.edu/admissions--aid/ financial-assistance/graduate-students/application-process-- deadlines/

ADDITIONAL INFORMATION

Interesting tidbit: The SHU Master of Physician Assistant Studies Program is a full-time, 27-month program consisting of a 12-month didactic phase followed by a 15-month clinical phase segmented into five-week rotations. Students will end the program with a combined 2,000 hours of experience in internal medicine, general surgery, pediatrics, and primary care/family medicine, as well as orthopedics, women's health, emergency medicine, behavioral health, and one additional elective area.

Important Updates due to COVID-19: The Program accepts prerequisite courses and labs completed online starting with the Spring 2020 academic year and beyond for the 2021-2022 admissions cycle. It has also reduced our required minimum paid patient care experience to 500 hours. Due to the challenges presented by the COVID-19 pandemic, the MPAS program will accept Telehealth experience but no more than half of the minimally required clinical hours.

Were tests required? No.

Are tests expected next year? No.

What international experiences are available? N/A

What dual degree options exist? N/A

What service-learning opportunities exist? N/A

PANCE First-Time Pass Rate: 91% (2020)

CONNECTICUT

MAINE

MASSACHUSETTS

NEW HAMPSHIRE

NEW JERSEY

NEW YORK

PENNSYLVANIA

RHODE ISLAND

VERMONT

NORTHEAST

CONNECTICUT

MAINE

MASSACHUSETTS

NEW HAMPSHIRE

NEW JERSEY

NEW YORK

PENNSYLVANIA

RHODE ISLAND

VERMONT

UNIVERSITY OF BRIDGEPORT

Address: 126 Park Avenue, Bridgeport, CT 06604
Website: *http://www.bridgeport.edu/academics/schools-colleges/physician-assistant-institute/physician-assistant-ms*
Contact: *admit@bridgeport.edu*
Phone: 202-576-4552

COST OF ATTENDANCE

Tuition and Fees: $48,835
Additional Expenses: N/A
Total: $48,835

Financial Aid: https://www.bridgeport.edu/cost-financial-aid/financial-aid/graduate-students

ADDITIONAL INFORMATION

Interesting tidbit: The program is a full-time 28-month schedule with a January start date. It is an intense and rigorous program that is demanding.

Important Updates due to COVID-19: Labs completed online will be accepted. The program will accept pass/fail grades for all prerequisites taken in the spring, summer, or fall of 2020.

Were tests required? No.

Are tests expected next year? No.

What international experiences are available? Annual global health trip.

What dual degree options exist? N/A

What service-learning opportunities exist? N/A

PANCE First-Time Pass Rate: 100% (2020)

UNIVERSITY OF SAINT JOSEPH

Address: 1678 Asylum Avenue, West Hartford, CT 06117
Website: *https://www.usj.edu/academics/academic-schools/sppas/physician-assistant-studies/admissions/*
Contact: *pastudiesprogram@usj.edu*
Phone: 860-231-5420

COST OF ATTENDANCE

Tuition and Fees: $51,291
Additional Expenses: N/A
Total: $51,291*

*This figure does not include cost of living or other indirect costs..

Financial Aid: https://www.usj.edu/admissions/tuition-financial-aid/graduate-financial-aid/

ADDITIONAL INFORMATION

Interesting tidbit: USJ's PA Studies Program has developed a unique modular curriculum, the only program of its kind in the region. Students will enroll in one course at a time, allowing for complete focus on mastery of clinical sciences specific to each organ system, with opportunities to begin integrating and applying concepts embedded throughout the curriculum.

Important Updates due to COVID-19: The USJ PA Studies Program will accept Pass/Fail grades to meet prerequisite requirements for courses taken in the Spring 2020 and Summer 2020 semesters.

Were tests required? No.

Are tests expected next year? No.

What international experiences are available? N/A

What dual degree options exist? N/A

What service-learning opportunities exist? N/A

PANCE First-Time Pass Rate: 100% (2020)

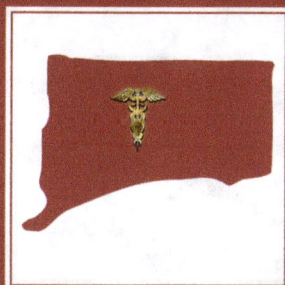

CONNECTICUT

MAINE

MASSACHUSETTS

NEW HAMPSHIRE

NEW JERSEY

NEW YORK

PENNSYLVANIA

RHODE ISLAND

VERMONT

NORTHEAST

YALE UNIVERSITY SCHOOL OF MEDICINE

Address: 100 Church Street South, Suite A250, New Haven, CT 06519
Website: *http://www.paprogram.yale.edu/*
Contact: *pa.program@yale.edu*
Phone: 203-785-2860

COST OF ATTENDANCE

Tuition and Fees: $46,708
Additional Expenses: $ 34,173
Total: $80,881

Financial Aid: https://medicine.yale.edu/education/financialaid/paprogram/

ADDITIONAL INFORMATION

Interesting tidbit: The Yale Physician Associate Program was developed in 1970. The founders of the PA Program wanted to convey the collegial relationship that exists between PAs and their supervising physicians and thus adopted the term "Physician Associate."

Important Updates due to COVID-19: The Program will accept pass/fail coursework for classes completed during the spring or summer 2020 terms. This policy only applies to applicants studying at an institution requiring students to complete coursework as pass/fail. It also accepts the in-home version of the GRE.

Were tests required? GRE required.

Are tests expected next year? Yes.

What international experiences are available? International clinical rotations available. See https://medicine.yale.edu/pa/curriculum/clinical/intlrotations/

What dual degree options exist? PA/MPH available. See https://medicine.yale.edu/pa/admissions/pa_mph_joint_degree/

What service-learning opportunities exist? N/A

PANCE First-Time Pass Rate: 100% (2020)

Other: The Yale School of Medicine offers the Physician Assistant Online Program as well. See https://paonline.yale.edu/

CONNECTICUT

MAINE

MASSACHUSETTS

NEW HAMPSHIRE

NEW JERSEY

NEW YORK

PENNSYLVANIA

RHODE ISLAND

VERMONT

UNIVERSITY OF NEW ENGLAND

Address: 716 Stevens Avenue, Portland, ME 04103
Website: *http://www.une.edu/wchp/pa*
Contact: *gradadmissions@une.edu*
Phone: 207-221-4225

COST OF ATTENDANCE

Tuition and Fees: $46,530
Additional Expenses: $35,869
Total: $82,399

Financial Aid: https://www.une.edu/sfs/graduate/financing-your-education

ADDITIONAL INFORMATION

Interesting tidbit: UNE's Portland, Maine-based Physician Assistant master's program operates on a 24-month, full-time calendar, beginning each June with a new entering class. Students begin patient care in their first year through the program's nationally recognized Interprofessional Geriatric Education Practicum.

Important Updates due to COVID-19: Virtual Interview

Were tests required? No.

Are tests expected next year? No.

What international experiences are available? N/A

What dual degree options exist? N/A

What service-learning opportunities exist? Interprofessional Geriatric Education Practicum.

PANCE First-Time Pass Rate: 94% (2020)

CONNECTICUT

MAINE

MASSACHUSETTS

NEW HAMPSHIRE

NEW JERSEY

NEW YORK

PENNSYLVANIA

RHODE ISLAND

VERMONT

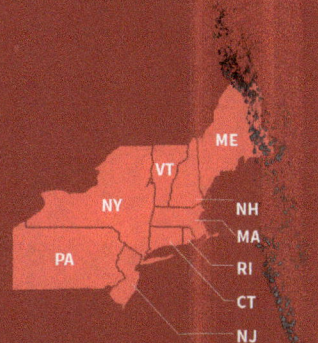

NORTHEAST

CONNECTICUT

MAINE

MASSACHUSETTS

NEW HAMPSHIRE

NEW JERSEY

NEW YORK

PENNSYLVANIA

RHODE ISLAND

VERMONT

BAY PATH UNIVERSITY

Address: 1 Denslow Road, East Longmeadow, MA 01028
Website: *http://graduate.baypath.edu/graduate-programs/programs-on-campus/ms-programs/physician-assistant-studies*
Contact: *paprogram@baypath.edu*
Phone: 413-565-1332

COST OF ATTENDANCE

Tuition and Fees: $54,385
Additional Expenses: N/A
Total: $54,385*

*This figure does not include cost of living or other indirect costs..

Financial Aid: https://www.baypath.edu/admissions-aid/graduate-admissions/financial-aid/

ADDITIONAL INFORMATION

Interesting tidbit: BPU PA curriculum offers unique 8-10 week schedules which allow for reflection and self-care. An emphasis on self-care practices helps the students feel and perform better.

Important Updates due to COVID-19: Bay Path will accept grades of Pass (P), Satisfactory (S), or the equivalent for required coursework for spring and summer 2020 courses. It will accept online labs. It will waive the 24-PA shadowing requirement.

Were tests required? No.

Are tests expected next year? No.

What international experiences are available? N/A

What dual degree options exist? N/A

What service-learning opportunities exist? N/A

PANCE First-Time Pass Rate: 100% (2020)

BOSTON UNIVERSITY SCHOOL OF MEDICINE

Address: 72 East Concord Street, Boston, MA 2118
Website: *http://bu.edu/paprogram*
Contact: *paoffice@bu.edu*
Phone: 617-638-9589

COST OF ATTENDANCE

Tuition and Fees: $47,782*
Additional Expenses: $10,799**
Total: $58,581**

*Matriculating students receive a PA scholarship of $36,162, which reduces the GMS tuition of $83,944.

**This figure does not include cost of living or other indirect costs..

Financial Aid: https://www.bu.edu/paprogram/admissions/tuition-and-financial-aid/financing-your-education/

ADDITIONAL INFORMATION

Interesting tidbit: Students in the PA program are required to complete a thesis proposal that demonstrates the student's ability to interpret scientific literature and develop a hypothesis-driven project proposal. This is a literature-based thesis and does not require collection or analysis of data.

Important Updates due to COVID-19: For courses in Spring 2020, Summer 2020, Fall 2020, and Spring 2021 semester, the program will allow prerequisite courses which had started in-person and moved to remote online teaching due to COVID.

Were tests required? GRE and CASPer required.

Are tests expected next year? Yes.

What international experiences are available? N/A

What dual degree options exist? N/A

What service-learning opportunities exist? N/A

PANCE First-Time Pass Rate: 96% (2020)

CONNECTICUT

MAINE

MASSACHUSETTS

NEW HAMPSHIRE

NEW JERSEY

NEW YORK

PENNSYLVANIA

RHODE ISLAND

VERMONT

NORTHEAST

CONNECTICUT

MAINE

MASSACHUSETTS

NEW HAMPSHIRE

NEW JERSEY

NEW YORK

PENNSYLVANIA

RHODE ISLAND

VERMONT

MCPHS UNIVERSITY - BOSTON

Address: 179 Longwood Avenue, Boston, MA 02115
Website: *https://www.mcphs.edu/academics/school-of-physician-assistant-studies/physician-assistant/physician-assistant-studies-mpas*
Contact: *admissions@mcphs.edu*
Phone: 617-870-5964

COST OF ATTENDANCE

Tuition and Fees: $40,051
Additional Expenses: N/A
Total: $40,051*

*This figure does not include cost of living or other indirect costs..

Financial Aid: https://www.mcphs.edu/admission-and-aid/financial-services/financial-aid/graduate-financial-aid

ADDITIONAL INFORMATION

Interesting tidbit: MCPHS PA - Boston is a three-year graduate program, which consists of four semesters of didactic classwork, followed by three semesters of supervised clinical rotations in a variety of settings.

Important Updates due to COVID-19: Virtual Interview.

Were tests required? No.

Are tests expected next year? No.

What international experiences are available? International clinical sites available.

What dual degree options exist? N/A

What service-learning opportunities exist? N/A

PANCE First-Time Pass Rate: 96% (2020)

Other: Online Doctor of Science in Physician Assistant Studies available. See https://www.mcphs.edu/academics/school-of-physician-assistant-studies/physician-assistant/physican-assistant-studies-doctor-of-science

MCPHS UNIVERSITY - WORCESTER

Address: 19 Foster St., Worcester, MA 01608
Website: *https://www.mcphs.edu/academics/school-of-physician-assistant-studies/physician-assistant/physican-assistant-studies-mpas-accelerated*
Contact: *admissions@mcphs.edu*
Phone: 617-870-5964

Other Locations: Manchester, NH

COST OF ATTENDANCE

Tuition and Fees: $56,441
Additional Expenses: N/A
Total: $56,441*

*This figure does not include cost of living or other indirect costs..

Financial Aid: https://www.mcphs.edu/admission-and-aid/financial-services/financial-aid/graduate-financial-aid

ADDITIONAL INFORMATION

Interesting tidbit: MCPHS PA - Worcester is an accelerated 2-year MPAS program.

Important Updates due to COVID-19: Virtual Interview.

Were tests required? No.

Are tests expected next year? No.

What international experiences are available? International clinical sites available.

What dual degree options exist? N/A

What service-learning opportunities exist? N/A

PANCE First-Time Pass Rate: 91% (2020)

Other: Online Doctor of Science in Physician Assistant Studies available. See https://www.mcphs.edu/academics/school-of-physician-assistant-studies/physician-assistant/physician-assistant-studies-doctor-of-science

CONNECTICUT

MAINE

MASSACHUSETTS

NEW HAMPSHIRE

NEW JERSEY

NEW YORK

PENNSYLVANIA

RHODE ISLAND

VERMONT

NORTHEAST

CONNECTICUT

MAINE

MASSACHUSETTS

NEW HAMPSHIRE

NEW JERSEY

NEW YORK

PENNSYLVANIA

RHODE ISLAND

VERMONT

MGH INSTITUTE OF HEALTH PROFESSIONS

Address: 36 1st Avenue, Charleston Navy Yard, Boston, MA 02129
Website: *https://www.mghihp.edu/physician-assistant-studies*
Contact: *pa@mghihp.edu*
Phone: 617-726-2947

COST OF ATTENDANCE

Tuition and Fees: $58,815
Additional Expenses: $34,795
Total: $87,895

Financial Aid: https://www.mghihp.edu/overview/financial-aid

ADDITIONAL INFORMATION

Interesting tidbit: As part of Mass General Brigham, New England's largest healthcare organization, the MGH Institute offers unparalleled access to Harvard Medical School-affiliated academic medical centers and other respected institutions throughout New England and beyond.

Important Updates due to COVID-19: Courses, including prerequisites, taken as pass/fail during the time of the COVID-19 response (Spring, Summer, and Fall 2020) will be accepted.

Were tests required? No.

Are tests expected next year? No.

What international experiences are available? N/A

What dual degree options exist? N/A

What service-learning opportunities exist? N/A

PANCE First-Time Pass Rate: 98% (2020)

NORTHEASTERN UNIVERSITY

Address: 202 Robinson Hall, Boston, MA 2115
Website: *https://bouve.northeastern.edu/physician-assistant/ms/*
Contact: *paprogram@neu.edu*
Phone: 312-503-1851

COST OF ATTENDANCE

Tuition and Fees: $48,525
Additional Expenses: $6,753*
Total: $55,278*

*This figure does not include cost of living or other indirect costs..

Financial Aid: https://studentfinance.northeastern.edu/applying-for-aid/graduate/#_ga=2.120169997.400786100.1623696222-251945952.1622159200

ADDITIONAL INFORMATION

Interesting tidbit: Northeastern University's Bouvé College of Health Sciences has been training physician assistants since 1971, making it one of the most experienced programs in the nation.

Important Updates due to COVID-19: The Northeastern University Physician Assistant Program will accept Pass/Fail grades in any 2 of our required prerequisite courses. These 2 courses must have been taken during the spring 2020 or summer 2020 terms only.

Were tests required? No.

Are tests expected next year? No.

What international experiences are available? N/A

What dual degree options exist? MSPA/MPH dual degree option (https://bouve.northeastern.edu/health-sciences/programs/pa-mph/); MSPA/MHI dual degree option (https://bouve.northeastern.edu/physician-assistant/programs/pa-mshi/)

What service-learning opportunities exist? N/A

PANCE First-Time Pass Rate: 98% (2020)

CONNECTICUT

MAINE

MASSACHUSETTS

NEW HAMPSHIRE

NEW JERSEY

NEW YORK

PENNSYLVANIA

RHODE ISLAND

VERMONT

NORTHEAST

CONNECTICUT

MAINE

MASSACHUSETTS

NEW HAMPSHIRE

NEW JERSEY

NEW YORK

PENNSYLVANIA

RHODE ISLAND

VERMONT

SPRINGFIELD COLLEGE

Address: 63 Alden Street, Springfield, MA 01109
Website: *https://springfield.edu/programs/graduate/physician-assistant-studies-masters-degree*
Contact: *isaloio@springfieldcollege.edu*
Phone: 413-748-3554

COST OF ATTENDANCE

Tuition and Fees: $59,670
Additional Expenses: $14,154*
Total: $73,824*

*This figure does not include cost of living or other indirect costs..

Financial Aid: https://springfield.edu/admissions/graduate-admissions/fellowships-asssociateships-scholarships

ADDITIONAL INFORMATION

Interesting tidbit: The Springfield College PA Program offers two tracks - a 2-year graduate program and a 6-year undergraduate program. The majority of its students enter the physician assistant program through the six-year track. Preference for admission is given to students entering through the six-year track as long as all program requirements are met.

Important Updates due to COVID-19: PA shadowing requirement is waived for the 2020-2021 application cycle.

Were tests required? No.

Are tests expected next year? No.

What international experiences are available? N/A

What dual degree options exist? BS/MSPAS. See https://springfield.edu/programs/physician-assistant-studies

What service-learning opportunities exist? N/A

PANCE First-Time Pass Rate: 80% (2020)

TUFTS UNIVERSITY SCHOOL OF MEDICINE

Address: 136 Harrison Avenue, Boston, MA 21111
Website: *http://medicine.tufts.edu/paprogram*
Contact: *paprogram@tufts.edu*
Phone: 617-636-0405

COST OF ATTENDANCE

Tuition and Fees: $34,608
Additional Expenses: $22,235
Total: $56,843

Financial Aid: https://medicine.tufts.edu/admissions-aid/financial-aid/financing-graduate-education

ADDITIONAL INFORMATION

Interesting tidbit: PA students complete their pre-clinical coursework at Tufts University's Health Sciences campus in downtown Boston, and participate in Grand Rounds at the world-class Tufts Medical Center. As a second-year student, you'll further hone your skills by completing clinical rotations at different practice sites in and around Boston.

Important Updates due to COVID-19: Pass/Fail grades for prerequisite courses will be accepted for the spring 2020 and summer 2020 semesters only. The GRE examination will be "test optional" for the 2021 cycle. Virtual Interview.

Were tests required? No, the GRE examination will be optional for the 2021 admission cycle.

Are tests expected next year? Yes, GRE or MCAT required.

What international experiences are available? N/A

What dual degree options exist? PA/MPH dual degree option. See https://publichealth.tufts.edu/graduate-programs/dual-degrees/pa-mph

What service-learning opportunities exist? Sharewood Project. See https://medicine.tufts.edu/local-global-engagement/sharewood

PANCE First-Time Pass Rate: 95% (2020)

CONNECTICUT

MAINE

MASSACHUSETTS

NEW HAMPSHIRE

NEW JERSEY

NEW YORK

PENNSYLVANIA

RHODE ISLAND

VERMONT

NORTHEAST

CONNECTICUT

MAINE

MASSACHUSETTS

NEW HAMPSHIRE

NEW JERSEY

NEW YORK

PENNSYLVANIA

RHODE ISLAND

VERMONT

WESTFIELD STATE UNIVERSITY

Address: 577 Western Avenue, Westfield, MA 01086
Website: *https://www.westfield.ma.edu/academics/master-of-science-in-physician-assistant-studies/*
Contact: *pastudies@westfield.ma.edu*
Phone: 415-572-8149

COST OF ATTENDANCE

Tuition and Fees: $50,660
Additional Expenses: N/A
Total: $50,660*

*This figure does not include cost of living or other indirect costs..

Financial Aid: https://www.westfield.ma.edu/academics/career-center/financing-graduate-school

ADDITIONAL INFORMATION

Interesting tidbit: The Master of Science in Physician Assistant Studies at Westfield State University is the only public physician assistant program in Massachusetts and all of New England. The program will grant an interview for all students who have graduated from a Massachusetts public four-year institution, if specific criteria are met.

Important Updates due to COVID-19: The program will accept Pass/Fail courses taken during spring 2020.

Were tests required? No.

Are tests expected next year? No.

What international experiences are available? N/A

What dual degree options exist? N/A

What service-learning opportunities exist? N/A

PANCE First-Time Pass Rate: 93% (2020)

ME

VT

NY

NH

MA

PA

RI

CT

NJ

FRANKLIN PIERCE UNIVERSITY

Address: 24 Airport Road, West Lebanon, NH 03784
Website: *http://www.franklinpierce.edu/academics/gradstudies/ programs_of_study/mpas/index.htm*
Contact: *paprogram@franklinpierce.edu*
Phone: 603-298-5549

COST OF ATTENDANCE

Tuition and Fees: $35,100
Additional Expenses: $25,830
Total: $60,930

Financial Aid: https://www.franklinpierce.edu/admissions/finaid/ forms/FinAidBasics-MPA.htm

ADDITIONAL INFORMATION

Interesting tidbit: Franklin Pierce MPAS program places an emphasis on serving the underserved. Students' clinical training will include rotations throughout the underserved regions of New Hampshire and Vermont. In 2016, the Program was ranked #2 in the nation by the Rural Health Research Center (2016) for producing a high proportion of graduates that go on to work in rural health-care.

Important Updates due to COVID-19: The shadowing hours may be virtual for the April – November 2021 CASPA cycle only.

Were tests required? No.

Are tests expected next year? No.

What international experiences are available? N/A

What dual degree options exist? N/A

What service-learning opportunities exist? N/A

PANCE First-Time Pass Rate: 88% (2020)

Other: MPAS Direct Admit Program (4+2) for highly qualified high school students. See https://www.franklinpierce.edu/academics/ ugrad/programs_of_study/div_natsci/health_science/HStoMPAS. htm

Other: Franklin Pierce offers the MPAS Hybrid/Online Program. See https://www.franklinpierce.edu/academics/gradstudies/programs_ of_study/mpas-az/

CONNECTICUT

MAINE

MASSACHUSETTS

NEW HAMPSHIRE

NEW JERSEY

NEW YORK

PENNSYLVANIA

RHODE ISLAND

VERMONT

NORTHEAST

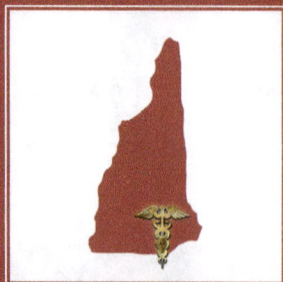

CONNECTICUT

MAINE

MASSACHUSETTS

NEW HAMPSHIRE

NEW JERSEY

NEW YORK

PENNSYLVANIA

RHODE ISLAND

VERMONT

MCPHS UNIVERSITY - MANCHESTER

Address: 1260 Elm Street, Manchester, MA 03101
Website: *https://www.mcphs.edu/academics/school-of-physician-assistant-studies/physician-assistant/physician-assistant-studies-mpas-accelerated*
Contact: *admissions@mcphs.edu*
Phone: 617-870-5964

COST OF ATTENDANCE

Tuition and Fees: $56,441
Additional Expenses: N/A
Total: $56,441*

*This figure does not include cost of living or other indirect costs..

Financial Aid: https://www.mcphs.edu/admission-and-aid/financial-services/financial-aid/graduate-financial-aid

ADDITIONAL INFORMATION

Interesting tidbit: MCPHS PA - Manchester is an accelerated 2-year MPAS program. In the second year (clinical phase), students complete supervised clinical rotations in a wide variety of settings, gaining experience in internal medicine and specialties such as surgery, women's health, psychiatry, pediatrics, and emergency medicine.

Important Updates due to COVID-19: Virtual Interview.

Were tests required? No.

Are tests expected next year? No.

What international experiences are available? International clinical sites available.

What dual degree options exist? N/A

What service-learning opportunities exist? N/A

PANCE First-Time Pass Rate: 91% (2020)

Other: Online Doctor of Science in Physician Assistant Studies available. See https://www.mcphs.edu/academics/school-of-physician-assistant-studies/physician-assistant/physican-assistant-studies-doctor-of-science

KEAN UNIVERSITY

Address: 1000 Morris Avenue, Union, NJ 07083
Website: *https://www.kean.edu/academics/programs/physician-assistant-studies-ms*
Contact: *pastudies@kean.edu*
Phone: 908-737-5916

COST OF ATTENDANCE

In-State Tuition and Fees: $38,631
Additional Expenses: N/A
Total: $38,631*

Out-of-State Tuition and Fees: $47,901
Additional Expenses: N/A
Total: $47,901*

*This figure does not include cost of living or other indirect costs..

Financial Aid: https://www.kean.edu/academics/nathan-weiss-graduate-college/graduate-financial-aid

ADDITIONAL INFORMATION

Interesting tidbit: In March 2021, Kean University PA Program was granted Accreditation - Provisional status. It is recruiting its inaugural class of 20 students. For the first class, students will apply directly through Kean University's COVID-19: N/A

Were tests required? GRE required.

Are tests expected next year? Yes graduate admissions.

Important Updates due to

What international experiences are available? N/A

What dual degree options exist? N/A

What service-learning opportunities exist? N/A

PANCE First-Time Pass Rate: N/A (PACE rate for the first cohort will be available at the conclusion of the spring 2024 semester.)

CONNECTICUT

MAINE

MASSACHUSETTS

NEW HAMPSHIRE

NEW JERSEY

NEW YORK

PENNSYLVANIA

RHODE ISLAND

VERMONT

NORTHEAST

CONNECTICUT

MAINE

MASSACHUSETTS

NEW HAMPSHIRE

NEW JERSEY

NEW YORK

PENNSYLVANIA

RHODE ISLAND

VERMONT

MONMOUTH UNIVERSITY

Address: Building C, 185 State Highway 36, West Long Branch, NJ 07764
Website: *https://www.monmouth.edu/graduate/ms-physician-assistant/*
Contact: *paprogram@monmouth.edu*
Phone: 732-923-4505

COST OF ATTENDANCE

Tuition and Fees: $57,570
Additional Expenses: N/A
Total: $57,570*

*This figure does not include cost of living or other indirect costs.

Financial Aid: https://www.monmouth.edu/finaid/prospective-students/master-of-science-in-physician-assistant-paestimated-costs-financial-aid/

ADDITIONAL INFORMATION

Interesting tidbit: Monmouth's PA graduate program consists of 28 months of coursework and supervised clinical practice experiences completed in 3-years time. Students have the summer semester off between the first and second year of didactic training.

Important Updates due to COVID-19: Students missing prerequisite courses as the result of the COVID-19 pandemic may still be eligible for an interview given they demonstrate a plan to complete these courses by the June 30 deadline.

Were tests required? GRE required.

Are tests expected next year? Yes.

What international experiences are available? N/A

What dual degree options exist? N/A

What service-learning opportunities exist? N/A

PANCE First-Time Pass Rate: 100% (2020)

RUTGERS UNIVERSITY

Address: 675 Hoes Lane West, 6th Floor, Piscataway, NJ 08854
Website: *https://shp.rutgers.edu/physician-assistant/master-of-science-physician-assistant-program/*
Contact: *pa-info@shrp.rutgers.edu*
Phone: 732-235-4445

COST OF ATTENDANCE

In-State Tuition and Fees: $31,000
Additional Expenses: $46,250
Total: $77,250

Out-of-State Tuition and Fees: $42,400
Additional Expenses: $46,250
Total: $88,650

Financial Aid: https://shp.rutgers.edu/tuition-scholarships/

ADDITIONAL INFORMATION

Interesting tidbit: Unlike the majority of PA programs (24-27 months long), Rutgers PA Program is a 33-month curriculum. Also, unlike the majority of PA programs, Rutgers PA Program is one of few PA Programs to offer both full time and part time options. Students can attend the program on a part-time basis for the first two years, and then they must become full-time students for the following two years.

Important Updates due to COVID-19: The program accepts prerequisite courses that are pass/fail. If an applicant chooses to take pass/fail courses or the applicant's college has deemed it mandatory during the Spring 2020 semester, we recommend that the applicant provide a brief statement to explain those circumstances.

Were tests required? No.

Are tests expected next year? No.

What international experiences are available? N/A

What dual degree options exist? MSPA/MPH. See 'Admissions' tab on https://shp.rutgers.edu/physician-assistant/master-of-science-physician-assistant-program/

What service-learning opportunities exist? HOPE (Health Outreach Patient Experience) Clinic

PANCE First-Time Pass Rate: 100% (2020)

Other: Articulated BA/MS or BS/MS Degree (3+3) Program. See 'Admissions' tab on https://shp.rutgers.edu/physician-assistant/master-of-science-physician-assistant-program/

CONNECTICUT

MAINE

MASSACHUSETTS

NEW HAMPSHIRE

NEW JERSEY

NEW YORK

PENNSYLVANIA

RHODE ISLAND

VERMONT

NORTHEAST

CONNECTICUT

MAINE

MASSACHUSETTS

NEW HAMPSHIRE

NEW JERSEY

NEW YORK

PENNSYLVANIA

RHODE ISLAND

VERMONT

SAINT ELIZABETH UNIVERSITY

Address: 2 Convent Road, Morristown, NJ 07960
Website: *https://www.steu.edu/academics/aas/physician-assistant/ms-in-physician-assistan*t
Contact: *mvaldez@steu.edu*
Phone: 973-290-4157

COST OF ATTENDANCE

Tuition and Fees: $47,624
Additional Expenses: N/A
Total: $47,624*

*This figure does not include cost of living or other indirect costs.

Financial Aid: https://www.steu.edu/admissions/financial-aid/graduate-financial-aid-checklist

ADDITIONAL INFORMATION

Interesting tidbit: Saint Elizabeth University launched its PA program in 2019, with the first class beginning in October 2019. SEU's 28-month MS PA program has welcomed its inaugural class of 33 students (Class of 2021) and second class of 40 students (Class of 2022).

Important Updates due to COVID-19: N/A

Were tests required? PA-CAT required.

Are tests expected next year? Yes.

What international experiences are available? N/A

What dual degree options exist? N/A

What service-learning opportunities exist? N/A

PANCE First-Time Pass Rate: N/A

SETON HALL UNIVERSITY

Address: 123 Metro Boulevard, Nutley, NJ 07110
Website: *https://www.shu.edu/academics/ms-physician-assistant.cfm*
Contact: *joann.codella@shu.edu*
Phone: 973-275-2596

COST OF ATTENDANCE

Tuition and Fees: $45,742
Additional Expenses: N/A
Total: $45,742*

*This figure does not include cost of living or other indirect costs.

Financial Aid: https://www.shu.edu/graduate-affairs/graduate-financial-aid.cfm

ADDITIONAL INFORMATION

Interesting tidbit: With a curriculum that runs for 33 months, SHU PA graduates are well prepared and have more clinical experience than their peers from other institutions.

Important Updates due to COVID-19: For completion of experience hours, Seton Hall University's Master of Science in Physician Assistant Program will accept hours completed virtually or through telemedicine. Applicants planning to apply for the 2021-2022 admissions cycle must complete a minimum of 100 hours of healthcare experience (25 of 100 hours should include shadowing a Physician Assistant).

Were tests required? GRE required.

Are tests expected next year? Yes.

What international experiences are available? N/A

What dual degree options exist? N/A

What service-learning opportunities exist? N/A

PANCE First-Time Pass Rate: 100% (2020)

Other: BS in Biology/MSPA available. See https://www.shu.edu/academics/course-catalogues.cfm

CONNECTICUT

MAINE

MASSACHUSETTS

NEW HAMPSHIRE

NEW JERSEY

NEW YORK

PENNSYLVANIA

RHODE ISLAND

VERMONT

NORTHEAST

CONNECTICUT

MAINE

MASSACHUSETTS

NEW HAMPSHIRE

NEW JERSEY

NEW YORK

PENNSYLVANIA

RHODE ISLAND

VERMONT

THOMAS JEFFERSON - NEW JERSEY

Address: 443 Laurel Oak Road, Voorhees, NJ 08043
Website: *https://www.jefferson.edu/university/health-professions/ departments/physician-assistant-studies/degrees-programs/ graduate/ms-new-jersery.html*
Contact: *enroll@jefferson.edu*
Phone: 856-784-1317

Other Locations: Center City, PA; East Falls, PA

COST OF ATTENDANCE

Tuition and Fees: $49,034
Additional Expenses: N/A
Total: $49,034*

*This figure does not include cost of living or other indirect costs.

Financial Aid: http://eastfalls.jefferson.edu/financialaid/Graduate/ index.html

ADDITIONAL INFORMATION

Interesting tidbit: The program partners with Richard Stockton University of New Jersey and Reliance Medical Group. This program builds on the relationships that Jefferson (Philadelphia University + Thomas Jefferson University) has formed with New Jersey medical communities.

Important Updates due to COVID-19: Courses taken Spring 2020 only that were transitioned from a letter grade to Pass/Fail due to COVID-19 will be accepted with a "Pass" grade. The PA Studies will accept online courses that were taken between Spring 2020 and Fall 2021 due to the outbreak of COVID-19.

Were tests required? No.

Are tests expected next year? No.

What international experiences are available? N/A

What dual degree options exist? N/A

What service-learning opportunities exist? N/A

PANCE First-Time Pass Rate: 87% (2020)

ALBANY MEDICAL COLLEGE

Address: 47 New Scotland Ave., Albany, NY 12208
Website: *https://www.amc.edu/academic/PhysicianAssistant/index.cfm*
Contact: *paprogram@amc.edu*
Phone: 518-262-5251

COST OF ATTENDANCE

Tuition and Fees: $28,828
Additional Expenses: $23,591
Total: $52,409

Financial Aid: https://www.amc.edu/academic/PhysicianAssistant/old_section/FinancialAid.cfm?cssearch=463155_1

ADDITIONAL INFORMATION

Interesting tidbit: The program design is 28 consecutive months of didactic instruction, clinical rotations, and research. The first four terms are dedicated to didactic curriculum. During the clinical year (Terms 5-7) students complete rotations in medicine, surgery, and medical and surgical specialties. A Portfolio for the Clinical Masters Student is developed with ongoing PA faculty advisement throughout the program.

Important Updates due to COVID-19: The program will accept online labs for the 2020 and 2021 academic terms if this is all the institution is offering. It will only accept a Pass/Fail grade from the 2020 academic terms.

Were tests required? No

Are tests expected next year? No.

What international experiences are available? N/A

What dual degree options exist? N/A

What service-learning opportunities exist? N/A

PANCE First-Time Pass Rate: 98% (2020)

Other: Articulated BS/MSPA available with a number of colleges. See 'Alternative Admissions Pathways' on https://www.amc.edu/academic/PhysicianAssistant/admissions.cfm.

CONNECTICUT

MAINE

MASSACHUSETTS

NEW HAMPSHIRE

NEW JERSEY

NEW YORK

PENNSYLVANIA

RHODE ISLAND

VERMONT

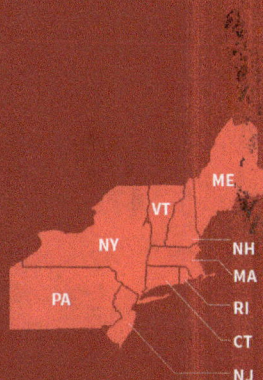

NORTHEAST

CONNECTICUT

MAINE

MASSACHUSETTS

NEW HAMPSHIRE

NEW JERSEY

NEW YORK

PENNSYLVANIA

RHODE ISLAND

VERMONT

CANISIUS COLLEGE

Address: 2001 Main Street, Buffalo, NY 14208
Website: *https://www.canisius.edu/academics/programs/physician-assistant*
Contact: *pastudies@canisius.edu*
Phone: 716-883-8500

COST OF ATTENDANCE

Tuition and Fees: $44.210
Additional Expenses: N/A
Total: $44,210*

*This figure does not include cost of living or other indirect costs.

Financial Aid: https://www.canisius.edu/admissions/graduate-admissions/financing-graduate-school

ADDITIONAL INFORMATION

Interesting tidbit: The Canisius College PA program has formed an affiliation with the University at Buffalo to participate in their nationally recognized interprofessional collaborative practice program. Students will be credentialed in a number of activities involving collaboration with students in medicine, nursing, physical therapy, occupational therapy, pharmacy, and more.

Important Updates due to COVID-19: N/A

Were tests required? No.

Are tests expected next year? No.

What international experiences are available? N/A

What dual degree options exist? N/A

What service-learning opportunities exist? A service-learning requirement that will ensure early exposure to underserved members of the Western New York community.

PANCE First-Time Pass Rate: N/A (available for the first cohort after May 2023 graduation)

CLARKSON UNIVERSITY

Address: 8 Clarkson Avenue, Potsdam, NY 13699
Website: *http://www.clarkson.edu/pa*
Contact: *pa@clarkson.edu*
Phone: 315-268-2161

COST OF ATTENDANCE

Tuition and Fees: $48,948
Additional Expenses: N/A
Total: $48,948

*This figure does not include cost of living or other indirect costs.

Financial Aid: https://www.clarkson.edu/graduate-admissions/
financial-aid-costs-scholarships

ADDITIONAL INFORMATION

Interesting tidbit: High school seniors who apply to Clarkson University for undergraduate studies are eligible to apply for the pre-physician assistant plan as part of their application. During their senior year, students must still formally apply through the centralized process (CASPA). Ten of the available seats in each cohort will be held for Clarkson University pre-physician assistant students.

Important Updates due to COVID-19: N/A

Were tests required? GRE and CASPer required.

Are tests expected next year? Yes.

What international experiences are available? N/A

What dual degree options exist? N/A

What service-learning opportunities exist? N/A

PANCE First-Time Pass Rate: 86% (2020)

CONNECTICUT

MAINE

MASSACHUSETTS

NEW HAMPSHIRE

NEW JERSEY

NEW YORK

PENNSYLVANIA

RHODE ISLAND

VERMONT

NORTHEAST

CONNECTICUT

MAINE

MASSACHUSETTS

NEW HAMPSHIRE

NEW JERSEY

NEW YORK

PENNSYLVANIA

RHODE ISLAND

VERMONT

CUNY YORK COLLEGE

Address: 94 - 20 Guy R. Brewer Blvd., Jamaica, NY 11451
Website: *http://www.york.cuny.edu/academics/departments/health-professions/physician-assistant*
Contact: *paprogram@york.cuny.edu*
Phone: 718-262-2460

COST OF ATTENDANCE

In-State Tuition and Fees: $22,770
Additional Expenses: N/A
Total: $22,770*

Out-of-State Tuition and Fees: $38,093
Additional Expenses: N/A
Total: $38,093*

*This figure does not include cost of living or other indirect costs.

Financial Aid: https://www.york.cuny.edu/produce-and-print/
contents/bulletin-graduate/financial-aid-graduate-students

ADDITIONAL INFORMATION

Interesting tidbit: In October of 2019, the York PA Program made it to the finals while competing in the New York State Society of Physician Assistants (NYSSPA) Medical Jeopardy. It was the first first time that the York PA Program made it to the finals.

Important Updates due to COVID-19: N/A

Were tests required? No.

Are tests expected next year? No.

What international experiences are available? N/A

What dual degree options exist? N/A

What service-learning opportunities exist? N?A

PANCE First-Time Pass Rate: 92% (2020)

D'YOUVILLE COLLEGE

Address: 320 Porter Avenue, Buffalo, NY 14201
Website: *http://www.dyc.edu/academics/pa/*
Contact: *chpadmit@cmich.edu*
Phone: 989-774-1730

COST OF ATTENDANCE

Tuition and Fees: $29,812
Additional Expenses: $19,551
Total: $49,363

Financial Aid: http://www.dyc.edu/admissions/financial-aid-scholarships/

ADDITIONAL INFORMATION

Interesting tidbit: D'Youville PA program is a direct entry BS + MS in Physician Assistant pathway. At D'Youville, in just four and half years you can earn a combined bachelor's and master's degree in physician assistant (BS+MS).

Important Updates due to COVID-19: Virtual interviews.

Were tests required? No.

Are tests expected next year? No.

What international experiences are available? N/A

What dual degree options exist? N/A

What service-learning opportunities exist? N/A

PANCE First-Time Pass Rate: 91% (2020)

CONNECTICUT

MAINE

MASSACHUSETTS

NEW HAMPSHIRE

NEW JERSEY

NEW YORK

PENNSYLVANIA

RHODE ISLAND

VERMONT

NORTHEAST

CONNECTICUT

MAINE

MASSACHUSETTS

NEW HAMPSHIRE

NEW JERSEY

NEW YORK

PENNSYLVANIA

RHODE ISLAND

VERMONT

DAEMEN COLLEGE

Address: 4380 Main Street, Amherst, NY 14226
Website: *https://www.daemen.edu/academics/areas-study/physician-assistant/physician-assistant-studies-ms*
Contact: *mmoore@daemen.edu*
Phone: 716-839-8383

COST OF ATTENDANCE

Tuition and Fees: $34,830
Additional Expenses: N/A
Total: $34,830*

*This figure does not include cost of living or other indirect costs.

Financial Aid: https://www.daemen.edu/admissions/tuition-fees-2021-2022

ADDITIONAL INFORMATION

Interesting tidbit: Daemen College offers two degree tracks - BS/MS and MS. The College first offers seats in the PA Program to students accepted as freshmen. Seats in the PA Program left unfilled are then offered to graduate students, leaving approximately 15-25 seats available each year for graduate students.

Important Updates due to COVID-19: Courses taken online from spring of 2020 through summer of 2021 will be accepted. Pass/fail and satisfactory/unsatisfactory grades are strongly discouraged for the courses of anatomy, physiology, organic chemistry and microbiology.

Were tests required? No.

Are tests expected next year? No.

What international experiences are available? Students Without Borders (SWOB) program organizes annual trips to Dominican Republic. See https://www.daemen.edu/academics/areas-study/physician-assistant/students-without-borders

What dual degree options exist? N/A

What service-learning opportunities exist? Students Without Borders (SWOB) program. See https://www.daemen.edu/academics/areas-study/physician-assistant/students-without-borders

PANCE First-Time Pass Rate: 98% (2020)

Other: BS in Health Science/MS in Physician Assistant Studies. See https://www.daemen.edu/academics/areas-study/physician-assistant/natural-science-health-science-bs-physician-assistant

HOFSTRA UNIVERSITY

Address: 113 Hofstra University, Hempstead, NY 11549
Website: *https://www.hofstra.edu/academics/colleges/nursing-physician-assistant/physician-assistant/*
Contact: *pagrogram@hofstra.edu*
Phone: 516-463-4074

COST OF ATTENDANCE

Tuition and Fees: $53,612
Additional Expenses: N/A
Total: $53,612*

*This figure does not include cost of living or other indirect costs.

Financial Aid: https://www.hofstra.edu/financial-aid/graduate.html

ADDITIONAL INFORMATION

Interesting tidbit: The professional curriculum is divided into 3 semesters of didactic instruction, 3 semesters of clinical clerkships, and 1 semester of research for a total of two and a half years of study. The research semester culminates in a master's thesis and professional poster presentation.

Important Updates due to COVID-19: N/A

Were tests required? No.

Are tests expected next year? No.

What international experiences are available? N/A

What dual degree options exist? N/A

What service-learning opportunities exist? N/A

PANCE First-Time Pass Rate: 96% (2020)

Other: Direct entry BS/MS available. See https://www.hofstra.edu/physician-assistant-studies/freshman-applicants.html

CONNECTICUT

MAINE

MASSACHUSETTS

NEW HAMPSHIRE

NEW JERSEY

NEW YORK

PENNSYLVANIA

RHODE ISLAND

VERMONT

NORTHEAST

CONNECTICUT

MAINE

MASSACHUSETTS

NEW HAMPSHIRE

NEW JERSEY

NEW YORK

PENNSYLVANIA

RHODE ISLAND

VERMONT

ITHACA COLLEGE

Address: 953 Danby Road, Ithaca, NY 14850
Website: *https://www.ithaca.edu/academics/school-health-sciences-and-human-performance/graduate-programs/physician-assistant-studies*
Contact: *paadmissions@ithaca.edu*
Phone: 607-274-7007

COST OF ATTENDANCE

Tuition and Fees: $50,580
Additional Expenses: $21,092
Total: $71,672

Financial Aid: https://www.ithaca.edu/tuition-financial-aid/graduate-costs-financial-aid

ADDITIONAL INFORMATION

Interesting tidbit: In March 2021, Ithaca College received provisional accreditation from the ARC-PA for its Master of Science in Physician Assistant Studies program. It anticipates that the the inaugural class entering in fall 2021 will consist of about 30 students for its 27-month MSPAS program

Important Updates due to COVID-19: For classes entering fall 2021 and 2022, DPCE is reduced to 250 hrs and the PA-CAT requirement is waived. Courses only offered pass-fail by the college or university due to COVID 19 (Spring 2020 through Spring 2021) will be accepted and will not contribute to the calculated GPA or Pre-Requisite GPA. Pass-Fail courses will not be accepted if there was an option to choose pass-fail or graded.

Were tests required? No, PA-CAT requirement waived due to COVID-19.

Are tests expected next year? PA-CAT required.

What international experiences are available? N/A

What dual degree options exist? N/A

What service-learning opportunities exist? N/A

PANCE First-Time Pass Rate: N/A (will be available after the graduation of the first cohort in 2023)

LE MOYNE COLLEGE

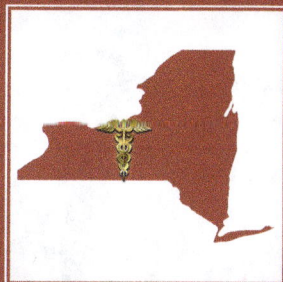

Address: 1419 Salt Springs Road, Syracuse, NY 13214
Website: *https://www.lemoyne.edu/pa*
Contact: *physassist@lemoyne.edu*
Phone: 315-445-4745

COST OF ATTENDANCE

Tuition and Fees: $46,268
Additional Expenses: $28,395
Total: $74,663

Financial Aid: https://www.lemoyne.edu/Admission/Financial-Aid/Incoming-Graduates

ADDITIONAL INFORMATION

Interesting tidbit: Le Moyne is one of only a handful of PA programs that presents medical humanities courses as integral to training. Community service learning moves the student from the classroom to the neighborhoods to facilitate an even greater, deeper understanding of the human condition in the "real world."

Important Updates due to COVID-19: Le Moyne accepts Pass/Satisfactory grades for prerequisite work however it is not recommended. Showcasing P/S grades will make applications significantly less competitive.

Were tests required? No.

Are tests expected next year? No.

What international experiences are available? Students who meet strict program criteria may submit appropriate paperwork (for elective rotations only) to be considered for international experiences.

What dual degree options exist? N/A

What service-learning opportunities exist? Community service learning available. Contact the admissions office.

PANCE First-Time Pass Rate: 96% (2020)

Other: Le Moyne offers a direct-entry program to high school seniors. See https://www.lemoyne.edu/Academics/Undergraduate-Programs/Health-Sciences/Direct-Entry-PA-Program

Other: Veteran - Physician Assistant Bridge pathway for students who identify as having former military service. See https://www.lemoyne.edu/Academics/Veterans-Programs-and-Military-Affairs/Veteran-Physican-Assistant-Bridge-Path

CONNECTICUT

MAINE

MASSACHUSETTS

NEW HAMPSHIRE

NEW JERSEY

NEW YORK

PENNSYLVANIA

RHODE ISLAND

VERMONT

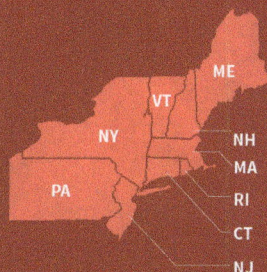

NORTHEAST

CONNECTICUT

MAINE

MASSACHUSETTS

NEW HAMPSHIRE

NEW JERSEY

NEW YORK

PENNSYLVANIA

RHODE ISLAND

VERMONT

LONG ISLAND UNIVERSITY

Address: 1 University Plaza, Brooklyn, NY 11201
Website: *https://www.liu.edu/Brooklyn/Academics/Schools/School-of-Health-Professions/Dept/Physician-Assistant/MS-PAS*
Contact: *bkln-pastudies@liu.edu*
Phone: 718-488-1505

COST OF ATTENDANCE

Tuition and Fees: $46,363
Additional Expenses: N/A
Total: $46,363*

*This figure does not include cost of living or other indirect costs.

Financial Aid: https://liu.edu/post/enrollment-services/financial-aid/types-of-financial-aid

Note: Graduate students are automatically considered for university merit-based scholarships and fellowships as part of the admission process.

ADDITIONAL INFORMATION

Interesting tidbit: LIU Brooklyn's Master of Science in Physician Assistant Studies is an intense, 28-month professional program. During the didactic year, medical courses are augmented with weekly clinical experiences. During the clinical year, students are assigned to clinical rotations for fifteen months on a full-time basis, returning to the program once every five weeks.

Important Updates due to COVID-19: N/A

Were tests required? GRE required.

Are tests expected next year? Yes.

What international experiences are available? N/A

What dual degree options exist? N/A

What service-learning opportunities exist? N/A

PANCE First-Time Pass Rate: 100% (2020)

MARIST COLLEGE

Address: 3399 North Road Rotunda, Poughkeepsie, NY 12601
Website: *http://www.marist.edu/science/physassist/*
Contact: *pa-program@marist.edu*
Phone: 845-575-3308

COST OF ATTENDANCE

Tuition and Fees: $50,850
Additional Expenses: $29,646
Total: $80,496

Financial Aid: https://www.marist.edu/science/physician-asst/
scholarships-financial-aid

ADDITIONAL INFORMATION

Interesting tidbit: The Master of Science in Physician Assistant Studies Program is a 24-month, full-time program consisting of one 12-month didactic phase and one 12-month clinical phase. Because the program is located in the Marist College Allied Health Building, the program shares resources and activities with other programs in the School of Science on campus, providing opportunities to develop inter-professional skills.

Important Updates due to COVID-19: If applying for the Summer 2021 cohort, prerequisite pass/fail course(s) completed during the Spring 2020 and/or Summer 2020 semesters will be evaluated on an individual basis. If an applicant is not given an option to receive a letter grade for a prerequisite course during Spring 2020 or Summer 2020, written documentation from their institution will need to be provided and submitted to the Office of Graduate Admission. Online labs will be accepted for prerequisite coursework completed during the Spring 2020 and Summer 2020 semesters.

Were tests required? No.

Are tests expected next year? No.

What international experiences are available? N/A

What dual degree options exist? N/A

What service-learning opportunities exist? N/A

PANCE First-Time Pass Rate: 92% (2020)

CONNECTICUT

MAINE

MASSACHUSETTS

NEW HAMPSHIRE

NEW JERSEY

NEW YORK

PENNSYLVANIA

RHODE ISLAND

VERMONT

NORTHEAST

CONNECTICUT

MAINE

MASSACHUSETTS

NEW HAMPSHIRE

NEW JERSEY

NEW YORK

PENNSYLVANIA

RHODE ISLAND

VERMONT

MERCY COLLEGE

Address: 1200 Waters Place, Bronx, NY 10461
Website: *https://www.mercy.edu/degrees-programs/ms-physician-assistant*
Contact: *paprogram@mercy.edu*
Phone: 718-678-8844

COST OF ATTENDANCE

Tuition and Fees: $55,753
Additional Expenses: N/A
Total: $55,753*

*This figure does not include cost of living or other indirect costs.

Financial Aid: https://www.mercy.edu/admissions-aid/graduate-admissions/graduate-financial-aid-and-fees

ADDITIONAL INFORMATION

Interesting tidbit: The Physician Assistant program at Mercy College embodies the principles of primary care medicine incorporating the biopsychosocial model of medical education. With this model, students learn to incorporate knowledge from biological science, while integrating psychological and social factors with population/community-based medicine in order to deliver comprehensive primary health care. Its emphasis on primary care is also manifested in requiring applicants to have fulfilled 250 hours of the 500 hours of direct patient care experience in a primary care setting,

Important Updates due to COVID-19: N/A

Were tests required? No.

Are tests expected next year? No.

What international experiences are available? International medical missions.

What dual degree options exist? N/A

What service-learning opportunities exist? Mobile health van community outreach.

PANCE First-Time Pass Rate: 81% (2020)

NEW YORK INSTITUTE OF TECHNOLOGY

Address: 352 Northern Boulevard, P.O. Box 8000, Old Westbury, NY 11568
Website: *http://www.nyit.edu/pa*
Contact: *pa@nyit.edu*
Phone: 516-686-3881

COST OF ATTENDANCE

Tuition and Fees: $44,164
Additional Expenses: N/A
Total: $44,164*

*This figure does not include cost of living or other indirect costs.

Financial Aid: https://www.nyit.edu/admissions/graduate_scholarships

ADDITIONAL INFORMATION

Interesting tidbit: There are two pathways to the Physician Assistant Studies at NYIT - BS/MSPAS and MSPAS. BS/MSPAS is a six-year program intended for qualified high school applicants.

Important Updates due to COVID-19: NYIT PA program will accept online courses, including labs, for the completion of our prerequisites. It will also accept a grade of pass (in lieu of a numeric letter grade) for all courses completed in Spring 2020. The program is reducing the required patient care experience requirement to 100 hours for the 2020-2021 and 2021-2022 application cycles.

Were tests required? No.

Are tests expected next year? No.

What international experiences are available? Global Health organized trips to Haiti and Ghana. Contact NYIT Center for Global Health for details.

What dual degree options exist? N/A

What service-learning opportunities exist? Service-learning initiatives both domestically and abroad.

PANCE First-Time Pass Rate: 98% (2020)

Other: Direct Entry program, BS Life Science/MS PAS available for high school students. See https://www.nyit.edu/degrees/physician_assistant_studies_bsms

CONNECTICUT

MAINE

MASSACHUSETTS

NEW HAMPSHIRE

NEW JERSEY

NEW YORK

PENNSYLVANIA

RHODE ISLAND

VERMONT

NORTHEAST

CONNECTICUT

MAINE

MASSACHUSETTS

NEW HAMPSHIRE

NEW JERSEY

NEW YORK

PENNSYLVANIA

RHODE ISLAND

VERMONT

PACE UNIVERSITY - LENOX HILL HOSPITAL

Address: 163 William Street, 5th floor, New York, NY 10038
Website: *https://chp.pace.edu/explore-programs/physician-assistant-program-nyc*
Contact: *paprogram_admissions@pace.edu*
Phone: 212-618-6052

COST OF ATTENDANCE

Tuition and Fees: $76,942
Additional Expenses: N/A
Total: $76,942*

*This figure does not include cost of living or other indirect costs.

Financial Aid: https://catalog.pace.edu/graduate/general-university/graduate-financial-aid/

ADDITIONAL INFORMATION

Interesting tidbit: The PA program's inception in 1995 was a unique arrangement between Lenox Hill Hospital and Pace University's Department of Biological Sciences. In 2010, the PA Program relocated from Pace University's Department of Biological Sciences into the College of Health Professions. After completion of all requirements, a combined master of science degree from Pace University and a certificate of completion from Lenox Hill Hospital is awarded.

Important Updates due to COVID-19: Pace University - Lenox Hill Hospital PA Program will accept pre-requisite course work taken on the Pass/Fail grading system for coursework completed in the Spring 2020 and Summer 2020 semesters only.

Were tests required? No.

Are tests expected next year? No.

What international experiences are available? N/A

What dual degree options exist? N/A

What service-learning opportunities exist? N/A

PANCE First-Time Pass Rate: 97% (2020)

PACE UNIVERSITY - PLEASANTVILLE

Address: 861 Bedford Road, Pleasantville, NY 10570
Website: *https://www.pace.edu/college-health-professions/
graduate-degree-programs/physician-assistant-program-
pleasantville*
Contact: *paplv@pace.edu*
Phone: 914-597-8319

COST OF ATTENDANCE

Tuition and Fees: $73,586
Additional Expenses: N/A
Total: $73,586*

*This figure does not include cost of living or other indirect costs.

Financial Aid: https://catalog.pace.edu/graduate/general-
university/graduate-financial-aid/

ADDITIONAL INFORMATION

Interesting tidbit: Pace University - Pleasantville PA program
is developing clinical clerkships to provide students with an
opportunity to learn and provide care in medically underserved
areas or with medically underserved populations including rural,
inner-city, immigrant, indigent, military and prison populations.
Clerkships will also focus on the needs, resources and counseling
available for these special populations and the influence that
culture and socioeconomic factors can have on healthcare delivery.

Important Updates due to COVID-19: Pace University Physician
Assistant Program-Pleasantville grading system for coursework
completed in the Spring 2020 and Summer 2020 semesters only.
It will also accept all coursework completed remotely (on-line),
including laboratory coursework, that was taken in Spring 2020
and Summer 2020. A minimum of 200 hours of direct patient care
experience will be accepted for the 2021-2022 cycle due to the
impact of Covid-19. PA work/shadowing hours are not required for
the 2021-2022 cycle.

Were tests required? No.

Are tests expected next year? No.

What international experiences are available? International
rotation available through Child Family Health International. See
"International Elective Rotation" on https://chp.pace.edu/pa-
pleasantville-clinical-affiliations

What dual degree options exist? N/A

What service-learning opportunities exist? Clinical clerkship.
See "Medically Underserved Area" on https://chp.pace.edu/pa-
pleasantville-clinical-affiliations

PANCE First-Time Pass Rate: 90% (2019)

CONNECTICUT

MAINE

MASSACHUSETTS

NEW HAMPSHIRE

NEW JERSEY

NEW YORK

PENNSYLVANIA

RHODE ISLAND

VERMONT

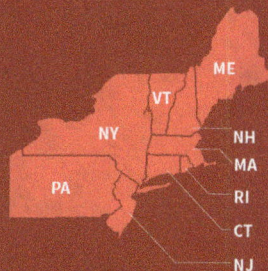

NORTHEAST

CONNECTICUT

MAINE

MASSACHUSETTS

NEW HAMPSHIRE

NEW JERSEY

NEW YORK

PENNSYLVANIA

RHODE ISLAND

VERMONT

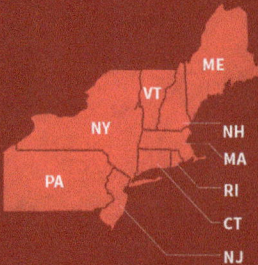

ROCHESTER INSTITUTE OF TECHNOLOGY

Address: 153 Lomb Memorial Drive, Rochester, NY 14623-5608
Website: *http://www.rit.edu/healthsciences/graduate-programs/physician-assistant*
Contact: *llwscl@rit.edu*
Phone: 585-475-5151

COST OF ATTENDANCE

Tuition and Fees: $50,136
Additional Expenses: $18,397
Total: $68,533

Financial Aid: https://www.rit.edu/admissions/financial-aid

ADDITIONAL INFORMATION

Interesting tidbit: The physician assistant major is offered as a BS/MS degree program, which enables students to earn both a bachelor's degree and a master's degree in five years. The curriculum is divided into a pre-professional phase (years 1 and 2) and a professional phase, (years 3, 4, and 5).

Important Updates due to COVID-19: N/A

Were tests required? No.

Are tests expected next year? No.

What international experiences are available? N/A

What dual degree options exist? N/A

What service-learning opportunities exist? N/A

PANCE First-Time Pass Rate: 81% (2020)

ST. BONAVENTURE UNIVERSITY

Address: 3261 West State Road, St. Bonaventure, NY 14778
Website: *https://www.sbu.edu/academics/physician-assistant-studies*
Contact: *Direct email link available on the PA Program page*
Phone: 716-375-2272

COST OF ATTENDANCE

Tuition and Fees: $48,310
Additional Expenses: N/A
Total: $48,310*

*This figure does not include cost of living or other indirect costs.

Financial Aid: https://www.sbu.edu/admissions/graduate-admissions/scholarships-aid-for-graduate-students

Note: Students enrolled in the Physician Assistant program are not eligible for St. Bonaventure institutional aid/scholarships.

ADDITIONAL INFORMATION

Interesting tidbit: In March 2020, the Master of Science in Physician Assistant Studies program at St. Bonaventure University received provisional accreditation. It plans to 25 students in January 2021, 35 students in January 2022, and 40 students every January thereafter.

Important Updates due to COVID-19: Due to the coronavirus pandemic, PA shadowing requirement is waived for the 2020-2021 admission cycle.

Were tests required? GRE required.

Are tests expected next year? Yes.

What international experiences are available? N/A

What dual degree options exist? N/A

What service-learning opportunities exist? N/A

PANCE First-Time Pass Rate: N/A (Inaugural class will graduate in 2023.)

CONNECTICUT

MAINE

MASSACHUSETTS

NEW HAMPSHIRE

NEW JERSEY

NEW YORK

PENNSYLVANIA

RHODE ISLAND

VERMONT

NORTHEAST

CONNECTICUT

MAINE

MASSACHUSETTS

NEW HAMPSHIRE

NEW JERSEY

NEW YORK

PENNSYLVANIA

RHODE ISLAND

VERMONT

ST. JOHN'S UNIVERSITY

Address: 8000 Utopia Parkway, Queens, NY 11439
Website: *https://www.stjohns.edu/academics/programs/physician-assistant-master-science*
Contact: *medranor@stjohns.edu*
Phone: 718-990-2000

COST OF ATTENDANCE

Tuition and Fees: $41,850*
Additional Expenses: N/A
Total: $41,850*

*Tuition only.

Financial Aid: https://www.stjohns.edu/admission/tuition-and-financial-aid/graduatelaw-aid

ADDITIONAL INFORMATION

Interesting tidbit: St. John's University PA Program developed an educational program that would reach those most in need—"the poor, alienated and the aged." The program will empower professionals to return to their own neighborhoods to promote preventive medicine and deliver affordable, high quality primary care.

Important Updates due to COVID-19: N/A

Were tests required? No.

Are tests expected next year? No.

What international experiences are available? N/A

What dual degree options exist? N/A

What service-learning opportunities exist? N/A

PANCE First-Time Pass Rate: 84% (2020)

STONY BROOK UNIVERSITY HEALTH SCIENCE CENTER

Address: 101 Nicolls Road, Health Science Center, Stony Brook, NY 11794
Website: *https://healthtechnology.stonybrookmedicine.edu/programs/pa/elpa*
Contact: *paprogram@stonybrook.edu*
Phone: 631-444-2252

Other Locations: Southampton, NY

COST OF ATTENDANCE

In-State Tuition and Fees: $20,952
Additional Expenses: $16,664
Total: $37,616

Out-of-State Tuition and Fees: $38,723
Additional Expenses: $16,934
Total: $55,657

Financial Aid: https://www.stonybrook.edu/commcms/hsstudents/financialaid/index.php

ADDITIONAL INFORMATION

Interesting tidbit: Stony Brook PA program is part of an academic Health Sciences Center (HSC) that includes a nationally-ranked University Hospital, and Schools of Medicine, Dentistry, Nursing, Social Work, as well as the School of Health Technology and Management (SHTM). As part of one of the top-ranked public research universities in the US, our HSC offers an exceptionally rich environment for health professions education, complemented by a group of affiliates that provide outstanding clinical training in a variety of environments.

Important Updates due to COVID-19: For coursework completed, or in progress from March 2020 through August 2021, grades of P/NC or S/U will be accepted in lieu of letter grades. Online courses from accredited institutions will be accepted toward requirements. Minimum acceptable number of direct patient care hours required for application is reduced to 500 hours from 1,000 hours.

Were tests required? No.

Are tests expected next year? No.

What international experiences are available? N/A

What dual degree options exist? N/A

What service-learning opportunities exist? N/A

PANCE First-Time Pass Rate: 98% (2020)

CONNECTICUT

MAINE

MASSACHUSETTS

NEW HAMPSHIRE

NEW JERSEY

NEW YORK

PENNSYLVANIA

RHODE ISLAND

VERMONT

NORTHEAST

STONY BROOK UNIVERSITY SOUTHAMPTON

Address: 39 Tuckahoe Road, Southampton, NY 11968
Website: *https://healthtechnology.stonybrookmedicine.edu/programs/pa/elpa*
Contact: *paprogram@stonybrook.edu*
Phone: 631-444-2252

Other Locations: Stony Brook, NY

COST OF ATTENDANCE

In-State Tuition and Fees: $20,952
Additional Expenses: $16,664
Total: $37,616

Out-of-State Tuition and Fees: $38,723
Additional Expenses: $16,934
Total: $55,657

Financial Aid: https://www.stonybrook.edu/commcms/hsstudents/financialaid/index.php

ADDITIONAL INFORMATION

Interesting tidbit: In 2018, the Stony Brook PA Program expanded to the Stony Brook Southampton campus. There are 25 PA students on the Southampton campus in addition to the 44 students on the Stony Brook location campus.

Important Updates due to COVID-19: For coursework completed, or in progress from March 2020 through August 2021, grades of P/NC or S/U will be accepted in lieu of letter grades. Online courses from accredited institutions will be accepted toward requirements. Minimum acceptable number of direct patient care hours required for application is reduced to 500 hours from 1,000 hours.

Were tests required? No.

Are tests expected next year? No.

What international experiences are available? N/A

What dual degree options exist? N/A

What service-learning opportunities exist? N/A

PANCE First-Time Pass Rate: 98% (2020)

CONNECTICUT

MAINE

MASSACHUSETTS

NEW HAMPSHIRE

NEW JERSEY

NEW YORK

PENNSYLVANIA

RHODE ISLAND

VERMONT

SUNY DOWNSTATE MEDICAL CENTER

Address: 450 Clarkson Avenue, Brooklyn, NY 11203
Website: *https://sls.downstate.edu/admissions/chrp/pa/index.html*
Contact: *pa.chrp@downstate.edu*
Phone: 718-270-2325

COST OF ATTENDANCE

In-State Tuition and Fees: $21,962
Additional Expenses: N/A
Total: $21,962*

Out-of-State Tuition and Fees: $40,306
Additional Expenses: N/A
Total: $40,306*

*This figure does not include cost of living or other indirect costs.

Financial Aid: https://sls.downstate.edu/financial_aid/

ADDITIONAL INFORMATION

Interesting tidbit: The SUNY DHSU PA program is a twenty-seven month, full-time program designed to provide the academic and clinical foundations for primary-care Physician Assistant. Graduates of the Program are trained with a focus on Primary Care.

Important Updates due to COVID-19: N/A

Were tests required? No.

Are tests expected next year? No.

What international experiences are available? N/A

What dual degree options exist? N/A

What service-learning opportunities exist? N/A

PANCE First-Time Pass Rate: 93% (2020)

Other: Physician Assistant Master's Completion Post Professional Degree program.

CONNECTICUT

MAINE

MASSACHUSETTS

NEW HAMPSHIRE

NEW JERSEY

NEW YORK

PENNSYLVANIA

RHODE ISLAND

VERMONT

NORTHEAST

CONNECTICUT

MAINE

MASSACHUSETTS

NEW HAMPSHIRE

NEW JERSEY

NEW YORK

PENNSYLVANIA

RHODE ISLAND

VERMONT

SUNY UPSTATE MEDICAL CENTER

Address: 750 East Adams Street, Syracuse, NY 13210
Website: *http://www.upstate.edu/chp/programs/pa/index.php*
Contact: *admissfa@upstate.edu*
Phone: 315-464-4570

COST OF ATTENDANCE

In-State Tuition and Fees: $24,330
Additional Expenses: $27,482
Total: $51,812

Out-of-State Tuition and Fees: $44,970
Additional Expenses: $27,482
Total: $72,452

Financial Aid: https://www.upstate.edu/financialaid/programs/
index.php

ADDITIONAL INFORMATION

Interesting tidbit: SUNY Upstate PA program's emphasis is on serving the rural and medically underserved populations throughout New York State. A unique feature of its training program is the design of the clinical year of training. Students live in an assigned medically underserved community in Upstate New York for 12 months, completing all clinical rotations in that designated region.

Important Updates due to COVID-19: The Program will accept Pass/Fail coursework if the applicant's undergraduate institution has required students to go to Pass/Fail coursework.

Were tests required? GRE required.

Are tests expected next year? Yes.

What international experiences are available? N/A

What dual degree options exist? N/A

What service-learning opportunities exist? N/A

PANCE First-Time Pass Rate: 88% (2020)

THE CUNY SCHOOL OF MEDICINE

Address: 160 Convent Avenue, New York, NY 10031
Website: *https://www.ccny.cuny.edu/csom/physician-assistant-program*
Contact: *paprogramadmissions@med.cuny.edu*
Phone: 212-650-7745

COST OF ATTENDANCE

In-State Tuition and Fees: $18,547
Additional Expenses: N/A
Total: $18,547*

Out-of-State Tuition and Fees: $36,112
Additional Expenses: N/A
Total: $36,112*

*This figure does not include cost of living or other indirect costs.

Financial Aid: https://www.ccny.cuny.edu/financialaid/graduate-financial-aid

ADDITIONAL INFORMATION

Interesting tidbit: The Physician Assistant Program requires 28 continuous months of instruction divided into three phases - didactic phase (12 months), clinical education phase (12 months) and research phase (4 months). The Program is committed to increasing the number of physician assistants of African-American, Latino, and other ethnic backgrounds, whose communities have historically been under-served.

Important Updates due to COVID-19: CUNY will not disadvantage students who present P (pass) or CR (credit) grades in their transcripts for courses taken during Spring 2020. In addition, CUNY will not disadvantage students whose prerequisite courses were transitioned to virtual during the Spring, Summer, and Fall 2020 and/or Spring and Summer 2021 semesters. Due to COVID-19, Spring/Summer/Fall 2020, and Spring/Summer 2021 online courses and laboratory components will be accepted.

Were tests required? No.

Are tests expected next year? No.

What international experiences are available? N/A

What dual degree options exist? N/A

What service-learning opportunities exist? N/A

PANCE First-Time Pass Rate: 88% (2021)

CONNECTICUT

MAINE

MASSACHUSETTS

NEW HAMPSHIRE

NEW JERSEY

NEW YORK

PENNSYLVANIA

RHODE ISLAND

VERMONT

NORTHEAST

CONNECTICUT

MAINE

MASSACHUSETTS

NEW HAMPSHIRE

NEW JERSEY

NEW YORK

PENNSYLVANIA

RHODE ISLAND

VERMONT

TOURO COLLEGE - LONG ISLAND

Address: 225 Eastview Drive, Central Islip, NY 11722
Website: *https://shs.touro.edu/programs/physician-assistant/physician-assistant-long-island/*
Contact: *enrollhealth@touro.edu*
Phone: 631-665-1600
Other Locations: Nassau University Medical Center, NY

COST OF ATTENDANCE

Tuition and Fees: $42,280
Additional Expenses: N/A
Total: $42,280*

*This figure does not include cost of living or other indirect costs.

Financial Aid: https://shs.touro.edu/admissions--aid/financial-aid/applying-for-aid/

ADDITIONAL INFORMATION

Interesting tidbit: The PA Long Island/NUMC program is a 28-month, 7-semester professional, graduate-level program, culminating in a joint BS/MS degree. Students can enroll in either the Central Islip campus or the Nassau University Medical Center Extension (NUMC). Long Island classes begin in August each year, and NUMC classes in January.

Important Updates due to COVID-19: Applications may be accepted and processed without completed Direct Patient Care experience hours with the understanding that these hours will be completed as soon as permissible and may be required in the event of acceptance if circumstances allow.

Were tests required? No.

Are tests expected next year? No.

What international experiences are available? N/A

What dual degree options exist? N/A

What service-learning opportunities exist? N/A

PANCE First-Time Pass Rate: 98% (2021)

TOURO COLLEGE - NUMC

Address: 2201 Hempstead Turnpike, East Meadow, NY 11554
Website: *https://shs.touro.edu/programs/physician-assistant/physician-assistant-long-island/*
Contact: *enrollhealth@touro.edu*
Phone: 631-665-1600

Other Locations: Central Islip, NY

COST OF ATTENDANCE

Tuition and Fees: $42,280
Additional Expenses: N/A
Total: $42,280*

*This figure does not include cost of living or other indirect costs.

Financial Aid: https://shs.touro.edu/admissions--aid/financial-aid/applying-for-aid/

ADDITIONAL INFORMATION

Interesting tidbit: NUMC is an extension site for the Touro Long Island PA program. With two campuses on Long Island, students have the option to start their BS/MS PA program in January or August.

Important Updates due to COVID-19: Applications may be accepted and processed without completed Direct Patient Care experience hours with the understanding that these hours will be completed as soon as permissible and may be required in the event of acceptance if circumstances allow.

Were tests required? No.

Are tests expected next year? No.

What international experiences are available? N/A

What dual degree options exist? N/A

What service-learning opportunities exist? N/A

PANCE First-Time Pass Rate: 100% (2021)

CONNECTICUT

MAINE

MASSACHUSETTS

NEW HAMPSHIRE

NEW JERSEY

NEW YORK

PENNSYLVANIA

RHODE ISLAND

VERMONT

NORTHEAST

CONNECTICUT

MAINE

MASSACHUSETTS

NEW HAMPSHIRE

NEW JERSEY

NEW YORK

PENNSYLVANIA

RHODE ISLAND

VERMONT

TOURO COLLEGE - MANHATTAN

Address: 232 West 40th Street, Manhattan, NY 10018
Website: *https://shs.touro.edu/programs/physician-assistant/physician-assistant-manhattan/*
Contact: *enrollhealth@touro.edu*
Phone: 631-795-4510

COST OF ATTENDANCE

Tuition and Fees: $42,060
Additional Expenses: N/A
Total: $41,060*

*This figure does not include cost of living or other indirect costs.

Financial Aid: https://shs.touro.edu/admissions--aid/financial-aid/applying-for-aid/

ADDITIONAL INFORMATION

Interesting tidbit: The Manhattan program has a non-traditional schedule better suited for those with outside responsibilities and is completed in 32 months with a research component, and an optional behavioral health focus. PA students in the Manhattan program can benefit from the unique elective opportunity of the Behavioral Health Track.

Important Updates due to COVID-19: Applications may be accepted and processed without completed Direct Patient Care experience hours with the understanding that these hours will be completed as soon as permissible and may be required in the event of acceptance if circumstances allow.

Were tests required? No.

Are tests expected next year? No.

What international experiences are available? N/A

What dual degree options exist? N/A

What service-learning opportunities exist? N/A

PANCE First-Time Pass Rate: 100% (2020)

WAGNER COLLEGE

Address: One Campus Road, Staten Island, NY 10301
Website: *http://wagner.edu/physician-assistant/*
Contact: *paprogram@wagner.edu*
Phone: 718-420-4142

COST OF ATTENDANCE

Tuition and Fees: $54,920
Additional Expenses: $18,346
Total: $73,266

Financial Aid: https://wagner.edu/financial-aid/apply/gradstudents/

ADDITIONAL INFORMATION

Interesting tidbit: The three-year BS/MS Program in PA Studies is a comprehensive program of didactic (academic), clinical and research (graduate) work. The requirements for the Master of Science include the development of a research thesis project. The Program is open to second bachelor's degree applicants who have earned a bachelor's degree in a field other than Physician Assistant Studies.

Important Updates due to COVID-19: N/A

Were tests required? No.

Are tests expected next year? No.

What international experiences are available? N/A

What dual degree options exist? N/A

What service-learning opportunities exist? N/A

PANCE First-Time Pass Rate: 100% (2020)

Other: Wagner offers the Graduate Program in Advanced PA Studies (36 credits) for practicing PAs for career advancement. See https://wagner.edu/physician-assistant/gradprogram/

CONNECTICUT

MAINE

MASSACHUSETTS

NEW HAMPSHIRE

NEW JERSEY

NEW YORK

PENNSYLVANIA

RHODE ISLAND

VERMONT

NORTHEAST

CONNECTICUT

MAINE

MASSACHUSETTS

NEW HAMPSHIRE

NEW JERSEY

NEW YORK

PENNSYLVANIA

RHODE ISLAND

VERMONT

WEILL CORNELL GRADUATE SCHOOL OF MEDICAL SCIENCES

Address: 570 Lexington Avenue, New York, NY 10022
Website: *https://gradschool.weill.cornell.edu/programs/health-sciences-physician-assistants*
Contact: *MSHPA@med.cornell.edu*
Phone: 646-962-1290

COST OF ATTENDANCE

Tuition and Fees: $32,822
Additional Expenses: N/A
Total: $32,822*

*This figure does not include cost of living or other indirect costs.

Financial Aid: See "Loan & Scholarship Programs" on https://gradschool.weill.cornell.edu/programs/health-sciences-physician-assistants

ADDITIONAL INFORMATION

Interesting tidbit: The MSHS PA Program, in its earliest model, began as a Surgical Assistant (SA) Program and the surgical focus remains strong. The 26-month program begins in early March each year and consists of two phases of study - preclinical and clinical phases.

Important Updates due to COVID-19: The program will accept test scores from the GRE administered remotely. Online coursework will be considered for the Spring, Summer and Fall 2020 and 2021 semesters. The Program will accept Pass/Fail grades for the Spring, Summer and Fall 2020 and 2021 semester courses. Interviews will proceed remotely until further notice.

Were tests required? GRE required.

Are tests expected next year? Yes.

What international experiences are available? N/A

What dual degree options exist? N/A

What service-learning opportunities exist? N/A

PANCE First-Time Pass Rate: 89% (2020)

YESHIVA UNIVERSITY

Address: 500 West 185th Street, New York, NY 10033
Website: *https://www.yu.edu/katz/programs/graduate/physician-assistant*
Contact: *jared.hakimi@yu.edu*
Phone: 646-592-4722

COST OF ATTENDANCE

Tuition and Fees: $32,978
Additional Expenses: N/A
Total: $32,978*

*This figure does not include cost of living or other indirect costs.

Financial Aid: https://www.yu.edu/osf/tuition-fees/graduate

ADDITIONAL INFORMATION

Interesting tidbit: The inaugural class of Yeshiva University's PA program begins in fall 2021. Thirty (30) students will be accepted into the inaugural cohort of the PA program (Class of 2023), 40 students will be accepted into the second cohort (Class of 2024), and 50 students will be accepted into the third and subsequent cohorts.

Important Updates due to COVID-19: N/A

Were tests required? No.

Are tests expected next year? No.

What international experiences are available? N/A

What dual degree options exist? N/A

What service-learning opportunities exist? N/A

PANCE First-Time Pass Rate: N/A (will be available on the website in spring 2024, after the graduation of the inaugural cohort)

CONNECTICUT

MAINE

MASSACHUSETTS

NEW HAMPSHIRE

NEW JERSEY

NEW YORK

PENNSYLVANIA

RHODE ISLAND

VERMONT

NORTHEAST

CONNECTICUT

MAINE

MASSACHUSETTS

NEW HAMPSHIRE

NEW JERSEY

NEW YORK

PENNSYLVANIA

RHODE ISLAND

VERMONT

ARCADIA UNIVERSITY

Address: 450 S. Easton Road, Glenside, PA 19038
Website: *https://www.arcadia.edu/academics/programs/physician-assistant*
Contact: *paadmissions@arcadia.edu*
Phone: 877-272-2342
Other Locations: Christiana, DE

COST OF ATTENDANCE

Tuition and Fees: $37,313
Additional Expenses: N/A
Total: $37,313*

*This figure does not include cost of living or other indirect costs.

Financial Aid: https://www.arcadia.edu/college-health-sciences/departments-faculty/physician-assistant/program-information/tuition-expenses

ADDITIONAL INFORMATION

Interesting tidbit: Arcadia's Physician Assistant (PA) program is in the Department of Medical Science, in the College of Health Sciences which includes the departments of Physical Therapy and Public Health. The program is offered on two campuses - Glenside, PA and Christina, DE.

Important Updates due to COVID-19: The Program will accept a passing grade for any prerequisite course taken during the Spring 2020 semester only. It will NOT accept Pass/Fail for any prerequisite courses required to enter the Program that have been taken after the spring semester of 2020.

Were tests required? GRE or MCAT required.

Are tests expected next year? Yes.

What international experiences are available? International Clinical Rotations; Medical Service Trips Abroad. See https://www.arcadia.edu/college-health-sciences/departments-faculty/physician-assistant/global-programs

What dual degree options exist? Physician Assistant and Master of Public Health (M.M.S., M.P.H.) at Glenside Campus

What service-learning opportunities exist? PA Olympics; Simon's Heart. See https://www.arcadia.edu/college-health-sciences/departments-faculty/physician-assistant/global-programs

PANCE First-Time Pass Rate: 98% (2020)

CHATHAM UNIVERSITY

Address: Berry Hall, Woodland Road, Pittsburgh, PA 15232
Website: *http://www.chatham.edu/mpas/*
Contact: *GradAdmissions@Chatham.edu*
Phone: 412-365-1825

COST OF ATTENDANCE

Tuition and Fees: $49,953
Additional Expenses: $10,447*
Total: $60,400*

*This figure does not include cost of living or other indirect costs.

Financial Aid: https://www.chatham.edu/admission-and-aid/graduate/funding-opportunities.html

ADDITIONAL INFORMATION

Interesting tidbit: Problem-Based Learning (PBL) is the cornerstone of Chatham MPAS students' first year. The incoming class is divided into groups of eight or nine students each and work together for five weeks, solving 5-8 simulated patient cases and taking two exams that cover what they might be expected to have covered during those weeks. The process occurs six times during the first year.

Important Updates due to COVID-19: The Program will not require the GRE exam as an admission requirement for the 2021-22 cycle. PA shadowing hours are also not required for applicants, but admitted students will be required to complete them by June 1st of the year of matriculation. A "Pass" grade for prerequisites will be accepted for coursework completed during the Spring 2020 semester only.

Were tests required? CASPer required.

Are tests expected next year? GRE and CASPer required.

What international experiences are available? N/A

What dual degree options exist? N/A

What service-learning opportunities exist? N/A

PANCE First-Time Pass Rate: 96% (2020)

Other: Chatham University offers a 3+2 integrated degree program (IDP). See https://www.chatham.edu/academics/undergraduate/integrated-degree-programs/index.html

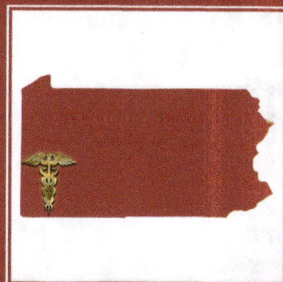

CONNECTICUT

MAINE

MASSACHUSETTS

NEW HAMPSHIRE

NEW JERSEY

NEW YORK

PENNSYLVANIA

RHODE ISLAND

VERMONT

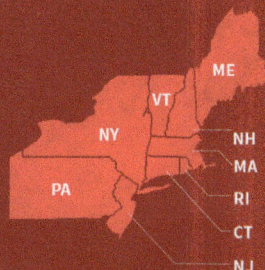

NORTHEAST

CONNECTICUT

MAINE

MASSACHUSETTS

NEW HAMPSHIRE

NEW JERSEY

NEW YORK

PENNSYLVANIA

RHODE ISLAND

VERMONT

DESALES UNIVERSITY

Address: 2755 Station Avenue, Center Valley, PA 18034
Website: *https://www.desales.edu/academics/graduate-studies/master-of-science-in-physician-assistant-studies-(mspas)*
Contact: *mspas@desales.edu*
Phone: 610-282-1100

COST OF ATTENDANCE

Tuition and Fees: $28,000
Additional Expenses: $15,662
Total: $43,662

Financial Aid: https://www.desales.edu/admissions-financial-aid/graduate-admissions-aid/financial-aid-scholarships-for-grad-students

ADDITIONAL INFORMATION

Interesting tidbit: DeSales firmly believes that replicating authentic healthcare delivery environments is critical to successful learning and skills application. The Gambet Center features simulation laboratories to mirror clinical scenarios specific to adult, pediatric, and birthing care for undergraduate and graduate healthcare degree programs.

Important Updates due to COVID-19: N/A

Were tests required? GRE required. MCAT scores will be accepted in place of GRE scores.

Are tests expected next year? Yes.

What international experiences are available? 5-week and 1-week elective international rotations. See https://www.desales.edu/academics/academic-programs/detail/master-of-science-in-physician-assistant-studies

What dual degree options exist? N/A

What service-learning opportunities exist? DeSales Free Clinic allows the PA students to deliver competent and compassionate medical care to one of the area's most vulnerable populations.

PANCE First-Time Pass Rate: 99% (2020)

Other: DeSales provides Advanced Pathway for undergraduate students (3+2 program and 4+2 program).

DREXEL UNIVERSITY

Address: 1601 Cherry Street, Philadelphia, PA 19102
Website: *http://drexel.edu/cnhp/academics/departments/Physician-Assistant/*
Contact: *paadmissions@drexel.edu*
Phone: 215-895-2000

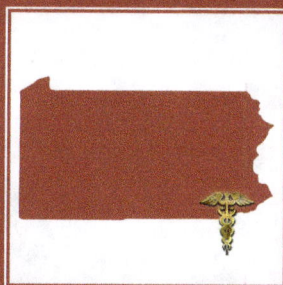

COST OF ATTENDANCE

Tuition and Fees: $57,798
Additional Expenses: N/A
Total: $57,798*

*This figure does not include cost of living or other indirect costs.

Financial Aid: https://drexel.edu/drexelcentral/finaid/prospective-students/grad/

ADDITIONAL INFORMATION

Interesting tidbit: Application review at Drexel PA program is multi-steps where faculty gets involved early in the process. Once the verified applications are screened by admissions personnel, applications that meet these criteria are then assigned to faculty members to be screened for interview. After the initial faculty review, the most promising applicants are invited for a personal interview.

Important Updates due to COVID-19: Drexel PA program will accept additional clinical patient contact hours submitted between the time of application and December 15, 2021 to meet the 500 hour minimum requirement. If the university/college an applicant attended only offered a pass/fail option for the Spring 2020 term or a subsequent term during the pandemic, applicants must provide a statement of university policy regarding forced pass/fail grading, and a statement from the university regarding criteria for "Pass." We will continue to allow online courses, including labs, provided they are completed through an accredited college or university for college credit and a letter grade. If applicants had virtual PA shadowing, the virtual nature of the experience must be clearly identified.

Were tests required? No.

Are tests expected next year? No.

What international experiences are available? N/A

What dual degree options exist? N/A

What service-learning opportunities exist? N/A

PANCE First-Time Pass Rate: 93% (2020)

Other: BS/MHS Bridge Program for Physician Assistant Option available. However, students enrolled in this program are not guaranteed admission into the Drexel PA program. See https://drexel.edu/cnhp/academics/undergraduate/BS-MHS-Physician-Assistant-Option/

Other: Drexel University College of Nursing and Health Professions has nine specific minor programs to offer graduate students from any program. See https://drexel.edu/cnhp/academics/graduate/graduate-minors/

CONNECTICUT

MAINE

MASSACHUSETTS

NEW HAMPSHIRE

NEW JERSEY

NEW YORK

PENNSYLVANIA

RHODE ISLAND

VERMONT

NORTHEAST

CONNECTICUT

MAINE

MASSACHUSETTS

NEW HAMPSHIRE

NEW JERSEY

NEW YORK

PENNSYLVANIA

RHODE ISLAND

VERMONT

DUQUESNE UNIVERSITY

Address: 600 Forbes Avenue, Pittsburgh, PA 15219
Website: *http://www.duq.edu/academics/schools/health-sciences/ academic-programs/physician-assistant*
Contact: *rshs@duq.edu*
Phone: 412-396-5914

COST OF ATTENDANCE

Tuition and Fees: $69,430
Additional Expenses: $19,012
Total: $88,442

Financial Aid: https://www.duq.edu/admissions-and-aid/financial-aid

ADDITIONAL INFORMATION

Interesting tidbit: The Duquesne University Physician Assistant Studies (PAS) Program was the first five-year, entry-level Master's degree program in the nation. "Entry level" students come into Duquesne University as freshmen, complete the 3-year pre-professional and advance into the accredited 2-year professional phase. Upon successful completion, students earn both a Bachelor of Science in Health Sciences degree and a Master of Physician Assistant Studies degree.

Important Updates due to COVID-19: Duquesne expanded test-optional admission to all programs for Fall 2021 freshmen.

Were tests required? No.

Are tests expected next year? SAT or ACT required.

What international experiences are available? Students may also have the opportunity to perform clinical rotations in international settings.

What dual degree options exist? N/A

What service-learning opportunities exist? N/A

PANCE First-Time Pass Rate: 96% (2020)

Other: The Duquesne University Physician Assistant Studies (PAS) Program does not accept transfer or second-degree applications.

GANNON UNIVERSITY

Address: 109 University Square, Erie, PA 16541
Website: *http://www.gannon.edu/academic-departments/physician-assistant-department/*
Contact: *schlick001@gannon.edu*
Phone: 814-871-5643

Other Locations: Ruskin, FL

COST OF ATTENDANCE

Tuition and Fees: $53,385
Additional Expenses: $22,347
Total: $75,732

Financial Aid: https://www.gannon.edu/Financial-Aid/Types-of-Financial-Aid/

ADDITIONAL INFORMATION

Interesting tidbit: The Gannon University Physician Assistant Program is a five-year, entry-level Master's degree program. "Entry level" students come into Gannon University as freshmen, complete the five year curriculum, and earn both a Bachelor of Science in Health Sciences degree and a Master of Physician Assistant Science degree. Applications for the post-baccalaureate option will be reviewed on a space available basis.

Important Updates due to COVID-19: SAT/ACT requirement waived for Fall 2021 admission only. Virtual Interviews.

Were tests required? No.

Are tests expected next year? SAT/ACT required.

What international experiences are available? N/A

What dual degree options exist? N/A

What service-learning opportunities exist? N/A

PANCE First-Time Pass Rate: 100% (2020)

Other: The Physician Assistant Department at the Ruskin Campus (FL) has received Provisional Status for its post-baccalaureate PA program.

CONNECTICUT

MAINE

MASSACHUSETTS

NEW HAMPSHIRE

NEW JERSEY

NEW YORK

PENNSYLVANIA

RHODE ISLAND

VERMONT

NORTHEAST

CONNECTICUT

MAINE

MASSACHUSETTS

NEW HAMPSHIRE

NEW JERSEY

NEW YORK

PENNSYLVANIA

RHODE ISLAND

VERMONT

KING'S COLLEGE

Address: 133 North River Street, Wilkes-Barre, PA 18711
Website: *https://www.kings.edu/academics/undergraduate_majors/physicianassistant*
Contact: *paadmissions@kings.edu*
Phone: 570-208-5853

COST OF ATTENDANCE

Tuition and Fees: $54,898
Additional Expenses: N/A
Total: $54,898*

*This figure does not include cost of living or other indirect costs.

Financial Aid: https://www.kings.edu/admissions/graduate/financial_aid#6

ADDITIONAL INFORMATION

Interesting tidbit: Seat availability in the Master's of Physician Assistant program is determined by the number of undergraduate BS/MS students who matriculate successfully into the professional program. The King's College Physician Assistant Program will not be opening graduate applications for the class entering in the fall of 2021 or the fall of 2022. If seats do become available, the program will notify applicants on its webpage.

Important Updates due to COVID-19: Online science course exceptions will be made for classes taken during the COVID-19 pandemic.

Were tests required? No.

Are tests expected next year? No.

What international experiences are available? N/A

What dual degree options exist? N/A

What service-learning opportunities exist? N/A

PANCE First-Time Pass Rate: 88% (2020)

MARYWOOD UNIVERSITY

Address: 2300 Adams Avenue, Scranton, PA 18509
Website: *http://www.marywood.edu/pa-program*
Contact: *paprogram@marywood.edu*
Phone: 570-348-6298

COST OF ATTENDANCE

Tuition and Fees: $48,540
Additional Expenses: N/A
Total: $48,540*

 *This figure does not include cost of living or other indirect costs.

Financial Aid: http://www.marywood.edu/fin_aid/apply/graduate.html

ADDITIONAL INFORMATION

Interesting tidbit: Marywood PA program offers a Mentor-Mentee program that matches a Didactic year student with a Clinical year student, as a "mentor" to help guide a new student through the program. Every student is also assigned a faculty advisor. Advising meetings will occur at least once per semester.

Important Updates due to COVID-19: Due to the COVID-19 pandemic, the Marywood University Physician Assistant Program is temporarily waiving the Health Care Related Experience Requirement and Shadowing Requirement for the 2021-2022 admissions cycle. All student interviews will be conducted on Zoom.

Were tests required? GRE or PA-CAT required.

Are tests expected next year? Yes.

What international experiences are available? N/A

What dual degree options exist? N/A

What service-learning opportunities exist? N/A

PANCE First-Time Pass Rate: 94% (2020)

Other: Guaranteed Seat Program for Marywood Pre-PA students. See http://www.marywood.edu/pa-program/requirements.html

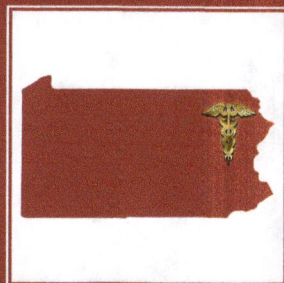

CONNECTICUT

MAINE

MASSACHUSETTS

NEW HAMPSHIRE

NEW JERSEY

NEW YORK

PENNSYLVANIA

RHODE ISLAND

VERMONT

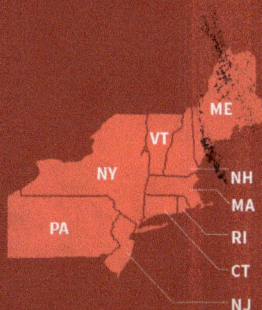

NORTHEAST

CONNECTICUT

MAINE

MASSACHUSETTS

NEW HAMPSHIRE

NEW JERSEY

NEW YORK

PENNSYLVANIA

RHODE ISLAND

VERMONT

MERCYHURST UNIVERSITY

Address: 501 East 38th Street, Erie, PA 16546
Website: *https://www.mercyhurst.edu/academics/grad/physician-assistant-studies*
Contact: *paprogram@mercyhurst.edu*
Phone: 814-824-2598

COST OF ATTENDANCE

Tuition and Fees: $59,990
Additional Expenses: N/A
Total: $59,990*

*This figure does not include cost of living or other indirect costs.

Financial Aid: https://www.mercyhurst.edu/admissions-aid/graduate-admissions/cost-and-financial-aid

ADDITIONAL INFORMATION

Interesting tidbit: the Physician Assistant Leadership Initiative in Oral Health integrates preventative oral health education into the Mercyhurst Physician Assistant curriculum and supports a community outreach project and improves oral health for Erie's inner-city children. The physician assistant students and faculty will collaborate with dental professionals as part of an interprofessional educational experience. Following the educational component, the physician assistant students will perform oral health screenings for Mercyhurst University's Carpe Diem Academy students.

Important Updates due to COVID-19: N/A

Were tests required? GRE required.

Are tests expected next year? Yes.

What international experiences are available? N/A

What dual degree options exist? N/A

What service-learning opportunities exist? Physician Assistant Leadership Initiative in Oral Health. See https://www.mercyhurst.edu/academics/grad/physician-assistant-studies/leadership

PANCE First-Time Pass Rate: 96% (2020)

MISERICORDIA UNIVERSITY

Address: 301 Lake Street, Dallas, PA 18612
Website: *https://www.misericordia.edu/page.cfm?p=655*
Contact: *mupainquiry@misericordia.edu*
Phone: 570-674-6716

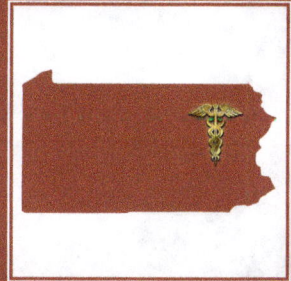

COST OF ATTENDANCE

Tuition and Fees: $38,175
Additional Expenses: $21,665
Total: $59,840

Financial Aid: https://catalog.misericordia.edu/content.php?catoid
=4&navoid=158#financial-assistance-program

ADDITIONAL INFORMATION

Interesting tidbit: Misericordia University has a 7,575 square foot, custom designed Physician Assistant educational facility within the Trocaire Building on its main campus. Also, a high level, state-of-the-art, new cadaver lab opened Fall 2020 in the new Frank M. and Dorothea Henry Science Center, immediately adjacent to the Trocaire building.

Important Updates due to COVID-19: Courses that are awarded satisfactory completion (P) will be accepted for the 2021-2022 admissions cycle. Labs that are completed online will be accepted for the 2021-2022 admissions cycle. If the lab component was removed, we will still accept that prerequisite course if completed with a grade of "B" or higher or with a satisfactory completion (P). During the 2021-2022 admissions cycle, the minimum of 500 hours of direct patient care experience required at the time of application submission will be reduced to 250 hours of direct patient care experience.

Were tests required? No.

Are tests expected next year? No.

What international experiences are available? N/A

What dual degree options exist? N/A

What service-learning opportunities exist? N/A

PANCE First-Time Pass Rate: 53% (2020)

CONNECTICUT

MAINE

MASSACHUSETTS

NEW HAMPSHIRE

NEW JERSEY

NEW YORK

PENNSYLVANIA

RHODE ISLAND

VERMONT

NORTHEAST

CONNECTICUT

MAINE

MASSACHUSETTS

NEW HAMPSHIRE

NEW JERSEY

NEW YORK

PENNSYLVANIA

RHODE ISLAND

VERMONT

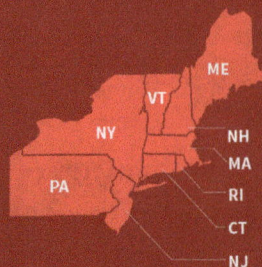

PENN STATE UNIVERSITY

Address: 700 HMC Crescent Road, Hershey, PA 17033
Website: *https://med.psu.edu/physician-assistant*
Contact: *psupaprogram@pennstatehealth.psu.edu*
Phone: 717-531-0003

COST OF ATTENDANCE

Tuition and Fees: $39,033
Additional Expenses: $19,940
Total: $58,973

Financial Aid: https://students.med.psu.edu/physician-assistant-student-information/financial-aid/

ADDITIONAL INFORMATION

Interesting tidbit: In addition to satisfactorily completing all curricular requirements in good academic standing, students must successfully complete a senior summative course and receive recommendation for graduation by the faculty of the specific program and the general faculty in order to graduate.

Important Updates due to COVID-19: The program accepts Satisfactory or Pass grades in lieu of letter grades for both pre-requisites and other courses for courses taken in the Spring 2020 and Summer 2020 semester.

Were tests required? GRE required.

Are tests expected next year? Yes.

What international experiences are available? N/A

What dual degree options exist? N/A

What service-learning opportunities exist? N/A

PANCE First-Time Pass Rate: 100% (2020)

PENNSYLVANIA COLLEGE OF TECHNOLOGY

Address: One College Avenue, Williamsport, PA 17701
Website: *https://www.pct.edu/academics/nhs/physician-assistant/physician-assistant-studies*
Contact: *admissions@pct.edu*
Phone: 570-327-4519

COST OF ATTENDANCE

In-State Tuition and Fees: $33,459
Additional Expenses: $16,502
Total: $49,961

Out-of-State Tuition and Fees: $47,823
Additional Expenses: $16,502
Total: $64,325

Financial Aid: https://www.pct.edu/admissions/financial-aid/graduate-students

ADDITIONAL INFORMATION

Interesting tidbit: The Physician Assistant Studies program at Penn College is a five-year combined bachelor/master of science degree program. Students who have bachelor's degrees apply for direct entry into the professional phase (the didactic and clinical years) of the program. Penn College utilizes the Casper test in its selection process to assess applicants rather than conducting interviews.

Important Updates due to COVID-19: N/A

Were tests required? CASPer required.

Are tests expected next year? Yes.

What international experiences are available? International clinical rotations

What dual degree options exist? N/A

What service-learning opportunities exist? N/A

PANCE First-Time Pass Rate: 95% (2020)

CONNECTICUT

MAINE

MASSACHUSETTS

NEW HAMPSHIRE

NEW JERSEY

NEW YORK

PENNSYLVANIA

RHODE ISLAND

VERMONT

NORTHEAST

CONNECTICUT

MAINE

MASSACHUSETTS

NEW HAMPSHIRE

NEW JERSEY

NEW YORK

PENNSYLVANIA

RHODE ISLAND

VERMONT

PHILADELPHIA COLLEGE OF OSTEOPATHIC MEDICINE (PCOM)

Address: 4170 City Avenue, Philadelphia, PA 19131
Website: *https://www.pcom.edu/academics/programs-and-degrees/physician-assistant-studies/*
Contact: *paadmissions@pcom.edu*
Phone: 215-871-6772

Other Locations: Suwanee, GA

COST OF ATTENDANCE

Tuition and Fees: $51,312
Additional Expenses: $33,394
Total: $84,706

Financial Aid: https://www.pcom.edu/about/departments/financial-aid/types-of-aid/

ADDITIONAL INFORMATION

Interesting tidbit: Students may enroll at either Suwanee, Georgia location or the main campus in Philadelphia, Pennsylvania. PCOM's PA Studies program offers students a holistic view of health care, being true to the principles of osteopathic medicine.

Important Updates due to COVID-19: N/A

Were tests required? No.

Are tests expected next year? No.

What international experiences are available? N/A

What dual degree options exist? N/A

What service-learning opportunities exist? N/A

PANCE First-Time Pass Rate: 96% (2020)

SAINT FRANCIS UNIVERSITY

Address: 117 Evergreen Drive, Loretto, PA 15940
Website: *https://www.francis.edu/Physician-Assistant-Science/*
Contact: *pa@francis.edu*
Phone: 814-472-3130

COST OF ATTENDANCE

Tuition and Fees: $59,032
Additional Expenses: $13,624
Total: $72,656

Financial Aid: https://www.francis.edu/Apply-for-Financial-Aid/

ADDITIONAL INFORMATION

Interesting tidbit: At SFU, clinical experiences are built into the first year of physician assistant curriculum. The program offers an integrated body system approach to medicine.

Important Updates due to COVID-19: Due to COVID, the program will temporarily be accepting virtual labs.

Were tests required? No.

Are tests expected next year? No.

What international experiences are available? Medical mission trips

What dual degree options exist? N/A

What service-learning opportunities exist? Free clinics, health fairs, and medical mission trips

PANCE First-Time Pass Rate: 100% (2020)

Other: The program offers a direct pathway for undergraduate applicants - Physician Assistant Science Program, B.S. in Health Science + Master of Physician Assistant Science (5-year).

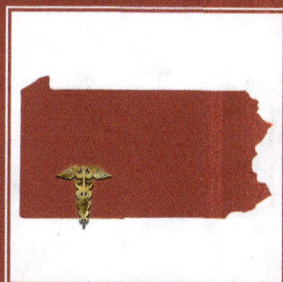

CONNECTICUT

MAINE

MASSACHUSETTS

NEW HAMPSHIRE

NEW JERSEY

NEW YORK

PENNSYLVANIA

RHODE ISLAND

VERMONT

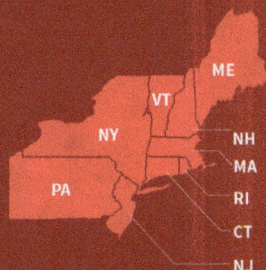

NORTHEAST

CONNECTICUT

MAINE

MASSACHUSETTS

NEW HAMPSHIRE

NEW JERSEY

NEW YORK

PENNSYLVANIA

RHODE ISLAND

VERMONT

SALUS UNIVERSITY

Address: 8360 Old York Road, Elkins Park, PA 19027
Website: *http://www.salus.edu/Colleges/Health-Sciences/Physician-Assistant.aspx*
Contact: *admissions@salus.edu*
Phone: 215-780-1515

COST OF ATTENDANCE

Tuition and Fees: $48,766
Additional Expenses: N/A
Total: $48,766*

*This figure does not include cost of living or other indirect costs.

Financial Aid: https://www.salus.edu/Admissions/Tuition-Financial-Aid/Types-of-Financial-Aid.aspx

ADDITIONAL INFORMATION

Interesting tidbit: The Salus University PA program is patient-centered with a primary care philosophy and holistic approach that assesses the whole patient for prevention, treatment, and rehabilitation. Patient care experiences are integrated throughout the first year.

Important Updates due to COVID-19: The program will continue to accept courses and labs that are delivered via online or distance learning from a regionally accredited institution. The program will accept Pass (P) as satisfying any of the program's academic course prerequisites that were taken during spring or summer 2020 and on a case-by-case basis otherwise.

Were tests required? GRE required.

Are tests expected next year? Yes.

What international experiences are available? N/A

What dual degree options exist? N/A

What service-learning opportunities exist? Inglis House Experience (see https://www.salus.edu/Colleges/Health-Sciences-Education-Rehabilitation/Physician-Assistant/Experiential-Learning/Inglis-House-Experience.aspx); Metropolitan Area Neighborhood Nutrition Alliance (see https://www.salus.edu/Colleges/Health-Sciences-Education-Rehabilitation/Physician-Assistant/Service-Learning.aspx)

PANCE First-Time Pass Rate: 100% (2020)

Other: Salus University has articulation agreements with several institutions for 3+2 PA Program and 4+2 PA Program. See https://www.salus.edu/Colleges/Health-Sciences-Education-Rehabilitation/Physician-Assistant/Affiliate-Undergraduate-Physician-Assistant-Progra.aspx

SETON HILL UNIVERSITY

Address: 1 Seton Hill Drive, Greensburg, PA 15601
Website: *http://www.setonhill.edu/academics/graduate_programs/physician_assistant*
Contact: *gadmit@setonhill.edu*
Phone: 724-552-4355

COST OF ATTENDANCE

Tuition and Fees: $46,510*
Additional Expenses: N/A
Total: $46,510*

*Tuition only.

Financial Aid: https://www.setonhill.edu/tuition-financial-aid/graduate-program-aid/

ADDITIONAL INFORMATION

Interesting tidbit: All prospective students must shadow at least three physician assistants in different practice settings for 4 hours per experience. Applications that do not meet the initial required 3.2 cumulative GPA or 3.2 prerequisite GPA will be automatically denied.

Important Updates due to COVID-19: Due to the pandemic applicants will be reviewed on a case by case basis and exceptions will be granted where necessary.

Were tests required? No.

Are tests expected next year? No.

What international experiences are available? N/A

What dual degree options exist? N/A

What service-learning opportunities exist? N/A

PANCE First-Time Pass Rate: 95% (2020)

Other: Combined BS/MS (3+2) pathway available.

CONNECTICUT

MAINE

MASSACHUSETTS

NEW HAMPSHIRE

NEW JERSEY

NEW YORK

PENNSYLVANIA

RHODE ISLAND

VERMONT

NORTHEAST

CONNECTICUT

MAINE

MASSACHUSETTS

NEW HAMPSHIRE

NEW JERSEY

NEW YORK

PENNSYLVANIA

RHODE ISLAND

VERMONT

SLIPPERY ROCK UNIVERSITY

Address: 105 North Hall, Slippery Rock, PA 16057
Website: *http://www.sru.edu/academics/graduate-programs/
physician-assistant-studies-master-of-science*
Contact: *pa.program@sru.edu*
Phone: 724-738-2425

COST OF ATTENDANCE

In-State Tuition and Fees: $43,236
Additional Expenses: N/A
Total: $43,236*

Out-of-State Tuition and Fees: $59,674
Additional Expenses: N/A
Total: $59,674*

*This figure does not include cost of living or other indirect costs.

Financial Aid: https://www.sru.edu/admissions/financial-aid/
types-of-aid

ADDITIONAL INFORMATION

Interesting tidbit: Unique to SRU's Physician Assistant Program is the emphasis on special populations and healthcare disparities that is intentionally interwoven throughout the didactic and clinical curriculum, providing graduates with the requisite knowledge and cultural sensitivity to effectively treat patients from diverse backgrounds.

Important Updates due to COVID-19: The PA program will review pre-requisites that were to be scheduled face to face, but were converted online due to COVID-19 on a case by case basis.

Were tests required? No.

Are tests expected next year? No.

What international experiences are available? N/A

What dual degree options exist? N/A

What service-learning opportunities exist? N/A

PANCE First-Time Pass Rate: 84% (2020)

TEMPLE UNIVERSITY

Address: 3500 North Broad Street, Philadelphia, PA 19140
Website: *https://medicine.temple.edu/education/physician-assistant-program*
Contact: *PA-Admissions@temple.edu*
Phone: 215-707-3656

COST OF ATTENDANCE

In-State Tuition and Fees: $42,718
Additional Expenses: N/A
Total: $42,718*

Out-of-State Tuition and Fees: $44,662
Additional Expenses: N/A
Total: $44,662*

*This figure does not include cost of living or other indirect costs.

Financial Aid: https://medicine.temple.edu/education/student-life-resources/resources-students/md-student-handbook/student-affairs-2

ADDITIONAL INFORMATION

Interesting tidbit: The PA training program is housed in the Lewis Katz School of Medicine, with a reputation for excellence in medical science, clinical education and unparalleled commitment to the urban, underserved community.

Important Updates due to COVID-19: N/A

Were tests required? No, for entering 2022 the GRE or MCAT will be optional.

Are tests expected next year? No.

What international experiences are available? N/A

What dual degree options exist? N/A

What service-learning opportunities exist? N/A

PANCE First-Time Pass Rate: 100% (2020)

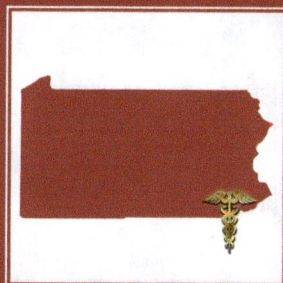

CONNECTICUT

MAINE

MASSACHUSETTS

NEW HAMPSHIRE

NEW JERSEY

NEW YORK

PENNSYLVANIA

RHODE ISLAND

VERMONT

NORTHEAST

CONNECTICUT

MAINE

MASSACHUSETTS

NEW HAMPSHIRE

NEW JERSEY

NEW YORK

PENNSYLVANIA

RHODE ISLAND

VERMONT

THIEL COLLEGE

Address: 75 College Ave., Greenville, PA 16125
Website: *https://www.thiel.edu/graduate-degrees/physician-assistant*
Contact: *paprogram@thiel.edu*
Phone: 724-589-2290

COST OF ATTENDANCE

Tuition and Fees: $54,388
Additional Expenses: N/A
Total: $54,388*

*This figure does not include cost of living or other indirect costs.

Financial Aid: https://www.thiel.edu/financial_aid

ADDITIONAL INFORMATION

Interesting tidbit: In March 2021, Thiel College PA program received Provisional Accreditation from the ARC-PA. It is recruiting its inaugural class of 40 students.

Important Updates due to COVID-19: Applicants can explain in the optional question section of CASPA if the current pandemic has affected coursework, shadowing and other components of the application. Virtual Interview.

Were tests required? No.

Are tests expected next year? No.

What international experiences are available? N/A

What dual degree options exist? N/A

What service-learning opportunities exist? N/A

PANCE First-Time Pass Rate: N/A (Inaugural class has not graduated)

Other: Thiel College offers a 5-Year Program (BA/MS) for highly motivated high school seniors.

THOMAS JEFFERSON UNIVERSITY - CENTER CITY

Address: 130 South 9th Street, Philadelphia, PA 19107
Website: https://www.jefferson.edu/academics/colleges-schools-institutes/health-professions/departments-programs/physician-assistant-studies/degrees-programs/graduate/ms-center-city.html
Phone: 215-503-0106

Other Locations: Center City, PA; East Falls, PA; Voorhees, NJ

COST OF ATTENDANCE

Tuition and Fees: $49,034
Additional Expenses: N/A
Total: $49,034*

*This figure does not include cost of living or other indirect costs.

Financial Aid: http://eastfalls.jefferson.edu/financialaid/Graduate/index.html

ADDITIONAL INFORMATION

Interesting tidbit: As part of an academic health center, the Physician Assistant Studies- Center City Program provides students with opportunities to learn side-by-side with medical, nursing and other healthcare students. One example is participation in the Health Mentors Program, which teams students with patients who have chronic health problems for a two-year relationship.

Important Updates due to COVID-19: Courses taken Spring 2020 only that were transitioned from a letter grade to Pass/Fail due to COVID-19 will be accepted with a "Pass" grade. The PA Studies will accept online courses that were taken between Spring 2020 and Fall 2021 due to the outbreak of COVID-19.

Were tests required? No.

Are tests expected next year? No.

What international experiences are available? N/A

What dual degree options exist? MS Physician Assistant Studies/ MPH. See https://www.jefferson.edu/academics/colleges-schools-institutes/population-health/degrees-programs/public-health/Pathways/dual-degrees/PAMPH.html

What service-learning opportunities exist? N/A

PANCE First-Time Pass Rate: 100% (2020)

CONNECTICUT

MAINE

MASSACHUSETTS

NEW HAMPSHIRE

NEW JERSEY

NEW YORK

PENNSYLVANIA

RHODE ISLAND

VERMONT

NORTHEAST

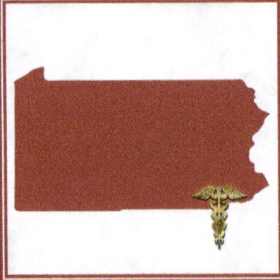

CONNECTICUT

MAINE

MASSACHUSETTS

NEW HAMPSHIRE

NEW JERSEY

NEW YORK

PENNSYLVANIA

RHODE ISLAND

VERMONT

THOMAS JEFFERSON - EAST FALLS

Address: 4201 Henry Avenue, Philadelphia, PA 19144
Website: *https://www.jefferson.edu/academics/colleges-schools-institutes/health-professions/departments-programs/physician-assistant-studies/degrees-programs/graduate/ms-east-falls.html*
Contact: *enroll@jefferson.edu*
Phone: 215-951-2908

Other Locations: Center City, PA; Voorhees, NJ

COST OF ATTENDANCE

Tuition and Fees: $49,034
Additional Expenses: N/A
Total: $49,034*

*This figure does not include cost of living or other indirect costs.

Financial Aid: http://eastfalls.jefferson.edu/financialaid/Graduate/index.html

ADDITIONAL INFORMATION

Interesting tidbit: Thomas Jefferson University offers Master of Science in Physician Assistant Studies on three different campuses - Center City, East Falls, and New Jersey, each requiring a separate application. Students will choose their preferred location between East Falls and New Jersey during the application process. If students apply to both the East Falls and New Jersey programs and are offered an interview, the campus location will be decided by the Admissions Committee based on which campus has the greater need.

Important Updates due to COVID-19: Courses taken Spring 2020 only that were transitioned from a letter grade to Pass/Fail due to COVID-19 will be accepted with a "Pass" grade. The PA Studies will accept online courses that were taken between Spring 2020 and Fall 2021 due to the outbreak of COVID-19.

Were tests required? No.

Are tests expected next year? No.

What international experiences are available? N/A

What dual degree options exist? N/A

What service-learning opportunities exist? N/A

PANCE First-Time Pass Rate: 87% (2020)

Other: Thomas Jefferson University offers an Undergraduate Entry option - Accelerated Health Sciences BS/Physician Assistant MS - East Falls. See https://www.jefferson.edu/academics/colleges-schools-institutes/health-professions/departments-programs/physician-assistant-studies/degrees-programs/undergraduate/3-2-pathway.html

UNIVERSITY OF PITTSBURGH

Address: 3010 William Pitt Way, Pittsburgh, PA 15238
Website: *https://www.shrs.pitt.edu/PAProgram*
Contact: *mlacovey@pitt.edu*
Phone: 412-624-6743

COST OF ATTENDANCE

In-State Tuition and Fees: $50,586
Additional Expenses: N/A
Total: $50,586*

Out-of-State Tuition and Fees: $59,289
Additional Expenses: N/A
Total: $59,289*

*This figure does not include cost of living or other indirect costs.

Financial Aid: https://www.shrs.pitt.edu/admissions/financial-information

ADDITIONAL INFORMATION

Interesting tidbit: The instruction for the didactic component is provided by physician assistants, physicians, surgeons, pharmacists, nurse practitioners, dentists, genetic counselors, and other professionals who have expertise in their respective specialties and fields.

Important Updates due to COVID-19: The program will accept "S" (satisfactory) or similar evidence of course completion for the 2020 Spring and Summer terms.

Were tests required? No.

Are tests expected next year? No.

What international experiences are available? N/A

What dual degree options exist? N/A

What service-learning opportunities exist? N/A

PANCE First-Time Pass Rate: 94% (2020)

Other: The University of Pittsburgh PA Studies Hybrid Program anticipates matriculating its first class in August 2022, pending achieving Accreditation - Provisional status at the March 2022 ARC-PA meeting.

CONNECTICUT

MAINE

MASSACHUSETTS

NEW HAMPSHIRE

NEW JERSEY

NEW YORK

PENNSYLVANIA

RHODE ISLAND

VERMONT

NORTHEAST

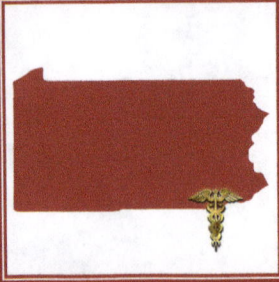

UNIVERSITY OF THE SCIENCES

Address: 600 South 43rd Street, Philadelphia, PA 19104
Website: *https://www.usciences.edu/samson-college-of-health-sciences/physician-assistant-studies/index.html*
Contact: *paprogram@usciences.edu*
Phone: 215-596-7141

COST OF ATTENDANCE

Tuition and Fees: $50,000
Additional Expenses: $23,382
Total: $73,382

Financial Aid: https://www.usciences.edu/admission/cost-financial-aid/information-for-graduate-students-professional-programs.html

ADDITIONAL INFORMATION

Interesting tidbit: USciences PA program welcomed its inaugural class of 40 students in 2020. The inaugural cohort will graduate in September 2022.

Important Updates due to COVID-19: N/A

Were tests required? No.

Are tests expected next year? No.

What international experiences are available? N/A

What dual degree options exist? N/A

What service-learning opportunities exist? N/A

PANCE First-Time Pass Rate: N/A (the inaugural class will graduate in 2022)

CONNECTICUT

MAINE

MASSACHUSETTS

NEW HAMPSHIRE

NEW JERSEY

NEW YORK

PENNSYLVANIA

RHODE ISLAND

VERMONT

UNIVERSITY OF THE SCIENCES

Address: 600 South 43rd Street, Philadelphia, PA 19104
Website: *https://www.usciences.edu/samson-college-of-health-sciences/physician-assistant-studies/index.html*
Contact: *paprogram@usciences.edu*
Phone: 215-596-7141

COST OF ATTENDANCE

Tuition and Fees: $50,000
Additional Expenses: $23,382
Total: $73,382

Financial Aid: https://www.usciences.edu/admission/cost-financial-aid/information-for-graduate-students-professional-programs.html

ADDITIONAL INFORMATION

Interesting tidbit: USciences PA program welcomed its inaugural class of 40 students in 2020. The inaugural cohort will graduate in September 2022.

Important Updates due to COVID-19: N/A

Were tests required? No.

Are tests expected next year? No.

What international experiences are available? N/A

What dual degree options exist? N/A

What service-learning opportunities exist? N/A

PANCE First-Time Pass Rate: N/A (the inaugural class will graduate in 2022)

CONNECTICUT

MAINE

MASSACHUSETTS

NEW HAMPSHIRE

NEW JERSEY

NEW YORK

PENNSYLVANIA

RHODE ISLAND

VERMONT

NORTHEAST

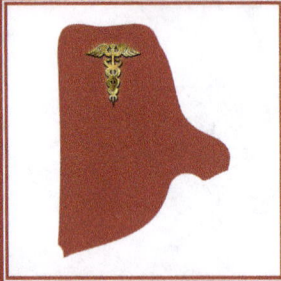

CONNECTICUT

MAINE

MASSACHUSETTS

NEW HAMPSHIRE

NEW JERSEY

NEW YORK

PENNSYLVANIA

RHODE ISLAND

VERMONT

BRYANT UNIVERSITY

Address: 1150 Douglas Pike, Smithfield, RI 02917
Website: *http://gradschool.bryant.edu/health-sciences.htm*
Contact: *pa_program@bryant.edu*
Phone: 401-232-6556

COST OF ATTENDANCE

Tuition and Fees: $52,637
Additional Expenses: N/A
Total: $52,637*

*This figure does not include cost of living or other indirect costs.

Financial Aid: https://gradschool.bryant.edu/financial-aid-and-tuition

ADDITIONAL INFORMATION

Interesting tidbit: PA students at Bryant University will work with patients in an unprecedented 12 clinical specialty rotations. Students will also study human gross anatomy at The Warren Alpert Medical School of Brown University in its award-winning medical education building in downtown Providence.

Important Updates due to COVID-19: N/A

Were tests required? GRE required.

Are tests expected next year? Yes.

What international experiences are available? N/A

What dual degree options exist? N/A

What service-learning opportunities exist? N/A

PANCE First-Time Pass Rate: 91% (2020)

JOHNSON & WALES UNIVERSITY

Address: 8 Abbott Park Place, Providence, RI 02903
Website: *http://www.jwu.edu/PA*
Contact: *kspolidoro@jwu.edu*
Phone: 401-598-2381

COST OF ATTENDANCE

Tuition and Fees: $49,083
Additional Expenses: $23,349
Total: $72,432

Financial Aid: https://www.jwu.edu/admissions/paying-for-college/index.html

ADDITIONAL INFORMATION

Interesting tidbit: The PA program is part of JWU's Center for Physician Assistant Studies, housed in an 18,000-sq. foot facility dedicated to the health sciences and located in Providence's Knowledge District. The facility is set up to maximize information sharing, teamwork and collaboration between students, faculty and community colleagues.

Important Updates due to COVID-19: JWU will accept prerequisite courses with non-letter grades (P/F, S/U) earned during the COVID-19 pandemic.

Were tests required? No.

Are tests expected next year? No.

What international experiences are available? N/A

What dual degree options exist? N/A

What service-learning opportunities exist? N/A

PANCE First-Time Pass Rate: 100% (2020)

CONNECTICUT

MAINE

MASSACHUSETTS

NEW HAMPSHIRE

NEW JERSEY

NEW YORK

PENNSYLVANIA

RHODE ISLAND

VERMONT

NORTHEAST

CHAPTER 3

REGION TWO

MIDWEST

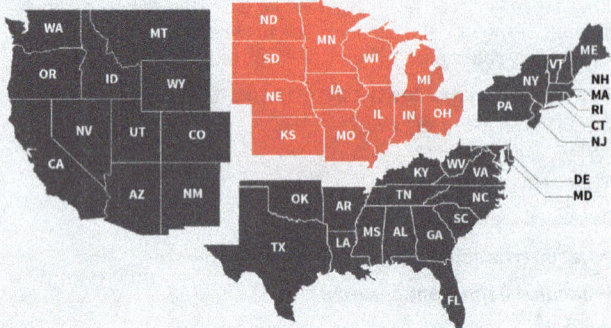

64 Programs | 12 States

PA PROGRAMS

PA School	Ave. GPA & GRE (Verbal, Quantitative, Analy. Writing) Int'l Students: Yes/No	Admissions Statistics	Prerequisite Coursework Other than Gen Bio, Gen Chem, Human Anatomy, Human Physiology, Microbiology, Statistics, Psychology
Dominican University of Illinois 7900 West Division Street, River Forest, IL 60305	3.59 (overall) 3.48 (science) GRE: 61% (V) 52% (Q) 72% (A) Int'l Student: Yes	Apps Received: 358 Interviews Offered: 57 Admission Offered: N/A Class Size: 30 Admitted Rate: 8.4%	Biochemistry; Genetics; Humanities and Social Sciences; Medical Terminology; OChem; Upper-level Biology
Midwestern University - Downers Grove 555 31st Street, Downers Grove, IL 60515	3.73 (overall) 3.69 (science) GRE: 66% (V) 59% (Q) 72% (A) Int'l Student: Yes	Apps Received: 1,400 Interviews Offered: N/A Admission Offered: N/A Class Size: 86 Admitted Rate: 6.1%	English Composition; OChem
Northwestern University 240 E. Huron Street, Chicago, IL 60611	3.68 (overall) 3.60 (science) GRE: Not Req. Int'l Student: Yes	Apps Received: N/A Interviews Offered: N/A Admission Offered: N/A Class Size: 36 Admitted Rate: N/A	Biochemistry; Medical Terminology
Rosalind Franklin University of Medicine 3333 Green Bay Road, North Chicago, IL 60064	3.55 (overall) 3.51 (science) GRE: Not Req. Int'l Student: Yes	Apps Received: 2,561 Interviews Offered: N/A Admission Offered: N/A Class Size: 67 Admitted Rate: 2.6%	
Rush University 600 S. Paulina Street, Chicago, IL 60612	3.50 (overall) 3.29 (science) GRE: 309 (Q&V combined) Int'l Student: Yes	Apps Received: N/A Interviews Offered: N/A Admission Offered: N/A Class Size: 30 Admitted Rate: N/A	Biochemistry

PA School	Ave. GPA & GRE (Verbal, Quantitative, Analy. Writing) Int'l Students: Yes/No	Admissions Statistics	Prerequisite Coursework Other than Gen Bio, Gen Chem, Human Anatomy, Human Physiology, Microbiology, Statistics, Psychology
Southern Illinois University 600 Agriculture Drive, Carbondale, IL 62901	3.2+ (overall) 3.2+ (science) GRE: N/A Int'l Student: No	Apps Received: N/A Interviews Offered: N/A Admission Offered: N/A Class Size: 40 Admitted Rate: N/A	English Composition; Medical Terminology
Butler University 4600 Sunset Avenue, Indianapolis, In 46208	3.70 (overall) GRE: 154 (V) 154 (Q) 4.3 (A) Int'l Student: Yes	Apps Received: N/A Interviews Offered: N/A Admission Offered: N/A Class Size: 75 Admitted Rate: N/A	OChem; Upper-level chemistry;
Franklin College 101 Branigin Blvd., Franklin, IN 46131	3.68 (overall) 3.61 (science) GRE: Not Req. Int'l Student: No	Apps Received: 435 Interviews Offered: N/A Admission Offered: N/A Class Size: 24 Admitted Rate: 5.5%	Behavior/Social Science; English Composition; OChem
Indiana State University 567 N. 5th Street, Terre Haute, IN 47809	3.43 (overall) 3.28 (science) GRE: 155+ (V) 155+ (Q) 4+ (A) Int'l Student: Yes	Apps Received: N/A Interviews Offered: N/A Admission Offered: N/A Class Size: 30 Admitted Rate: N/A	Medical Terminology; OChem; Upper-level Biology
Indiana University School of Health and Human Sciences 1140 W. Michigan Street, Indianapolis, IN 46202	3.66 (overall) 3.62 (science) GRE: Not Req. Int'l Student: Yes	Apps Received: 454 Interviews Offered: N/A Admission Offered: N/A Class Size: 44 Admitted Rate: 9.7%	Medical Terminology; OChem; Upper level Human Biology

MIDWEST

PA PROGRAMS

PA School	Ave. GPA & GRE (Verbal, Quantitative, Analy. Writing) Int'l Students: Yes/No	Admissions Statistics	Prerequisite Coursework Other than Gen Bio, Gen Chem, Human Anatomy, Human Physiology, Microbiology, Statistics, Psychology
Trine University 1 University Avenue, Angola, IN 46703	3.0+ (overall) 3.0+ (science) GRE: Not Req. Int'l Student: No	Apps Received: N/A Interviews Offered: N/A Admission Offered: N/A Class Size: 36 Admitted Rate: N/A	Biochemistry; OChem; Medical Terminology
University of Evansville 515 Bob Jones Way, Room 3001, Evansville, IN 47708	3.62 (overall) 3.50 (science) GRE: Not Req. Int'l Student: Yes	Apps Received: N/A Interviews Offered: N/A Admission Offered: N/A Class Size: 36 Admitted Rate: N/A	Medical Terminology; OChem; Social Science
University of Saint Francis - Fort Wayne 2701 Spring Street, Fort Wayne, IN 46808	3.50 (overall) 3.0+ (science) GRE: 4+ (A) Int'l Student: Yes	Apps Received: N/A Interviews Offered: N/A Admission Offered: N/A Class Size: 25 Admitted Rate: N/A	OChem
Valparaiso University 1700 Chapel Dr., Valparaiso, IN 46383	3.3+ (overall) GRE: Not Req. Int'l Student: No	Apps Received: N/A Interviews Offered: N/A Admission Offered: N/A Class Size: 45 Admitted Rate: N/A	Four years of lab science in high school; Pre-calculus; *This program is a Direct Entry PA program (3+2 BS/MS) intended for high school applicants.
Des Moines University 3200 Grand Avenue, Des Moines, IA 50312	3.65 (overall) 3.55 (science) GRE: 154 (V) 154 (Q) Int'l Student: No	Apps Received: 716 Interviews Offered: 142 Admission Offered: N/A Class Size: 50 Admitted Rate: 7%	Biochemistry; Genetics; Medical Terminology; OChem
Northwestern College 107 7th Street SW, Orange City, IA 51041	3.0+ (overall) 3.0+ (science) GRE: Not Req. Int'l Student: Yes	Apps Received: N/A Interviews Offered: N/A Admission Offered: N/A Class Size: 32 Admitted Rate: N/A	Biochemistry; Genetics; OChem

PA School	Ave, GPA & GRE (Verbal, Quantitative, Analy. Writing) Int'l Students: Yes/No	Admissions Statistics	Prerequisite Coursework Other than Gen Bio, Gen Chem, Human Anatomy, Human Physiology, Microbiology, Statistics, Psychology
St. Ambrose University 518 W. Locust Street, Davenport, IA 52804	3.0+ (overall) GRE: N/A Int'l Student: No	Apps Received: N/A Interviews Offered: N/A Admission Offered: N/A Class Size: 30 Admitted Rate: N/A	Biochemistry; English Composition; Medical Terminology; OChem
University of Dubuque 1000 University Ave., Dubuque, IA 52001	3.70 (overall) 3.64 (science) GRE: 307 (Q&V combined) Int'l Student: No	Apps Received: 580 Interviews Offered: 300 Admission Offered: N/A Class Size: 25 Admitted Rate: 4.3%	Biochemistry; Genetics; Medical Terminology; OChem
University of Iowa The University of Iowa, Iowa City, IA 52242-1110	3.76 (overall) 3.63 (science) GRE: 158 (V) 158 (Q) 4.6 (A) Int'l Student: No	Apps Received: N/A Interviews Offered: N/A Admission Offered: N/A Class Size: 25 Admitted Rate: N/A	Biochemistry; OChem; Upper-level Biology (3)
Wichita State University 213 North Mead Street, Wichita, KS 67202	3.70 (overall) GRE: Not Req. Int'l Student: Yes	Apps Received: N/A Interviews Offered: N/A Admission Offered: N/A Class Size: 48 Admitted Rate: N/A	Biochemistry/OChem; Genetics; Medical Terminology
Central Michigan University 1280 E. Campus Drive, Mount Pleasant, MI 48859	3.0+ (overall) 3.0+ (science) GRE: Not Req. Int'l Student: Yes	Apps Received: N/A Interviews Offered: N/A Admission Offered: N/A Class Size: 40 Admitted Rate: N/A	Biochemistry; Pathophysiology

MIDWEST

PA PROGRAMS

PA School	Ave. GPA & GRE (Verbal, Quantitative, Analy. Writing) Int'l Students: Yes/No	Admissions Statistics	Prerequisite Coursework Other than Gen Bio, Gen Chem, Human Anatomy, Human Physiology, Microbiology, Statistics, Psychology
Concordia University - Ann Arbor 4090 Geddes Road, Ann Arbor, MI 48105	3.2+ (overall) 3.2+ (science) GRE: Not Req. Int'l Student: Yes	Apps Received: N/A Interviews Offered: N/A Admission Offered: N/A Class Size: 32 Admitted Rate: N/A	Biochemistry; College Algebra or higher math; English Composition; Medical Terminology; OChem
Eastern Michigan University 222 Rackham Building, Ypsilanti, MI 48197	3.70 (overall) GRE: 315 (Q&V combined) Int'l Student: Yes	Apps Received: 774 Interviews Offered: N/A Admission Offered: N/A Class Size: 30 Admitted Rate: 3.9%	
Grand Valley State University - Grand Rapids 301 Michigan Street NE, Grand Rapids, MI 49315	3.78 (overall) 3.84 (science) GRE: 153 (V) 154 (Q) 4.2 (A) Int'l Student: Yes	Apps Received: 491* Interviews Offered: N/A Admission Offered: N/A Class Size: 36 Admitted Rate: 2.4% *Aggregate number for both Grand Rapids and Traverse City campuses.	Biochemistry; Genetics; OChem; Physics
Grand Valley State University - Traverse City 2200 Dendrinos Drive, Suite 15, Traverse City, MI 49684	3.76 (overall) 3.82 (science) GRE: N/A Int'l Student: Yes	Apps Received: 491* Interviews Offered: N/A Admission Offered: N/A Class Size: 12 Admitted Rate: 2.4% *Aggregate number for both Grand Rapids and Traverse City campuses.	Biochemistry; Genetics; OChem; Physics
University of Detroit Mercy 4001 West McNichols Road, MI 48221	3.0+ (overall) GRE: N/A Int'l Student: Yes	Apps Received: N/A Interviews Offered: N/A Admission Offered: N/A Class Size: 60 Admitted Rate: N/A	Medical Ethics; Nutrition
University of Michigan - Flint 303 East Kearsley Street, MI 48502	3.0+ (overall) 3.0+ (science) GRE: Not Req. Int'l Student: Yes	Apps Received: N/A Interviews Offered: N/A Admission Offered: N/A Class Size: 50 Admitted Rate: N/A	Medical Terminology

PA School	Ave. GPA & GRE (Verbal, Quantitative, Analy. Writing) Int'l Students: Yes/No	Admissions Statistics	Prerequisite Coursework Other than Gen Bio, Gen Chem, Human Anatomy, Human Physiology, Microbiology, Statistics, Psychology
Wayne State University 259 Mack Avenue, Detroit, MI 48201	3.69 (overall) 3.86 (science) GRE: 151 (V) 150 (Q) 4.2 (A) Int'l Student: Yes	Apps Received: N/A Interviews Offered: N/A Admission Offered: N/A Class Size: 50 Admitted Rate: N/A	Biochemistry or OChem; English Composition; Medical Terminology; Nutrition; Upper-level science
Western Michigan University 1903 W Michigan Ave., Kalamazoo, MI 49008	3.62 (overall) 3.50 (science) GRE: Not Req. Int'l Student: Yes	Apps Received: N/A Interviews Offered: N/A Admission Offered: N/A Class Size: 40 Admitted Rate: N/A	Biochemistry
Augsburg University 701 25th Avenue South, Minneapolis, Minnesota 55454	3.0+ (overall) 3.0+ (science) GRE: Not Req. Int'l Student: Yes	Apps Received: N/A Interviews Offered: N/A Admission Offered: N/A Class Size: 33 Admitted Rate: N/A	Bethel University 3900 Bethel Drive, St. Paul, MN 55112
Bethel University 3900 Bethel Drive, St. Paul, MN 55112	3.80 (overall) 3.80 (science) GRE: Not Req. Int'l Student: Yes	Apps Received: N/A Interviews Offered: N/A Admission Offered: N/A Class Size: 32 Admitted Rate: N/A	Biochemistry; Genetics; OChem
College of Saint Scholastica 1200 Kenwood Avenue, Duluth, MN 55811	3.0+ (overall) 3.0+ (science) GRE: N/A Int'l Student: Yes	Apps Received: N/A Interviews Offered: N/A Admission Offered: N/A Class Size: 30 Admitted Rate: N/A	Biochemistry; Medical Terminology; OChem

MIDWEST

PA PROGRAMS

PA School	Ave. GPA & GRE (Verbal, Quantitative, Analy. Writing) Int'l Students: Yes/No	Admissions Statistics	Prerequisite Coursework Other than Gen Bio, Gen Chem, Human Anatomy, Human Physiology, Microbiology, Statistics, Psychology
Mayo Clinic School of Health Sciences 200 First Street SW, Rochester, MN 55905	3.5+ (overall) 3.5+ (science) GRE: Not Req. Int'l Student: No	Apps Received: N/A Interviews Offered: N/A Admission Offered: N/A Class Size: 24 Admitted Rate: N/A	*This is a 3+2 program intended for high school applicants.
Saint Catherine University 2004 Randolph Avenue, Saint Paul, MN 55105	3.60 (overall) 3.58 (science) GRE: 154 (V) 155 (Q) 4 (A) Int'l Student: Yes	Apps Received: 249 Interviews Offered: N/A Admission Offered: N/A Class Size: 32 Admitted Rate: 12.9%	Biochemistry; Medical Terminology; OChem; Pre-Calculus
Missouri State University 901 S. National Avenue, Springfield, MO 65897	3.70 (overall) 3.60 (science) GRE: 303 (Q&V combined) Int'l Student: Yes	Apps Received: N/A Interviews Offered: N/A Admission Offered: N/A Class Size: 30 Admitted Rate: N/A	Biochemistry or OChem; Genetics; Social Science
Saint Louis University 3437 Caroline Street, Saint Louis, MO 64104	3.0+ (overall) 3.0+ (science) GRE: Not Req. Int'l Student: Yes	Apps Received: N/A Interviews Offered: N/A Admission Offered: N/A Class Size: 46 Admitted Rate: N/A	Genetics; OChem; Medical Terminology
Stephens College 1200 E Broadway, Columbia, MO 65215	3.49 (overall) 3.44 (science) GRE: 150.10 (V) 150.16 (Q) 3.73 (A) Int'l Student: Yes	Apps Received: N/A Interviews Offered: N/A Admission Offered: N/A Class Size: 30 Admitted Rate: N/A	Genetics; OChem; Medical Terminology

PA School	Ave. GPA & GRE (Verbal, Quantitative, Analy. Writing) Int'l Students: Yes/No	Admissions Statistics	Prerequisite Coursework Other than Gen Bio, Gen Chem, Human Anatomy, Human Physiology, Microbiology, Statistics, Psychology
University of Missouri - Kansas City 2411 Holmes Street, Kansas City, MO 64108	3.0+ (overall) 3.0+ (science) GRE: N/A Int'l Student: No	Apps Received: 333 Interviews Offered: 80 Admission Offered: N/A Class Size: 20 Admitted Rate: 6%	Biochemistry; Medical Terminology; OChem
College of Saint Mary 7000 Mercy Road, Omaha, NE 68106	3.0+ (overall) 3.0+ (science) GRE: 25%+ (V) 25% + (Q) 25%+ (A) Int'l Student: Yes	Apps Received: N/A Interviews Offered: N/A Admission Offered: N/A Class Size: 40 Admitted Rate: N/A	Biochemistry; Medical Terminology; OChem; Upper-level Biology
Creighton University 2500 California Plaza, Omaha, NE 68178	3.70 (overall) 3.65 (science) GRE: Not Req. Int'l Student: No	Apps Received: N/A Interviews Offered: N/A Admission Offered: N/A Class Size: 28 Admitted Rate: N/A	Abnormal Psychology; Biochemistry; OChem; Medical Terminology
Union College 3800 South 48th Street, Lincoln, NE 68506	3.58 (overall) 3.46 (science) GRE: Not Req. Int'l Student: Yes	Apps Received: 263 Interviews Offered: ~100 Admission Offered: N/A Class Size: 30 Admitted Rate: 11.4%	Biochemistry; Medical Terminology; OChem
University of Nebraska Medical Center - Kearney 2402 University Dr., Kearney, NE 68849	3.79 (overall) 3.70 (science) GRE: Not Req. Int'l Student: Yes	Apps Received: 567* Interviews Offered: N/A Admission Offered: N/A Class Size: 15 Admitted Rate: 2.6% *Aggregate number for both Kearney and Omaha campuses.	Biochemistry; English Composition; Medical Terminology; OChem

MIDWEST

PA School	Ave. GPA & GRE (Verbal, Quantitative, Analy. Writing) Int'l Students: Yes/No	Admissions Statistics	Prerequisite Coursework Other than Gen Bio, Gen Chem, Human Anatomy, Human Physiology, Microbiology, Statistics, Psychology
University of Nebraska Medical Center - Omaha 984300 Nebraska Medical Center, Omaha, NE 68198	3.70 (overall) 3.58 (science) GRE: Not Req. Int'l Student: Yes	Apps Received: 567* Interviews Offered: N/A Admission Offered: N/A Class Size: 50 Admitted Rate: 8.8% *Aggregate number for both Kearney and Omaha campuses.	
University of North Dakota 501 N. Columbia Road, Grand Forks, ND 58202	3.40 (overall) GRE: Not Req. Int'l Student: Yes	Apps Received: N/A Interviews Offered: N/A Admission Offered: N/A Class Size: 35 Admitted Rate: N/A	Upper-level science (6) from: • Biochemistry • Biochemistry of proteins and information flow • Genetics • Cell biology • Developmental biology • Endocrinology • Systems biology • Physiology of organs and systems • Molecular genetics • Molecular biology of the cell • OChem • immunology
Ashland University 401 College Ave., Ashland, OH 44805	Apps Received: N/A Interviews Offered: N/A Admission Offered: N/A Class Size: 30 Admitted Rate: N/A	Apps Received: N/A Interviews Offered: N/A Admission Offered: N/A Class Size: 30 Admitted Rate: N/A	Biochemistry; Medical Terminology; OChem
Baldwin Wallace University 275 Eastland Rd., Berea, OH 44017	3.83 (overall) 3.89 (science) GRE: N/A Int'l Student: Yes	Apps Received: 700 Interviews Offered: N/A Admission Offered: N/A Class Size: 35 Admitted Rate: 5%	English Composition; Medical Terminology; OChem
Case Western Reserve University 9501 Euclid Avenue, Cleveland, OH 44106	3.5+ (overall) 3.5+ (science) GRE: N/A Int'l Student: Yes	Apps Received: N/A Interviews Offered: N/A Admission Offered: N/A Class Size: 36 Admitted Rate: N/A	

PA School	Ave, GPA & GRE (Verbal, Quantitative, Analy. Writing) Int'l Students: Yes/No	Admissions Statistics	Prerequisite Coursework Other than Gen Bio, Gen Chem, Human Anatomy, Human Physiology, Microbiology, Statistics, Psychology
Kettering College 3737 Southern Boulevard, Kettering, OH 45429	3.68 (overall) 3.62 (science) GRE: N/A Int'l Student: Yes	Apps Received: N/A Interviews Offered: N/A Admission Offered: N/A Class Size: 60 Admitted Rate: N/A	Biochemistry; OChem
Lake Erie College 391 W. Washington Street, Painesville, OH 44077	3.55 (overall) GRE: N/A Int'l Student: Yes	Apps Received: N/A Interviews Offered: N/A Admission Offered: N/A Class Size: 26 Admitted Rate: N/A	College Algebra; English Composition; Genetics; OChem
Marietta College 215 Fifth Street, Marietta, OH 45750	3.66 (overall) 3.70 (science) GRE: 152 (V) 151 (Q) Int'l Student: Yes	Apps Received: N/A Interviews Offered: N/A Admission Offered: N/A Class Size: 36 Admitted Rate: N/A	OChem; Upper-level Biology
Mercy College of Ohio 2221 Madison AVe., Toledo, OH 43604	3.0+ (overall) 3.0+ (science) GRE: 150+ (V) 150+ (Q) 3.5+ (A) Int'l Student: Yes	Apps Received: N/A Interviews Offered: N/A Admission Offered: N/A Class Size: 20 Admitted Rate: N/A	Biochemistry; Medical Terminology; OChem
Mount St. Joseph University 5701 Delhi Road, Cincinnati, OH 45052	3.0+ (overall) 3.0+ (science) GRE: 300+ (Q&V combined) 4+ (A) Int'l Student: Yes	Apps Received: N/A Interviews Offered: N/A Admission Offered: N/A Class Size: 32 Admitted Rate: N/A	Biochemistry; OChem

MIDWEST

PA PROGRAMS

PA School	Ave. GPA & GRE (Verbal, Quantitative, Analy. Writing) Int'l Students: Yes/No	Admissions Statistics	Prerequisite Coursework Other than Gen Bio, Gen Chem, Human Anatomy, Human Physiology, Microbiology, Statistics, Psychology
Ohio Dominican University 1216 Sunbury Road, Columbus, OH 43219	3.0+ (overall) 3.0+ (science) GRE: N/A Int'l Student: No	Apps Received: N/A Interviews Offered: N/A Admission Offered: N/A Class Size: 50 Admitted Rate: N/A	Biochemistry; College Algebra or higher; Humanities
Ohio University 6805 Bobcat Way, Dublin, OH 43016	3.69 (overall) 3.62 (science) GRE: 153 (V) 154 (Q) 4.2 (A) Int'l Student: No	Apps Received: N/A Interviews Offered: N/A Admission Offered: N/A Class Size: 35 Admitted Rate: N/A	Biochemistry; College Algebra or higher; Medical Terminology; OChem
University of Dayton 300 College Park, Dayton, OH 45469	3.62 (overall) 3.66 (science) GRE: Not Req. Int'l Student: Yes	Apps Received: N/A Interviews Offered: N/A Admission Offered: N/A Class Size: 40 Admitted Rate: N/A	Biochemistry; Medical Terminology; OChem
University of Findlay 1000 North Main Street, Findlay, OH 45840	3.0+ (overall) 3.0+ (science) GRE: Not Req. Int'l Student: Yes	Apps Received: N/A Interviews Offered: N/A Admission Offered: N/A Class Size: 22 Admitted Rate: N/A	Biochemistry; Genetics; Medical Terminology; OChem; Physics
University of Mount Union 1972 Clark Avenue, Alliance, OH 44601	3.0+ (overall) 3.0+ (science) GRE: N/A Int'l Student: Yes	Apps Received: N/A Interviews Offered: N/A Admission Offered: N/A Class Size: 40 Admitted Rate: N/A	English Composition; Genetics; Medical Terminology; OChem
University of Toledo 3000 Arlington Ave., Collier Building, Toledo, OH 43614	3.4+ (overall) 3.4+ (science) GRE: 290 (Q&V combined) Int'l Student: No	Apps Received: N/A Interviews Offered: N/A Admission Offered: N/A Class Size: 40 Admitted Rate: N/A	Biochemistry or OChem; College Algebra or higher; Genetics; Medical Terminology

PA School	Ave. GPA & GRE (Verbal, Quantitative, Analy. Writing) Int'l Students: Yes/No	Admissions Statistics	Prerequisite Coursework Other than Gen Bio, Gen Chem, Human Anatomy, Human Physiology, Microbiology, Statistics, Psychology
University of South Dakota 414 E. Clark St., Vermillion, SD 57069	3.72 (overall) 3.64 (science) GRE: Not Req. Int'l Student: No	Apps Received: 485 Interviews Offered: 90 Admission Offered: N/A Class Size: 25 Admitted Rate: 5.2%	Biochemistry
Carroll University 100 N. East Avenue, Waukesha, WI 53186	3.74 (overall) 3.68 (science) GRE: 65% (V) 56% (Q) Int'l Student: Yes	Apps Received: 659 Interviews Offered: N/A Admission Offered: N/A Class Size: 28 Admitted Rate: 4.2%	Biochemistry; OChem
Concordia University - Wisconsin 12800 North Lake Shore Drive, Mequon, WI 53097	3.2+ (overall) 3.2+ (science) GRE: Not Req. Int'l Student: No	Apps Received: N/A Interviews Offered: N/A Admission Offered: N/A Class Size: 30 Admitted Rate: N/A	Biochemistry; College Algebra or higher; Genetics; Medical Terminology; OChem
Marquette University 507 N 17th Street,, Milwaukee, WI 53233	3.0+ (overall) GRE: Not Req. Int'l Student: Yes	Apps Received: N/A Interviews Offered: N/A Admission Offered: N/A Class Size: 75 Admitted Rate: N/A	Biochemistry; Medical Terminology
University of Wisconsin - La Crosse 1725 State St., La Crosse, WI 54601	3.92 (overall) 3.89 (science) GRE: 156 (V) 158 (Q) 4.4 (A) Int'l Student: Yes	Apps Received: 492 Interviews Offered: 90 Admission Offered: N/A Class Size: 28 Admitted Rate: 5.7%	Biochemistry; OChem; Pre-Calculus;

MIDWEST

PA PROGRAMS

PA School	Ave. GPA & GRE (Verbal, Quantitative, Analy. Writing) Int'l Students: Yes/No	Admissions Statistics	Prerequisite Coursework Other than Gen Bio, Gen Chem, Human Anatomy, Human Physiology, Microbiology, Statistics, Psychology
University of Wisconsin - Madison 750 Highland Avenue, Madison, WI 53705	3.2+ (overall) 3.2+ (science) GRE: Not Req. Int'l Student: No	Apps Received: N/A Interviews Offered: N/A Admission Offered: N/A Class Size: 52 Admitted Rate: N/A	Biochemistry

ILLINOIS

INDIANA

IOWA

KANSAS

MICHIGAN

MINNESOTA

MISSOURI

NEBRASKA

NORTH DAKOTA

OHIO

SOUTH DAKOTA

WISCONSIN

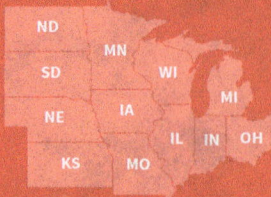

DOMINICAN UNIVERSITY OF ILLINOIS

Address: 7900 West Division Street, River Forest, IL 60305
Website: *https://www.dom.edu/admission/graduate/health-sciences-programs/mmspas*
Contact: *pa.program@dom.edu*
Phone: 708-366-2490

COST OF ATTENDANCE

Tuition and Fees: $52,510
Additional Expenses: $14,950*
Total: $67,460

*Health Insurance cost not included.

Financial Aid: https://www.dom.edu/admission/office-financial-aid/prospective-graduate-students

ADDITIONAL INFORMATION

Interesting tidbit: Dominican's Physician Assistant Studies Program reflects the university's longstanding commitment to social justice, grounded in our Dominican Catholic tradition. The distinctive, relationship-centered approach to graduate education means students will gain not only professional skills but also a greater understanding of team dynamics, ethical issues, and the unique needs of the individuals in their care.

Important Updates due to COVID-19: The program will accept online labs if an applicant was unable to take 'in-seat' labs in 2020 and 2021 due to the Covid-19 Pandemic. Virtual interview.

Were tests required? GRE required.

Are tests expected next year? Yes.

What international experiences are available? N/A

What dual degree options exist? N/A

What service-learning opportunities exist? N/A

PANCE First-Time Pass Rate: 96% (2020)

MIDWESTERN UNIVERSITY - DOWNERS GROVE

Address: 555 31st Street, Downers Grove, IL 60515
Website: *https://www.midwestern.edu/academics/degrees-and-programs/master-of-medical-science-in-physician-assistant-program-il.xml*
Contact: *admissil@midwestern.edu*
Phone: 630-515-6034

COST OF ATTENDANCE

Tuition and Fees: $59,287
Additional Expenses: N/A
Total: $59,287*

*This figure does not include cost of living or other indirect costs.

Financial Aid: https://www.midwestern.edu/admissions/tuition-and-financial-aid.xml

ADDITIONAL INFORMATION

Interesting tidbit: Subsidized housing is provided for distant in-state and out-of-state core clinical rotations only. Otherwise, students are expected to secure their own housing for local and elective rotations, and must provide their own transportation to all core and elective clinical rotations regardless of location.

Important Updates due to COVID-19: The Program accepts prerequisite coursework with a laboratory component completed during Spring 2020, Summer 2020, Fall 2020, Spring 2021, or Summer 2021 which was only offered online. It will also accept all prerequisite coursework completed during Spring, Summer, or Fall 2020 in which only pass/fail grades were awarded.

Were tests required? GRE required. CASPer required only for those who are invited to interview.

Are tests expected next year? Yes.

What international experiences are available? N/A

What dual degree options exist? N/A

What service-learning opportunities exist? N/A

PANCE First-Time Pass Rate: 95% (2020)

ILLINOIS

INDIANA

IOWA

KANSAS

MICHIGAN

MINNESOTA

MISSOURI

NEBRASKA

NORTH DAKOTA

OHIO

SOUTH DAKOTA

WISCONSIN

MIDWEST

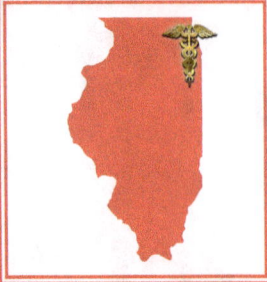

ILLINOIS

INDIANA

IOWA

KANSAS

MICHIGAN

MINNESOTA

MISSOURI

NEBRASKA

NORTH DAKOTA

OHIO

SOUTH DAKOTA

WISCONSIN

NORTHWESTERN UNIVERSITY

Address: 240 E. Huron Street, Suite 1-200, Chicago, IL 60611
Website: *http://www.feinberg.northwestern.edu/sites/pa/*
Contact: *paprogram@northwestern.edu*
Phone: 312-503-1851

COST OF ATTENDANCE

Tuition and Fees: $49,629
Additional Expenses: $38,929
Total: $88,558

Financial Aid: https://chicagofinancialaid.northwestern.edu/
resources-by-program/physician-assistant/index.html

ADDITIONAL INFORMATION

Interesting tidbit: The Northwestern University Physician Assistant
Program offers a unique, organ system-based curriculum with
small-group, Problem-Based Learning (PBL) as the unifying feature
throughout the pre-clinical year. The program emphasizes early
acquisition and ongoing reinforcement of clinical reasoning skills,
and the students are introduced to their first "PBL patient" on the
first day of class.

Important Updates due to COVID-19: For the 2021-22 admission
cycle, the GRE requirement is temporarily waived.

Were tests required? No.

Are tests expected next year? GRE required.

What international experiences are available? N/A

What dual degree options exist? N/A

What service-learning opportunities exist? N/A

PANCE First-Time Pass Rate: 100% (2020)

ROSALIND FRANKLIN UNIVERSITY

Address: 3333 Green Bay Road, North Chicago, IL 60064
Website: *https://www.rosalindfranklin.edu/academics/college-of-health-professions/degree-programs/physician-assistant-practice-ms/*
Contact: *pa.admissions@rosalindfranklin.edu*
Phone: 847-578-3204

COST OF ATTENDANCE

Tuition and Fees: $50,089
Additional Expenses: $29,148
Total: $77,857

Financial Aid: https://www.rosalindfranklin.edu/admission-aid/financial-services/financial-aid/sources-of-aid/

ADDITIONAL INFORMATION

Interesting tidbit: The second 12 months of the curriculum entails attending seven core clinical rotations and two elective rotations. For the two elective rotations, each student has the opportunity to request a site of his/her choosing.The department has a long list of established sites from which students may request rotations.

Important Updates due to COVID-19: The Physician Assistant program at Rosalind Franklin University will temporarily accept Pass/Fail and Satisfactory/Fail grades. Supporting documentation from the institution where the course was completed must be presented stating change of grading policy was the only option presented and not a choice.

Were tests required? No.

Are tests expected next year? No.

What international experiences are available? N/A

What dual degree options exist? N/A

What service-learning opportunities exist? N/A

PANCE First-Time Pass Rate: 98% (2020)

ILLINOIS

INDIANA

IOWA

KANSAS

MICHIGAN

MINNESOTA

MISSOURI

NEBRASKA

NORTH DAKOTA

OHIO

SOUTH DAKOTA

WISCONSIN

MIDWEST

ILLINOIS

INDIANA

IOWA

KANSAS

MICHIGAN

MINNESOTA

MISSOURI

NEBRASKA

NORTH DAKOTA

OHIO

SOUTH DAKOTA

WISCONSIN

RUSH UNIVERSITY

Address: 600 S. Paulina Street, Suite 746 AAC, Chicago, IL 60612
Website: *http://www.rushu.rush.edu/pa-program*
Contact: *pa_admissions@rush.edu*
Phone: 312-563-3234

COST OF ATTENDANCE

Tuition and Fees: $25,590
Additional Expenses: $42,746
Total: $68,336

Financial Aid: https://www.rushu.rush.edu/rush-experience/
student-services/office-student-financial-aid

ADDITIONAL INFORMATION

Interesting tidbit: Rush University's PA program offers a 30-month curriculum, 28 of which are devoted to clinical training. Its extensive training provides advanced practice training opportunities in various fields of clinical practice to prepare students to take leadership roles in clinical practice, research and service.

Important Updates due to COVID-19: The program will accept passing grades taken in a Pass/Fail system for any course taken from May to December 2020, and up to 2 required, prerequisite courses taken from May to December 2020. Completion of the CASPer assessment is not a requirement for admission for the 2021-2022 cycle.

Were tests required? No.

Are tests expected next year? CASPer required.

What international experiences are available? N/A

What dual degree options exist? N/A

What service-learning opportunities exist? N/A

PANCE First-Time Pass Rate: 93% (2020)

SOUTHERN ILLINOIS UNIVERSITY

Address: 600 Agriculture Drive, Carbondale, IL 62901
Website: *https://www.siumed.edu/paprogram*
Contact: *paadvisement-L@listserv.siu.edu*
Phone: 618-453-5527

COST OF ATTENDANCE

In-State Tuition and Fees: $42,026
Additional Expenses: $25,308
Total: $67,334

Out-of-State Tuition and Fees: $81,821
Additional Expenses: $25,308
Total: $107,129

Financial Aid: https://gradschool.siu.edu/cost-aid/

ADDITIONAL INFORMATION

Interesting tidbit: SIU Physician Assistant Program is part of the SIU School of Medicine, which utilizes a problem-based learning (PBL) format for delivery of its medical curriculum. As such, the PA Program has been a pioneer in using PBL, simulated patients, innovative evaluation techniques, and clinical mentoring programs.

Important Updates due to COVID-19: N/A

Were tests required? GRE required.

Are tests expected next year? Yes.

What international experiences are available? N/A

What dual degree options exist? N/A

What service-learning opportunities exist? N/A

PANCE First-Time Pass Rate: 100% (2020)

ILLINOIS

INDIANA

IOWA

KANSAS

MICHIGAN

MINNESOTA

MISSOURI

NEBRASKA

NORTH DAKOTA

OHIO

SOUTH DAKOTA

WISCONSIN

MIDWEST

ILLINOIS

INDIANA

IOWA

KANSAS

MICHIGAN

MINNESOTA

MISSOURI

NEBRASKA

NORTH DAKOTA

OHIO

SOUTH DAKOTA

WISCONSIN

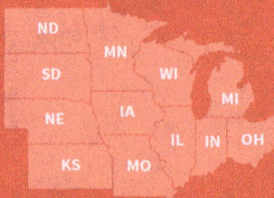

BUTLER UNIVERSITY

Address: 4600 Sunset Avenue, Indianapolis, IN 46208
Website: *http://www.butler.edu/physician-assistant/*
Contact: *mliveret@butler.edu*
Phone: 317-940-6529

COST OF ATTENDANCE

Tuition and Fees: $47,050
Additional Expenses: $19,722
Total: $66,772

Financial Aid: https://www.butler.edu/financial-aid/graduate-students-financial-aid

ADDITIONAL INFORMATION

Interesting tidbit: In addition to the Standard Admission Pathway, Butler University offers a Selective Internal Admission Pathway to the PA program for current Butler University students and/or alumni. For the CASPA Application Cycles of 2020-21, 2021-22, and 2022-23 up to 60% of each class will be students who have previously earned Butler degrees at the time they begin in the PA Program. For CASPA Application Cycles 2023-24 and beyond 40% of each class will be reserved for students who have previously earned Butler degrees at the time they begin in the PA Program.

Important Updates due to COVID-19: If you were required to take prerequisite courses for Pass/Fail or Credit/No Credit during Spring or Summer 2020, the PA Admission Committee will take these applications into consideration. Applicants must submit a form that includes verification from your institution that a grade of P/F, Credit/No Credit, or similar was required. For the 2020-2021 and 2021-2022 CASPA Application Cycles, applicants may have three outstanding prerequisites of any configuration (including chemistry and biology-related courses) at the time of application.

Were tests required? GRE required.

Are tests expected next year? Yes.

What international experiences are available? International rotations.

What dual degree options exist? N/A

What service-learning opportunities exist? N/A

PANCE First-Time Pass Rate: 100% (2020)

FRANKLIN COLLEGE

Address: 101 Branigin Boulevard, Franklin, IN 46131
Website: *https://franklincollege.edu/academics/graduate-programs/master-science-physician-assistant/*
Contact: *paprogram@franklincollege.edu*
Phone: 317-738-8095

COST OF ATTENDANCE

Tuition and Fees: $52,027
Additional Expenses: $14,085
Total: $66,112

Financial Aid: https://franklincollege.edu/admissions/financial-aid/types-financial-aid/

ADDITIONAL INFORMATION

Interesting tidbit: The Physician Assistant Studies Program at Franklin College is a 25-month curriculum divided into 12-month didactic, 12-month clinical and 1-month capstone. The Program has a patient-centered humanistic healthcare focus with an emphasis on community engagement and underserved populations.

Important Updates due to COVID-19: Requirement of a minimum of 200 documented patient care hours is waived for those applying in 2021.

Were tests required? No.

Are tests expected next year? No.

What international experiences are available? N/A

What dual degree options exist? N/A

What service-learning opportunities exist? N/A

PANCE First-Time Pass Rate: 89% (2020)

Other: Franklin College undergraduate students have the opportunity to apply as early as their junior year for early admission.

ILLINOIS

INDIANA

IOWA

KANSAS

MICHIGAN

MINNESOTA

MISSOURI

NEBRASKA

NORTH DAKOTA

OHIO

SOUTH DAKOTA

WISCONSIN

MIDWEST

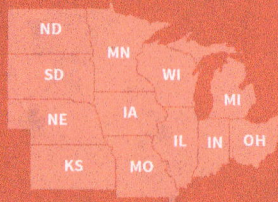

INDIANA STATE UNIVERSITY

Address: 567 N. 5th Street, Terre Haute, IN 47809
Website: *https://www.indstate.edu/health/program/pa*
Contact: *isu-pa@indstate.edu*
Phone: 812-237-3632

COST OF ATTENDANCE

In-State Tuition and Fees: $45,378
Additional Expenses: N/A
Total: $45,378*

Out-of-State Tuition and Fees: $83,601
Additional Expenses: N/A
Total: $83,601*

*This figure does not include cost of living or other indirect costs.

Financial Aid: https://www.indstate.edu/financial-aid/graduate-awards

ADDITIONAL INFORMATION

Interesting tidbit: Students at Indiana State'sPA Program have numerous opportunities for interprofessional education with Indiana State University Physical Therapy, Nursing, and Athletic Training students, as well as IUSM-TH medical students. As a partner and through collaboration with the Rural Health Innovation Collaborative, Indiana State embodies excellence in interprofessional education to produce highly skilled healthcare professionals who ser the public and especially the vulnerable and underserved.

Important Updates due to COVID-19: Applications lacking the minimum 500 hours of healthcare/direct patient care experience (and/or 1000 hours of healthcare/direct patient care + shadowing), and 100 community service hours will still be considered until further notice.

Were tests required? GRE required.

Are tests expected next year? Yes.

What international experiences are available? N/A

What dual degree options exist? N/A

What service-learning opportunities exist? N/A

PANCE First-Time Pass Rate: 89% (2020)

INDIANA UNIVERSITY SCHOOL OF HEALTH & HUMAN SCIENCES

Address: 1140 W. Michigan Street, Indianapolis, IN 46202
Website: *https://shhs.iupui.edu/graduate-professional/physician-assistant-studies/master-physician-assistant-studies/index.html*
Contact: *shrsinfo@iupui.edu*
Phone: 317-278-9550

COST OF ATTENDANCE

In-State Tuition and Fees: $34,616
Additional Expenses: N/A
Total: $34,616*

Out-of-State Tuition and Fees: $48,246
Additional Expenses: N/A
Total: $48,246*

*This figure does not include cost of living or other indirect costs.

Financial Aid: See 'Financial Aid and Tuition' on FAQ
https://shhs.iupui.edu/graduate-professional/physician-assistant-studies/master-physician-assistant-studies/faqs.html

ADDITIONAL INFORMATION

Interesting tidbit: IU MPAS 27-month/seven-semester program is based on medical school curriculum and includes classroom education and extensive clinical training. Students benefit from a partnership with the IU School of Medicine, the nation's largest medical school and have access to over 400 community and clinical partnerships.

Important Updates due to COVID-19: The IU PA Admissions Committee will accept online labs for prerequisite courses completed during 2020 and 2021. Due to the ongoing pandemic, there will be no minimum number of shadowing hours required.

Were tests required? No.

Are tests expected next year? No.

What international experiences are available? N/A

What dual degree options exist? N/A

What service-learning opportunities exist? IU Student Outreach Clinic.

PANCE First-Time Pass Rate: 100% (2020)

ILLINOIS

INDIANA

IOWA

KANSAS

MICHIGAN

MINNESOTA

MISSOURI

NEBRASKA

NORTH DAKOTA

OHIO

SOUTH DAKOTA

WISCONSIN

MIDWEST

ILLINOIS

INDIANA

IOWA

KANSAS

MICHIGAN

MINNESOTA

MISSOURI

NEBRASKA

NORTH DAKOTA

OHIO

SOUTH DAKOTA

WISCONSIN

TRINE UNIVERSITY

Address: 1 University Avenue, Angola, IN 46703
Website: *http://www.trine.edu/academics/majors-and-minors/
graduate/master-physician-assistant-studies/index.aspx*
Contact: *pa@trine.edu*
Phone: 260-203-2914

COST OF ATTENDANCE

Tuition and Fees: $46,541
Additional Expenses: N/A
Total: $46,541*

*This figure does not include cost of living or other indirect costs.

Financial Aid: https://www.trine.edu/admission-aid/tuition-aid/
types-of-aid/index.aspx

ADDITIONAL INFORMATION

Interesting tidbit: The Trine University MPAS program provides
students with an unparalleled experience. It is in partnerships with
Lutheran and Parkview health systems, and is a member of the Fort
Wayne Area Interprofessional Education Consortium for Graduate
Health Care Education, which allows for interprofessional and
multidisciplinary learning opportunities.

Important Updates due to COVID-19: N/A

Were tests required? GRE required.

Are tests expected next year? Yes.

What international experiences are available? N/A

What dual degree options exist? N/A

What service-learning opportunities exist? N/A

PANCE First-Time Pass Rate: 96% (2020)

Other: Trine University offers two additional pathways to its PA
Program - Direct Entry Pathway (for qualified high school students)
and Direct Admissions Pathways (for current, qualified Trine
university undergrad students).

UNIVERSITY OF EVANSVILLE

Address: 515 Bob Jones Way, Room 3001, Evansville, IN 47708
Website: *https://www.evansville.edu/majors/physicianassistant/*
Contact: *pa@evansville.edu*
Phone: 812-488-3400

COST OF ATTENDANCE

Tuition and Fees: $48,650
Additional Expenses: N/A
Total: $48,650*

*This figure does not include cost of living or other indirect costs.

Financial Aid: https://www.evansville.edu/student-financial-services/scholarships-for-master-of-physician-assistant-science.cfm

ADDITIONAL INFORMATION

Interesting tidbit: The PA Program is at the Stone Family Center for Health Sciences, a multi-institutional campus provides unique opportunities for inter-professional experiences among various health professional students, collaborative learning, and research opportunities. The curriculum is designed to prepare students to provide patient-centered care and work within an interprofessional team environment.

Important Updates due to COVID-19: The UEPA Program will only accept letter grades for our listed pre-requisite courses. No exceptions.

Were tests required? Altus Suite required.

Are tests expected next year? Yes.

What international experiences are available? N/A

What dual degree options exist? N/A

What service-learning opportunities exist? N/A

PANCE First-Time Pass Rate: 100% (2020)

Other: University of Evansville offers a Baccalaureat to Physician Assistant (B/PA) Program, a direct entry admission for high school seniors.

ILLINOIS

INDIANA

IOWA

KANSAS

MICHIGAN

MINNESOTA

MISSOURI

NEBRASKA

NORTH DAKOTA

OHIO

SOUTH DAKOTA

WISCONSIN

MIDWEST

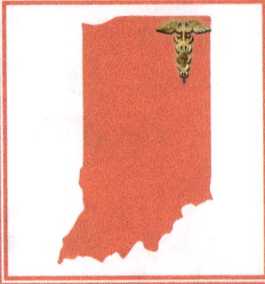

ILLINOIS

INDIANA

IOWA

KANSAS

MICHIGAN

MINNESOTA

MISSOURI

NEBRASKA

NORTH DAKOTA

OHIO

SOUTH DAKOTA

WISCONSIN

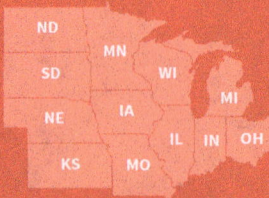

UNIVERSITY OF SAINT FRANCIS

Address: 2701 Spring Street, Fort Wayne, IN 46808
Website: *http://pa.sf.edu/*
Contact: *dlabarbera@sf.edu*
Phone: 260-399-7700

COST OF ATTENDANCE

Tuition and Fees: $43,095*
Additional Expenses: $20,850
Total: $63,945

*Alumni tuition and fees is $24,510 and total, $53,793.

Financial Aid: https://admissions.sf.edu/costs-aid/graduate-financial-aid/

ADDITIONAL INFORMATION

Interesting tidbit: USF offers extensive clinical experience and specialty track options to PA students. With more than 1,000 clinical education partners throughout the region, USF will help students find rotation sites that align with their goals. Students have the flexibility to choose two additional rotations from one of the following four tracks based on their professional goals - trauma/surgery, family practice, hospital-based care and internal medicine.

Important Updates due to COVID-19: N/A

Were tests required? GRE required.

Are tests expected next year? Yes.

What international experiences are available? N/A

What dual degree options exist? N/A

What service-learning opportunities exist? N/A

PANCE First-Time Pass Rate: 100% (2020)

VALPARAISO UNIVERSITY

Address: 1700 Chapel Dr., Valparaiso, IN 46383
Website: *https://www.valpo.edu/physician-assistant-program/ programs/admission/*
Contact: *jodi.gass@valpo.edu*
Phone: 219-464-5611

COST OF ATTENDANCE

Tuition and Fees: $64,213
Additional Expenses: N/A
Total: $64,213*

*This figure does not include cost of living or other indirect costs.

Financial Aid: https://www.valpo.edu/student-financial-services/ planning/

ADDITIONAL INFORMATION

Interesting tidbit: Valpo's Physician Assistant program is a 5-Year BS/MS program, which consists of three years of undergraduate study and two years of graduate study. The accredited, graduate phase of the 5-Year PA Program (MSPA) does not accept transfer students nor grant early entry.

Important Updates due to COVID-19: N/A

Were tests required? No.

Are tests expected next year? No.

What international experiences are available? N/A

What dual degree options exist? N/A

What service-learning opportunities exist? N/A

PANCE First-Time Pass Rate: 84% (2020)

ILLINOIS

INDIANA

IOWA

KANSAS

MICHIGAN

MINNESOTA

MISSOURI

NEBRASKA

NORTH DAKOTA

OHIO

SOUTH DAKOTA

WISCONSIN

MIDWEST

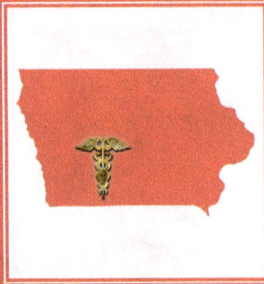

ILLINOIS

INDIANA

IOWA

KANSAS

MICHIGAN

MINNESOTA

MISSOURI

NEBRASKA

NORTH DAKOTA

OHIO

SOUTH DAKOTA

WISCONSIN

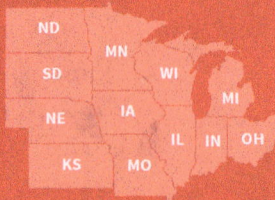

DES MOINES UNIVERSITY

Address: 3200 Grand Avenue, Des Moines, IA 50312
Website: *https://www.dmu.edu/pa/*
Contact: *paadmit@dmu.edu*
Phone: 515-271-1603

COST OF ATTENDANCE

Tuition and Fees: $41,382
Additional Expenses: $30,265
Total: $71,647

Financial Aid: https://www.dmu.edu/financial-aid/scholarships/physician-assistant/

ADDITIONAL INFORMATION

Interesting tidbit: DMU's 25-month physician assistant program emphasizes hands-on experience and critical thinking. In addition to DMU's Simulation Center and the Standardized Performance Assessment Lab (SPAL), the Surgery Skills Center provides opportunities for the students to train in suturing, surgical instrumentation, dissection, intravenous placements and other clinical and surgical skills.

Important Updates due to COVID-19: Due to the disruptions caused by COVID-19, virtual shadowing experiences are accepted.

Were tests required? GRE required. While the GRE is required, MCAT results will also be considered.

Are tests expected next year? Yes.

What international experiences are available? International clinical rotation through DMU's Global Health Department. See https://www.dmu.edu/globalhealth/

What dual degree options exist? N/A

What service-learning opportunities exist? Service trips through DMU's Global Health Department. See https://www.dmu.edu/globalhealth/

PANCE First-Time Pass Rate: 96% (2020)

NORTHWESTERN COLLEGE

Address: 101 7th Street SW, Orange City, Iowa 51041
Website: *https://www.nwciowa.edu/graduate/physician-assistant*
Contact: *physician.assistant@nwciowa.edu*
Phone: 712-707-7359

COST OF ATTENDANCE

Tuition and Fees: $54,000
Additional Expenses: $35,395
Total: $89,395

Financial Aid: https://www.nwciowa.edu/graduate/physician-assistant/tuition

ADDITIONAL INFORMATION

Interesting tidbit: Northwestern College's Master of Science in Physician Assistant Studies (MSPAS) is a faith-based 27-month graduate program. The clinical phase (3 terms out of 7) entails clinical rotations with concurrent online courses designed to facilitate the integration of classroom material with clinical experience.

Important Updates due to COVID-19: Contact admissions directly.

Were tests required? CASPer required.

Are tests expected next year? Yes.

What international experiences are available? N/A

What dual degree options exist? N/A

What service-learning opportunities exist? N/A

PANCE First-Time Pass Rate: N/A (The inaugural class will graduate in 2022).

ILLINOIS

INDIANA

IOWA

KANSAS

MICHIGAN

MINNESOTA

MISSOURI

NEBRASKA

NORTH DAKOTA

OHIO

SOUTH DAKOTA

WISCONSIN

MIDWEST

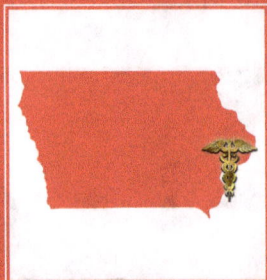

ILLINOIS

INDIANA

IOWA

KANSAS

MICHIGAN

MINNESOTA

MISSOURI

NEBRASKA

NORTH DAKOTA

OHIO

SOUTH DAKOTA

WISCONSIN

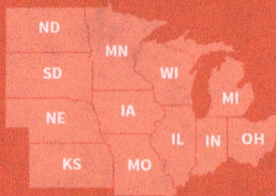

ST. AMBROSE UNIVERSITY

Address: 518 W. Locust Street, Davenport, IA 52804
Website: *http://www.sau.edu/master-of-physician-assistant-studies*
Contact: *pa@sau.edu*
Phone: 563-333-5886

COST OF ATTENDANCE

Tuition and Fees: $39,003
Additional Expenses: N/A
Total: $39,003*

*This figure does not include cost of living or other indirect costs.

Financial Aid: http://www.sau.edu/cost-and-aid

ADDITIONAL INFORMATION

Interesting tidbit: Based on projected needs in rural states, primary care is an emphasis of the SAU MPAS program, especially in rural and underserved populations. Specifically in Iowa, the Primary Care Recruitment and Retention Endeavor offers two-year grants when PAs work in a health professional shortage area.

Important Updates due to COVID-19: SAU MPAS Program will accept Spring 2020 coursework that is graded on a Pass/Fail or Satisfactory/Unsatisfactory basis to fulfill a prerequisite course requirement.

Were tests required? GRE required.

Are tests expected next year? Yes.

What international experiences are available? N/A

What dual degree options exist? N/A

What service-learning opportunities exist? N/A

PANCE First-Time Pass Rate: 93% (2020)

Other: St. Ambrose offers an Early Admit pathway for high school applicants.

UNIVERSITY OF DUBUQUE

Address: 1000 University Ave., Dubuque, IA 52001
Website: *http://www.dbq.edu/Academics/OfficeofAcademicAffairs/
GraduatePrograms/MasterofScienceinPhysicianAssistantStudies/*
Contact: *mpas@dbq.edu*
Phone: 563-589-3664

COST OF ATTENDANCE

Tuition and Fees: $33,863
Additional Expenses: N/A
Total: $33,863

*This figure does not include cost of living or other indirect costs.

Financial Aid:

ADDITIONAL INFORMATION

Interesting tidbit: The University of Dubuque Master of Science in Physician Assistant Studies Program is preparing clinicians who are educated in all aspects of health care with special emphasis placed on primary care in rural and underserved areas. A facility was constructed specifically to house the PA Program, which adjoins the University Science Center and provides students with state of the art equipment and facilities including a cadaver lab, skills lab, and exam room suite.

Important Updates due to COVID-19: For the 2021 admission cycle, the program will accept in-person or online labs. The UD PA Program will accept any S/U or Pass/Fail grading for Spring and Summer 2020 through Summer 2021 courses where the transcripts identify an assigned value of an S or Pass as equaling a C or higher.

Were tests required? GRE required.

Are tests expected next year? Yes.

What international experiences are available? N/A

What dual degree options exist? N/A

What service-learning opportunities exist? N/A

PANCE First-Time Pass Rate: 92% (2020)

ILLINOIS

INDIANA

IOWA

KANSAS

MICHIGAN

MINNESOTA

MISSOURI

NEBRASKA

NORTH DAKOTA

OHIO

SOUTH DAKOTA

WISCONSIN

MIDWEST

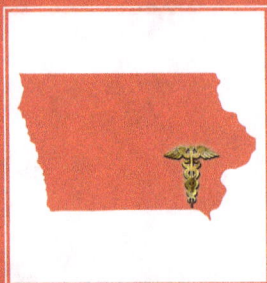

ILLINOIS

INDIANA

IOWA

KANSAS

MICHIGAN

MINNESOTA

MISSOURI

NEBRASKA

NORTH DAKOTA

OHIO

SOUTH DAKOTA

WISCONSIN

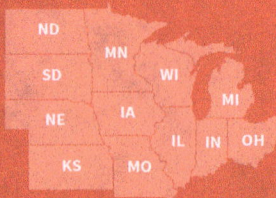

UNIVERSITY OF IOWA

Address: The University of Iowa, Iowa City, IA 52242-1110
Website: *http://www.medicine.uiowa.edu/pa/*
Contact: *paprogram@uiowa.edu*
Phone: 319-335-8922

COST OF ATTENDANCE

In-State Tuition and Fees: $25,725
Additional Expenses: $27,148
Total: $49,873

Out-of-State Tuition and Fees: $44,660
Additional Expenses: $27,198
Total: $71,858

Financial Aid: https://medicine.uiowa.edu/pa/education/prospective-students/expenses-and-financial-aid/financial-aid-information-physician

ADDITIONAL INFORMATION

Interesting tidbit: The University of Iowa's PA Program curriculum is purposefully designed to have the PA students complete their didactic curriculum with medical students.

Important Updates due to COVID-19: If an applicant does not have the option to take a course for letter grade and the institution has moved courses to Pass/Fail during the COVID-19 pandemic, the PA Program will review these on an individual basis. The applicant should state this on their application.

Were tests required? GRE/MCAT required.

Are tests expected next year? Yes.

What international experiences are available? N/A

What dual degree options exist? N/A

What service-learning opportunities exist? N/A

PANCE First-Time Pass Rate: 100% (2020)

WICHITA STATE UNIVERSITY

Address: 213 North Mead Street, Wichita, KS 67202
Website: *http://www.wichita.edu/thisis/home/?u=pa*
Contact: *physician.assistant@wichita.edu*
Phone: 316-978-3011

COST OF ATTENDANCE

In-State Tuition and Fees: $15,400
Additional Expenses: $11,641*
Total: $27,041*

Out-of-State Tuition and Fees: $37,819
Additional Expenses: $11,641*
Total: $49,460*

*This figure does not include cost of living or other indirect costs.

Financial Aid: https://www.wichita.edu/academics/gradschool/Forms/GraduateSchoolAwards.php

ADDITIONAL INFORMATION

Interesting tidbit: The Physician Assistant (PA) program at Wichita State University is the only one of its kind in Kansas. It offers one of the largest university-based programs for health professionals west of the Mississippi.

Important Updates due to COVID-19: The WSU PA Program will accept Pass/Fail and Credit/No Credit grades for course prerequisites taken during the Spring 2020 semester.

Were tests required? No.

Are tests expected next year? No.

What international experiences are available? N/A

What dual degree options exist? N/A

What service-learning opportunities exist? N/A

PANCE First-Time Pass Rate: 100% (2020)

ILLINOIS

INDIANA

IOWA

KANSAS

MICHIGAN

MINNESOTA

MISSOURI

NEBRASKA

NORTH DAKOTA

OHIO

SOUTH DAKOTA

WISCONSIN

MIDWEST

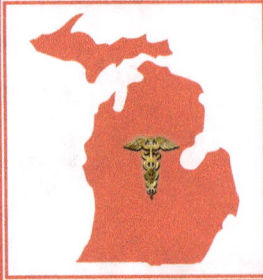

ILLINOIS

INDIANA

IOWA

KANSAS

MICHIGAN

MINNESOTA

MISSOURI

NEBRASKA

NORTH DAKOTA

OHIO

SOUTH DAKOTA

WISCONSIN

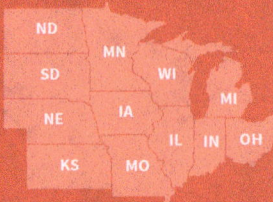

CENTRAL MICHIGAN UNIVERSITY

Address: 1280 E. Campus Drive, Mount Pleasant, MI 48859
Website: https://www.cmich.edu/colleges/CHP/hp_academics/srms/physician_assistant/Pages/PA-Program-at-CMU.aspx
Contact: chpadmit@cmich.edu
Phone: 989-774-1730

COST OF ATTENDANCE

Tuition and Fees: $52,234
Additional Expenses: $26,469
Total: $78,703

Financial Aid: https://go.cmich.edu/tuitionandaid/graduate/Pages/default.aspx

ADDITIONAL INFORMATION

Interesting tidbit: The program was created by CMU to address the healthcare needs of residents in the northern lower peninsula and the Upper Peninsula of Michigan, which includes many rural and medically underserved communities. PAs work as part of the clinical and medical interdisciplinary medical team.

Important Updates due to COVID-19: N/A

Were tests required? PA-CAT required.

Are tests expected next year? Yes.

What international experiences are available? N/A

What dual degree options exist? N/A

What service-learning opportunities exist? N/A

PANCE First-Time Pass Rate: 85% (2020)

CONCORDIA UNIVERSITY - ANN ARBOR

Address: 4090 Geddes Road, Ann Arbor, MI 48105
Website: *https://www.cuaa.edu/academics/programs/physician-assistant-masters/index.html#overview*
Contact: *admission@cuaa.edu*
Phone: 734-995-7300

COST OF ATTENDANCE

Tuition and Fees: $49,637
Additional Expenses: N/A
Total: $49,637*

*This figure does not include cost of living or other indirect costs.

Financial Aid:

ADDITIONAL INFORMATION

Interesting tidbit: CUAA's mission is to train students in all aspects of primary care medicine. This will not be a program curriculum focused on specialty surgery, or latest advances in specialty care.

Important Updates due to COVID-19: Students may be allowed to submit P/F grades (if able to verify due to COVID issues) by completing the COVID WAIVER FORM.

Were tests required? CASPer required.

Are tests expected next year? Yes.

What international experiences are available? N/A

What dual degree options exist? N/A

What service-learning opportunities exist? N/A

PANCE First-Time Pass Rate: N/A (CUAA MSPAS inaugural class began January 2021 and will graduate in May 2023.)

ILLINOIS

INDIANA

IOWA

KANSAS

MICHIGAN

MINNESOTA

MISSOURI

NEBRASKA

NORTH DAKOTA

OHIO

SOUTH DAKOTA

WISCONSIN

MIDWEST

ILLINOIS

INDIANA

IOWA

KANSAS

MICHIGAN

MINNESOTA

MISSOURI

NEBRASKA

NORTH DAKOTA

OHIO

SOUTH DAKOTA

WISCONSIN

EASTERN MICHIGAN UNIVERSITY

Address: 222 Rackham Building, Ypsilanti, MI 48197
Website: *http://www.emich.edu/pa*
Contact: *chhs_paprogram@emich.edu*
Phone: 734-487-2843

COST OF ATTENDANCE

In-State Tuition and Fees: $10,260*
Additional Expenses: $19,550
Total: $29,810*

Out-of-State Tuition and Fees: $18,240*
Additional Expenses: $19,550
Total: $37,790*

*Figures are based on Cost of Attendance for graduate students as EMU had not provided tuition and fees for the PA program.

Financial Aid: https://www.emich.edu/graduate/scholarships-aid/index.php

ADDITIONAL INFORMATION

Interesting tidbit: EMU PA Program offers multi-faceted teaching styles. The program combines interactive lectures with a clinical focus, small-group learning, hands-on practical training, out-of-classroom learning and high-fidelity medical simulation.

Important Updates due to COVID-19: For winter 2020 semester courses only, the program will accept successful Pass/Fail credit from EMU and from other accredited academic institutions to satisfy pre-admission course requirement(s).

Were tests required? GRE required.

Are tests expected next year? Yes.

What international experiences are available? N/A

What dual degree options exist? N/A

What service-learning opportunities exist? N/A

PANCE First-Time Pass Rate: 93% (2020)

GRAND VALLEY STATE UNIVERSITY - GRAND RAPIDS

Address: 301 Michigan Street NE, Suite 200, Grand Rapids, MI 49315
Website: *http://www.gvsu.edu/pas*
Contact: *pas@gvsu.edu*
Phone: 616-331-5700

Other Locations: Traverse City, MI

COST OF ATTENDANCE

Tuition and Fees: $38,775
Additional Expenses: N/A
Total: $38,775*

*This figure does not include cost of living or other indirect costs.

Financial Aid: See "Financial Support" on https://www.gvsu.edu/pas/tuition-financial-aid-81.htm

ADDITIONAL INFORMATION

Interesting tidbit: The Grand Valley State University MPAS Program is offered at two locations - Grand Rapids and Traverse City. Grand Rapids campus enrolls 36 students annually and Traverse City, 12 students. Applicants may apply to the Grand Rapids OR Traverse City Campus but are NOT permitted to apply to both campuses.

Important Updates due to COVID-19: The GVSU PAS program has created an Academic Request Form (ARF) specific to issues surrounding closures related to the COVID-19 pandemic. Students should only submit an Admissions Academic Request Form (ARF) IF they have highly unusual circumstances that impact their ability to meet the published admission criteria.

Were tests required? GRE and CASPer required.

Are tests expected next year? Yes.

What international experiences are available? N/A

What dual degree options exist? N/A

What service-learning opportunities exist? N/A

PANCE First-Time Pass Rate: 100% (2019 is the latest data)

ILLINOIS

INDIANA

IOWA

KANSAS

MICHIGAN

MINNESOTA

MISSOURI

NEBRASKA

NORTH DAKOTA

OHIO

SOUTH DAKOTA

WISCONSIN

MIDWEST

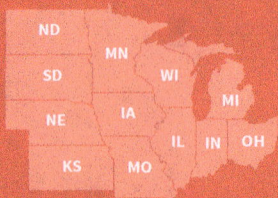

GRAND VALLEY STATE UNIVERSITY - TRAVERSE CITY

Address: 2200 Dendrinos Drive, Suite 15, Traverse City, MI 49684
Website: *https://www.gvsu.edu/pas/traverse-city-campus-89.htm*
Contact: *nminfo@gvsu.edu*
Phone: 231-995-1785

Other Locations: Grand Rapids, MI

COST OF ATTENDANCE

In-State Tuition and Fees: $38,930
Additional Expenses: N/A
Total: $38,930*

*This figure does not include cost of living or other indirect costs.

Financial Aid: See "Financial Support" on https://www.gvsu.edu/pas/tuition-financial-aid-81.htm

ADDITIONAL INFORMATION

Interesting tidbit: In 2015, Grand Valley State University expanded its Physician Assistant Studies program to Traverse City to encourage students to practice in Northern Michigan after they graduate. Thus, in addition to general admission requirements, admission to Traverse City campus will include previous/current residence and/or connections to Northern Michigan.

Important Updates due to COVID-19: The GVSU PAS program has created an Academic Request Form (ARF) specific to issues surrounding closures related to the COVID-19 pandemic. Students should only submit an Admissions Academic Request Form (ARF) IF they have highly unusual circumstances that impact their ability to meet the published admission criteria.

Were tests required? GRE and CASPer required.

Are tests expected next year? Yes.

What international experiences are available? N/A

What dual degree options exist? N/A

What service-learning opportunities exist? N/A

PANCE First-Time Pass Rate: 100% (2019 is the latest data)

UNIVERSITY OF DETROIT MERCY

Address: 4001 West McNichols Road, CHP 115, Detroit, MI 48221
Website: *http://healthprofessions.udmercy.edu/academics/pa/grad.php*
Contact: *chpgrad@udmercy.edu*
Phone: 313-578-0438

COST OF ATTENDANCE

Tuition and Fees: $41,183
Additional Expenses: N/A
Total: $41,183*

*This figure does not include cost of living or other indirect costs.

Financial Aid:

ADDITIONAL INFORMATION

Interesting tidbit: The curriculum emphasizes the natural and behavioral sciences and work experience. The curriculum contains basic science and applied behavioral science courses as well as coursework specific to the Physician Assistant program and graduate courses in health promotion/disease prevention and methodology in medical research. During the second year, students acquire clinical expertise through a broad range of intensive clinical rotations, community health education and health projects with medically underserved communities.

Important Updates due to COVID-19: N/A

Were tests required? GRE required.

Are tests expected next year? Yes.

What international experiences are available? N/A

What dual degree options exist? N/A

What service-learning opportunities exist? Community health projects during the second year.

PANCE First-Time Pass Rate: 92% (2020)

Other: University of Detroit Mercy offers a five-year accelerated track (BS/MS PA) for high school applicants. See https://healthprofessions.udmercy.edu/academics/pa/five-year.php

ILLINOIS

INDIANA

IOWA

KANSAS

MICHIGAN

MINNESOTA

MISSOURI

NEBRASKA

NORTH DAKOTA

OHIO

SOUTH DAKOTA

WISCONSIN

MIDWEST

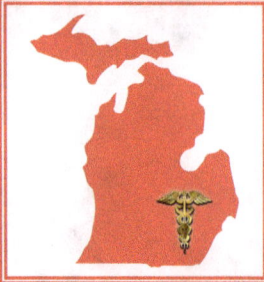

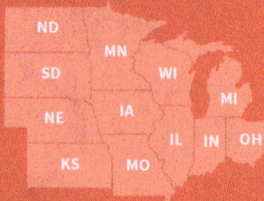

UNIVERSITY OF MICHIGAN - FLINT

Address: 303 East Kearsley Street, Flint, MI, 48502
Website: *https://www.umflint.edu/graduateprograms/physician-assistant-ms/*
Contact: *flint.padept@umich.edu*
Phone: 810-762-3300

COST OF ATTENDANCE

In-State Tuition and Fees: $30,720
Additional Expenses: N/A
Total: $30,720*

Out-of-State Tuition and Fees: $47,312
Additional Expenses: N/A
Total: $47,312*

*This figure does not include cost of living or other indirect costs.

Financial Aid: https://www.umflint.edu/graduateprograms/paying-for-college/

ADDITIONAL INFORMATION

Interesting tidbit: Over a 28-month period, UM-Flint PA program students attend on-campus and online courses and experience a variety of clinical rotations. The first 16 months are of didactic instruction-lecture and laboratory format with clinical immersions. The final 12 months are primarily clinical rotations with some online and on-campus requirements.

Important Updates due to COVID-19: Pass/No Pass option will not be accepted.

Were tests required? CASPer required.

Are tests expected next year? Yes.

What international experiences are available? N/A

What dual degree options exist? MSPA/MBA Program

What service-learning opportunities exist? UM-Flint pro-bono interprofessional student health clinic

PANCE First-Time Pass Rate: N/A (New MSPA Program launched in January 2021.)

ILLINOIS

INDIANA

IOWA

KANSAS

MICHIGAN

MINNESOTA

MISSOURI

NEBRASKA

NORTH DAKOTA

OHIO

SOUTH DAKOTA

WISCONSIN

WAYNE STATE UNIVERSITY

Address: 259 Mack Avenue, Detroit, MI 48201
Website: *http://www.pa.cphs.wayne.edu/*
Contact: *paadmit@wayne.edu*
Phone: 313-577-1368

COST OF ATTENDANCE

In-State Tuition and Fees: $25,727
Additional Expenses: $11,108*
Total: $36,835*

Out-of-State Tuition and Fees: $49,463
Additional Expenses: $11,108*
Total: $60,571*

*This figure does not include cost of living or other indirect costs.

Financial Aid: https://gradschool.wayne.edu/students/funding

ADDITIONAL INFORMATION

Interesting tidbit: The program implements its commitment to the compassionate delivery of services to those in need through a curriculum which emphasizes the practical and policy issues of: health promotion and disease prevention; primary care delivery in inner city and urban medically underserved areas, and the delivery of care to populations with special needs.

Important Updates due to COVID-19: N/A

Were tests required? GRE and CASPer required.

Are tests expected next year? Yes.

What international experiences are available? N/A

What dual degree options exist? N/A

What service-learning opportunities exist? N/A

PANCE First-Time Pass Rate: 98% (2020)

ILLINOIS

INDIANA

IOWA

KANSAS

MICHIGAN

MINNESOTA

MISSOURI

NEBRASKA

NORTH DAKOTA

OHIO

SOUTH DAKOTA

WISCONSIN

MIDWEST

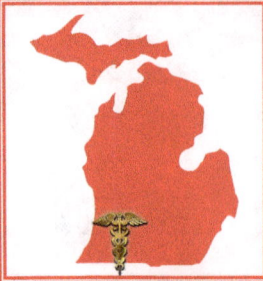

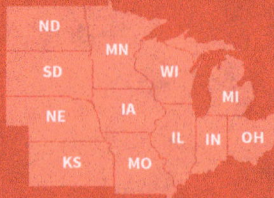

WESTERN MICHIGAN UNIVERSITY

Address: 1903 W Michigan Avenue, Kalamazoo, MI 49008
Website: *http://www.wmich.edu/pa*
Contact: *pa-info@wmich.edu*
Phone: 269-387-5311

COST OF ATTENDANCE

In-State Tuition and Fees: $33,587
Additional Expenses: N/A
Total: $33,587*

Out-of-State Tuition and Fees: $53,522
Additional Expenses: N/A
Total: $53,522*

*This figure does not include cost of living or other indirect costs.

Financial Aid: https://wmich.edu/finaid/graduate

ADDITIONAL INFORMATION

Interesting tidbit: William Birch, M.D., is credited with founding the physician assistant program at Western Michigan University in 1972, making it one of the first PA programs in the nation and the second in Michigan. WMich PA program is dedicated to preparing its students to become primary care physician assistants.

Important Updates due to COVID-19: For Spring 2020 ONLY (January start date), WMU's Physician Assistant Program will accept Credit/No Credit or Pass/Fail grades, as long as the minimum grade required for credit or a pass grade is a C or higher.

Were tests required? No.

Are tests expected next year? No.

What international experiences are available? N/A

What dual degree options exist? N/A

What service-learning opportunities exist? N/A

PANCE First-Time Pass Rate: 92% (2020)

ILLINOIS

INDIANA

IOWA

KANSAS

MICHIGAN

MINNESOTA

MISSOURI

NEBRASKA

NORTH DAKOTA

OHIO

SOUTH DAKOTA

WISCONSIN

AUGSBURG UNIVERSITY

Address: 701 25th Avenue South, Minneapolis, MN 55454
Website: *http://www.augsburg.edu/pa/*
Contact: *paprog@augsburg.edu*
Phone: 612-330-1388

COST OF ATTENDANCE

Tuition and Fees: $58,692
Additional Expenses: N/A
Total: $58,692*

*This figure does not include cost of living or other indirect costs.

Financial Aid: https://www.augsburg.edu/studentfinancial/financial-aid/graduate-financial-aid/

ADDITIONAL INFORMATION

Interesting tidbit: The Augsburg PA Program trains students using an active-learning model which incorporates case-based small group discussions, in-lecture clinical vignettes, and hands-on skill-based workshops.

Important Updates due to COVID-19: Augsburg PA will accept Pass (P), Satisfactory (S) or the equivalent for required prerequisite coursework taken in the Spring and Summer of 2020.

Were tests required? No.

Are tests expected next year? No.

What international experiences are available? Elective international experiences.

What dual degree options exist? N/A

What service-learning opportunities exist? N/A

PANCE First-Time Pass Rate: 97% (2020)

ILLINOIS

INDIANA

IOWA

KANSAS

MICHIGAN

MINNESOTA

MISSOURI

NEBRASKA

NORTH DAKOTA

OHIO

SOUTH DAKOTA

WISCONSIN

MIDWEST

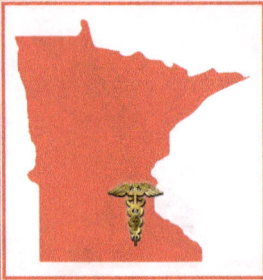

ILLINOIS

INDIANA

IOWA

KANSAS

MICHIGAN

MINNESOTA

MISSOURI

NEBRASKA

NORTH DAKOTA

OHIO

SOUTH DAKOTA

WISCONSIN

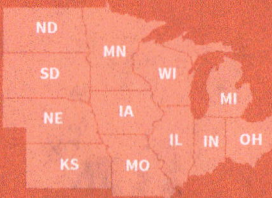

BETHEL UNIVERSITY

Address: 3900 Bethel Drive, St. Paul, MN 55112
Website: *https://www.bethel.edu/graduate/academics/physician-assistant/*
Contact: *physician-assistant@bethel.edu*
Phone: 651-635-8074

COST OF ATTENDANCE

Tuition and Fees: $49,147
Additional Expenses: $23,326
Total: $72,473

Financial Aid: https://www.bethel.edu/graduate/financial-aid/

ADDITIONAL INFORMATION

Interesting tidbit: PA students at Bethel will develop skills for excellent medical practice, building a balanced core of knowledge upon the fields of humanities, natural and social sciences, medical sciences, behavioral sciences, and evidence-based medicine, all from a Christian perspective.

Important Updates due to COVID-19: If applicants took any courses for Pass/Fail between January 2020 and May 2021, they are still invited to apply, but additional documentation may be required.

Were tests required? No.

Are tests expected next year? No.

What international experiences are available? N/A

What dual degree options exist? N/A

What service-learning opportunities exist? N/A

PANCE First-Time Pass Rate: 97% (2020)

COLLEGE OF SAINT SCHOLASTICA

Address: 1200 Kenwood Avenue, Duluth, MN 55811
Website: *http://www.css.edu/graduate/masters-doctoral-and-professional-programs/areas-of-study/ms-physician-assistant.html*
Contact: *ceickman@css.edu*
Phone: 218-625-4823

COST OF ATTENDANCE

Tuition and Fees: $49,419
Additional Expenses: $8,892*
Total: $58,311*

*This figure does not include cost of living or other indirect costs.

Financial Aid: http://www.css.edu/graduate/masters-doctoral-and-professional-programs/financial-aid.html

ADDITIONAL INFORMATION

Interesting tidbit: the College of St. Scholastica's MSPAS program provides interprofessional experiences to create "team-care-ready" PAs. PA students practice interprofessional teamwork that's required in the workplace by collaborating with graduate students in a variety of health professions, including Physical Therapy, Occupational Therapy, Athletic Training, Health Informatics, Exercise Physiology, Nursing and Social Work.

Important Updates due to COVID-19: Any prerequisite course taken for credit (pass/fail, credit/no credit, satisfactory/unsatisfactory, etc.) between spring 2020 - spring 2021 will be accepted.

Were tests required? GRE required.

Are tests expected next year? Yes.

What international experiences are available? N/A

What dual degree options exist? N/A

What service-learning opportunities exist? N/A

PANCE First-Time Pass Rate: 93% (2020)

ILLINOIS

INDIANA

IOWA

KANSAS

MICHIGAN

MINNESOTA

MISSOURI

NEBRASKA

NORTH DAKOTA

OHIO

SOUTH DAKOTA

WISCONSIN

MIDWEST

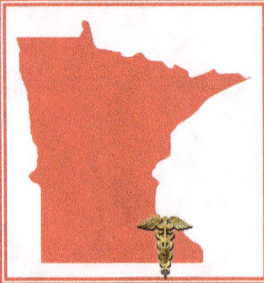

ILLINOIS

INDIANA

IOWA

KANSAS

MICHIGAN

MINNESOTA

MISSOURI

NEBRASKA

NORTH DAKOTA

OHIO

SOUTH DAKOTA

WISCONSIN

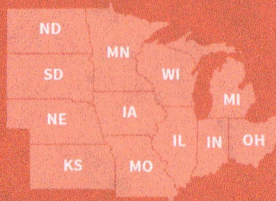

MAYO CLINIC SCHOOL OF HEALTH SCIENCES

Address: 200 First Street SW, Rochester, MN 55905
Website: *https://college.mayo.edu/academics/health-sciences-education/physician-assistant-program-minnesota/*
Contact: *tynsky.troy@mayo.edu*
Phone: 507-284-3293

COST OF ATTENDANCE

Tuition and Fees: $40,920
Additional Expenses: $6,250
Total: $47,170

*This figure does not include cost of living or other indirect costs.

Financial Aid: https://college.mayo.edu/admissions-and-tuition/financial-aid/

ADDITIONAL INFORMATION

Interesting tidbit: The PA Program has collaborated with Saint Mary's University in Winona, MN, and University of Minnesota Rochester in a 3+2 pathway for admission. Each year, 24 students are admitted to their first year of undergraduate studies in the 3+2 pathway program. After completing three years of undergraduate pre-PA courses, students then move directly into two years of the graduate-level Mayo Clinic PA Program.

Important Updates due to COVID-19: N/A

Were tests required? No.

Are tests expected next year? No.

What international experiences are available? N/A

What dual degree options exist? N/A

What service-learning opportunities exist? N/A

PANCE First-Time Pass Rate: N/A (the inaugural class graduates in 2022)

SAINT CATHERINE UNIVERSITY

Address: 2004 Randolph Avenue, Saint Paul, MN 55105
Website: *https://www.stkate.edu/academic-programs/gc/physician-assistant-studies-mpas*
Contact: *rgort181@stkate.edu*
Phone: 612-271-6166

COST OF ATTENDANCE

Tuition and Fees: $49,680
Additional Expenses: $10,730
Total: $60,410

Financial Aid: https://www.stkate.edu/admission-and-aid/gc/tuition-and-financial-aid

ADDITIONAL INFORMATION

Interesting tidbit: St. Kate's master's in physician assistant studies provides the building blocks of critical thinking by incorporating medical decision-making, ethical considerations, and principles of team-based practice into every course. By the end of the program, students will have had 2,000 hours in clinical clerkships.

Important Updates due to COVID-19: The Program will accept a Satisfactory or Pass designation for any prerequisite course completed Spring 2020 through Summer 2021. However, no more than 1/3 of all prerequisite courses can be used with a S/U or P/F designation.

Were tests required? GRE required.

Are tests expected next year? Yes.

What international experiences are available? N/A

What dual degree options exist? N/A

What service-learning opportunities exist? N/A

PANCE First-Time Pass Rate: 100% (2019)

ILLINOIS

INDIANA

IOWA

KANSAS

MICHIGAN

MINNESOTA

MISSOURI

NEBRASKA

NORTH DAKOTA

OHIO

SOUTH DAKOTA

WISCONSIN

MIDWEST

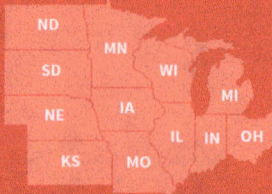

MISSOURI STATE UNIVERSITY

Address: 901 S. National Avenue, Springfield, MO 65897
Website: *http://www.missouristate.edu/pas*
Contact: *physicianasststudies@missouristate.edu*
Phone: 417-836-6151

COST OF ATTENDANCE

In-State Tuition and Fees: $23,000
Additional Expenses: $2,222*
Total: $25,222*

Out-of-State Tuition and Fees: $36,311
Additional Expenses: $2,222*
Total: $38,533*

*This figure does not include cost of living or other indirect costs.

Financial Aid: https://www.missouristate.edu/FinancialAid/Graduate.htm

ADDITIONAL INFORMATION

Interesting tidbit: MSU PA Program students will gain clinical experience in every phase of the program – with special emphasis placed on primary care and rural care. Students should expect to complete one primary care preceptorship (family practice, internal medicine, or pediatrics) in a rural setting.

Important Updates due to COVID-19: N/A

Were tests required? GRE or MCAT required.

Are tests expected next year? Yes.

What international experiences are available? N/A

What dual degree options exist? N/A

What service-learning opportunities exist? N/A

PANCE First-Time Pass Rate: 96% (2020)

SAINT LOUIS UNIVERSITY

Address: 3437 Caroline Street, Saint Louis, MO 63104
Website: *https://www.slu.edu/doisy/degrees/graduate/physician-assistant-mms.php*
Contact: *paprog@health.slu.edu*
Phone: 314-977-7821

COST OF ATTENDANCE

Tuition and Fees: $48,900
Additional Expenses: $23,866
Total: $72,786

Financial Aid: https://www.slu.edu/financial-aid/index.php

ADDITIONAL INFORMATION

Interesting tidbit: Saint Louis University is a member of the National Council for State Authorization and Reciprocity Act (NC-SARA), which allows students to complete a portion of their education in a different state. In some cases, students may be allowed to develop up to three of their own clerkships, following a careful screening process and programmatic approval.

Important Updates due to COVID-19: SLU strongly recommends that each applicant complete the optional COVID-19 essay through CASPA so that the Admissions Committee has a more comprehensive view of each applicant during the review process.

Were tests required? No.

Are tests expected next year? No.

What international experiences are available? N/A

What dual degree options exist? MMS/MPH. See https://catalog.slu.edu/colleges-schools/public-health-social-justice/graduate-programs/physician-assistant-mms-mph-dua-degree/?_ga=2.14310903.1599767768.1624579454-1194455489.1624579454

What service-learning opportunities exist? Health Resource Center, student-run free clinic

PANCE First-Time Pass Rate: 100% (2020)

Other: DCHS PA Scholars Track allows an opportunity for freshmen to be guaranteed a position in SLU's physician assistant program. See https://www.slu.edu/doisy/degrees/undergraduate/pre-pa-scholars.php

ILLINOIS

INDIANA

IOWA

KANSAS

MICHIGAN

MINNESOTA

MISSOURI

NEBRASKA

NORTH DAKOTA

OHIO

SOUTH DAKOTA

WISCONSIN

MIDWEST

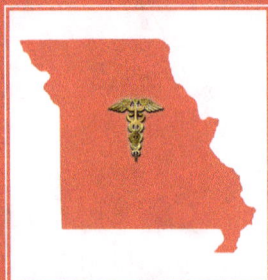

ILLINOIS

INDIANA

IOWA

KANSAS

MICHIGAN

MINNESOTA

MISSOURI

NEBRASKA

NORTH DAKOTA

OHIO

SOUTH DAKOTA

WISCONSIN

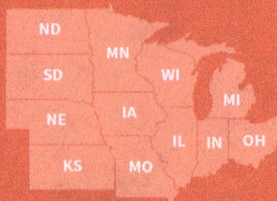

STEPHENS COLLEGE

Address: 1200 E Broadway, Columbia MO 65215
Website: *https://www.stephens.edu/academics/graduate-programs/master-in-physician-assistant-studies/*
Contact: *ejohnson@stephens.edu*
Phone: 572-876-2310

COST OF ATTENDANCE

Tuition and Fees: $45,750
Additional Expenses: $45,960
Total: $91,710

Financial Aid: https://www.stephens.edu/admission-aid/graduate/master-of-physician-assistant-studies/apply/tuition-aid/

*No scholarship available for MPAS program students. PA students should explore the National Health Service Corps scholarship and loan repayment programs.

ADDITIONAL INFORMATION

Interesting tidbit: The Stephens PA program is a full-time, 27-month professional program, providing 13 months of didactic education and 14 months of clinical training. Clinical rotations include family medicine, women's health, pediatrics, general surgery, internal medicine, behavioral medicine and emergency medicine.

Important Updates due to COVID-19: Pass/Fail or Credit/No Credit grading options will be accepted for any courses taken in the Spring and Summer 2020 semesters. Also, the previously required 16 hours of Shadowing is waived due to the ongoing pandemic.

Were tests required? No.

Are tests expected next year? No.

What international experiences are available? N/A

What dual degree options exist? N/A

What service-learning opportunities exist? N/A

PANCE First-Time Pass Rate: 97% (2020)

UNIVERSITY OF MISSOURI - KANSAS CITY

Address: 2411 Holmes Street, Kansas City, MO 64108
Website: *http://med.umkc.edu/pa/*
Contact: *medicine@umkc.edu*
Phone: 816-235-1860

COST OF ATTENDANCE

In-State Tuition and Fees: $31,17
Additional Expenses: N/A
Total: $31,175*

Out-of-State Tuition and Fees: $37,239
Additional Expenses: N/A
Total: $37.239*

*This figure does not include cost of living or other indirect costs.

Financial Aid: https://finaid.umkc.edu/financial-aid/index.html

ADDITIONAL INFORMATION

Interesting tidbit: The Master of Medical Science Physician Assistant Program is a seven-semester program based in the UMKC School of Medicine. PA students benefit from the extensive medical education resources.

Important Updates due to COVID-19: UMKC SOM will not penalize applicants for circumstances outside of their control for classes taken during the Spring 2020 or Summer 2020 semesters as pass/fail. The shadowing requirement is also waived.

Were tests required? GRE or MCAT required.

Are tests expected next year? Yes.

What international experiences are available? N/A

What dual degree options exist? N/A

What service-learning opportunities exist? N/A

PANCE First-Time Pass Rate: 90% (2020)

Other: The UMKC School of Medicine offers a PA Scholars program that would offer early and guaranteed admission to undergraduate students matriculated at designated colleges. See https://med.umkc.edu/pa/scholars/

ILLINOIS

INDIANA

IOWA

KANSAS

MICHIGAN

MINNESOTA

MISSOURI

NEBRASKA

NORTH DAKOTA

OHIO

SOUTH DAKOTA

WISCONSIN

MIDWEST

ILLINOIS

INDIANA

IOWA

KANSAS

MICHIGAN

MINNESOTA

MISSOURI

NEBRASKA

NORTH DAKOTA

OHIO

SOUTH DAKOTA

WISCONSIN

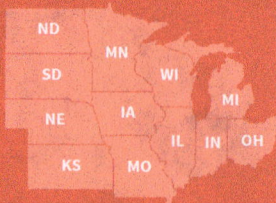

COLLEGE OF SAINT MARY

Address: 7000 Mercy Road, Omaha, NE 68106
Website: *http://www.csm.edu/academics/health-human-services/master-science-degree-physician-assistant-studies*
Contact: *pa@csm.edu*
Phone: 402-399-2477

COST OF ATTENDANCE

Tuition and Fees: $42,150
Additional Expenses: $27,504
Total: $69,654

Financial Aid: http://www.csm.edu/admissions/graduate-financial-aid

*The American Association of Medical Colleges provides a database to search loan repayment/forgiveness and scholarship programs.

ADDITIONAL INFORMATION

Interesting tidbit: College of Saint Mary's Master of Science in Physician Assistant Studies degree is a 24-month program that begins in August with a maximum class size of 40 students. The class is selected with a combination of students admitted through CASPA and the CSM Physician Assistant Studies Accelerated Entry Program (PAS-AEP).

Important Updates due to COVID-19: N/A

Were tests required? GRE and Altus Suite required.

Are tests expected next year? Yes.

What international experiences are available? N/A

What dual degree options exist? N/A

What service-learning opportunities exist? N/A

PANCE First-Time Pass Rate: 90% (2020)

Other: College of Saint Mary offers Physician Assistant Studies Accelerated Entry Program (PAS-AEP), a 5-year path (3+2) to the Physician Assistant Program.

CREIGHTON UNIVERSITY

Address: 2500 California Plaza, Omaha, NE 68178
Website: *https://medschool.creighton.edu/program/physician-assistant-mpas*
Contact: *pa.admissions@creighton.edu*
Phone: 402-280-4531

COST OF ATTENDANCE

Tuition and Fees: $25,500
Additional Expenses: $29,594
Total: $55,094

Financial Aid: https://financialaid.creighton.edu/types-aid

ADDITIONAL INFORMATION

Interesting tidbit: Creighton's new MPAS Program welcomed its inaugural class in August 2019. In Creighton's Jesuit, Catholic tradition, the Program is dedicated to providing an interprofessional, broad-based medical education in an environment of reflective learning.

Important Updates due to COVID-19: N/A

Were tests required? No.

Are tests expected next year? No.

What international experiences are available? N/A

What dual degree options exist? N/A

What service-learning opportunities exist? N/A

PANCE First-Time Pass Rate: N/A (The inaugural class will complete training in December of 2021. PANCE pass rates will be available in 2022.)

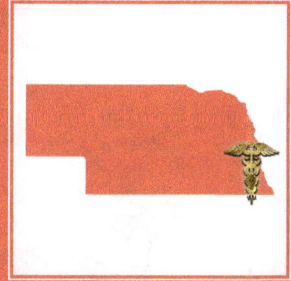

ILLINOIS

INDIANA

IOWA

KANSAS

MICHIGAN

MINNESOTA

MISSOURI

NEBRASKA

NORTH DAKOTA

OHIO

SOUTH DAKOTA

WISCONSIN

MIDWEST

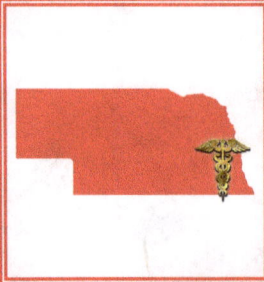

ILLINOIS

INDIANA

IOWA

KANSAS

MICHIGAN

MINNESOTA

MISSOURI

NEBRASKA

NORTH DAKOTA

OHIO

SOUTH DAKOTA

WISCONSIN

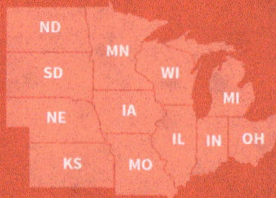

UNION COLLEGE

Address: 3800 South 48th Street, Lincoln, NE 68506
Website: *http://www.ucollege.edu/pa*
Contact: *paprog@ucollege.edu*
Phone: 402-486-2527

COST OF ATTENDANCE

Tuition and Fees: $34,800
Additional Expenses: $17,372*
Total: $52.172*

*This figure does not include cost of living or other indirect costs.

Financial Aid: https://ucollege.edu/admissions/financial-checklist

ADDITIONAL INFORMATION

Interesting tidbit: Union College MPAS Program is a 33-month curriculum with a 24-month didactic phase followed by 11 months of clinical rotations. Union College is committed to equipping students to serve humanity through an academically strong, Christian education.

Important Updates due to COVID-19: The program will accept online course work and pass/fail course work (equaling a C or above) for the spring, summer, and fall 2020 terms. We will also accept online science prerequisite coursework for the spring and summer 2021 terms.

Were tests required? No.

Are tests expected next year? No.

What international experiences are available? N/A

What dual degree options exist? N/A

What service-learning opportunities exist? Matt Talbot Kitchen and Outreach. See https://ucollege.edu/pa/foot-clinic/

PANCE First-Time Pass Rate: 100% (2020)

Other: Union College offers Accelerated Pre-PA Emphasis Program (3+3) for high school applicants.

UNIVERSITY OF NEBRASKA MEDICAL CENTER - KEARNEY

Address: 2402 University Dr., Kearney, NE 68849
Website: *https://www.unmc.edu/alliedhealth/education/pa/*
Contact: *cahpadmissions@unmc.edu*
Phone: 402-559-6673

Other Locations: Omaha, NE

COST OF ATTENDANCE

In-State Tuition and Fees: $18,950
Additional Expenses: $34,545
Total: $53,495

Out-of-State Tuition and Fees: $49,260
Additional Expenses: $34,545
Total: $83,805

Financial Aid: https://www.unmc.edu/alliedhealth/education/financialaid.html

ADDITIONAL INFORMATION

Interesting tidbit: The Kearney divisions of the UNMC College of Nursing and the UNMC College of Allied Health Professions are located on the University of Nebraska at Kearney campus. UNMC Omaha is the main campus. UNMC anticipates accepting 50 students to its Omaha campus and 16 students to its Kearney campus each year.

Important Updates due to COVID-19: N/A

Were tests required? No.

Are tests expected next year? No.

What international experiences are available? N/A

What dual degree options exist? MPAS/MPH (see https://www.unmc.edu/alliedhealth/education/pa/mpas-mph/index.html), and MPAS/MBA (see https://www.unmc.edu/alliedhealth/education/dual-mba/index.html).

What service-learning opportunities exist? N/A

PANCE First-Time Pass Rae: 100% (2020)

Other: UNMC offers an MPAS Degree Advancement Option (distance learning program) for current Physician Assistants who are seeking to further their education. See https://www.unmc.edu/alliedhealth/education/online/padao/index.html.

Other: The PA program participates in RHOP and KHOP, early admission programs. Up to seven (7) positions in each entering class are reserved for applicants to these programs. See https://www.unmc.edu/alliedhealth/education/pathway/index.html.

ILLINOIS

INDIANA

IOWA

KANSAS

MICHIGAN

MINNESOTA

MISSOURI

NEBRASKA

NORTH DAKOTA

OHIO

SOUTH DAKOTA

WISCONSIN

MIDWEST

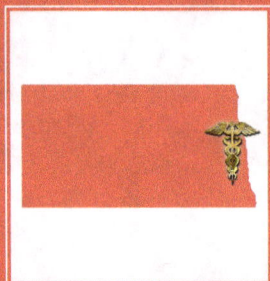

ILLINOIS

INDIANA

IOWA

KANSAS

MICHIGAN

MINNESOTA

MISSOURI

NEBRASKA

NORTH DAKOTA

OHIO

SOUTH DAKOTA

WISCONSIN

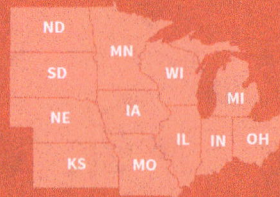

UNIVERSITY OF NORTH DAKOTA

Address: 501 N. Columbia Road, Grand Forks, ND 58202
Website: *http://med.und.edu/physician-assistant/index.cfm*
Contact: *und.med.paprogram@med.und.edu*
Phone: 701-777-2344

COST OF ATTENDANCE

In-State Tuition and Fees: $23,608
Additional Expenses: N/A
Total: $23,608*

Out-of-State Tuition and Fees: $31,218
Additional Expenses: N/A
Total: $31,218*

*This figure does not include cost of living or other indirect costs.

Financial Aid: https://med.und.edu/physician-assistant/financial-info.html

ADDITIONAL INFORMATION

Interesting tidbit: The UND Department of Physician Assistant Studies Master's Program offers a unique hybrid of synchronous and asynchronous online coursework combined with alternating classroom and clinical experiences. The 24-month curriculum begins with two semesters of online coursework focusing on basic science content and is delivered entirely from a distance.

Important Updates due to COVID-19: The UND DPAS will accept S/U courses in prerequisites if that grade was mandated by the school without student choice. Applicants must provide rationale of S/U courses in your CASPA application under the custom questions section.

Were tests required? No.

Are tests expected next year? No.

What international experiences are available? N/A

What dual degree options exist? N/A

What service-learning opportunities exist? N/A

PANCE First-Time Pass Rate: 89% (2020)

ASHLAND UNIVERSITY

Address: 401 College Ave., Ashland, OH 44805
Website: *https://www.ashland.edu/conhs/majors/master-science-physician-assistant-studies*
Contact: *paprogram@ashland.edu*
Phone: 419-521-6854

COST OF ATTENDANCE

Tuition and Fees: $46,250
Additional Expenses: $22,559
Total: $68,809

Financial Aid: https://www.ashland.edu/administration/financial-aid/graduate-students

ADDITIONAL INFORMATION

Interesting tidbit: The Master of Science in Physician Assistant Studies is a practice-focused degree that prepares Physician Assistants to function in diverse healthcare environments. Emphasis is placed on evidence-based medicine, to competently practice patient-centered care, exercise cultural humility, and cultivate a team approach that will produce practice-ready Physician Assistants upon graduation.

Important Updates due to COVID-19: N/A

Were tests required? GRE required.

Are tests expected next year? Yes.

What international experiences are available? N/A

What dual degree options exist? N/A

What service-learning opportunities exist? N/A

PANCE First-Time Pass Rate: N/A (the inaugural class is scheduled to graduate in 2023)

ILLINOIS

INDIANA

IOWA

KANSAS

MICHIGAN

MINNESOTA

MISSOURI

NEBRASKA

NORTH DAKOTA

OHIO

SOUTH DAKOTA

WISCONSIN

MIDWEST

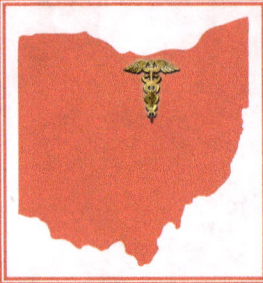

ILLINOIS

INDIANA

IOWA

KANSAS

MICHIGAN

MINNESOTA

MISSOURI

NEBRASKA

NORTH DAKOTA

OHIO

SOUTH DAKOTA

WISCONSIN

BALDWIN WALLACE UNIVERSITY

Address: 275 Eastland Rd., Berea, OH 44017
Website: *https://www.bw.edu/graduate/physician-assistant/*
Contact: *paprogram@bw.edu*
Phone: 440-826-2221

COST OF ATTENDANCE

Tuition and Fees: $43,750
Additional Expenses: N/A
Total: $43,750*

*This figure does not include cost of living or other indirect costs.

Financial Aid: https://www.bw.edu/academics/physician-assistant/tuition-costs/

ADDITIONAL INFORMATION

Interesting tidbit: PA students will acquire more than 2,000 hours of clinical experience through 11 clinical rotations (including 3 elective choices), working with practicing professionals in a variety of settings, from major research hospitals to clinics and extended care facilities.

Important Updates due to COVID-19: The 40 hours of PA shadowing has been waived due to restrictions related to COVID-19.

Were tests required? GRE required.

Are tests expected next year? Yes.

What international experiences are available? N/A

What dual degree options exist? N/A

What service-learning opportunities exist? N/A

PANCE First-Time Pass Rate: 100% (2021)

CASE WESTERN RESERVE UNIVERSITY

Address: 9501 Euclid Avenue, Cleveland, OH 44106
Website: *http://case.edu/medicine/physician-assistant/*
Contact: *paprogram@case.edu*
Phone: 216.368-0575

COST OF ATTENDANCE

Tuition and Fees: $40,020
Additional Expenses: $33,713
Total: $73,733

Financial Aid: https://case.edu/medicine/students/financial-aid

ADDITIONAL INFORMATION

Interesting tidbit: In their second semester, CWRU PA students begin pre-clinical clerkships (PCC). Students are placed in clinical sites in the community for one half-day a week where they practice their clinical skills, acclimate to the clinical environment and build confidence in approaching patients. Pre-clinical clerkships and clinical experiences are integrated across the 27-month curriculum.

Important Updates due to COVID-19: CWRU PA Program will accept pass/no pass for any course taken between January and May of 2020. For courses that occurred between January and May of 2020, the Program will accept online lab work only if the lab was started in person but converted to online/remote due to COVID-19. The Program will require a letter from the applicant's professor stating that the lab started on-ground and outlining the content delivered remotely. This will be reviewed on an individual basis. For Summer, Fall 2020 and Spring 2021, the Program will accept online prerequisites, including labs. For Summer and Fall 2021, the Program will accept online prerequisites, including labs on a case-by-case basis only.

Were tests required? GRE required.

Are tests expected next year? Yes.

What international experiences are available? N/A

What dual degree options exist? N/A

What service-learning opportunities exist? Pre-clinical clerkships (PCC).

PANCE First-Time Pass Rate: 94% (2020)

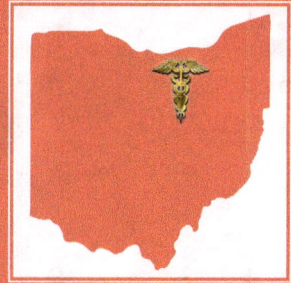

ILLINOIS

INDIANA

IOWA

KANSAS

MICHIGAN

MINNESOTA

MISSOURI

NEBRASKA

NORTH DAKOTA

OHIO

SOUTH DAKOTA

WISCONSIN

MIDWEST

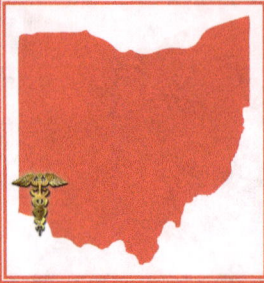

ILLINOIS

INDIANA

IOWA

KANSAS

MICHIGAN

MINNESOTA

MISSOURI

NEBRASKA

NORTH DAKOTA

OHIO

SOUTH DAKOTA

WISCONSIN

KETTERING COLLEGE

Address: 3737 Southern Boulevard, Kettering, OH 45429
Website: *http://kc.edu/academics/physician-assistant/*
Contact: *paeducation@lec.edu*
Phone: 440-375-7365

COST OF ATTENDANCE

Tuition and Fees: $41,761
Additional Expenses: N/A
Total: $41,761*

*This figure does not include cost of living or other indirect costs.

Financial Aid:** https://kc.edu/admissions/financial-aid/

**Also, scholarship opportunities through https://onlinepadegrees.com/scholarships/

ADDITIONAL INFORMATION

Interesting tidbit: Kettering College is distinguished as one of the oldest PA programs in the nation. Duke University developed the nations' first Physician Assistant program, accepting its first class of PA students in 1965, and Kettering College was not far behind. We have been educating quality Physician Assistants since 1973.

Important Updates due to COVID-19: The Department of Physician Assistant Studies at Kettering College will accept pass/fail or satisfactory/unsatisfactory grades that colleges/university institutions decided to assign for courses taken from January through July 2020. It will require the undergraduate institution, where the pass or satisfactory grades were earned, to provide written documentation stating that letter grades were not available for the student during this period.

Were tests required? GRE required. CASPer required for applicants selected for an interview.

Are tests expected next year? Yes.

What international experiences are available? N/A

What dual degree options exist? N/A

What service-learning opportunities exist? N/A

PANCE First-Time Pass Rate: 96% (2020)

LAKE ERIE COLLEGE

Address: 391 W. Washington Street, Painsville, OH 44077
Website: *http://www.lec.edu/pa*
Contact: *paeducation@lec.edu*
Phone: 440-375-7365

COST OF ATTENDANCE

Tuition and Fees: $37,200
Additional Expenses: $27,375
Total: $64,575
Financial Aid: https://www.lec.edu/financial-aid/

ADDITIONAL INFORMATION

Interesting tidbit: Early clinical experiences are integrated within the first several weeks of the didactic training phases. Students will have early exposure to clinical medicine to enhance learning and create excitement for patient care.

Important Updates due to COVID-19: N/A

Were tests required? GRE required.

Are tests expected next year? Yes.

What international experiences are available? N/A

What dual degree options exist? MSPAS/MBA. Graduation of the PA Program creates automatic acceptance into the Lake Erie College Parker MBA Program.

What service-learning opportunities exist? Fresh Air Camp, Geauga Faith Rescue Mission, Hospice of Western Reserve, Kids Kicking Cancer, Lake County Free Clinic, Medwish, oral health at local elementary schools, Relay for Life, and Victory Gallop.

PANCE First-Time Pass Rate: 96% (2020)

Other: Early Acceptance Opportunity (EAO) for LEC undergraduates. See https://www.lec.edu/pa/physician-assistant-early-acceptance-opportunity/

ILLINOIS

INDIANA

IOWA

KANSAS

MICHIGAN

MINNESOTA

MISSOURI

NEBRASKA

NORTH DAKOTA

OHIO

SOUTH DAKOTA

WISCONSIN

MIDWEST

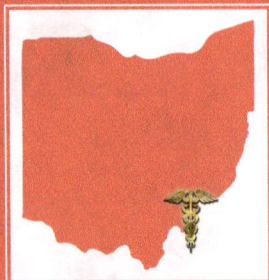

ILLINOIS

INDIANA

IOWA

KANSAS

MICHIGAN

MINNESOTA

MISSOURI

NEBRASKA

NORTH DAKOTA

OHIO

SOUTH DAKOTA

WISCONSIN

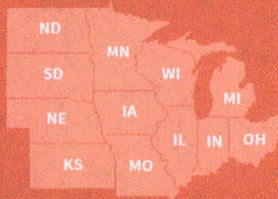

MARIETTA COLLEGE

Address: 215 Fifth Street, Marietta, OH 45750
Website: *https://www.marietta.edu/pa-program*
Contact: *pagrog@marietta.edu*
Phone: 740-376-4458

COST OF ATTENDANCE

Tuition and Fees: $42,500
Additional Expenses: $22,800
Total: $65,300

Financial Aid*: https://www.marietta.edu/tuition-financial-aid

*Paul Spear Appalachia Scholarship (see https://www.marietta.edu/webform/paul-spear-appalachia-scholarship-application)

ADDITIONAL INFORMATION

Interesting tidbit: In January 2001, Marietta College received a grant from the Appalachian Regional Commission (ARC) to help launch the master's program. The Marietta College Physician Assistant Program is dedicated to educating future physician assistants to provide quality healthcare (physical, social, and behavioral) to meet the needs of patients in Ohio and throughout the Appalachian region.

Important Updates due to COVID-19: The program will accept two (2) "pass" grades for pre-requisites taken during the spring 2020 and summer 2020 semesters.

Were tests required? GRE required.

Are tests expected next year? Yes.

What international experiences are available? N/A

What dual degree options exist? N/A

What service-learning opportunities exist? N/A

PANCE First-Time Pass Rate: 97% (2020)

Other: Direct Admissions Physician Assistant Program available for high school applicants. See https://www.marietta.edu/sites/default/files/documents/pa_direct_admit_2018.pdf

MERCY COLLEGE OF OHIO

Address: 2221 Madison Ave, Toledo, OH 43604
Website: *https://mercycollege.edu/academics/programs/graduate/physician-assistant-studies*
Contact: *admissions@mercycollege.edu*
Phone: 419-251-1313

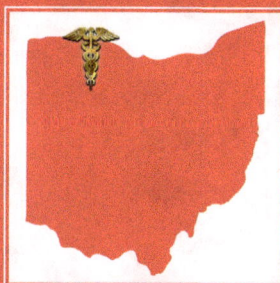

COST OF ATTENDANCE

Tuition and Fees: $41,700
Additional Expenses: N/A
Total: $46,720*

*This figure does not include cost of living or other indirect costs.

Financial Aid: https://mercycollege.edu/admissions/financial-aid

ADDITIONAL INFORMATION

Interesting tidbit: Mercy College of Ohio is a Catholic institution with a focus on healthcare. The first cohort of 20 PA students (PAS) starts May 2021, with clinicals August 2022 through the beginning of August 2023; second cohort of 25 PAS; third and subsequent cohorts of 30 PAS.

Important Updates due to COVID-19: Pass/Fail grades earning Pass will generally be acceptable for the pandemic affected semester(s) courses. The Pass/Fail courses will be interpreted within the candidate's existing GPA and other admissions data. The home-based GRE will be accepted. Virtual interviews.

Were tests required? GRE and Altus Suite required.

Are tests expected next year? Yes.

What international experiences are available? N/A

What dual degree options exist? N/A

What service-learning opportunities exist? N/A

PANCE First-Time Pass Rate: N/A (inaugural cohort of 20 students will graduate in 2023)

Other: The PA Program has a Direct Entry pathway for high school applicants. See https://assets.mercycollege.edu/uploads/documents/undergraduate_pre_pa_direct_entry_admission_requirements_updated_4.28.21.pdf?mtime=20210428201804&focal=none

ILLINOIS

INDIANA

IOWA

KANSAS

MICHIGAN

MINNESOTA

MISSOURI

NEBRASKA

NORTH DAKOTA

OHIO

SOUTH DAKOTA

WISCONSIN

MIDWEST

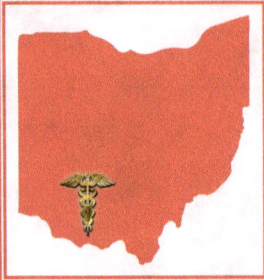

ILLINOIS

INDIANA

IOWA

KANSAS

MICHIGAN

MINNESOTA

MISSOURI

NEBRASKA

NORTH DAKOTA

OHIO

SOUTH DAKOTA

WISCONSIN

OHIO DOMINICAN UNIVERSITY

Address: 1216 Sunbury Road, Columbus, OH 43219
Website: *http://www.ohiodominican.edu/academics/graduate/ physician-assistant-program*
Contact: *paprogram@ohiodominican.edu*
Phone: 614-251-4320

COST OF ATTENDANCE

Tuition and Fees: $49,840
Additional Expenses: N/A
Total: $49,840*

*This figure does not include cost of living or other indirect costs.

Financial Aid: N/A

ADDITIONAL INFORMATION

Interesting tidbit: ODU's master's program in Physician Assistant Studies promotes the Roman Catholic moral teaching on the transcendent and inherent dignity of the human person.

Important Updates due to COVID-19: N/A

Were tests required? GRE or MCAT required.

Are tests expected next year? Yes.

What international experiences are available? Medical mission trips.

What dual degree options exist? N/A

What service-learning opportunities exist? All students will perform a service-component during the didactic phase for the course "Diverse & Vulnerable Patient Populations."

PANCE First-Time Pass Rate: 98% (2020)

OHIO UNIVERSITY

Address: 6805 Bobcat Way, Dublin, OH 43016
Website: *https://www.ohio.edu/chsp/rcs/pa/*
Contact: *paadmissions@ohio.edu*
Phone: 614-793-5619

COST OF ATTENDANCE

In-State Tuition and Fees: $30,056
Additional Expenses: $18,300
Total: $48,356

Out-of-State Tuition and Fees: $31,444
Additional Expenses: $18,300
Total: $49,744

Financial Aid:

ADDITIONAL INFORMATION

Interesting tidbit: The Ohio University Physician Assistant (OHIO PA) program offers interprofessional opportunities with the OHIO Heritage College of Osteopathic Medicine and other professions within the College of Health Sciences and Professions. It actively recruits students from regions that are considered medically underserved and students with military experience.

Important Updates due to COVID-19: Alternative grading options given during the COVID-19 pandemic may be subject to further review.

Were tests required? GRE required.

Are tests expected next year? Yes.

What international experiences are available? N/A

What dual degree options exist? N/A

What service-learning opportunities exist? N/A

PANCE First-Time Pass Rate: 100% (2020)

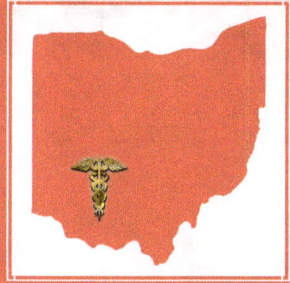

ILLINOIS

INDIANA

IOWA

KANSAS

MICHIGAN

MINNESOTA

MISSOURI

NEBRASKA

NORTH DAKOTA

OHIO

SOUTH DAKOTA

WISCONSIN

MIDWEST

ILLINOIS

INDIANA

IOWA

KANSAS

MICHIGAN

MINNESOTA

MISSOURI

NEBRASKA

NORTH DAKOTA

OHIO

SOUTH DAKOTA

WISCONSIN

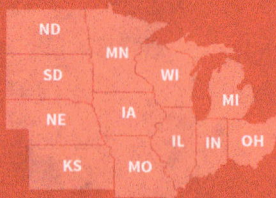

UNIVERSITY OF DAYTON

Address: 300 College Park, Dayton, OH 45469
Website: *https://udayton.edu/education/departments_and_programs/pa/index.php*
Contact: *akidwell1@udayton.edu*
Phone: 937-229-2900

COST OF ATTENDANCE

Tuition and Fees: $36,765
Additional Expenses: $4,159*
Total: $40,924*

*This figure does not include cost of living or other indirect costs.

Financial Aid: https://udayton.edu/affordability/graduate/index.php

ADDITIONAL INFORMATION

Interesting tidbit: The University of Dayton is the first and only program to offer The Healer's Art course to Physician Assistant Education students. The course explores the "art of medicine" via reflection and discussion of such topics as self-care, grief and loss, healing lineage, courage, and service as a way of life.

Important Updates due to COVID-19: The Program will consider accepting P/F grading for spring and summer 2020 courses on a case-by-case basis.

Were tests required? No.

Are tests expected next year? No.

What international experiences are available? International elective rotations through Global Health Electives and Child Family Health International.

What dual degree options exist? N/A

What service-learning opportunities exist? Child Family Health International.

PANCE First-Time Pass Rate: 100% (2020)

UNIVERSITY OF FINDLAY

Address: 1000 North Main Street, Findlay, OH 45840
Website: *https://www.findlay.edu/healthprofessions/*
physicianassistant-ma/
Contact: *paprogram@findlay.edu*
Phone: 419-434-4529

COST OF ATTENDANCE

Tuition and Fees: $41,668
Additional Expenses: $9,315*
Total: $50,983*

*This figure does not include cost of living or other indirect costs.

Financial Aid: https://www.findlay.edu/financial-aid/graduate-student-info

ADDITIONAL INFORMATION

Interesting tidbit: The UF PA Program is in the middle of an incremental increase in students approved by the ARC-PA. Twenty students were admitted in 2020 (increased from previous 18), 22 will be admitted in 2021, and 24 will be admitted in 2022. The number of students in a cohort will remain at 24 from 2022 onward.

Important Updates due to COVID-19: N/A

Were tests required? No.

Are tests expected next year? No.

What international experiences are available? N/A

What dual degree options exist? N/A

What service-learning opportunities exist? N/A

PANCE First-Time Pass Rate: 100% (2020)

ILLINOIS

INDIANA

IOWA

KANSAS

MICHIGAN

MINNESOTA

MISSOURI

NEBRASKA

NORTH DAKOTA

OHIO

SOUTH DAKOTA

WISCONSIN

MIDWEST

ILLINOIS

INDIANA

IOWA

KANSAS

MICHIGAN

MINNESOTA

MISSOURI

NEBRASKA

NORTH DAKOTA

OHIO

SOUTH DAKOTA

WISCONSIN

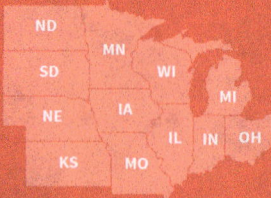

UNIVERSITY OF MOUNT UNION

Address: 1972 Clark Avenue, Alliance, OH 44601
Website: *https://www.mountunion.edu/physician-assistant-studies*
Contact: *scarpill@mountunion.edu*
Phone: 330-823-2419

COST OF ATTENDANCE

Tuition and Fees: $37,500
Additional Expenses: $9,000*
Total: $46,500*

*This figure does not include cost of living or other indirect costs.

Financial Aid: https://www.mountunion.edu/tuition-and-aid

ADDITIONAL INFORMATION

Interesting tidbit: The 15-month didactic phase consists of traditional lectures, web-based interactive learning, student laboratories and seminars, followed by a 12-month clinical phase.

Important Updates due to COVID-19: Online prerequisite course work and labs taken between January 2020 and December 2021 will be accepted, online lab courses prior to and after this time frame will be reviewed on a case-by-case basis. The program will accept virtual shadowing hours.

Were tests required? GRE required.

Are tests expected next year? Yes.

What international experiences are available? Service learning trips in partnership with Refuge International.

What dual degree options exist? N/A

What service-learning opportunities exist? Service learning trips in partnership with Refuge International.

PANCE First-Time Pass Rate: 92% (2020)

Other: The University of Mount Union Physician Assistant Studies Program offers priority admission to some applicants. See https://www.mountunion.edu/academics/graduate-degrees/physician-assistant-studies/pa-priority-admission

UNIVERSITY OF TOLEDO

Address: 3000 Arlington Ave., Collier Building, Toledo, OH 43614
Website: *http://www.utoledo.edu/med/grad/pa/*
Contact: *physicianassistant@utoledo.edu*
Phone: 419-383-5408

COST OF ATTENDANCE

In-State Tuition and Fees: $29,118
Additional Expenses: N/A
Total: $29,118*

Out-of-State Tuition and Fees: $46,870
Additional Expenses: N/A
Total: $46,870*

*This figure does not include cost of living or other indirect costs.

Financial Aid: https://www.utoledo.edu/financialaid/hsc/

ADDITIONAL INFORMATION

Interesting tidbit: The University of Toledo Physician Assistant Program (UTPA) is a 27-month graduate program leading to a Master of Science in Biomedical Sciences (MSBS) degree with a Physician Assistant concentration. The UT PA Program and the College of Nursing share the fine facilities of the Collier Building on the Health Science Campus, optimal for interprofessional education.

Important Updates due to COVID-19: The prerequisite courses must have a letter grade on the transcript. Pass/fail grades will not be acceptable. Online labs will be acceptable for the 2020-2021 admission cycle due to the COVID pandemic.

Were tests required? PA-CAT/GRE, and Altus Suite required.

Are tests expected next year? Yes.

What international experiences are available? Medical mission teams with the Global Health Program (see https://www.utoledo.edu/med/studentaffairs/organizations/ccc.html); Annual Honduras mission trip and the Nicaragua Medical Mission Trip (see https://www.utoledo.edu/hhs/pt/spto/pdfs/Nicaragua%20Mission%20PT%202016.pdf).

What dual degree options exist? N/A

What service-learning opportunities exist? Community Care Clinics (see https://www.utoledo.edu/med/studentaffairs/organizations/ccc.html); That Neighborhood Free Health Clinic

PANCE First-Time Pass Rate: 100% (2020)

ILLINOIS

INDIANA

IOWA

KANSAS

MICHIGAN

MINNESOTA

MISSOURI

NEBRASKA

NORTH DAKOTA

OHIO

SOUTH DAKOTA

WISCONSIN

MIDWEST

ILLINOIS

INDIANA

IOWA

KANSAS

MICHIGAN

MINNESOTA

MISSOURI

NEBRASKA

NORTH DAKOTA

OHIO

SOUTH DAKOTA

WISCONSIN

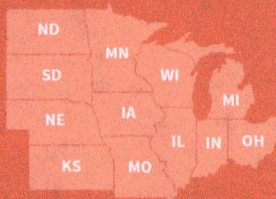

UNIVERSITY OF SOUTH DAKOTA

Address: 414 E. Clark St., Vermillion, SD 57069
Website: *http://www.usd.edu/pa*
Contact: *pa@usd.edu*
Phone: 605-658-5926

COST OF ATTENDANCE

In-State Tuition and Fees: $20,019
Additional Expenses: $34,043
Total: $54,062

Out-of-State Tuition and Fees: $39,718
Additional Expenses: $34,043
Total: $73,761

Financial Aid: https://www.usd.edu/financial-aid/applying-for-aid/graduate-financial-aid

ADDITIONAL INFORMATION

Interesting tidbit: In accordance with the PA program mission and goals, the program will give preference to applicants who indicate a high potential for future practice in primary care or in a medically underserved area as well as individuals from targeted populations. Also, over half of the matriculants are South Dakota residents or those with strong ties to the state.

Important Updates due to COVID-19: N/A

Were tests required? No.

Are tests expected next year? No.

What international experiences are available? N/A

What dual degree options exist? N/A

What service-learning opportunities exist? N/A

PANCE First-Time Pass Rate: 96% (2020)

CARROLL UNIVERSITY

Address: 100 N. East Avenue, Waukesha, WI 53186
Website: *http://www.carrollu.edu/gradprograms/physasst/admission.asp*
Contact: *painfo@carrollu.edu*
Phone: 262-524-7361

COST OF ATTENDANCE

Tuition and Fees: $45,201
Additional Expenses: $20,094
Total: $65,295

Financial Aid: https://www.carrollu.edu/financial-aid/graduate-students

ADDITIONAL INFORMATION

Interesting tidbit: As part of the Health Science Primary Care Training and Enhancement Program, Carroll University provides healthcare to medically underserved populations through an interprofessional team composed of physician assistant, physical therapy, occupational therapy, nursing, and public health students. Through this initiative, Carroll has designed, implemented, and is evaluating a training model that prepares physician assistants (as well as the other interprofessional students listed above) to work in a transformed health care delivery system while meeting the primary care needs of Hispanic seniors in Milwaukee and medically underserved patients in Waukesha.

Important Updates due to COVID-19: Prerequisite courses successfully completed as pass/fail (without letter grades) will be accepted. Prerequisite lab science courses successfully completed online will be accepted.

Were tests required? GRE required.

Are tests expected next year? Yes.

What international experiences are available? N/A

What dual degree options exist? N/A

What service-learning opportunities exist? United Community Center and Waukesha Free Clinic.

PANCE First-Time Pass Rate: 100% (2020)

ILLINOIS

INDIANA

IOWA

KANSAS

MICHIGAN

MINNESOTA

MISSOURI

NEBRASKA

NORTH DAKOTA

OHIO

SOUTH DAKOTA

WISCONSIN

MIDWEST

ILLINOIS

INDIANA

IOWA

KANSAS

MICHIGAN

MINNESOTA

MISSOURI

NEBRASKA

NORTH DAKOTA

OHIO

SOUTH DAKOTA

WISCONSIN

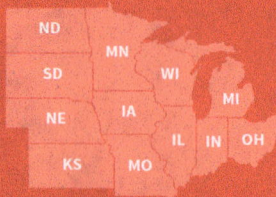

CONCORDIA UNIVERSITY - WISCONSIN

Address: 12800 North Lake Shore Drive, Mequon, WI 53097
Website: *https://www.cuw.edu/academics/programs/physician-assistant-masters/*
Contact: *admissions@cuw.edu*
Phone: 262-243-5700

COST OF ATTENDANCE

Tuition and Fees: $44,868
Additional Expenses: N/A
Total: $44,864*

*This figure does not include cost of living or other indirect costs.

Financial Aid: https://www.cuw.edu/admissions/financial-aid/graduate.html

ADDITIONAL INFORMATION

Interesting tidbit: The overarching theme of CUW PA education will be an emphasis on preventative medicine and primary care.

Important Updates due to COVID-19: Online labs will be accepted for courses completed January 2020- May 2022. A 'Pass' grade for a Pass/Fail course will be accepted for courses completed January 2020 – May 2022 for all prerequisite courses. PA shadowing requirement is waived. Proof of completed COVID vaccination is required upon acceptance to the program.

Were tests required? No.

Are tests expected next year? No.

What international experiences are available? International rotations available. Contact the Program directly.

What dual degree options exist? N/A

What service-learning opportunities exist? Opportunities for service learning available. Contact the Program directly.

PANCE First-Time Pass Rate: 90% (2020)

MARQUETTE UNIVERSITY

Address: 507 N 17th Street, Milwaukee, WI 53233
Website: *http://www.marquette.edu/physician-assistant*
Contact: *doris.osterhaus@marquette.edu*
Phone: 414-288-5688

COST OF ATTENDANCE

Tuition and Fees: $48,955
Additional Expenses: N/A
Total: $48,955*

*This figure does not include cost of living or other indirect costs.

Financial Aid: https://www.marquette.edu/grad/financial-aid.php

ADDITIONAL INFORMATION

Interesting tidbit: Beginning in Summer 2021, each year, the PA program accepts 75 individuals. Students are selected from both internal applicants consisting of Marquette undergraduates and external applicants consisting of graduates and undergraduates from other universities. The Department of Physician Assistant Studies combines Marquette's Jesuit tradition of cura personalis ("care for the whole person") with the College of Health Sciences' Jesuit ideals of concern for the spiritual, emotional and physical development of the individual.

Important Updates due to COVID-19: N/A

Were tests required? Altus Suite required.

Are tests expected next year? Yes.

What international experiences are available? Belize clinical rotation. See https://www.marquette.edu/physician-assistant/belize-clinical-rotation.php

What dual degree options exist? N/A

What service-learning opportunities exist? Hillside Clinic (Belize). See https://www.hillsidebelize.org/

PANCE First-Time Pass Rate: 100% (2020)

ILLINOIS

INDIANA

IOWA

KANSAS

MICHIGAN

MINNESOTA

MISSOURI

NEBRASKA

NORTH DAKOTA

OHIO

SOUTH DAKOTA

WISCONSIN

MIDWEST

ILLINOIS

INDIANA

IOWA

KANSAS

MICHIGAN

MINNESOTA

MISSOURI

NEBRASKA

NORTH DAKOTA

OHIO

SOUTH DAKOTA

WISCONSIN

UNIVERSITY OF WISCONSIN - LA CROSSE

Address: 1725 State St., La Crosse, WI 54601
Website: *https://www.uwlax.edu/grad/physician-assistant-studies/*
Contact: *paprogram@uwlax.edu*
Phone: 608-785-8470

COST OF ATTENDANCE

In-State Tuition and Fees: $17,991
Additional Expenses: $6,094*
Total: $24,085*

Out-of-State Tuition and Fees: $36,644
Additional Expenses: $6,094*
Total: $42,738*

*This figure does not include cost of living or other indirect costs.

Financial Aid: https://www.uwlax.edu/grad/physician-assistant-studies/financial-aid/

ADDITIONAL INFORMATION

Interesting tidbit: The UWLAX Physician Assistant program is unique in that it is a partnership between four organizations, including the University of Wisconsin-La Crosse, Gundersen Medical Foundation, Mayo Clinic School of Health Sciences, and Marshfield Clinic Health System. Didactic instruction during the first year of the program occurs at the Health Science Center located on the campus of UWL, while clinical instruction during the second year occurs within the three clinical partners' healthcare systems.

Important Updates due to COVID-19: N/A

Were tests required? GRE required.

Are tests expected next year? Yes.

What international experiences are available? N/A

What dual degree options exist? N/A

What service-learning opportunities exist? N/A

PANCE First-Time Pass Rate: 100% (2020)

UNIVERSITY OF WISCONSIN - MADISON

Address: 750 Highland Avenue, Madison, WI 53705
Website: *https://www.med.wisc.edu/education/physician-assistant-pa-program/*
Contact: *paprogram@mailplus.wisc.edu*
Phone: 608-262-5620

COST OF ATTENDANCE

In-State Tuition and Fees: $19,379
Additional Expenses: $9,125*
Total: $28,504*

Out-of-State Tuition and Fees: $39,319
Additional Expenses: $9,125*
Total: $48,444*

*This figure does not include cost of living or other indirect costs.

Financial Aid: https://financialaid.wisc.edu/

ADDITIONAL INFORMATION

Interesting tidbit: A dynamic, primary care-oriented curriculum emphasizes population/public health, evidence- based medicine, cultural humility, and rural health. The modular, system-based approach to teaching clinical medicine, pharmacology and diagnostic methods, allows integration of innovative case-based and active learning strategies. All students are required to complete one clinical rotation in a rural or medically underserved community.

Important Updates due to COVID-19: The UW-Madison PA Program will accept grades of Pass (P), Satisfactory (S), or the equivalent for required coursework taken in spring 2020 and beyond. The CASPA application gives applicants the opportunity to share how COVID-19 affected their personal, professional, and academic experiences and the Admissions Committee will use the information provided as part of their assessment.

Were tests required? Altus Suite required.

Are tests expected next year? Yes.

What international experiences are available? N/A

What dual degree options exist? MPH/MPAS. See https://www.med.wisc.edu/education/physician-assistant-pa-program/curriculum/mph-pa-dual-degree/

What service-learning opportunities exist? N/A

PANCE First-Time Pass Rate: 98% (2020)

Other: The Program offers 36-month distance tracks for students who live within driving distance of Madison or those who wish to practice in a medically underserved area. See https://www.med.wisc.edu/education/physician-assistant-pa-program/curriculum/distance-tracks/

Other: The Program offers a full-time, 24-month northern Wisconsin PA education program for students who live and plan to practice in northern Wisconsin (wisPACT track). See https://www.med.wisc.edu/education/physician-assistant-pa-program/curriculum/wispact/

ILLINOIS

INDIANA

IOWA

KANSAS

MICHIGAN

MINNESOTA

MISSOURI

NEBRASKA

NORTH DAKOTA

OHIO

SOUTH DAKOTA

WISCONSIN

MIDWEST

ALABAMA

ARKANSAS

DELAWARE

DISTRICT OF
COLUMBIA

FLORIDA

GEORGIA

KENTUCKY

LOUISIANA

MARYLAND

MISSISSIPPI

NORTH CAROLINA

OKLAHOMA

SOUTH CAROLINA

TENNESSEE

TEXAS

VIRGINIA

WEST VIRGINIA

CHAPTER 4
REGION THREE
SOUTH

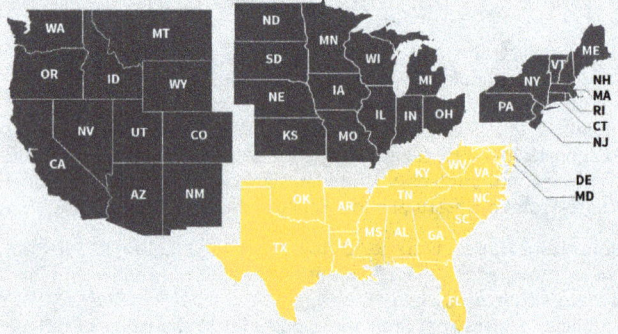

106 *Programs* | 16 *States*

1. AL - Faulkner University
2. AL - Samford University
3. AL - University of Alabama at Birmingham
4. AL - University of South Alabama
5. AR - Harding University
6. AR - University of Arkansas
7. D.C. - George Washington University
8. FL - AdventHealth University
9. FL – Barry University – Miami
10. FL – Barry University – St. Petersburg
11. FL - Florida Gulf Coast University
12. FL - Florida International University Herbert Wertheim College of Medicine
13. FL - Florida State University
14. FL - Gannon University - Ruskin
15. FL - Keiser University
16. FL - Miami Dade College
17. FL - Nova Southeastern University - Fort Lauderdale
18. FL - Nova Southeastern University - Fort Myers
19. FL - Nova Southeastern University - Jacksonville
20. FL - Nova Southeastern University - Orlando
21. FL - South University, Tampa
22. FL - South University, West Palm Beach
23. FL - University of Florida
24. FL - University of South Florida
25. FL - University of Tampa
26. GA - Augusta University
27. GA - Brenau University
28. GA - Emory University
29. GA - Mercer University
30. GA - Morehouse School of Medicine
31. GA - PCOM - Georgia
32. GA - South College - Atlanta
33. GA - South University, Savannah
34. KY - Sullivan University
35. KY - University of Kentucky - Lexington
36. KY - University of Kentucky - Morehead
37. KY - University of the Cumberlands
38. KY - University of the Cumberlands, Northern Kentucky Campus
39. LA - Franciscan Missionaries of Our Lady University
40. LA - Louisiana State University Health Sciences Center Shreveport
41. LA - Louisiana State University - New Orleans
42. LA - Xavier University of Louisiana
43. MD - Frostburg State University
44. MD - Towson University CCBC - Essex
45. MD - University of Maryland Baltimore (Ann Arundel Community College)
46. MD - University of Maryland Eastern Shore
47. MS - Mississippi College
48. MS - Mississippi State University - Meridian
49. NC - Campbell University
50. NC - Duke University
51. NC - East Carolina University
52. NC - Elon University
53. NC - Gardner-Webb University
54. NC - High Point University
55. NC - Methodist University
56. NC - Pfeiffer University
57. NC - UNC-Chapel Hill
58. NC - Wake Forest University - Winston-Salem
59. NC - Wake Forest University - Boone
60. NC - Wingate University
61. NC - Wingate University - Hendersonville
62. OK - Northeastern State University
63. OK - Oklahoma City University
64. OK - Oklahoma State University
65. OK - University of Oklahoma - Oklahoma City
66. OK - University of Oklahoma - Tulsa
67. SC - Charleston Southern University
68. SC - Medical University of South Carolina
69. SC - North Greenville University
70. SC - Presbyterian College
71. SC - University of South Carolina SOM
72. TN - Bethel University, Tennessee
73. TN - Christian Brothers University
74. TN - Lincoln Memorial University
75. TN - Lincoln Memorial University - Knoxville
76. TN - Lipscomb University
77. TN - Milligan University
78. TN - South College - Knoxville
79. TN - South College - Nashville
80. TN - Trevecca Nazarene University
81. TN - University of Tennessee Health Science Center
82. TX - Baylor College of Medicine
83. TX - Hardin-Simmons University
84. TX - Texas Tech University Health Sciences Center
85. TX - University of Mary Hardin Baylor
86. TX - University of North Texas HS Center Fort Worth
87. TX - U.S. Army Medical Center of Excellence IPAP
88. TX - University of Texas Health Science Center at Laredo
89. TX - University of Texas Health Science Center at San Antonio
90. TX - University of Texas Medical Branch at Galveston
91. TX - University of Texas Rio Grande Valley
92. TX - University of Texas Southwestern Medical Center School of Health Professions
93. VA - Eastern Virginia Medical School
94. VA - Emory & Henry College
95. VA - James Madison University
96. VA - Mary Baldwin University
97. VA - Radford University
98. VA - Shenandoah University - Loudoun
99. VA - Shenandoah University - Winchester
100. VA - South University, Richmond
101. VA - University of Lynchburg
102. WV - Alderson-Broaddus University
103. WV - Marshall University Joan C. Edwards School of Medicine
104. WV - University of Charleston
105. WV - West Liberty University
106. WV - West Virginia University

PA PROGRAMS

PA School	Ave. GPA & GRE (Verbal, Quantitative, Analy. Writing) Int'l Students: Yes/No	Admission Statistics	Prerequisite Coursework Other Than Gen Bio, Gen Chem, Human Anatomy, Human Physiology, Microbiology, Statistics, Psychology
Faulkner University 5345 Atlanta Highway, Montgomery, AL 36109	3.0+ (overall) GRE: 20%+ (V) 20%+ (Q) 20%+ (A) Int'l Student: Yes	Apps Received: N/A Interviews Offered: N/A Admission Offered: N/A Class Size: 35 Admitted Rate: N/A	N/A
Samford University School of Health Professions 800 Lakeshore Dr., Homewood, Al 35229	3.73 (overall) 3.67 (science) GRE: 305 (Q&V combined) Int'l Student: Yes	Apps Received: N/A Interviews Offered: N/A Admission Offered: N/A Class Size: 36 Admitted Rate: N/A	Medical Terminology
University of Alabama at Birmingham 1716 9th Avenue South, Birmingham, AL 35233	3.59 (overall) 3.47 (science) GRE: 54% (V) 39% (Q) Int'l Student: Yes	Apps Received: 997 Interviews Offered: N/A Admission Offered: N/A Class Size: 71 Admitted Rate: 7.1%	Medical Terminology
University of South Alabama 5721 USA Drive North, Mobile, AL 36688	3.66 (overall) 3.62 (science) GRE: 152 (V) 151 (Q) Int'l Student: Yes	Apps Received: N/A Interviews Offered: N/A Admission Offered: N/A Class Size: 40 Admitted Rate: N/A	Biochemistry or OChem; College Algebra or higher; Medical Terminology
Harding University 915 E. Market Ave., Searcy, AR 72149	3.50 (overall) 3.57 (science) GRE: N/A Int'l Student: Yes	Apps Received: N/A Interviews Offered: N/A Admission Offered: N/A Class Size: 36 Admitted Rate: N/A	Biochemistry or Ochem; College Algebra or higher; Medical Terminology; Psychology elective; Upper-level Biology

PA PROGRAMS

PA School	Ave. GPA & GRE (Verbal, Quantitative, Analy. Writing) Int'l Students: Yes/No	Admission Statistics	Prerequisite Coursework Other Than Gen Bio, Gen Chem, Human Anatomy, Human Physiology, Microbiology, Statistics, Psychology
University of Arkansas 4301 W. Markham St., Little Rock, AR 72205	3.76 (overall) 3.71 (science) GRE: 302 (Q&V combined) Int'l Student: Yes	Apps Received: N/A Interviews Offered: N/A Admission Offered: N/A Class Size: 40 Admitted Rate: N/A	Genetics; OChem
George Washington University Rose Hall, 2300 Eye Street NW, Washington, D.C. 20037	3.56 (overall) 3.54 (science) GRE: 80% (V) 60% (Q) Int'l Student: Yes	Apps Received: N/A Interviews Offered: N/A Admission Offered: N/A Class Size: 68 Admitted Rate: N/A	Biochemistry or OChem
AdventHealth University 660 Winyah Drive, Orlando, FL 32803	3.49 (overall) 3.46 (science) GRE: Not Req. Int'l Student: Yes	Apps Received: N/A Interviews Offered: N/A Admission Offered: N/A Class Size: 30 Admitted Rate: N/A	Genetics; Medical Terminology; OChem
Barry University - Miami 11300 NE 2nd Avenue, Miami, FL 33161	3.40 (overall) 3.50 (science) GRE: 150+ (V) 150+ (Q) 3+ (A) Int'l Student: Yes	Apps Received: N/A Interviews Offered: N/A Admission Offered: N/A Class Size: 76 Admitted Rate: N/A	Biochemistry or OChem

SOUTH

PA PROGRAMS

PA School	Ave. GPA & GRE (Verbal, Quantitative, Analy. Writing) Int'l Students: Yes/No	Admission Statistics	Prerequisite Coursework Other Than Gen Bio, Gen Chem, Human Anatomy, Human Physiology, Microbiology, Statistics, Psychology
Barry University - St. Petersburg 7200 66th Street North, Pinellas Park, FL 33781	3.40 (overall) 3.50 (science) GRE: 150+ (V) 150+ (Q) 3+ (A) Int'l Student: Yes	Apps Received: N/A Interviews Offered: N/A Admission Offered: N/A Class Size: 24 Admitted Rate: N/A	Biochemistry or OChem
Florida Gulf Coast University 10501 FGCU Blvd. South, Fort Myers, FL 33965	3.0+ (overall) 3.0+ (science) GRE: N/A Int'l Student: Yes	Apps Received: N/A Interviews Offered: N/A Admission Offered: N/A Class Size: 20 Admitted Rate: N/A	Biochemistry or OChem; Genetics; Medical Terminology
Florida International University 11200 SW 8th Street, MARC Bldg. #260, Miami, FL 33199	3.56 (overall) 3.49 (science) GRE: 150.67 (V) 150.84 (Q) 4.07 (A) Int'l Student: Yes	Apps Received: 2,000 Interviews Offered: N/A Admission Offered: N/A Class Size: 45 Admitted Rate: 2.3%	N/A
Florida State University 1115 W. Call Street, Tallahassee, FL 32306	3.56 (overall) 3.54 (science) GRE: 152 (V) 152 (Q) Int'l Student: No	Apps Received: 1,321 Interviews Offered: N/A Admission Offered: N/A Class Size: 60 Admitted Rate: 4.5%	Biochemistry; College Algebra or higher; English Composition; Genetics; Medical Terminology; OChem
Gannon University - Ruskin 105 Commercial Center Drive, Ruskin, FL 33573	3.57 (overall) 3.50 (science) GRE: N/A Int'l Student: Yes	Apps Received: N/A Interviews Offered: N/A Admission Offered: N/A Class Size: 30 Admitted Rate: N/A	Genetics; Medical Terminology

PA PROGRAMS

PA School	Ave. GPA & GRE (Verbal, Quantitative, Analy. Writing) Int'l Students: Yes/No	Admission Statistics	Prerequisite Coursework Other Than Gen Bio, Gen Chem, Human Anatomy, Human Physiology, Microbiology, Statistics, Psychology
Keiser University 1500 NW 49th Street, Fort Lauderdale, FL 33309	2.75+ (overall) 3.0+ (science) GRE: 294+ (Q&V combined) Int'l Student: Yes	Apps Received: N/A Interviews Offered: N/A Admission Offered: N/A Class Size: 40 Admitted Rate: N/A	Biochemistry or OChem; College Math or higher; English Composition; English/Literature; Genetics; Medical Terminology; Social Science
Miami-Dade College* 950 NW 20th Street, Suite 2204, Bldg. #2, Miami, FL 33127	3.0+ (overall) 3.0+ (science) GRE: Not Req. Int'l Student: Yes	Apps Received: N/A Interviews Offered: N/A Admission Offered: N/A Class Size: 55 Admitted Rate: N/A	College Algebra or higher; Introduction to Health Care & Lab *This is a Direct Entry PA program (BS/MS) intended for high school applicants.
Nova Southeastern University, Fort Lauderdale 3200 S. University Drive, Fort Lauderdale, FL 33328	3.4+ (overall) 3.4+ (science) GRE: 40%+ (V) 40%+ (Q) 40%+ (A) Int'l Student: Yes	Apps Received: 1,400 Interviews Offered: ~250 Admission Offered: N/A Class Size: 75 Admitted Rate: 5.4%	Biochemistry; College Math; English & English Composition; Genetics; Humanities/Arts; Medical Terminology; Social Sciences
Nova Southeastern University, Fort Myers 3650 Colonial Court, Fort Myers, FL 33913	3.4+ (overall) 3.4+ (science) GRE: 40%+ (V) 40%+ (Q) 40%+ (A) Int'l Student: Yes	Apps Received: 1,000* Interviews Offered: N/A Admission Offered: N/A Class Size: 53 Admitted Rate: 5.3% *Aggregate number for Fort Myers, Jacksonville and Orlando campuses.	Biochemistry; College Math; English & English Composition; Genetics; Humanities/Arts; Medical Terminology; Social Sciences

SOUTH

PA PROGRAMS

PA School	Ave. GPA & GRE (Verbal, Quantitative, Analy. Writing) Int'l Students: Yes/No	Admission Statistics	Prerequisite Coursework Other Than Gen Bio, Gen Chem, Human Anatomy, Human Physiology, Microbiology, Statistics, Psychology
Nova Southeastern University, Jacksonville 6675 Corporate Center Parkway, Suite 115, Jacksonville, FL 32216	3.4+ (overall) 3.4+ (science) GRE: 40%+ (V) 40%+ (Q) 40%+ (A) Int'l Student: Yes	Apps Received: 1,000* Interviews Offered: N/A Admission Offered: N/A Class Size: 60 Admitted Rate: 6.0% *Aggregate number for Fort Myers, Jacksonville and Orlando campuses	Biochemistry; College Math; English & English Composition; Genetics; Humanities/Arts; Medical Terminology; Social Sciences
Nova Southeastern University, Orlando 4850 Millenia Boulevard, Orlando, FL 32839	3.4+ (overall) 3.4+ (science) GRE: 40%+ (V) 40%+ (Q) 40%+ (A) Int'l Student: Yes	Apps Received: 1,000* Interviews Offered: N/A Admission Offered: N/A Class Size: 64 Admitted Rate: 6.4% *Aggregate number for Fort Myers, Jacksonville and Orlando campuses	Biochemistry; College Math; English & English Composition; Genetics; Humanities/Arts; Medical Terminology; Social Sciences
South University, Tampa 4401 N. Himes Avenue, Tampa, FL 33614	3.39 (overall) 3.2+ (science) GRE: 50%+ (V) 50%+ (Q) 50%+ (A) Int'l Student: Yes	Apps Received: N/A Interviews Offered: N/A Admission Offered: N/A Class Size: 48 Admitted Rate: N/A	Biochemistry or OChem
South University, West Palm Beach 9801 Belvedere Road, Palm Beach, FL 33411	3.3+ (overall) 315+ (science) GRE: 50%+ (V) 50%+ (Q) 50%+ (A) Int'l Student: Yes	Apps Received: N/A Interviews Offered: N/A Admission Offered: N/A Class Size: 40 Admitted Rate: N/A	Biochemistry or OChem

PA School	Ave. GPA & GRE (Verbal, Quantitative, Analy. Writing) Int'l Students: Yes/No	Admission Statistics	Prerequisite Coursework Other Than Gen Bio, Gen Chem, Human Anatomy, Human Physiology, Microbiology, Statistics, Psychology
University of Florida University of Florida, Gainesville, FL 32610	3.60 (overall) 3.60 (science) GRE: 155 (V) 155 (Q) 4.3 (A) Int'l Student: No	Apps Received: 2,185 Interviews Offered: N/A Admission Offered: N/A Class Size: 60 Admitted Rate: 2.7%	Medical Terminology
University of South Florida 12901 Bruce B. Down Blvd MDC5, Tampa, FL 33612	3.72 (overall) 3.67 (science) GRE: 155 (V) 155 (Q) 4 (A) Int'l Student: No	Apps Received: N/A Interviews Offered: N/A Admission Offered: N/A Class Size: 50 Admitted Rate: N/A	Biochemistry; Medical Terminology; OChem
University of Tampa 401 W Kennedy Blvd., FL 33606	3.72 (overall) 3.60 (science) GRE: Not Req. Int'l Student: No	Apps Received: N/A Interviews Offered: N/A Admission Offered: N/A Class Size: 48 Admitted Rate: N/A	N/A
Augusta University 987 St. Sebastian Way, Augusta, GA 30912	3.69 (overall) 3.52 (science) GRE: 308 (Q&V combined) Int'l Student: Yes	Apps Received: N/A Interviews Offered: N/A Admission Offered: N/A Class Size: 44 Admitted Rate: N/A	College Algebra or higher; English Composition; Humanities and Fine Arts; OChem; Social Sciences

SOUTH

PA PROGRAMS

PA School	Ave. GPA & GRE (Verbal, Quantitative, Analy. Writing) Int'l Students: Yes/No	Admission Statistics	Prerequisite Coursework Other Than Gen Bio, Gen Chem, Human Anatomy, Human Physiology, Microbiology, Statistics, Psychology
Brenau University 500 Washington St. SE, Gainesville, GA 30501	3.45 (overall) 3.33 (science) GRE: 151 (V) 150 (Q) 3.86 (A) Int'l Student: Yes	Apps Received: 500 Interviews Offered: 122 Admission Offered: N/A Class Size: 33 Admitted Rate: 6.6%	College Algebra or higher; Genetics; OChem
Emory University 1462 Clifton Rd NE, Suite 280,, Atlanta, GA 30322	3.63 (overall) 3.65 (science) GRE: 154 (V) 159 (Q) 4.4 (A) Int'l Student: Yes	Apps Received: 2.071 Interviews Offered: 205 Admission Offered: N/A Class Size: 54 Admitted Rate: 2.6%	Biochemistry or OChem
Mercer University 3001 Mercer University Drive, McAfee Building, Atlanta, GA 30341	3.89 (overall) 3.47 (science) GRE: 310 (Q&V combined) 4.0 (A) Int'l Student: Yes	Apps Received: N/A Interviews Offered: N/A Admission Offered: N/A Class Size: 70 Admitted Rate: N/A	Biochemistry; English Composition; OChem
Morehouse School of Medicine 720 Westview Dr. Atlanta, GA 30310	3.0+ (overall) 3.0+ (science) GRE: N/A Int'l Student: No	Apps Received: N/A Interviews Offered: N/A Admission Offered: N/A Class Size: 20 Admitted Rate: N/A	Biochemistry; OChem
PCOM - Georgia 625 Old Peachtree Road NW, Suwanee, GA 30024	3.76 (overall) 3.71 (science) GRE: Not Req. Int'l Student: Yes	Apps Received: 1,377 Interviews Offered: 51 Admission Offered: N/A Class Size: 20 Admitted Rate: 1.5%	Biochemistry or OChem; Health-related Science Course or Physics; Social Sciences

PA School	Ave. GPA & GRE (Verbal, Quantitative, Analy. Writing) Int'l Students: Yes/No	Admission Statistics	Prerequisite Coursework Other Than Gen Bio, Gen Chem, Human Anatomy, Human Physiology, Microbiology, Statistics, Psychology
South College - Atlanta 2600 Century Parkway NE Atlanta, Georgia 30345	3.50 (overall) GRE: 153 (V) 153 (Q) 3.9 (A) Int'l Student: Yes	Apps Received: 2,300 Interviews Offered: N/A Admission Offered: N/A Class Size: 40 Admitted Rate: 1.7%	English; Humanities/Social Sciences
South University, Savannah 709 Mall Boulevard Savannah, GA 31406	3.65 (overall) GRE: N/A Int'l Student: Yes	Apps Received: N/A Interviews Offered: N/A Admission Offered: N/A Class Size: 70 Admitted Rate: N/A	Biochemistry or OChem
Sullivan University 2100 Gardiner Lane, Louisville, KY 40205	3.59 (overall) 3.57 (science) GRE: Not Req. Int'l Student: Yes	Apps Received: N/A Interviews Offered: N/A Admission Offered: N/A Class Size: 48 Admitted Rate: N/A	Biochemistry or OChem; English Composition; Medical Terminology
University of Kentucky - Lexington 900 South Limestone Street, Charles T. Wethington Bldg., Lexington, KY 40536	3.65 (overall) 3.55 (science) GRE: N/A Int'l Student: Yes	Apps Received: N/A Interviews Offered: N/A Admission Offered: N/A Class Size: 40 Admitted Rate: N/A	Anthropology or Sociology; Medical Terminology; OChem
University of Kentucky - Morehead 316 W 2nd Street, Morehead, KY 40351	3.65 (overall) 3.55 (science) GRE: N/A Int'l Student: Yes	Apps Received: N/A Interviews Offered: N/A Admission Offered: N/A Class Size: 16 Admitted Rate: N/A	Anthropology or Sociology; Medical Terminology; OChem

SOUTH

PA PROGRAMS

PA School	Ave. GPA & GRE (Verbal, Quantitative, Analy. Writing) Int'l Students: Yes/No	Admission Statistics	Prerequisite Coursework Other Than Gen Bio, Gen Chem, Human Anatomy, Human Physiology, Microbiology, Statistics, Psychology
University of the Cumberlands 6178 College Station Drive, Williamsburg, KY 40769	3.0+ (overall) 3.0+ (science) GRE: Not Req. Int'l Student: Yes	Apps Received: N/A Interviews Offered: N/A Admission Offered: N/A Class Size: 30 Admitted Rate: N/A	Biochemistry or OChem; Medical Terminology
University of the Cumberlands, Northern Kentucky 410 Meijer Drive, Florence, KY 41402	3.0+ (overall) 3.0+ (science) GRE: 50%+ (V) 50% (Q) 50%+ (A) Int'l Student: No	Apps Received: N/A Interviews Offered: N/A Admission Offered: N/A Class Size: 30 Admitted Rate: N/A	Biochemistry or OChem; Medical Terminology
Franciscan Missionaries of Our Lady University 5414 Brittany Drive, Baton Rouge, LA 70808	3.57 (overall) 3.57 (science) GRE: 151 (V) 150 (Q) 4.08 (A) Int'l Student: Yes	Apps Received: N/A Interviews Offered: N/A Admission Offered: N/A Class Size: 30 Admitted Rate: N/A	Genetics; Medical Terminology; OChem
Louisiana State University Health Sciences Center Shreveport 1501 Kings Highway, Shreveport, LA 71103	3.0+ (overall) 3.0+ (science) GRE: 143 (V) 145 (Q) 3 (A) Int'l Student: Yes	Apps Received: N/A Interviews Offered: N/A Admission Offered: N/A Class Size: 40 Admitted Rate: N/A	Upper-level Bio electives
Louisiana State University - New Orleans 411 South Prieur St., New Orleans, LA 70112	3.65 (overall) 3.60 (science) GRE: 153+ (V) 144+ (Q) 3.5+ (A) Int'l Student: No	Apps Received: N/A Interviews Offered: N/A Admission Offered: N/A Class Size: 35 Admitted Rate: N/A	Biochemistry or OChem; College Algebra or higher; Genetics; Upper-level Biological Sciences

PA School	Ave. GPA & GRE (Verbal, Quantitative, Analy. Writing) Int'l Students: Yes/No	Admission Statistics	Prerequisite Coursework Other Than Gen Bio, Gen Chem, Human Anatomy, Human Physiology, Microbiology, Statistics, Psychology
Xavier University of Louisiana 411 South Prieur St., New Orleans, LA 70112	3.0+ (overall) 3.0+ (science) GRE: 150+ (V) 150+ (Q) 3.5+ (A) Int'l Student: Yes	Apps Received: N/A Interviews Offered: N/A Admission Offered: N/A Class Size: 40 Admitted Rate: N/A	Biochemistry; English Composition; Genetics; Medical Terminology; OChem; Sociology; Upper-level Biology
Frostburg University 32 West Washington Street, Hagerstown, MD 21740	3.0+ (overall) 3.0+ (science) GRE: 40%+ (V) 40%+ (Q) 40%+ (A) Int'l Student: No	Apps Received: N/A Interviews Offered: N/A Admission Offered: N/A Class Size: 25 Admitted Rate: N/A	Biochemistry; Medical Terminology
Towson University/ CCBC Essex 7201 Rossville Blvd., Baltimore, MD 21237	3.50 (overall) 3.50 (science) GRE: Not Req. Int'l Student: Yes	Apps Received: N/A Interviews Offered: N/A Admission Offered: N/A Class Size: 36 Admitted Rate: N/A	Biochemistry; Medical Terminology
University of Maryland Baltimore/ Anne Arundel Community College 101 College Parkway, Arnold, MD 21012	3.56 (overall) 3.52 (science) GRE: 40%+ (V) 40%+ (Q) 40%+ (A) Int'l Student: Yes	Apps Received: 800 Interviews Offered: N/A Admission Offered: N/A Class Size: 40 Admitted Rate: 5.0%	N/A

SOUTH

PA PROGRAMS

PA School	Ave. GPA & GRE (Verbal, Quantitative, Analy. Writing) Int'l Students: Yes/No	Admission Statistics	Prerequisite Coursework Other Than Gen Bio, Gen Chem, Human Anatomy, Human Physiology, Microbiology, Statistics, Psychology
University of Maryland Eastern Shore Hazel Hall, Suite 1062, Princess Anne, MD 21653	3.0+ (overall) 3.0+ (science) GRE: N/A Int'l Student: Yes	Apps Received: N/A Interviews Offered: N/A Admission Offered: N/A Class Size: 20 Admitted Rate: N/A	Medical Terminology; OChem
Mississippi College 200 S. Capitol Street, Clinton, MS 39056	3.54 (overall) 3.44 (science) GRE: 155 (V) 150 (Q) 4.5 (A) Int'l Student: Yes	Apps Received: N/A Interviews Offered: N/A Admission Offered: N/A Class Size: 36 Admitted Rate: N/A	OChem
Mississippi State University - Meridian 2214 5th Street, Meridian, MS 39301	3.0+ (overall) 3.0+ (science) GRE: N/A Int'l Student: Yes	Apps Received: N/A Interviews Offered: N/A Admission Offered: N/A Class Size: 20 Admitted Rate: N/A	Behavioral Sciences; Biochemistry or OChem; College Algebra or higher; Genetics; Upper-level sciences
Campbell University 143 Main Street, Buies Creek, NC 27506	3.48 (overall) 3.4+ (science) GRE: 153 (V) 152 (Q) 4.1 (A) Int'l Student: Yes	Apps Received: N/A Interviews Offered: N/A Admission Offered: N/A Class Size: 54 Admitted Rate: N/A	Biochemistry or OChem
Duke University Medical Center 800 S. Duke Street, Durham, NC 27701	3.51 (overall) 3.40 (science) GRE: 154 (V) 152 (Q) 4.5 (A) Int'l Student: Yes	Apps Received: 4,100 Interviews Offered: 250 Admission Offered: N/A Class Size: 90 Admitted Rate: 2.2%	Upper-level Biology (2); Upper-level Chemistry (2)

PA PROGRAMS

PA School	Ave. GPA & GRE (Verbal, Quantitative, Analy. Writing) Int'l Students: Yes/No	Admission Statistics	Prerequisite Coursework Other Than Gen Bio, Gen Chem, Human Anatomy, Human Physiology, Microbiology, Statistics, Psychology
East Carolina University 600 Moye Blvd., Greenville, NC 27834	3.86 (overall) 3.81 (science) GRE: 314 (Q&V combined) 4.34 (A) Int'l Student: No	Apps Received: N/A Interviews Offered: N/A Admission Offered: N/A Class Size: 36 Admitted Rate: N/A	Genetics
Elon University 762 East Haggard Ave., Elon, NC 27244	3.82 (overall) 3.77 (science) GRE: Not Req. Int'l Student: Yes	Apps Received: N/A Interviews Offered: N/A Admission Offered: N/A Class Size: 38 Admitted Rate: N/A	Additional Chemistry; Upper-level Science
Gardner Webb University 110 S. Main Street, Boiling Springs, NC 28017	3.66 (overall) 3.61 (science) GRE: Not Req. Int'l Student: No	Apps Received: N/A Interviews Offered: N/A Admission Offered: N/A Class Size: 36 Admitted Rate: N/A	Additional Biology; Additional Chemistry; Medical Terminology; OChem
High Point University One University Parkway, High Point, NC 27288	3.81 (overall) 3.79 (science) GRE: 152 (V) 153 (Q) Int'l Student: Yes	Apps Received: N/A Interviews Offered: N/A Admission Offered: N/A Class Size: 35 Admitted Rate: N/A	Additional Chemistry; Humanities and Social Sciences; Upper-level Human Biological Sciences
Methodist University 5107 College Center Drive, Fayetteville, NC 28311	3.50 (overall) 3.62 (science) GRE: 154 (V) 152 (Q) 4 (A) Int'l Student: Yes	Apps Received: 1,164 Interviews Offered: N/A Admission Offered: N/A Class Size: 40 Admitted Rate: 3.4%	Additional Human Biology courses (2); Biochemistry; Medical Terminology; OChem

SOUTH

PA PROGRAMS

PA School	Ave. GPA & GRE (Verbal, Quantitative, Analy. Writing) Int'l Students: Yes/No	Admission Statistics	Prerequisite Coursework Other Than Gen Bio, Gen Chem, Human Anatomy, Human Physiology, Microbiology, Statistics, Psychology
Pfeiffer University 48380 US Hwy 52, Misenheimer, NC 28109	3.0+ (overall) 3.2+ (science) GRE: Not Req. Int'l Student: No	Apps Received: N/A Interviews Offered: N/A Admission Offered: N/A Class Size: 36 Admitted Rate: N/A	Biochemistry; Genetics; Medical Terminology; OChem
University of North Carolina - Chapel Hill 321 S Columbia Street, Chapel Hill, NC 27514	3.49 (overall) 3.62 (science) GRE: 64% (V) 47% (Q) Int'l Student: No	Apps Received: 800 Interviews Offered: N/A Admission Offered: N/A Class Size: 20 Admitted Rate: 2.5%	Biochemistry or OChem; Medical Terminology
Wake Forest University - Winston - Salem 525 Vine Street, Winston-Salem, NC 27101	3.57 (overall) 3.50 (science) GRE: 155 (V) 153 (Q) Int'l Student: No	Apps Received: 1,405* Interviews Offered: 247* Admission Offered: 144* Class Size: 64 Admitted Rate: 4.6% *Aggregate data for both Winston-Salem and Boone campuses.	Biochemistry; Genetics; Medical Terminology
Wake Forest University - Boone 1179 State Farm Road, Boone, NC 28608	3.57 (overall) 3.50 (science) GRE: 155 (V) 153 (Q) Int'l Student: No	Apps Received: 1,405* Interviews Offered: 247* Admission Offered: 144* Class Size: 24 Admitted Rate: 1.7% *Aggregate data for both Winston-Salem and Boone campuses.	Biochemistry; Genetics; Medical Terminology
Wingate University 220 N Camden Rd., Wingate, NC 28174	No Min. (overall) 3.2+ (science) GRE: 50%+ (V) 50%+ (Q) 50%+ (A) Int'l Student: No	Apps Received: 592* Interviews Offered: N/A Admission Offered: N/A Class Size: 40 Admitted Rate: 6.8% *Aggregate data for both Wingate and Hendersonville campuses.	Biochemistry; Genetics; Medical Terminology; OChem

PA PROGRAMS

PA School	Ave. GPA & GRE (Verbal, Quantitative, Analy. Writing) Int'l Students: Yes/No	Admission Statistics	Prerequisite Coursework Other Than Gen Bio, Gen Chem, Human Anatomy, Human Physiology, Microbiology, Statistics, Psychology
Wingate University - Hendersonville 805 6th Avenue W, Suite 200, Hendersonville, NC 28739	No Min. (overall) 3.2+ (science) GRE: 50%+ (V) 50%+ (Q) 50%+ (A) Int'l Student: No	Apps Received: 592* Interviews Offered: N/A Admission Offered: N/A Class Size: 15 Admitted Rate: 2.5% *Aggregate data for both Wingate and Hendersonville campuses.	Biochemistry; Genetics; Medical Terminology; OChem
Northeastern State University 2400 West Shawnee St., Muskogee, OK 74401	3.0+ (overall) 3.0+ (science) GRE: Not Req. Int'l Student: Yes	Apps Received: N/A Interviews Offered: N/A Admission Offered: N/A Class Size: 20 Admitted Rate: N/A	Biochemistry; College Algebra or higher; Genetics; OChem
Oklahoma City University 2501 N Blackwelder, Oklahoma City, OK 73106	3.0+ (overall) GRE: Not Req. Int'l Student: Yes	Apps Received: N/A Interviews Offered: N/A Admission Offered: N/A Class Size: 36 Admitted Rate: N/A	Biochemistry
Oklahoma State University 1111 W. 17 Street, Tulsa, OK 74107	3.0+ (overall) GRE: Not Req. Int'l Student: Yes	Apps Received: N/A Interviews Offered: N/A Admission Offered: N/A Class Size: 26 Admitted Rate: N/A	College Algebra or higher; Upper-level Science (2)
University of Oklahoma, Oklahoma City 940 Stanton L. Young Blvd., Ste. 357, Oklahoma City, OK 73104	3.0+ (overall) 3.0+ (science) GRE: Not Req. Int'l Student: Yes	Apps Received: N/A Interviews Offered: N/A Admission Offered: N/A Class Size: 50 Admitted Rate: N/A	College Algebra or higher; Pathogenic Microbiology/ Immunology/virology / Genetics;

SOUTH

PA School	Ave. GPA & GRE (Verbal, Quantitative, Analy. Writing) Int'l Students: Yes/No	Admission Statistics	Prerequisite Coursework Other Than Gen Bio, Gen Chem, Human Anatomy, Human Physiology, Microbiology, Statistics, Psychology
University of Oklahoma, Tulsa 4502 E. 41st Street, Tulsa, OK 74135	3.0+ (overall) 3.0+ (science) GRE: N/A Int'l Student: Yes	Apps Received: 700 Interviews Offered: 100 Admission Offered: N/A Class Size: 24 Admitted Rate: 3.4%	College Algebra or higher; English Composition; Upper level Sciences (2)
Charleston Southern University 9200 University Blvd., Health Science Bldg., Charleston, SC 29406	3.60 (overall) 3.60 (science) GRE: N/A Int'l Student: No	Apps Received: N/A Interviews Offered: N/A Admission Offered: N/A Class Size: 60 Admitted Rate: N/A	Biochemistry or OChem; Medical Terminology; Upper-level Biology, Chemistry or Physics (2)
Medical University of South Carolina 151 Rutledge Ave A., Charleston, SC 29403	3.73 (overall) 3.60 (science) GRE: Not Req. Int'l Student: No	Apps Received: N/A Interviews Offered: N/A Admission Offered: N/A Class Size: 60 Admitted Rate: N/A	Biochemistry or OChem; Medical Terminology
North Greenville University 405 Lancaster Ave., Greer, SC 29650	3.55 (overall) 3.75 (science) GRE: 153 (V) 152 (Q) 4 (A) Int'l Student: Yes	Apps Received: 700 Interviews Offered: 150 Admission Offered: N/A Class Size: 30 Admitted Rate: 4.3%	Additional Biology; Additional Chemistry
Presbyterian College 503 South Broad St., Clinton, SC 29325	3.2+ (overall) 3.2+ (science) GRE: N/A Int'l Student: Yes	Apps Received: N/A Interviews Offered: N/A Admission Offered: N/A Class Size: 34 Admitted Rate: N/A	English; Genetics; Medical Terminology; OChem

PA PROGRAMS

PA School	Ave. GPA & GRE (Verbal, Quantitative, Analy. Writing) Int'l Students: Yes/No	Admission Statistics	Prerequisite Coursework Other Than Gen Bio, Gen Chem, Human Anatomy, Human Physiology, Microbiology, Statistics, Psychology
University of South Carolina SOM 6311 Garners Ferry Rd., Bldg 101, Columbia, SC 29209	3.59 (overall) 3.56 (science) GRE: 307 (Q&V combine) Int'l Student: No	Apps Received: 1,000 Interviews Offered: N/A Admission Offered: N/A Class Size: 30 Admitted Rate: 3.0%	Medical Terminology; OChem
Bethel University - Tennessee 302B Tyson Avenue, Paris, TN 38242	3.33 (overall) 3.30 (science) GRE: 151.7 (V) 151.9 (Q) 3.8 (A) Int'l Student: Yes	Apps Received: 448 Interviews Offered: 108 Admission Offered: N/A Class Size: 50 Admitted Rate: 11.2%	Genetics
Christian Brothers University 650 East Parkway South, Memphis, Tn 38104	3.48 (overall) GRE: N/A Int'l Student: Yes	Apps Received: N/A Interviews Offered: N/A Admission Offered: N/A Class Size: 32 Admitted Rate: N/A	N/A
Lincoln Memorial University 6965 Cumberland Gap Parkway, Harrogate, TN 37752	3.49 (overall) 3.38 (science) GRE: 152 (V) 150 (Q) 3.9 (A) Int'l Student: Yes	Apps Received: N/A Interviews Offered: N/A Admission Offered: N/A Class Size: 96 Admitted Rate: N/A	Biochemistry or OChem; College Algebra or higher; English Composition; Medical Terminology; Psychology elective;
Lincoln Memorial University - Knoxville 421 Park 40 N Blvd., Knoxville, TN 37923	3.0+ (overall) 3.0+ (science) GRE: N/A Int'l Student: No	Apps Received: N/A Interviews Offered: N/A Admission Offered: N/A Class Size: 60 Admitted Rate: N/A	Biochemistry or OChem; English Composition; Medical Terminology

SOUTH

PA PROGRAMS

PA School	Ave. GPA & GRE (Verbal, Quantitative, Analy. Writing) Int'l Students: Yes/No	Admission Statistics	Prerequisite Coursework Other Than Gen Bio, Gen Chem, Human Anatomy, Human Physiology, Microbiology, Statistics, Psychology
Lipscomb University One University Park Drive, Nashville, TN 37204	3.70 (overall) 3.70 (science) GRE: Not Req. Int'l Student: Yes	Apps Received: N/A Interviews Offered: N/A Admission Offered: N/A Class Size: 50 Admitted Rate: N/A	Chemistry for Health Sciences; OChem; Upper level Biology
Milligan University 1 Blowers Blvd., Milligan, TN 37682	3.75 (overall) 3.71 (science) GRE: 302 (Q&V combined) Int'l Student: Yes	Apps Received: N/A Interviews Offered: N/A Admission Offered: N/A Class Size: 26 Admitted Rate: N/A	Biochemistry or OChem; Developmental Psychology/ Life Span Psychology; English Composition; Medical Terminology; Public Speaking;
South College - Knoxville 400 Goody's Lane, Parkside Campus, Knoxville, TN 37922	3.60 (overall) GRE: 155 (V) 154 (Q) 4.1 (A) Int'l Student: Yes	Apps Received: 2,300 Interviews Offered: N/A Admission Offered: N/A Class Size: 85 Admitted Rate: 3.7%	English; Humanities/Social Sciences
South College - Nashville 616 Marriott Drive, Nashville, TN 37214	3.60 (overall) 3.50 (science) GRE: N/A Int'l Student: Yes	Apps Received: 1,500 Interviews Offered: N/A Admission Offered: N/A Class Size: 30 Admitted Rate: 2.0%	English; Humanities/Social Sciences
Trevecca Nazarene University 333 Murfreesboro Road, Nashville, TN 37210	3.70 (overall) 3.76 (science) GRE: 307 (Q&V combine) Int'l Student: Yes	Apps Received: N/A Interviews Offered: N/A Admission Offered: N/A Class Size: 50 Admitted Rate: N/A	Developmental Psychology; Medical Terminology
University of Tennessee Health Science Center, Memphis 66 North Pauline, Ste. 116, Memphis, TN 38163	3.50 (overall) 3.50 (science) GRE: 305 (Q&V combined) Int'l Student: Yes	Apps Received: 1,600 Interviews Offered: N/A Admission Offered: N/A Class Size: 30 Admitted Rate: 1.9%	Medical Terminology

PA School	Ave. GPA & GRE (Verbal, Quantitative, Analy. Writing) Int'l Students: Yes/No	Admission Statistics	Prerequisite Coursework Other Than Gen Bio, Gen Chem, Human Anatomy, Human Physiology, Microbiology, Statistics, Psychology
Baylor College of Medicine 1 Baylor Plaza, Houston, TX 77030	3.70 (overall) 3.70 (science) GRE: Not Req. Int'l Student: Yes	Apps Received: 1,200 Interviews Offered: 150 Admission Offered: N/A Class Size: 40 Admitted Rate: 3.3%	N/A
Hardin-Simmons University 2200 Hickory Street, Abilene, TX 79698	3.58 (overall) 3.45 (science) GRE: 153.17 (V) 152.33 (Q) 4.02 (A) Int'l Student: Yes	Apps Received: N/A Interviews Offered: N/A Admission Offered: N/A Class Size: 30 Admitted Rate: N/A	English Composition; Genetics; Humanities Elective; OChem;
Texas Tech University Health Sciences Center 3600 N Garfield St., Midland, TX 79705	3.58 (overall) 3.49 (science) GRE: 151 (V) 151 (Q) 3.8 (A) Int'l Student: No	Apps Received: 1,832 Interviews Offered: 180-200 Admission Offered: N/A Class Size: 60 Admitted Rate: 3.3%	Biochemistry or OChem; Genetics
University of Mary Hardin Baylor 900 College Street, Belton, TX 76513	3.0+ (overall) 3.0+ (science) GRE: N/A Int'l Student: Yes	Apps Received: N/A Interviews Offered: N/A Admission Offered: N/A Class Size: 40 Admitted Rate: N/A	Genetics; OChem
University of North Texas Health Science Center, Ft. Worth 3500 Camp Bowie Blvd., Fort Worth, TX 76107	3.76 (overall) 3.70 (science) GRE: 65%+ (V) 65%+ (Q) 65%+ (A) Int'l Student: Yes	Apps Received: 2,024 Interviews Offered: 189 Admission Offered: N/A Class Size: 75 Admitted Rate: 3.7%	Genetics; OChem

SOUTH

PA PROGRAMS

PA School	Ave. GPA & GRE (Verbal, Quantitative, Analy. Writing) Int'l Students: Yes/No	Admission Statistics	Prerequisite Coursework Other Than Gen Bio, Gen Chem, Human Anatomy, Human Physiology, Microbiology, Statistics, Psychology
U.S. Army Medical Center of Excellence ISPA* 3599 Winfield Scott Road, Academy of Health Sciences, Fort Sam Houston, TX 78234	N/A	N/A	*Only Military applicants are accepted.
University of Texas Health Science Center - Laredo 1937 Bustamante Street, Laredo, TX 78041	3.79 (overall) 3.76 (science) GRE: N/A Int'l Student: Yes	Apps Received: N/A Interviews Offered: N/A Admission Offered: N/A Class Size: 10 Admitted Rate: N/A	GEnetics; OChem
University of Texas Health Science Center - San Antonio 7703 Floyd Curl Drive, San Antonio, TX 78229	3.60 (overall) 3.60 (science) GRE: N/A Int'l Student: Yes	Apps Received: 1,505 Interviews Offered: 140 Admission Offered: N/A Class Size: 45 Admitted Rate: 3.0%	Genetics; OChem
University of Texas - Medical Branch at Galveston 301 University Blvd., Galveston, TX 77555	3.72 (overall) 3.64 (science) GRE: 154 (V) 154 (Q) Int'l Student: Yes	Apps Received: 1,480 Interviews Offered: 213 Admission Offered: N/A Class Size: 90 Admitted Rate: 6.1%	Genetics; Immunology; Medical Terminology; OChem
University of Texas Rio Grande Valley 1201 West University Drive, Edinburg, TX 78539	3.57 (overall) 3.52 (science) GRE: N/A Int'l Student: Yes	Apps Received: N/A Interviews Offered: N/A Admission Offered: N/A Class Size: 100 Admitted Rate: N/A	Biochemistry or OChem; Genetics

PA PROGRAMS

PA School	Ave. GPA & GRE (Verbal, Quantitative, Analy. Writing) Int'l Students: Yes/No	Admission Statistics	Prerequisite Coursework Other Than Gen Bio, Gen Chem, Human Anatomy, Human Physiology, Microbiology, Statistics, Psychology
UT Southwestern School of Health Professions 6011 Harry Hines Blvd., Dallas, TX 75390	3.67 (overall) 3.77 (science) GRE: N/A Int'l Student: Yes	Apps Received: 1,500 Interviews Offered: 180 Admission Offered: N/A Class Size: 60 Admitted Rate: 4.0%	Genetics; OChem
Eastern Virginia Medical School 651 Colley Avenue, Norfolk, VA 23501	3.84 (overall) 3.85 (science) GRE: Not Req. Int'l Student: No	Apps Received: 1,166 Interviews Offered: 100 Admission Offered: 156 Class Size: 80 Admitted Rate: 6.9%	Advanced Psychology; Biochemistry or OChem;
Emory & Henry College 565 Radio Hill Road, Marion, VA 24354	3.29 (overall) 3.13 (science) GRE: 39.79% (V) 46.53% (Q) 58.09% (A) Int'l Student: Yes	Apps Received: N/A Interviews Offered: N/A Admission Offered: N/A Class Size: 34 Admitted Rate: N/A	Biochemistry or OChem; Genetics; Medical Terminology
James Madison University 235 Martin Luther King Jr. Way, MSC 4315, Harrisonburg, VA 22807	3.48 (overall) 3.41 (science) GRE: 68% (V) 54% (Q) 70% (A) Int'l Student: Yes	Apps Received: N/A Interviews Offered: N/A Admission Offered: N/A Class Size: 32 Admitted Rate: N/A	Biochemistry; Genetics; Medical Terminology
Mary Baldwin University 100 Baldwin Blvd., Fisherville, VA 22939	3.0+ (overall) 3.0+ (science) GRE: N/A Int'l Student: No	Apps Received: N/A Interviews Offered: N/A Admission Offered: N/A Class Size: 30 Admitted Rate: N/A	Biochemistry or OChem; Medical Terminology

SOUTH

PA PROGRAMS

PA School	Ave. GPA & GRE (Verbal, Quantitative, Analy. Writing) Int'l Students: Yes/No	Admission Statistics	Prerequisite Coursework Other Than Gen Bio, Gen Chem, Human Anatomy, Human Physiology, Microbiology, Statistics, Psychology
Radford University Carilion 101 Elm Avenue SE, Roanoke, VA 24013	3.0+ (overall) 3.0+ (science) GRE: N/A Int'l Student: Yes	Apps Received: 900 Interviews Offered: ~140 Admission Offered: N/A Class Size: 42 Admitted Rate: 4.7%	N/A
Shenandoah University - Loudoun 44160 Scholar Plaza, Leesburg, VA 20176	3.60 (overall) 3.56 (science) GRE: Not Req. Int'l Student: Yes	Apps Received: 647* Interviews Offered: N/A Admission Offered: N/A Class Size: 18 Admitted Rate: 2.8% *Aggregate data for both Loudoun and Winchester campuses.	Abnormal Psychology; Biochemistry or OChem; Developmental Psychology; Medical Terminology
Shenandoah University - Winchester 1775 North Sector Ct., Winchester, VA 22601	3.60 (overall) 3.56 (science) GRE: Not Req. Int'l Student: Yes	Apps Received: 647* Interviews Offered: N/A Admission Offered: N/A Class Size: 42 Admitted Rate: 6.5% *Aggregate data for both Loudoun and Winchester campuses.	Abnormal Psychology; Biochemistry or OChem; Developmental Psychology; Medical Terminology
South University, Richmond 2151 Old Brick Road, Glen Allen, VA 23060	3.38 (overall) GRE: N/A Int'l Student: Yes	Apps Received: N/A Interviews Offered: N/A Admission Offered: N/A Class Size: 36 Admitted Rate: N/A	Biochemistry or OChem
University of Lynchburg 1501 Lakeside Drive, Lynchburg, VA 24501	3.52 (overall) GRE: N/A Int'l Student: Yes	Apps Received: N/A Interviews Offered: N/A Admission Offered: N/A Class Size: 40 Admitted Rate: N/A	Biochemistry or OChem; Genetics; Social Science

PA PROGRAMS

PA School	Ave. GPA & GRE (Verbal, Quantitative, Analy. Writing) Int'l Students: Yes/No	Admission Statistics	Prerequisite Coursework Other Than Gen Bio, Gen Chem, Human Anatomy, Human Physiology, Microbiology, Statistics, Psychology
Alderson-Broaddus University 101 College Hill Drive, Philippi, WV 26416	3.57 (overall) 3.49 (science) GRE: 145 (V) 147 (Q) 3.5 (A) Int'l Student: Yes	Apps Received: 2,000 Interviews Offered: N/A Admission Offered: N/A Class Size: 36 Admitted Rate: 1.8%	Biochemistry or OChem; Upper level Sciences
Marshall University 1542 Spring Valley Drive, Huntington, WV 25704	3.53 (overall) 3.49 (science) GRE: 54% (V) 43% (Q) Int'l Student: Yes	Apps Received: N/A Interviews Offered: N/A Admission Offered: N/A Class Size: 25 Admitted Rate: N/A	Biochemistry or OChem; College Algebra or higher; Medical Terminology
University of Charleston 2300 MacCorkle Avenue SE, Charleston, WV 25304	3.56 (overall) 3.45 (science) GRE: N/A Int'l Student: Yes	Apps Received: N/A Interviews Offered: N/A Admission Offered: N/A Class Size: 30 Admitted Rate: N/A	College Algebra or higher; OChem
West Liberty University 208 University Drive, West Liberty, WV 26074	3.0+ (overall) 3.0+ (science) GRE: N/A Int'l Student: Yes	Apps Received: N/A Interviews Offered: N/A Admission Offered: N/A Class Size: 18 Admitted Rate: N/A	College Algebra or higher; English Composition; Humanities/Social Science
West Virginia University Morgantown, WV 26506	3.86 (overall) 3.81 (science) GRE: N/A Int'l Student: Yes	Apps Received: 420 Interviews Offered: 131 Admission Offered: N/A Class Size: 24 Admitted Rate: 5.7%	Biochemistry or OChem; Medical Terminology

SOUTH

FAULKNER UNIVERSITY

Address: 5345 Atlanta Highway, Montgomery, AL 36109
Website: *https://www.faulkner.edu/graduate/graduate-degrees/physican-assistant-studies-ms-pas/*
Contact: *pjordan@faulkner.edu*
Phone: 334-386-7450

COST OF ATTENDANCE

Tuition and Fees: $25,500
Additional Expenses: $15,660
Total: $41,160

Financial Aid: https://www.faulkner.edu/graduate/tuition-financial-aid-graduate-students/

ADDITIONAL INFORMATION

Interesting tidbit: Faulkner University PA program was granted Accreditation-Provisional in June 2020. The inaugural class of 35 students is to matriculate in Fall 2020. The program expects to enroll 50 students going forward.

Important Updates due to COVID-19: N/A

Were tests required? GRE or MCAT required.

Are tests expected next year? Yes.

What international experiences are available? N/A

What dual degree options exist? N/A

What service-learning opportunities exist? N/A

PANCE First-Time Pass Rate: N/A

SAMFORD UNIVERSITY SCHOOL OF HEALTH PROFESSIONS

Address: 800 Lakeshore Dr., Homewood, AL 35229
Website: *https://www.samford.edu/healthprofessions/master-of-science-in-physician-assistant-studies*
Contact: *avanhook@samford.edu*
Phone: 205-726-2619

COST OF ATTENDANCE

Tuition and Fees: $25,018
Additional Expenses: $14,006
Total: $39,024

Financial Aid: https://www.samford.edu/admission/graduate/financial-aid

ADDITIONAL INFORMATION

Interesting tidbit: As a part of Samford's College of Health Sciences, PA students will learn in an interprofessional setting, studying alongside students in other health care disciplines, like nursing, pharmacy, physical therapy, social work, nutrition, and more.

Important Updates due to COVID-19: For prerequisite courses taken during the spring 2020 semester, pass/fail grading will be accepted.

Were tests required? GRE or MCAT or PA-CAT required.

Are tests expected next year? Yes.

What international experiences are available? N/A

What dual degree options exist? N/A

What service-learning opportunities exist? N/A

PANCE First-Time Pass Rate: N/A

ALABAMA

ARKANSAS

DELAWARE

DISTRICT OF COLUMBIA

FLORIDA

GEORGIA

KENTUCKY

LOUISIANA

MARYLAND

MISSISSIPPI

NORTH CAROLINA

OKLAHOMA

SOUTH CAROLINA

TENNESSEE

TEXAS

VIRGINIA

WEST VIRGINIA

SOUTH

UNIVERSITY OF ALABAMA AT BIRMINGHAM

Address: 1716 9th Avenue South, Birmingham, AL 35233
Website: *http://www.uab.edu/shp/cds/physician-assistant*
Contact: *askcds@uab.edu*
Phone: 205-934-3209

COST OF ATTENDANCE

In-State Tuition and Fees: $27,656
Additional Expenses: N/A
Total: $27,656*

Out-of-State Tuition and Fees: $65,624
Additional Expenses: N/A
Total: $65,624*

*This figure does not include cost of living or other related costs.

Financial Aid: https://www.uab.edu/shp/cds/graduate/financial-aid

ADDITIONAL INFORMATION

Interesting tidbit: The UAB Physician Assistant Studies program is the second oldest PA program in the nation and was established only two years after the birth of the PA profession. The UAB PA program provides intense didactic and clinical experiences in primary care, medicine and surgery.

Important Updates due to COVID-19: N/A

Were tests required? GRE or MCAT required.

Are tests expected next year? Yes.

What international experiences are available? N/A

What dual degree options exist? MSPAS/MPH dual degree program. See https://www.uab.edu/shp/cds/physician-assistant-studies/mspas-mph

What service-learning opportunities exist? N/A

PANCE First-Time Pass Rate: 97% (2020)

UNIVERSITY OF SOUTH ALABAMA

Address: 5721 USA Drive North, Mobile, AL 36688
Website: *https://www.southalabama.edu/colleges/alliedhealth/pa/*
Contact: *pastudies@southalabama.edu*
Phone: 251-445-9334

COST OF ATTENDANCE

In-State Tuition and Fees: $25,575
Additional Expenses: $24,242
Total: $49,817

Out-of-State Tuition and Fees: $59,620
Additional Expenses: $24,242
Total: $83,862

Financial Aid: https://www.southalabama.edu/colleges/
graduateschool/financialassistance.html

Note: For PA specific scholarships, see https://www.southalabama.
edu/colleges/alliedhealth/pa/scholarships.html

ADDITIONAL INFORMATION

Interesting tidbit: Clinical rotations are mostly in Mobile, with
other locations in Pensacola and the Mississippi Gulf Coast.
All rotations within a 75-mile radius (one-way) are considered
commutable. Rural rotations for Primary Care and Pediatrics are
required.

Important Updates due to COVID-19: The program accepts Pass/
Fail or Satisfactory/Unsatisfactory grades for the term of Spring
2020 only. Its customary minimum requirement of 500 hours for
direct patient care has been reduced to 100 hours for the 2021
admissions cycle.

Were tests required? GRE required.

Are tests expected next year? Yes.

What international experiences are available? N/A

What dual degree options exist? N/A

What service-learning opportunities exist? N/A

PANCE First-Time Pass Rate: 93% (2020)

ALABAMA
ARKANSAS
DELAWARE
DISTRICT OF
COLUMBIA
FLORIDA
GEORGIA
KENTUCKY
LOUISIANA
MARYLAND
MISSISSIPPI
NORTH CAROLINA
OKLAHOMA
SOUTH CAROLINA
TENNESSEE
TEXAS
VIRGINIA
WEST VIRGINIA

SOUTH

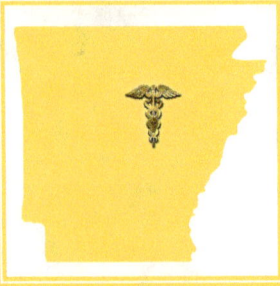

HARDING UNIVERSITY

Address: 915 E. Market Ave., Searcy, AR 72149
Website: *http://www.harding.edu/PAprogram/*
Contact: *paprogram@harding.edu*
Phone: 501-279-5642

COST OF ATTENDANCE

Tuition and Fees: $45,471
Additional Expenses: $33,600
Total: $79,071

Financial Aid: https://www.harding.edu/assets/www/academics/
colleges-departments/allied-health/physician-assistant-program/
pdf/pa%20class%20of%202023%20tuition.pdf

ADDITIONAL INFORMATION

Interesting tidbit: The Physician Assistant Program is an integral part of Harding University, and embraces Christ-centered education and service to others. The HUPA program is dedicated to training future PAs to develop practice-oriented critical thinking and provide primary care reflective of their Christian faith and service to their community and to the world.

Important Updates due to COVID-19: The program will allow CR/NC (or similar) for the Spring 2020 grades. The interview process will be virtual this 2020-2021 CASPA application cycle.

Were tests required? GRE required.

Are tests expected next year? Yes.

What international experiences are available? International mission trip Guatemala through Health Talents International (HTI). See http://healthtalents.org/

What dual degree options exist? N/A

What service-learning opportunities exist? Voluntary mission trip to Guatemala through Health Talents International (HTI). See http://healthtalents.org/

PANCE First-Time Pass Rate: 94% (2020)

UNIVERSITY OF ARKANSAS

Address: 4301 W. Markham St., Little Rock, AR 72205
Website: *http://healthprofessions.uams.edu/programs/ physicianassistant/*
Contact: *paprogram@uams.edu*
Phone: 501-686-7211

COST OF ATTENDANCE

In-State Tuition and Fees: $20,001
Additional Expenses: $10,231*
Total: $30,232*

Out-of-State Tuition and Fees: $31,500
Additional Expenses: $10,231*
Total: $41,731*

*This figure does not include cost of living or other related costs.

Financial Aid: https://healthprofessions.uams.edu/financial-assistance/

ADDITIONAL INFORMATION

Interesting tidbit: The UAMS Physician Assistant Program is a continuous 28 month, full-time professional program that matriculates a cohort of 40 students in mid-May each year. It is divided into a 13-month didactic phase and a 15-month clinical phase.

Important Updates due to COVID-19: The program is acceptable of P/F grading system during the semesters/quarters impacted by COVID-19 as long as the college or university documents "pass/P or credit/CR" and the credit hours on the transcript.

Were tests required? GRE required.

Are tests expected next year? Yes.
What international experiences are available? N/A
What dual degree options exist? N/A
What service-learning opportunities exist? N/A
PANCE First-Time Pass Rate: 82% (2020)

ALABAMA
ARKANSAS
DELAWARE
DISTRICT OF COLUMBIA
FLORIDA
GEORGIA
KENTUCKY
LOUISIANA
MARYLAND
MISSISSIPPI
NORTH CAROLINA
OKLAHOMA
SOUTH CAROLINA
TENNESSEE
TEXAS
VIRGINIA
WEST VIRGINIA

SOUTH

ALABAMA

ARKANSAS

DELAWARE

DISTRICT OF
COLUMBIA

FLORIDA

GEORGIA

KENTUCKY

LOUISIANA

MARYLAND

MISSISSIPPI

NORTH CAROLINA

OKLAHOMA

SOUTH CAROLINA

TENNESSEE

TEXAS

VIRGINIA

WEST VIRGINIA

GEORGE WASHINGTON UNIVERSITY

Address: Rose Hall, 2300 Eye Street NW, Washington, DC 20037
Website: *https://smhs.gwu.edu/physician-assistant/*
Contact: *paadm@gwu.edu*
Phone: 202-994-7644

COST OF ATTENDANCE

Tuition and Fees: $48,615
Additional Expenses: N/A
Total: $48,615*

*This figure does not include cost of living or other related costs.

Financial Aid: https://physicianassistant.smhs.gwu.edu/pa-financial-aid-and-tuition

ADDITIONAL INFORMATION

Interesting tidbit: Housed within the Department of Physician Assistant Studies, the Physician Assistant Program builds strong primary care and public health foundations among its students. GW launched a joint Physician Assistant/Master of Public Health degree (PA/MPH) in 1986 for students interested in the clinical application of preventive medicine taught in an integrated and simultaneous fashion at a time when there were no other PA/MPH programs in the nation.

Important Updates due to COVID-19: The program will accept up to two (2) prerequisite courses completed on a pass/no pass grading scale. This applies only to courses taken in 2020 and spring 2021.

Were tests required? GRE required.

Are tests expected next year? Yes.

What international experiences are available? N/A

What dual degree options exist? Three-year MSHS-PA/MPH dual degree. See https://physicianassistant.smhs.gwu.edu/pamph-curriculum

What service-learning opportunities exist? N/A

PANCE First-Time Pass Rate: 98% (2019)

ADVENTHEALTH UNIVERSITY

Address: 660 Winyah Drive, Orlando, FL 32803
Website: *https://www.adu.edu/academics/ms-physician-assistant*
Contact: *pa.info@ahu.edu*
Phone: 407-303-8778

COST OF ATTENDANCE

Tuition and Fees: $40,500
Additional Expenses: $6,475*
Total: $46,975*

*This figure does not include cost of living or other related costs.

Financial Aid: https://www.ahu.edu/admissions/tuition-aid

ADDITIONAL INFORMATION

Interesting tidbit: The AHU PA program believes that a holistic education goes beyond the textbooks and arithmetic. Core and program-specific classes must prepare graduates for handling real-world situations with a human touch while upholding the highest professional standards. PA students are required to complete a minimum of 40 hours of community service.

Important Updates due to COVID-19: The AHU PA program will allow an applicant up to 8-credit hours of prerequisite pass/ fail grades received during the 2020 calendar year only. Prerequisite pass/ fail credit hours will not be accepted outside of the 2020 calendar year.

Were tests required? CASPer and PA-CAT required.

Are tests expected next year?

What international experiences are available? AHU sponsors two international mission trips annually.

What dual degree options exist? N/A

What service-learning opportunities exist? N/A

PANCE First-Time Pass Rate: 96% (2020)

ALABAMA

ARKANSAS

DELAWARE

DISTRICT OF COLUMBIA

FLORIDA

GEORGIA

KENTUCKY

LOUISIANA

MARYLAND

MISSISSIPPI

NORTH CAROLINA

OKLAHOMA

SOUTH CAROLINA

TENNESSEE

TEXAS

VIRGINIA

WEST VIRGINIA

SOUTH

BARRY UNIVERSITY - MIAMI

Address: 11300 NE 2nd Avenue, Miami Shores, FL 33161
Website: *http://www.barry.edu/physician-assistant/*
Contact: *paadmissions@mail.barry.edu*
Phone: 305-899-3964
Other Locations: St. Petersburg, FL

COST OF ATTENDANCE

Tuition and Fees: $34,395
Additional Expenses: N/A
Total: $34,395*

*This figure does not include cost of living or other related costs.

Financial Aid: https://www.barry.edu/physician-assistant/
financial-aid/

ADDITIONAL INFORMATION

Interesting tidbit: The program seats students at two locations -
76 students at Barry University campus in Miami and 24 students
at St. Petersburg College campus, through a partnership with the
University Partnership Center. Both locations are considered one
program. It conducts multi-campus communication (classes and
meetings) via interactive videoconferencing (IAVC).

Important Updates due to COVID-19: The Barry University
Physician Assistant program may make exceptions to letter-grade
policy if applicants who were required to complete a prerequisite
course as Pass/Fail or Credit/No Credit during spring and summer
2020 courses. Any applicant affected in spring and summer of
2020 must submit a prerequisite course request with proof of their
institution's grade policy at that time. The Admissions Committee
will consider on a case-by-case basis.

Were tests required? GRE required.

Are tests expected next year? Yes.

What international experiences are available? N/A

What dual degree options exist? N/A

What service-learning opportunities exist? N/A

PANCE First-Time Pass Rate: 92% (2020)

BARRY UNIVERSITY - ST. PETERSBURG

Address: 7200 66th Street North, Pinellas Park, FL 33781
Website: *http://www.barry.edu/physician-assistant/*
Contact: *paadmissions@mail.barry.edu*
Phone: 305-899-3964
Other Locations: Miami Shores, FL

COST OF ATTENDANCE

Tuition and Fees: $34,395
Additional Expenses: N/A
Total: $34,395*

*This figure does not include cost of living or other related costs.

Financial Aid: https://www.barry.edu/physician-assistant/
financial-aid/

ADDITIONAL INFORMATION

Interesting tidbit: Applicants can only apply and be considered for one, either Miami campus or St. Petersburg campus. Up to four students per year, who graduated from St. Petersburg College and who are admitted into the program in St. Petersburg, will receive a tuition discount of 20%.

Important Updates due to COVID-19: The Barry University Physician Assistant program may make exceptions to letter-grade policy if applicants who were required to complete a prerequisite course as Pass/Fail or Credit/No Credit during spring and summer 2020 courses. Any applicant affected in spring and summer of 2020 must submit a prerequisite course request with proof of their institution's grade policy at that time. The Admissions Committee will consider on a case-by-case basis.

Were tests required? GRE required.

Are tests expected next year?

What international experiences are available? N/A

What dual degree options exist? N/A

What service-learning opportunities exist? N/A

PANCE First-Time Pass Rate: 92% (2020)

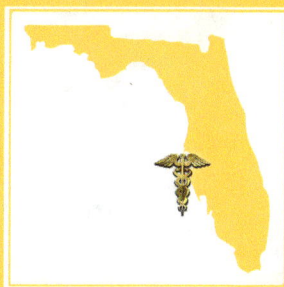

ALABAMA

ARKANSAS

DELAWARE

DISTRICT OF COLUMBIA

FLORIDA

GEORGIA

KENTUCKY

LOUISIANA

MARYLAND

MISSISSIPPI

NORTH CAROLINA

OKLAHOMA

SOUTH CAROLINA

TENNESSEE

TEXAS

VIRGINIA

WEST VIRGINIA

SOUTH

ALABAMA

ARKANSAS

DELAWARE

DISTRICT OF
COLUMBIA

FLORIDA

GEORGIA

KENTUCKY

LOUISIANA

MARYLAND

MISSISSIPPI

NORTH CAROLINA

OKLAHOMA

SOUTH CAROLINA

TENNESSEE

TEXAS

VIRGINIA

WEST VIRGINIA

FLORIDA GULF COAST UNIVERSITY

Address: 10501 FGCU Boulevard South, Fort Myers, FL 33965
Website: *https://www2.fgcu.edu/mariebcollege/HS/MPAS/index.html*
Contact: *paprogram@fgcu.edu*
Phone: 239-745-4477

COST OF ATTENDANCE

In-State Tuition and Fees: $24,455
Additional Expenses: $15,167
Total: $39,622

Out-of-State Tuition and Fees: $61,546
Additional Expenses: $15,167
Total: $76,713

Financial Aid: https://www.fgcu.edu/admissionsandaid/
financialaid/graduate/

ADDITIONAL INFORMATION

Interesting tidbit: During the clinical phase, three selective rotations will be arranged based upon the request of the student and needs of the program. Core clinical rotations are in primary-care medicine, internal medicine, pediatrics, behavioral health, women's health, general surgery and emergency medicine.

Important Updates due to COVID-19: N/A

Were tests required? GRE required.

Are tests expected next year? Yes.

What international experiences are available? N/A

What dual degree options exist? N/A

What service-learning opportunities exist? N/A

PANCE First-Time Pass Rate: 95% (2020)

FLORIDA STATE UNIVERSITY

Address: 1115 W. Call Street Tallahassee, FL 32306
Website: *https://med.fsu.edu/index.cfm?page=pa.home*
Contact: *pasinfo@med.fsu.edu*
Phone: 850-644-1732

COST OF ATTENDANCE

In-State Tuition and Fees: $27,999
Additional Expenses: $13,943*
Total: $41,942*

Out-of-State Tuition and Fees: $38,001
Additional Expenses: $13,943*
Total: $51,944*

*This figure does not include cost of living or other related costs.

Financial Aid: https://med.fsu.edu/financialaid/home

ADDITIONAL INFORMATION

Interesting tidbit: The PA Program at FSU is extremely challenging with a strong emphasis in the biomedical sciences, simulation and procedural skills.

Important Updates due to COVID-19: The FSU SPAP will permit applicants to have up to 2 (two) prerequisite courses outstanding at the time of application for the 2021 cycle which begins May 1, 2021. If accepted, outstanding prerequisites must be completed by the end of the Spring 2022 semester in order to matriculate. Applicants may apply to the FSU PA Program with outstanding Direct Patient Care Hours with the expectation that the hours will be completed by the end of the Spring 2022 semester.

Were tests required? GRE and Altus Suite required.

Are tests expected next year? Yes.

What international experiences are available? N/A

What dual degree options exist? N/A

What service-learning opportunities exist? N/A

PANCE First-Time Pass Rate: 96% (2020)

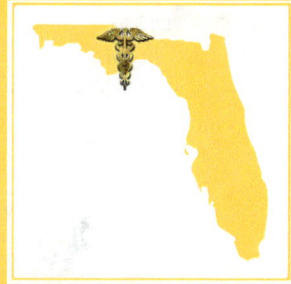

ALABAMA
ARKANSAS
DELAWARE
DISTRICT OF COLUMBIA
FLORIDA
GEORGIA
KENTUCKY
LOUISIANA
MARYLAND
MISSISSIPPI
NORTH CAROLINA
OKLAHOMA
SOUTH CAROLINA
TENNESSEE
TEXAS
VIRGINIA
WEST VIRGINIA

SOUTH

ALABAMA

ARKANSAS

DELAWARE

DISTRICT OF
COLUMBIA

FLORIDA

GEORGIA

KENTUCKY

LOUISIANA

MARYLAND

MISSISSIPPI

NORTH CAROLINA

OKLAHOMA

SOUTH CAROLINA

TENNESSEE

TEXAS

VIRGINIA

WEST VIRGINIA

GANNON UNIVERSITY - RUSKIN

Address: 105 Commercial Center Drive Ruskin, Florida 33573
Website: *https://www.gannon.edu/Academic-Offerings/Health-Professions-and-Sciences/Graduate/Master-of-Physician-Assistant-Science/*
Contact: *graduate@gannon.edu*
Phone: 814-871-7474

COST OF ATTENDANCE

Tuition and Fees: $54,900
Additional Expenses: $6,381*
Total: $61,281*

*This figure does not include cost of living or other related costs.

Financial Aid: https://www.gannon.edu/financial-aid/

ADDITIONAL INFORMATION

Interesting tidbit: The program features a curriculum designed to provide didactic classroom experiences through traditional and online instruction. It offers opportunities for interprofessional interactions with Gannon's other allied health programs.

Important Updates due to COVID-19: N/A

Were tests required? CASPer required.

Are tests expected next year? Yes.

What international experiences are available? N/A

What dual degree options exist? N/A

What service-learning opportunities exist? N/A

PANCE First-Time Pass Rate: N/A (available February 2020 after the inaugural class of 2021 takes the test)

KEISER UNIVERSITY

Address: 1500 NW 49th Street, Fort Lauderdale, FL 33309
Website: *https://www.keiseruniversity.edu/master-of-science-in-physician-assistant/*
Contact: *paprogram@keiseruniversity.edu*
Phone: 954-776-4456

COST OF ATTENDANCE

Tuition and Fees: $42,336
Additional Expenses: $6,589*
Total: $48,925*

*This figure does not include cost of living or other related costs.

Financial Aid: https://www.keiseruniversity.edu/financial-services/

ADDITIONAL INFORMATION

Interesting tidbit: During the 12-month didactic phase, students can expect a challenging curriculum of lectures, activities, practical lab sessions, interpretation of medical literature, case presentations, case-based learning and critical thinking labs. No elective courses are offered in this program, although two clinical rotation electives are required.

Important Updates due to COVID-19: N/A

Were tests required? GRE required.

Are tests expected next year? Yes.

What international experiences are available? N/A

What dual degree options exist? N/A

What service-learning opportunities exist? N/A

PANCE First-Time Pass Rate: 92% (2020)

ALABAMA
ARKANSAS
DELAWARE
DISTRICT OF COLUMBIA
FLORIDA
GEORGIA
KENTUCKY
LOUISIANA
MARYLAND
MISSISSIPPI
NORTH CAROLINA
OKLAHOMA
SOUTH CAROLINA
TENNESSEE
TEXAS
VIRGINIA
WEST VIRGINIA

SOUTH

MIAMI-DADE COLLEGE

Address: 950 NW 20th Street, Suite 2204 Building #2 Miami, FL 33127
Website: *http://www.mdc.edu/physicianassistantas/*
Contact: *mdcpaprogram@mdc.edu*
Phone: 305-237-4124

COST OF ATTENDANCE

In-State Tuition and Fees: $35,787
Additional Expenses: $24,526*
Total: $60,312*

Out-of-State Tuition and Fees: $56,077
Additional Expenses: $24,526*
Total: $80,602*

*This figure does not include cost of living or other related costs.

Financial Aid: https://www.nova.edu/financialaid/apply-for-aid/index.html

ADDITIONAL INFORMATION

Interesting tidbit: Beginning with the matriculating class of 2021, students will be concurrently enrolled in both the MDC PA program and the Masters of Health Science (M.H.Sc.) program through an affiliation with Nova Southeastern University (NSU). PA students who successfully complete all the requirements of the MDC PA Program and the NSU M.H.Sc. program will simultaneously graduate with the professional credential from MDC and the Master's degree from NSU.

Important Updates due to COVID-19: Due to COVID 19 the program will not hold students responsible for completing the minimum of 50 hours shadowing an MD, DO, PA, or ARNP during the 2020 application cycle.

Were tests required? PA-CAT and Admissions Written Essay test required.

Are tests expected next year? Yes.

What international experiences are available? N/A

What dual degree options exist? N/A

What service-learning opportunities exist? N/A

PANCE First-Time Pass Rate: 90% (2020)

NOVA SOUTHEASTERN UNIVERSITY, FORT LAUDERDALE

Address: 3200 S. University Drive, Fort Lauderdale, FL 33328
Website: *http://www.nova.edu/chcs/pa/fortlauderdale/index.html*
Contact: *dickman@nova.edu*
Phone: 954-262-1109
Other Locations: Fort Myers, FL; Jacksonville, FL; Orlando, FL

COST OF ATTENDANCE

Tuition and Fees: $36,923
Additional Expenses: $42,563
Total: $79,486

Financial Aid: https://www.nova.edu/financialaid/index.html?pk_vid=abcaa8234452b22b1625514640333bdb

ADDITIONAL INFORMATION

Interesting tidbit: The NSU PA degree is offered in four locations - Fort Lauderdale, Fort Myers, Jacksonville and Orlando. The programs in Ft. Lauderdale, Ft. Myers, Jacksonville, and Orlando are distinct. The Fort Lauderdale program is located on the main campus of Nova Southeastern University in Davie, Florida.

Important Updates due to COVID-19: N/A

Were tests required? GRE and Writing Assessment required.

Are tests expected next year? Yes.

What international experiences are available? N/A

What dual degree options exist? MMS-PA/MPH dual degree. See https://healthsciences.nova.edu/academics/masters/pa-mph-concurrent/index.html

What service-learning opportunities exist? N/A

PANCE First-Time Pass Rate: 94% (2020)

ALABAMA
ARKANSAS
DELAWARE
DISTRICT OF COLUMBIA
FLORIDA
GEORGIA
KENTUCKY
LOUISIANA
MARYLAND
MISSISSIPPI
NORTH CAROLINA
OKLAHOMA
SOUTH CAROLINA
TENNESSEE
TEXAS
VIRGINIA
WEST VIRGINIA

SOUTH

NOVA SOUTHEASTERN UNIVERSITY, FORT MEYER

Address: 3650 Colonial Court, Fort Myers, FL 33913
Website: *https://healthsciences.nova.edu/pa/fort-myers/index.html*
Contact: *rs1152@nova.edu*
Phone: 239-274-6952

COST OF ATTENDANCE

Tuition and Fees: $36,923
Additional Expenses: $42,563
Total: $79,486

Financial Aid: https://www.nova.edu/financialaid/index.html?pk_vid=abcaa8234452b22b1625514640333bdb

ADDITIONAL INFORMATION

Interesting tidbit: The Physician Assistant (PA) Program Ft. Myers is based upon the successful model of the Fort Lauderdale program. It matriculates 53 students in June each year.

Important Updates due to COVID-19: N/A

Were tests required? GRE required.

Are tests expected next year? Yes.

What international experiences are available? Medical mission trip to Dominican Republic.

What dual degree options exist? MMS-PA/MPH dual degree. See https://healthsciences.nova.edu/academics/masters/pa-mph-concurrent/index.html

What service-learning opportunities exist? Medical mission trip to Dominican Republic.

PANCE First-Time Pass Rate: 93% (2020)

NOVA SOUTHEASTERN UNIVERSITY, JACKSONVILLE

Address: 6675 Corporate Center Parkway, Suite 115, Jacksonville, FL 32216
Website: *https://healthsciences.nova.edu/pa/jacksonville/index.html*
Contact: *kandee.griffith@nova.edu*
Phone: 904-245-8913

COST OF ATTENDANCE

Tuition and Fees: $36,923
Additional Expenses: $42,563
Total: $79,486

Financial Aid: https://www.nova.edu/financialaid/index.html?pk_vid=abcaa8234452b22b1625514640333bdb

ADDITIONAL INFORMATION

Interesting tidbit: Being a part of encompassing College of Health Care Sciences, the PA program stands not as a separate program but as a collaborative and collegial health education entity.

Important Updates due to COVID-19: N/A

Were tests required? GRE required.

Are tests expected next year? Yes.

What international experiences are available? Medical mission trips to Dominican Republic and Panama.

What dual degree options exist? MMS-PA/MPH dual degree. See https://healthsciences.nova.edu/academics/masters/pa-mph-concurrent/index.html

What service-learning opportunities exist? Medical mission trips to Dominican Republic and Panama.

PANCE First-Time Pass Rate: 93% (2020)

Other: Preferred Admission Program with Florida State College of Jacksonville. See https://healthsciences.nova.edu/pa/jacksonville/dual.html

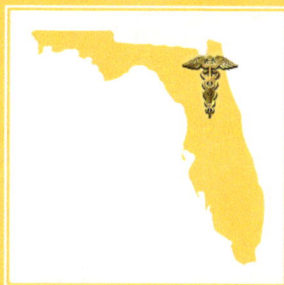

ALABAMA
ARKANSAS
DELAWARE
DISTRICT OF COLUMBIA
FLORIDA
GEORGIA
KENTUCKY
LOUISIANA
MARYLAND
MISSISSIPPI
NORTH CAROLINA
OKLAHOMA
SOUTH CAROLINA
TENNESSEE
TEXAS
VIRGINIA
WEST VIRGINIA

SOUTH

ALABAMA

ARKANSAS

DELAWARE

DISTRICT OF
COLUMBIA

FLORIDA

GEORGIA

KENTUCKY

LOUISIANA

MARYLAND

MISSISSIPPI

NORTH CAROLINA

OKLAHOMA

SOUTH CAROLINA

TENNESSEE

TEXAS

VIRGINIA

WEST VIRGINIA

NOVA SOUTHEASTERN UNIVERSITY, ORLANDO

Address: 4850 Millenia Boulevard, Orlando, FL 32839
Website: *https://healthsciences.nova.edu/pa/orlando/index.html*
Contact: *sarah.kimble@nova.edu*
Phone: 407-264-5153

COST OF ATTENDANCE

Tuition and Fees: $36,923
Additional Expenses: $42,563
Total: $79,486

Financial Aid: https://www.nova.edu/financialaid/index.html?pk_vid=abcaa8234452b22b1625514640333bdb

ADDITIONAL INFORMATION

Interesting tidbit: NSU trains health practitioners in a multidisciplinary setting, with an emphasis on medically underserved areas. NSU PA students experience life-changing service working domestically and internationally with people in need.

Important Updates due to COVID-19: N/A

Were tests required? GRE required.

Are tests expected next year? Yes.

What international experiences are available? Medical mission trips to Guatemala and Puerto Rico.

What dual degree options exist? MMS-PA/MPH dual degree. See https://healthsciences.nova.edu/academics/masters/pa-mph-concurrent/index.html

What service-learning opportunities exist? Medical mission trips to Guatemala and Puerto Rico; Sports physicals for the underserved; Medical Tent for DisneyRun Marathons.

PANCE First-Time Pass Rate: 100% (2020)

SOUTH UNIVERSITY, TAMPA

Address: 4401 N. Himes Avenue, Tampa, FL 33614
Website: http://www.southuniversity.edu/tampa/areas-of-study/
physician-assistant/physician-assistant-master-of-science-ms
Contact: paprogram@southuniversity.edu
Phone: 813-393-3720

COST OF ATTENDANCE

Tuition and Fees: $40,000
Additional Expenses: $8,410*
Total: $48,410*

*This figure does not include cost of living or other related costs.

Financial Aid: https://www.southuniversity.edu/paying-for-college

ADDITIONAL INFORMATION

Interesting tidbit: The South University, Tampa Master of Science in Physician Assistant program is committed to recruiting highly qualified, diverse student cohorts that will foster success in the program.

Important Updates due to COVID-19: The South University PA programs will accept "Satisfactory/Unsatisfactory" or "Pass/Fail" grades for courses affected by the COVID-19 pandemic as submitted through CASPA.

Were tests required? GRE required.

Are tests expected next year? Yes.

What international experiences are available? N/A

What dual degree options exist? N/A

What service-learning opportunities exist? N/A

PANCE First-Time Pass Rate: 98% (2021)

ALABAMA
ARKANSAS
DELAWARE
DISTRICT OF COLUMBIA
FLORIDA
GEORGIA
KENTUCKY
LOUISIANA
MARYLAND
MISSISSIPPI
NORTH CAROLINA
OKLAHOMA
SOUTH CAROLINA
TENNESSEE
TEXAS
VIRGINIA
WEST VIRGINIA

SOUTH

SOUTH UNIVERSITY, WEST PALM BEACH

Address: 9801 Belvedere Road, Royal Palm Beach, FL 33411
Website: *https://www.southuniversity.edu/west-palm-beach/physician-assistant-ms*
Contact: *paprogram@southuniversity.edu*
Phone: 561-273-6500

COST OF ATTENDANCE

Tuition and Fees: $40,000
Additional Expenses: $8,410*
Total: $48,410*

*This figure does not include cost of living or other related costs.

Financial Aid: https://www.southuniversity.edu/paying-for-college

ADDITIONAL INFORMATION

Interesting tidbit: The South University, West Palm Beach PA students rotate in busy clinics, private physician offices, teaching hospitals, large institutions, and military hospitals and clinics. Rotations exist both in small towns and metropolitan cities. Students are offered a wide variety of experiences and locations for their clinical rotations that are designed to round out the application of knowledge and skills to actual patient care.

Important Updates due to COVID-19: The South University PA programs will accept "Satisfactory/Unsatisfactory" or "Pass/Fail" grades for courses affected by the COVID-19 pandemic as submitted through CASPA.

Were tests required? GRE required.

Are tests expected next year? Yes.

What international experiences are available? N/A

What dual degree options exist? N/A

What service-learning opportunities exist? N/A

PANCE First-Time Pass Rate: N/A (will be available once the first cohort completes the exam in 2023)

UNIVERSITY OF FLORIDA

Address: University of Florida, Gainesville, FL 32610
Website: *https://pap.med.ufl.edu/*
Contact: *admissions@pap.ufl.edu*
Phone: 352-294-8150

COST OF ATTENDANCE

In-State Tuition and Fees: $27,940
Additional Expenses: $25,565
Total: $53,505

Out-of-State Tuition and Fees: $61,277
Additional Expenses: $25,565
Total: $86,842

Financial Aid: https://pa.med.ufl.edu/university-of-florida-pa-program/tuition-and-financial-aid/

ADDITIONAL INFORMATION

Interesting tidbit: During the clinical year of the curriculum, each student must complete at least one rural rotation. The capstone project, a requirement, will begin in the academic year, culminating in a manuscript and presentation in the clinical year.

Important Updates due to COVID-19: N/A

Were tests required? GRE and CASPer required.

Are tests expected next year? Yes.

What international experiences are available? N/A

What dual degree options exist? N/A

What service-learning opportunities exist? N/A

PANCE First-Time Pass Rate: 98% (2020)

ALABAMA
ARKANSAS
DELAWARE
DISTRICT OF COLUMBIA
FLORIDA
GEORGIA
KENTUCKY
LOUISIANA
MARYLAND
MISSISSIPPI
NORTH CAROLINA
OKLAHOMA
SOUTH CAROLINA
TENNESSEE
TEXAS
VIRGINIA
WEST VIRGINIA

SOUTH

UNIVERSITY OF SOUTH FLORIDA

Address: 12901 Bruce. B Down Boulevard MDC5, Tampa, Florida 33612
Website: *https://health.usf.edu/medicine/pa/*
Contact: *paprogram@usf.edu*
Phone: 813-974-8926

COST OF ATTENDANCE

In-State Tuition and Fees: $34,083
Additional Expenses: $28,582
Total: $62,665

Out-of-State Tuition and Fees: $64,533
Additional Expenses: $28,582
Total: $93,115

Financial Aid: https://health.usf.edu/well/financial-aid/pa-program

ADDITIONAL INFORMATION

Interesting tidbit: During the clinical phase, students will engage in approximately 2300 hours of supervised clinical practice experiences. Students will follow the schedule of their clerkship preceptor. This schedule may require a 40-60 hour work week that may include evenings and weekends.

Important Updates due to COVID-19: N/A

Were tests required? GRE required.

Are tests expected next year? Yes.

What international experiences are available? N/A

What dual degree options exist? N/A

What service-learning opportunities exist? N/A

PANCE First-Time Pass Rate: 98%b (2021)

UNIVERSITY OF TAMPA

Address: 401 W Kennedy Blvd, Tampa, FL 33606
Website: *https://www.ut.edu/graduate-degrees/physician-assistant-medicine-program*
Contact: *pam@ut.edu*
Phone: 813-257-3071

COST OF ATTENDANCE

Tuition and Fees: $43,911
Additional Expenses: $21,881
Total: $65,792

Financial Aid: https://www.ut.edu/admissions/financial-aid/financial-aid-for-graduates

ADDITIONAL INFORMATION

Interesting tidbit: The University of Tampa's graduate-level physician assistant program. It leads to a Master of Physician Assistant Medicine (MPAM) degree upon successful completion of a 27-month curriculum. The inaugural cohort will graduate in December of 2021.

Important Updates due to COVID-19: N/A

Were tests required? PA-CAT required.

Are tests expected next year? Yes.

What international experiences are available? N/A

What dual degree options exist? N/A

What service-learning opportunities exist? N/A

PANCE First-Time Pass Rate: N/A (UT's first cohort graduates in December 2021 and their PANCE performance data will be published at that time)

ALABAMA
ARKANSAS
DELAWARE
DISTRICT OF COLUMBIA
FLORIDA
GEORGIA
KENTUCKY
LOUISIANA
MARYLAND
MISSISSIPPI
NORTH CAROLINA
OKLAHOMA
SOUTH CAROLINA
TENNESSEE
TEXAS
VIRGINIA
WEST VIRGINIA

SOUTH

AUGUSTA UNIVERSITY

Address: 987 St. Sebastian Way, Augusta, GA 30912
Website: *http://www.augusta.edu/alliedhealth/pa/*
Contact: *paprogram@augusta.edu*
Phone: 706-721-3247

COST OF ATTENDANCE

In-State Tuition and Fees: $20,925
Additional Expenses: $8,920*
Total: $29,845*

Out-of-State Tuition and Fees: $41,850
Additional Expenses: $8,920*
Total: $50,770*

Financial Aid: https://www.augusta.edu/finaid/graduatehealthscience.php

ADDITIONAL INFORMATION

Interesting tidbit: Augusta University has a long tradition of PA education. Augusta University's PA program received its accreditation in 1973, making it one of the oldest programs in the South. It is committed to providing affordable graduate PA education compared to other comparable programs within Georgia and across the southeast.

Important Updates due to COVID-19: No modifications will be made but applicants should explain in their application which admissions criteria they have yet to fulfill as it relates to the pandemic and any plans to complete those criteria prior to May 2022.

Were tests required? GRE and CASPer required.

Are tests expected next year? Yes.

What international experiences are available? N/A

What dual degree options exist? N/A

What service-learning opportunities exist? Monthly Christ Church Health Promotion and Disease Prevention Clinic. See https://sites.google.com/site/christchurchhealthclinic/home

PANCE First-Time Pass Rate: 98% (2020)

BRENAU UNIVERSITY

Address: 500 Washington St. SE, Gainesville, GA 30501
Website: *https://www.brenau.edu/healthsciences/physician-assistant-studies/*
Contact: *pastudies@brenau.edu*
Phone: 770-534-6299

COST OF ATTENDANCE

Tuition and Fees: $40,500
Additional Expenses: $26,532
Total: $67,032

Financial Aid: https://www.brenau.edu/admissions/financialaid/

ADDITIONAL INFORMATION

Interesting tidbit: In September 2020, the ARC-PA granted Accreditation-Provisional status to the Brenau University Department of Physician Assistant Studies Program. The program matriculated 33 students in its augural class of 2023.

Important Updates due to COVID-19: Contact the PA program with details so the admissions team can review the application and concerns on an individual, case-by-case basis.

Were tests required? GRE required.

Are tests expected next year? Yes.

What international experiences are available? N/A

What dual degree options exist? N/A

What service-learning opportunities exist? N/A

PANCE First-Time Pass Rate: N/A (available upon graduation of inaugural class of 2023)

ALABAMA

ARKANSAS

DELAWARE

DISTRICT OF COLUMBIA

FLORIDA

GEORGIA

KENTUCKY

LOUISIANA

MARYLAND

MISSISSIPPI

NORTH CAROLINA

OKLAHOMA

SOUTH CAROLINA

TENNESSEE

TEXAS

VIRGINIA

WEST VIRGINIA

SOUTH

ALABAMA

ARKANSAS

DELAWARE

DISTRICT OF COLUMBIA

FLORIDA

GEORGIA

KENTUCKY

LOUISIANA

MARYLAND

MISSISSIPPI

NORTH CAROLINA

OKLAHOMA

SOUTH CAROLINA

TENNESSEE

TEXAS

VIRGINIA

WEST VIRGINIA

EMORY UNIVERSITY

Address: 1462 Clifton Rd NE, Suite 280,, Atlanta, GA 30322
Website: *http://www.emorypa.org/*
Contact: *pa_admissions@emory.edu*
Phone: 404-727-7857

COST OF ATTENDANCE

Tuition and Fees: $45,201
Additional Expenses: $12,120*
Total: $57,321*

*This figure does not include cost of living or other related costs.

Financial Aid: https://med.emory.edu/departments/family-preventive/divisions-programs/physician-assistant-program/admissions/financial-matters.html

ADDITIONAL INFORMATION

Interesting tidbit: All students have service opportunities to work with cultural minorities. Grady Memorial Hospital serves a multicultural population with patients from African nations, the Middle East, South and Central America, and Eastern Europe. This diversity offers the opportunity to work with onsite interpreters or use a language line for ~50 languages. Most students complete at least one rotation at a medically underserved site.

Important Updates due to COVID-19: N/A

Were tests required? GRE required.

Are tests expected next year? Yes.

What international experiences are available? International elective rotations through Global Health Institute of Emory University.

What dual degree options exist? MMSc-PA/MPH dual degree. See https://med.emory.edu/departments/family-preventive/divisions-programs/physician-assistant-program/education/mmsc-pa-mph.html

What service-learning opportunities exist? Annual Farmworker Project; PA-student directed clinic at the Good Samaritan Health Center; Portal de Salud. For details, see https://med.emory.edu/departments/family-preventive/divisions-programs/physician-assistant-program/about-us/program-goal-3.html

PANCE First-Time Pass Rate: 98% (2020)

MERCER UNIVERSITY

Address: 3001 Mercer University Drive, McAfee Building, Atlanta, GA 30341
Website: *http://chp.mercer.edu/academics-departments/physician-assistant-studies/*
Contact: *paprogram@mercer.edu*
Phone: 678-547-6391

COST OF ATTENDANCE

Tuition and Fees: $46,414
Additional Expenses: $41,340
Total: $87,754

Financial Aid: https://financialaid.mercer.edu/

ADDITIONAL INFORMATION

Interesting tidbit: Mercer PA program prides itself on its innovative didactic and clinical curriculum that emphasizes evidence-based medicine, informatics, critical decision-making, interdisciplinary teamwork, and the appreciation of ethical values and human diversity.

Important Updates due to COVID-19: The program will accept science courses/labs that have had to go online for the Spring 2020, Summer 2020, and Fall 2020 semesters.

Were tests required? GRE required.

Are tests expected next year? Yes.

What international experiences are available? Global Health Outreach

What dual degree options exist? MMSc-PA/MPH dual degree. See http://chp.mercer.edu/academics-departments/physician-assistant-studies/pa-program/mmsc-mph/

What service-learning opportunities exist? South Georgia Migrant Farmworker Health Project; Portal de Salud Hispanic Health Fair; Clarkston Refugee Clinic.

PANCE First-Time Pass Rate: 97% (2020)

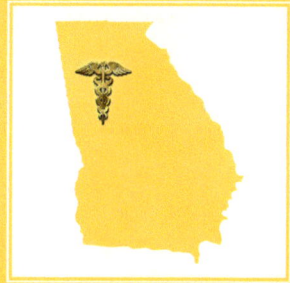

ALABAMA
ARKANSAS
DELAWARE
DISTRICT OF COLUMBIA
FLORIDA
GEORGIA
KENTUCKY
LOUISIANA
MARYLAND
MISSISSIPPI
NORTH CAROLINA
OKLAHOMA
SOUTH CAROLINA
TENNESSEE
TEXAS
VIRGINIA
WEST VIRGINIA

SOUTH

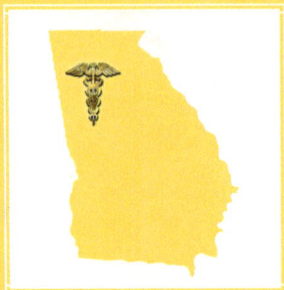

MOREHOUSE SCHOOL OF MEDICINE

Address: 720 Westview Dr., Atlanta, GA 30310
Website: *http://www.msm.edu//physicianassistantprogram/index.php*
Contact: pas@msm.edu
Phone: 404-756-1254

COST OF ATTENDANCE

Tuition and Fees: $45,006
Additional Expenses: $27,379
Total: $72,385

Financial Aid: Refer to "Financial Aid" section on https://www.msm.edu/physicianassistantprogram/tuition.php

Note: There are no scholarships available for MSM-PA program students or applicants.

ADDITIONAL INFORMATION

Interesting tidbit: The MSM PA Program exists to equip aspiring learners from underrepresented backgrounds to become competent and compassionate healthcare providers. These future leaders will be trained to respond to the increasing healthcare demands across Georgia and specifically in underserved and underprivileged regions.

Important Updates due to COVID-19: N/A

Were tests required? GRE or PA-CAT or MCAT required.

Are tests expected next year? Yes.

What international experiences are available? N/A

What dual degree options exist? N/A

What service-learning opportunities exist? N/A

PANCE First-Time Pass Rate: N/A (inaugural class of 2021 is has not been updated)

PCOM - GEORGIA

Address: 625 Old Peachtree Road NW, Suwanee, GA 30024
Website: *https://www.pcom.edu/academics/programs-and-degrees/physician-assistant-studies/georgia.html*
Contact: *gaadmissions@pcom.edu*
Phone: 678-225-7500

Other Locations: Philadelphia, PA

COST OF ATTENDANCE

Tuition and Fees: $51,312
Additional Expenses: $33,178
Total: $84,490

Financial Aid: https://www.pcom.edu/about/departments/financial-aid/

ADDITIONAL INFORMATION

Interesting tidbit: Students may enroll at either Suwanee, GA location or the main campus in Philadelphia, PA.

Important Updates due to COVID-19: N/A

Were tests required? No.

Are tests expected next year? No.

What international experiences are available? N/A

What dual degree options exist? N/A

What service-learning opportunities exist? N/A

PANCE First-Time Pass Rate: 96% (2020)

ALABAMA

ARKANSAS

DELAWARE

DISTRICT OF COLUMBIA

FLORIDA

GEORGIA

KENTUCKY

LOUISIANA

MARYLAND

MISSISSIPPI

NORTH CAROLINA

OKLAHOMA

SOUTH CAROLINA

TENNESSEE

TEXAS

VIRGINIA

WEST VIRGINIA

SOUTH

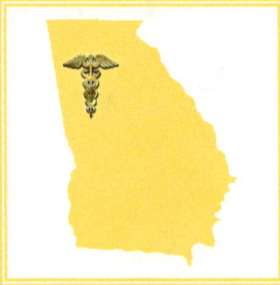

ALABAMA

ARKANSAS

DELAWARE

DISTRICT OF
COLUMBIA

FLORIDA

GEORGIA

KENTUCKY

LOUISIANA

MARYLAND

MISSISSIPPI

NORTH CAROLINA

OKLAHOMA

SOUTH CAROLINA

TENNESSEE

TEXAS

VIRGINIA

WEST VIRGINIA

SOUTH COLLEGE - ATLANTA

Address: 2600 Century Parkway NE, Atlanta, GA 30345
Website: *https://www.south.edu/programs/master-health-science-physician-assistant-studies/atlanta/*
Contact: *dboromei@south.edu*
Phone: 470-322-1200

Other Locations: Knoxville, TN; Nashville, TN

COST OF ATTENDANCE

Tuition and Fees: $45,000
Additional Expenses: $4,274*
Total: $49,274*

*This figure does not include cost of living or other related costs.

Financial Aid: See "Physician Assistant Financial Aid Resources" on https://www.south.edu/programs/master-health-science-physician-assistant-studies/tuition-and-fees/

ADDITIONAL INFORMATION

Interesting tidbit: The South College Masters of Health Science Physician Assistant Program is a single program with two campuses - Knoxville (TN) and Nashville (TN), and an extension campus in Atlanta (GA). The program promotes the importance of health maintenance, health education, and the prevention of disease.

Important Updates due to COVID-19: N/A

Were tests required? GRE required.

Are tests expected next year? Yes.

What international experiences are available? N/A

What dual degree options exist? N/A

What service-learning opportunities exist? N/A

PANCE First-Time Pass Rate: N/A (the first PANCE pass rates results for the Atlanta program will be late 2021/early 2022)

SOUTH UNIVERSITY, SAVANNAH

Address: 709 Mall Boulevard, Savannah, GA 31406
Website: *https://www.southuniversity.edu/savannah/areas-of-study/physician-assistant/physician-assistant-master-of-science-ms*
Contact: *paprogram@southuniversity.edu*
Phone: 912-201-8171

COST OF ATTENDANCE

Tuition and Fees: $40,000
Additional Expenses: $8,410*
Total: $48,410*

*This figure does not include cost of living or other related costs.

Financial Aid: https://www.southuniversity.edu/paying-for-college

ADDITIONAL INFORMATION

Interesting tidbit: The South University PA program is offered on four campuses - Richmond (VA), Savannah (GA), Tampa (FL), and West Palm Beach (FL).

Important Updates due to COVID-19: The South University PA programs will accept "Satisfactory/Unsatisfactory" or "Pass/Fail" grades for courses affected by the COVID-19 pandemic as submitted through CASPA.

Were tests required? GRE required.

Are tests expected next year? Yes.

What international experiences are available? N/A

What dual degree options exist? N/A

What service-learning opportunities exist? N/A

PANCE First-Time Pass Rate: 91% (2020)

ALABAMA
ARKANSAS
DELAWARE
DISTRICT OF COLUMBIA
FLORIDA
GEORGIA
KENTUCKY
LOUISIANA
MARYLAND
MISSISSIPPI
NORTH CAROLINA
OKLAHOMA
SOUTH CAROLINA
TENNESSEE
TEXAS
VIRGINIA
WEST VIRGINIA

SOUTH

ALABAMA

ARKANSAS

DELAWARE

DISTRICT OF
COLUMBIA

FLORIDA

GEORGIA

KENTUCKY

LOUISIANA

MARYLAND

MISSISSIPPI

NORTH CAROLINA

OKLAHOMA

SOUTH CAROLINA

TENNESSEE

TEXAS

VIRGINIA

WEST VIRGINIA

SULLIVAN UNIVERSITY

Address: 2100 Gardiner Lane, Louisville, KY 40205
Website: *https://www.sullivan.edu/programs/master-of-science-in-physician-assistant*
Contact: *paprogram@sullivan.edu*
Phone: 502-413-8939

COST OF ATTENDANCE

Tuition and Fees: $52,348
Additional Expenses: $20,881
Total: $73,229

Financial Aid: https://www.sullivan.edu/college-of-pharmacy-and-health-sciences/tuition-financial-aid

ADDITIONAL INFORMATION

Interesting tidbit: Academic and professional growth is monitored closely throughout the program by the program director, the medical director, directors of Didactic and Clinical Education, and the academic, clinical, and course coordinators. Each student is assigned a faculty advisor for assistance and counseling regarding academic progress.

Important Updates due to COVID-19: N/A

Were tests required? No.

Are tests expected next year? No.

What international experiences are available? N/A

What dual degree options exist? N/A

What service-learning opportunities exist? N/A

PANCE First-Time Pass Rate: 98% (2020)

UNIVERSITY OF KENTUCKY - LEXINGTON

Address: 900 South Limestone Street, Charles T. Wethington, Jr. Building, Lexington KY 40536
Website: *https://www.uky.edu/chs/physician-assistant-studies/campuses/lexington*
Contact: *julia.berry@uky.edu*
Phone: 859-257-5001

COST OF ATTENDANCE

In-State Tuition and Fees: $20,926
Additional Expenses: $4,573*
Total: $25,499*

Out-of-State Tuition and Fees: $49,262
Additional Expenses: $4,573*
Total: $53,835*

*This figure does not include cost of living or other related costs.

Financial Aid: https://www.uky.edu/chs/physician-assistant-studies/admissions/financial-aid

ADDITIONAL INFORMATION

Interesting tidbit: UKY College of Health Sciences houses the longest-running Physician Assistant program in Kentucky. The Lexington campus is the program's main campus. The UKPAS Lexington campus classes and labs are housed in the Charles T. Wethington (CTW) Building, which has central access to the UK Chandler Hospital, Kentucky Clinic, College of Medicine, College of Dentistry, College of Nursing and College of Pharmacy.

Important Updates due to COVID-19: The UKPA Program accepted Pass/Fail grading for prerequisite coursework for the Spring & Summer 2020 semesters only. The UKPA program also extended prerequisite course completion for the 2020-2021 Admissions Cycle. It allowed up to two outstanding prerequisite courses to be completed by December 2020. For the 2021-2022 Admissions Cycle, applicants may apply with two outstanding prerequisite courses, as long as they are completed by August 2021.

Were tests required? GRE required.

Are tests expected next year? Yes.

What international experiences are available? International rotations (availability is dependent upon CDC travel guidelines, COVID-19 considerations/restrictions, and Department discretion.)

What dual degree options exist? N/A

What service-learning opportunities exist? N/A

PANCE First-Time Pass Rate: 85% (2020)

ALABAMA
ARKANSAS
DELAWARE
DISTRICT OF COLUMBIA
FLORIDA
GEORGIA
KENTUCKY
LOUISIANA
MARYLAND
MISSISSIPPI
NORTH CAROLINA
OKLAHOMA
SOUTH CAROLINA
TENNESSEE
TEXAS
VIRGINIA
WEST VIRGINIA

SOUTH

ALABAMA

ARKANSAS

DELAWARE

DISTRICT OF
COLUMBIA

FLORIDA

GEORGIA

KENTUCKY

LOUISIANA

MARYLAND

MISSISSIPPI

NORTH CAROLINA

OKLAHOMA

SOUTH CAROLINA

TENNESSEE

TEXAS

VIRGINIA

WEST VIRGINIA

UNIVERSITY OF KENTUCKY - MOREHEAD

Address: 316 W 2nd Street, Center for Health Education & Research, Morehead, KY 40351
Website: *https://www.uky.edu/chs/physician-assistant-studies/campuses/morehead*
Contact: *julia.berry@uky.edu*
Phone: 606-783-2558

COST OF ATTENDANCE

In-State Tuition and Fees: $20,926
Additional Expenses: $4,029*
Total: $24,955*

Out-of-State Tuition and Fees: $49,262
Additional Expenses: $4,029*
Total: $53,291*

*This figure does not include cost of living or other related costs.

Financial Aid: https://www.uky.edu/chs/physician-assistant-studies/admissions/financial-aid

ADDITIONAL INFORMATION

Interesting tidbit: In addition to the Lexington campus, the program has a campus located in Morehead, Kentucky for rural training. The Morehead Campus is a satellite campus and many classes are observed using the ITV telecommunication system on campus. Applicants may apply to only one campus and are not allowed to apply to both.

Important Updates due to COVID-19: The UKPA Program accepted Pass/Fail grading for prerequisite coursework for the Spring & Summer 2020 semesters only. The UKPA program also extended prerequisite course completion for the 2020-2021 Admissions Cycle. It allowed up to two outstanding prerequisite courses to be completed by December 2020. For the 2021-2022 Admissions Cycle, applicants may apply with two outstanding prerequisite courses, as long as they are completed by August 2021.

Were tests required? GRE required.

Are tests expected next year? Yes.

What international experiences are available? International rotations (availability is dependent upon CDC travel guidelines, COVID-19 considerations/restrictions, and Department discretion.)

What dual degree options exist? N/A

What service-learning opportunities exist? N/A

PANCE First-Time Pass Rate: 85% (2020)

UNIVERSITY OF THE CUMBERLANDS

Address: 6178 College Station Drive, Williamsburg, KY 40769
Website: *http://gradweb.ucumberlands.edu/academics/graduate/programs/master-science-physician-assistant-studies*
Contact: *pa@ucumberlands.edu*
Phone: 606-539-4616

COST OF ATTENDANCE

Tuition and Fees: $34,950
Additional Expenses: N/A
Total: $34,950*

*This figure does not include cost of living or other related costs.

Financial Aid: https://www.ucumberlands.edu/admissions/graduate/financial-aid

ADDITIONAL INFORMATION

Interesting tidbit: University of the Cumberlands offers the Master of Science in Physician Assistant Studies program through both its Williamsburg and Northern Kentucky Campuses. International students seeking to study in the physician assistant program under an F1 student visa can only apply to study at Williamsburg campus.

Important Updates due to COVID-19: For 2021-2022 application only, candidates who do not have any PA shadowing hours will need to submit a 500 word essay following this prompt: "For this 500 word max essay, discuss why you wish to be a PA.

Were tests required? PA-CAT required.

Are tests expected next year? Yes.

What international experiences are available? N/A

What dual degree options exist? N/A

What service-learning opportunities exist? N/A

PANCE First-Time Pass Rate: 93% (2020)

ALABAMA
ARKANSAS
DELAWARE
DISTRICT OF COLUMBIA
FLORIDA
GEORGIA
KENTUCKY
LOUISIANA
MARYLAND
MISSISSIPPI
NORTH CAROLINA
OKLAHOMA
SOUTH CAROLINA
TENNESSEE
TEXAS
VIRGINIA
WEST VIRGINIA

SOUTH

UNIVERSITY OF THE CUMBERLANDS, NORTHERN KENTUCKY

Address: 410 Meijer Drive, Florence, KY 41042
Website: *http://gradweb.ucumberlands.edu/academics/graduate/programs/master-science-physician-assistant-studies*
Contact: *pa@ucumberlands.edu*
Phone: 606-539-4398

COST OF ATTENDANCE

Tuition and Fees: $34,950
Additional Expenses: N/A
Total: $34,950*

*This figure does not include cost of living or other related costs.

Financial Aid: https://www.ucumberlands.edu/admissions/graduate/financial-aid

ADDITIONAL INFORMATION

Interesting tidbit: The Northern Kentucky Campus began matriculating 30 students each year in its MSPAS program with its inaugural class of 2022. Applicants to the Northern Kentucky Campus are required to take the GRE while applicants to the Williamsburg Campus are required to take the PA-CAT.

Important Updates due to COVID-19: Contact PA admissions if applicants have any questions related to direct patient contact hours or PA shadowing hours during the COVID-19 pandemic.

Were tests required? GRE required.

Are tests expected next year? Yes.

What international experiences are available? N/A

What dual degree options exist? N/A

What service-learning opportunities exist? N/A

PANCE First-Time Pass Rate: N/A (will be available when the first cohort graduates in 2022)

ALABAMA

ARKANSAS

DELAWARE

DISTRICT OF COLUMBIA

FLORIDA

GEORGIA

KENTUCKY

LOUISIANA

MARYLAND

MISSISSIPPI

NORTH CAROLINA

OKLAHOMA

SOUTH CAROLINA

TENNESSEE

TEXAS

VIRGINIA

WEST VIRGINIA

FRANCISCAN MISSIONARIES OF OUR LADY UNIVERSITY

Address: 5414 Brittany Drive, Baton Rouge, LA 70808
Website: *https://www.franu.edu/academics/academic-programs/physician-assistant-studies*
Contact: *pa@franu.edu*
Phone: 225-490-1650

COST OF ATTENDANCE

Tuition and Fees: $40,300
Additional Expenses: $4,988*
Total: $45,288*

*This figure does not include cost of living or other related costs.

Financial Aid: https://franu.edu/offices-services/office-of-financial-aid

ADDITIONAL INFORMATION

Interesting tidbit: The didactic classes may be taught online, face-to-face, or in a blended format. Two clinical rotations are offered as "elective" rotations. Students rank their top two choices based on clinical site/preceptor availability. Electives are then assigned via lottery style.

Important Updates due to COVID-19: Virtual interviews.

Were tests required? GRE and CASPer required.

Are tests expected next year? Yes.

What international experiences are available? International elective rotations.

What dual degree options exist? N/A

What service-learning opportunities exist? N/A

PANCE First-Time Pass Rate: 100% (2021)

Other: 3+2 Accelerated Pathway to Physician Assistant Studies. See https://franu.edu/academics/academic-programs/biology/accelerated-3-2-pathway-to-physician-assistant-studies

ALABAMA
ARKANSAS
DELAWARE
DISTRICT OF COLUMBIA
FLORIDA
GEORGIA
KENTUCKY
LOUISIANA
MARYLAND
MISSISSIPPI
NORTH CAROLINA
OKLAHOMA
SOUTH CAROLINA
TENNESSEE
TEXAS
VIRGINIA
WEST VIRGINIA

SOUTH

ALABAMA

ARKANSAS

DELAWARE

DISTRICT OF
COLUMBIA

FLORIDA

GEORGIA

KENTUCKY

LOUISIANA

MARYLAND

MISSISSIPPI

NORTH CAROLINA

OKLAHOMA

SOUTH CAROLINA

TENNESSEE

TEXAS

VIRGINIA

WEST VIRGINIA

LOUISIANA STATE UNIVERSITY HEALTH SCIENCES CENTER SHREVEPORT

Address: 1501 Kings Highway, Shreveport, LA 71103
Website: *https://lsuhscshreveportedu.finalsite.com/departments/ allied-health-professions-departments/physician-assistant*
Contact: *paprogramshreveport@lsuhs.edu*
Phone: 318-813-2920

COST OF ATTENDANCE

In-State Tuition and Fees: $30,816
Additional Expenses: $45,328
Total: $76,144

Out-of-State Tuition and Fees: $43,122
Additional Expenses: $55,068
Total: $98,190

Financial Aid: https://www.lsuhs.edu/admissions/student-financial-services/student-financial-aid/graduate-aid

ADDITIONAL INFORMATION

Interesting tidbit: The LSU Health Shreveport Physician Assistant Program is 27 months long and begins during the summer semester. For the class of 2020, 91% of graduates are licensed to practice in Louisiana.

Important Updates due to COVID-19: In response to COVID-19, pass/fail coursework will be accepted for prerequisite coursework during Spring 2020 or Summer 2020 only. P/F coursework cannot be for more than 50% of prerequisite courses.

Were tests required? GRE required. CASPer will be incorporated into the interview process.

Are tests expected next year? Yes.

What international experiences are available? N/A

What dual degree options exist? N/A

What service-learning opportunities exist? N/A

PANCE First-Time Pass Rate: 100% (2020)

LOUISIANA STATE UNIVERSITY - NEW ORLEANS

Address: 411 South Prieur St., New Orleans, LA 70112
Website: *http://alliedhealth.lsuhsc.edu/pa/*
Contact: *PAProgram@lsuhsc.edu*
Phone: 504-556-3420

COST OF ATTENDANCE

In-State Tuition and Fees: $21,022
Additional Expenses: $6,810*
Total: $27,831*

Out-of-State Tuition and Fees: $42,868
Additional Expenses: $6,810*
Total: $49,678*

*This figure does not include cost of living or other related costs.

Financial Aid: https://www.lsuhsc.edu/financialaid/

ADDITIONAL INFORMATION

Interesting tidbit: The program will include learning opportunities in clinical genetics, culture and diversity, ethics and health promotion and disease prevention. Both discipline-specific and interdisciplinary learning experiences with medical and allied health professions students delivered in traditional and team-based fashion are used to define the shared knowledge base requisite to entry-level practice.

Important Updates due to COVID-19: N/A

Were tests required? PA-CAT or GRE required. PA-CAT is highly recommended.

Are tests expected next year? Yes.

What international experiences are available? N/A

What dual degree options exist? N/A

What service-learning opportunities exist? N/A

PANCE First-Time Pass Rate: 100% (2021)

ALABAMA
ARKANSAS
DELAWARE
DISTRICT OF COLUMBIA
FLORIDA
GEORGIA
KENTUCKY
LOUISIANA
MARYLAND
MISSISSIPPI
NORTH CAROLINA
OKLAHOMA
SOUTH CAROLINA
TENNESSEE
TEXAS
VIRGINIA
WEST VIRGINIA

SOUTH

XAVIER UNIVERSITY OF LOUISIANA

Address: 1 Drexel Drive, New Orleans, LA 70125
Website: *https://www.xula.edu/physician-assistant-program-about*
Contact: *paprogram@xula.edu*
Phone: 504-520-5119

COST OF ATTENDANCE

Tuition and Fees: $36,900
Additional Expenses: $24,158
Total: $61,058

Financial Aid: https://www.xula.edu/physician-assistant-program-financial-aid

ADDITIONAL INFORMATION

Interesting tidbit: Xavier University of Louisiana has partnered with Ochsner Health System, one of the leading hospital systems in the Gulf South and the largest health system in metro New Orleans. Ochsner Health Network and its healthcare professionals are committed to being XULA's clinical affiliate and playing a vital role in preparing XULA PA students for entry into clinical practice.

Important Updates due to COVID-19: N/A

Were tests required? GRE or MCAT required.

Are tests expected next year? Yes.

What international experiences are available? N/A

What dual degree options exist? N/A

What service-learning opportunities exist? N/A

PANCE First-Time Pass Rate: N/A (data from the inaugural class of 2022 not available yet)

FROSTBURG STATE UNIVERSITY

Address: 32 West Washington Street, Hagerstown, MD 21740
Website: *https://www.frostburg.edu/academics/majorminors/graduate/ms-physician-assistant/index.php*
Contact: *gradservices@frostburg.edu*
Phone: 301-687-7053

COST OF ATTENDANCE

In-State Tuition and Fees: $35,905
Additional Expenses: $29,804
Total: $65,709

Out-of-State Tuition and Fees: $52,360
Additional Expenses: $29,804
Total: $82,164

Financial Aid: https://www.frostburg.edu/admissions-and-cost/financial-aid/index.php

ADDITIONAL INFORMATION

Interesting tidbit: Frostburg State University is the program's sponsoring institution and operates the program at University System of Maryland Higher Education Center site located in Hagerstown, Maryland. The program operates out of the USMH Agnita M. Stine Schreiber Health Sciences Center with over 8,000 sq. ft. of newly renovated space with state-of-the art teaching and learning space and equipment.

Important Updates due to COVID-19: P/F grades will be accepted for prerequisite courses only if the institution did not provide the student with a choice for graded option. Also, online courses and labs for the spring 2020 semester will be accepted. Application will be reviewed with two letters for the 2021 application cycle. Virtual interviews are planned.

Were tests required? GRE required.

Are tests expected next year? Yes.

What international experiences are available? N/A

What dual degree options exist? N/A

What service-learning opportunities exist? N/A

PANCE First-Time Pass Rate: N/A (PANCE results for graduates will be reported here upon their completion in the summer of 2021)

ALABAMA
ARKANSAS
DELAWARE
DISTRICT OF COLUMBIA
FLORIDA
GEORGIA
KENTUCKY
LOUISIANA
MARYLAND
MISSISSIPPI
NORTH CAROLINA
OKLAHOMA
SOUTH CAROLINA
TENNESSEE
TEXAS
VIRGINIA
WEST VIRGINIA

SOUTH

ALABAMA

ARKANSAS

DELAWARE

DISTRICT OF
COLUMBIA

FLORIDA

GEORGIA

KENTUCKY

LOUISIANA

MARYLAND

MISSISSIPPI

NORTH CAROLINA

OKLAHOMA

SOUTH CAROLINA

TENNESSEE

TEXAS

VIRGINIA

WEST VIRGINIA

TOWSON UNIVERSITY/CCBC - ESSEX

Address: 7201 Rossville Blvd., Baltimore, MD 21237
Website: *https://www.towson.edu/chp/departments/health-sciences/grad/physician-assistant/*
Contact: *davenport@towson.edu*
Phone: 410-704-2262

COST OF ATTENDANCE

In-State Tuition and Fees: $33,102
Additional Expenses: $18,032
Total: $51,134

Out-of-State Tuition and Fees: $59,670
Additional Expenses: $18,032
Total: $77,702

Financial Aid: https://www.towson.edu/admissions/financialaid/

ADDITIONAL INFORMATION

Interesting tidbit: The CCBC-Essex physician assistant program, a collaborative program of CCBC Essex and Towson University, is the oldest and most established program in Maryland. Entry into the program requires both admission to the CCBC Essex Physician Assistant Professional Certificate component and the Towson University Master of Physician Assistant Studies component. Graduates of this 26-month post-baccalaureate program receive a Master of Physician Assistant Studies degree from Towson University and a professional certificate from CCBC Essex.

Important Updates due to COVID-19: Online labs are accepted for the 2020-2021 application cycle.

Were tests required? No.

Are tests expected next year? No.

What international experiences are available? N/A

What dual degree options exist? N/A

What service-learning opportunities exist? N/A

PANCE First-Time Pass Rate: 100% (2020)

UNIVERSITY OF MARYLAND BALTIMORE/ ANNE ARUNDEL COMMUNITY COLLEGE

Address: 101 College Parkway Arnold, MD 21012
Website: *https://graduate.umaryland.edu/mshs-pa-umb/*
Contact: *paprogram@umaryland.edu*
Phone: 410-777-1888

COST OF ATTENDANCE

In-State Tuition and Fees: $39,799
Additional Expenses: $8,681*
Total: $48,480*

Out-of-State Tuition and Fees: $54,359
Additional Expenses: $8,681*
Total: $63,040*

*This figure does not include cost of living or other related costs.

Financial Aid: www.umaryland.edu/fin

ADDITIONAL INFORMATION

Interesting tidbit: Effective Jan. 1, 2020, the Physician Assistant Program changed its sponsorship to the University of Maryland Baltimore. Thus, it is now the University of Maryland Baltimore/ Anne Arundel Community College Collaborative Physician Assistant Program. The admission process is guided by UMB.

Important Updates due to COVID-19: N/A

Were tests required? GRE required.

Are tests expected next year? Yes.

What international experiences are available? N/A

What dual degree options exist? N/A

What service-learning opportunities exist? N/A

PANCE First-Time Pass Rate: 100% (2020)

Other: Anne Arundel Community College (AACC) offers an Interprofessional Healthcare Certificate Program (IPH), a unique pathway to the UMB PA Program.

Other: AACC offers the first three years of UMB's 3+2 Accelerated PA Program.

ALABAMA
ARKANSAS
DELAWARE
DISTRICT OF COLUMBIA
FLORIDA
GEORGIA
KENTUCKY
LOUISIANA
MARYLAND
MISSISSIPPI
NORTH CAROLINA
OKLAHOMA
SOUTH CAROLINA
TENNESSEE
TEXAS
VIRGINIA
WEST VIRGINIA

SOUTH

ALABAMA

ARKANSAS

DELAWARE

DISTRICT OF
COLUMBIA

FLORIDA

GEORGIA

KENTUCKY

LOUISIANA

MARYLAND

MISSISSIPPI

NORTH CAROLINA

OKLAHOMA

SOUTH CAROLINA

TENNESSEE

TEXAS

VIRGINIA

WEST VIRGINIA

UNIVERSITY OF MARYLAND EASTERN SHORE

Address: Hazel Hall, Suite 1062, Princess Anne, MD 21653
Website: *http://www.umes.edu/pa*
Contact: *padept@umes.edu*
Phone: 410-651-6783

COST OF ATTENDANCE

In-State Tuition and Fees: $25,882
Additional Expenses: $8,395*
Total: $34,277*

Out-of-State Tuition and Fees: $46,028
Additional Expenses: $8,395*
Total: $54,423*

*This figure does not include cost of living or other related costs.

Financial Aid: https://www.umes.edu/PA/Content/Tuition-and-Financial-Aid/

Note: There are no scholarships available for students or applicants of the UMES PA Program.

ADDITIONAL INFORMATION

Interesting tidbit: The UMES PA Program is committed to facilitating a learning environment that promotes interprofessional collaboration to ensure continuity of patient care and positive patient outcomes. It endeavors to foster the interpersonal and collaborative attributes necessary for its PA students to become exemplary medical providers working in team-based practices.

Important Updates due to COVID-19: The program will accept Pass/No Pass grading (only passes are acceptable to meet prerequisites) for courses/labs taken during spring and summer 2020 terms. It will accept courses and labs taken during the spring and summer 2020 terms that are delivered via online or distance learning.

Were tests required? GRE required.

Are tests expected next year? Yes.

What international experiences are available? N/A

What dual degree options exist? N/A

What service-learning opportunities exist? N/A

PANCE First-Time Pass Rate: N/A (will be available after the initial cohort of students graduates in 2022)

MISSISSIPPI COLLEGE

Address: 200 S. Capitol Street, Clinton, MS 39056
Website: *http://www.mc.edu/academics/departments/pa/*
Contact: *PA@mc.edu*
Phone: 601-925-7371

COST OF ATTENDANCE

Tuition and Fees: $33,900
Additional Expenses: $32,253
Total: $66,153

Financial Aid: https://www.mc.edu/academics/departments/pa/admissions/financial-information

ADDITIONAL INFORMATION

Interesting tidbit: PAs are educated in the medical model designed to complement physician training. The program curriculum is advanced science-based. Students at our program are assigned to faculty-mentored learning teams.

Important Updates due to COVID-19: Contact PA@mc.edu for specific questions or concerns due to COVID-19.

Were tests required? GRE required.

Are tests expected next year? Yes.

What international experiences are available? N/A

What dual degree options exist? N/A

What service-learning opportunities exist? N/A

PANCE First-Time Pass Rate: 97% (2020)

ALABAMA
ARKANSAS
DELAWARE
DISTRICT OF COLUMBIA
FLORIDA
GEORGIA
KENTUCKY
LOUISIANA
MARYLAND
MISSISSIPPI
NORTH CAROLINA
OKLAHOMA
SOUTH CAROLINA
TENNESSEE
TEXAS
VIRGINIA
WEST VIRGINIA

SOUTH

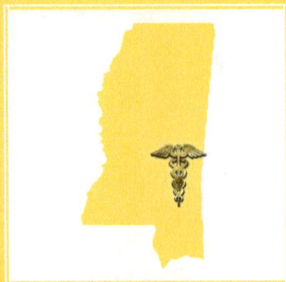

ALABAMA

ARKANSAS

DELAWARE

DISTRICT OF
COLUMBIA

FLORIDA

GEORGIA

KENTUCKY

LOUISIANA

MARYLAND

MISSISSIPPI

NORTH CAROLINA

OKLAHOMA

SOUTH CAROLINA

TENNESSEE

TEXAS

VIRGINIA

WEST VIRGINIA

MISSISSIPPI STATE UNIVERSITY - MERIDIAN

Address: 2214 5th Street, Meridian, MS 39301
Website: *https://www.meridian.msstate.edu/academics/physician-assistant/*
Contact: *pa@meridian.msstate.edu*
Phone: 601-696-2320

COST OF ATTENDANCE

In-State Tuition and Fees: $30,000
Additional Expenses: $21,065
Total: $51,065

Out-of-State Tuition and Fees: $55,000
Additional Expenses: $21,065
Total: $76,065

Financial Aid: https://www.sfa.msstate.edu/

ADDITIONAL INFORMATION

Interesting tidbit: The first cohort of 20 students matriculated in January 2021. THE MSU MPAS Program is 29 months in duration, requiring a total of 108 credit hours to complete.

Important Updates due to COVID-19: The program will accept documented virtual shadowing experiences.

Were tests required? GRE required.

Are tests expected next year? Yes.

What international experiences are available? N/A

What dual degree options exist? N/A

What service-learning opportunities exist? N/A

PANCE First-Time Pass Rate: N/A (will be available after first cohort graduates in 2023)

CAMPBELL UNIVERSITY

Address: 143 Main Street, Buies Creek, NC 27506
Website: *https://cphs.campbell.edu/academic-programs/physician-assistant/master-physician-assistant-practice/*
Contact: *stiltnerk@campbell.edu*
Phone: 910-893-1210

COST OF ATTENDANCE

Tuition and Fees: $47,880
Additional Expenses: $9,026*
Total: $56,906*

*This figure does not include cost of living or other related costs.

Financial Aid: https://cphs.campbell.edu/admissions/financial-aid/physician-assistant/

ADDITIONAL INFORMATION

Interesting tidbit: The Campbell Physician Assistant Program believes in interprofessional education and team-based practice. It embraces the CUPA tenants of Faith, Learning, and Service. All students are required to complete 25 hours of community service during their didactic year.

Important Updates due to COVID-19: The program will consider pass/fail grades for prerequisite courses taken during the spring and summer 2020 terms. It accepts online labs in courses taken during 2020 and during spring/summer 2021.

Were tests required? GRE required.

Are tests expected next year? Yes.

What international experiences are available? N/A

What dual degree options exist? MPAP/MSPH (see https://cphs.campbell.edu/academic-programs/dual-degrees/mpap-msph/) and MPAP/MSCR (see https://cphs.campbell.edu/academic-programs/dual-degrees/pa-ms-in-clinical-research/)

What service-learning opportunities exist? N/A

PANCE First-Time Pass Rate: 98% (2020)

ALABAMA
ARKANSAS
DELAWARE
DISTRICT OF COLUMBIA
FLORIDA
GEORGIA
KENTUCKY
LOUISIANA
MARYLAND
MISSISSIPPI
NORTH CAROLINA
OKLAHOMA
SOUTH CAROLINA
TENNESSEE
TEXAS
VIRGINIA
WEST VIRGINIA

SOUTH

ALABAMA

ARKANSAS

DELAWARE

DISTRICT OF
COLUMBIA

FLORIDA

GEORGIA

KENTUCKY

LOUISIANA

MARYLAND

MISSISSIPPI

NORTH CAROLINA

OKLAHOMA

SOUTH CAROLINA

TENNESSEE

TEXAS

VIRGINIA

WEST VIRGINIA

DUKE UNIVERSITY MEDICAL CENTER

Address: 800 S. Duke Street, Durham, NC 27701
Website: *http://pa.duke.edu/*
Contact: *paadmission@mc.duke.edu*
Phone: 919-681-3161

COST OF ATTENDANCE

Tuition and Fees: $45,259
Additional Expenses: $33,447
Total: $78,706

Financial Aid: https://fmch.duke.edu/duke-physician-assistant-program/admissions/financial-aid

ADDITIONAL INFORMATION

Interesting tidbit: The physician assistant (PA) profession originated at Duke in 1965. It is the birthplace of the PA profession.

Important Updates due to COVID-19: The Duke Physician Assistant Program will conduct virtual interviews for the 2021-2022 cycle. It will accept pass/fail courses that have a grade of 'Pass.'

Were tests required? GRE required.

Are tests expected next year? Yes.

What international experiences are available? N/A

What dual degree options exist? N/A

What service-learning opportunities exist? N/A

PANCE First-Time Pass Rate: 96% (2020)

EAST CAROLINA UNIVERSITY

Address: 600 Moye Boulevard, Greenville, NC 27834
Website: *http://www.ecu.edu/pa*
Contact: *paadmissions@ecu.edu*
Phone: 252-744-1100

COST OF ATTENDANCE

In-State Tuition and Fees: $17,986
Additional Expenses: $6,357*
Total: $24,343*

Out-of-State Tuition and Fees: $37,706
Additional Expenses: $6,357*
Total: $44,063*

*This figure does not include cost of living or other related costs.

Financial Aid: See "Financial Aid" and "Scholarships" on https://pa.ecu.edu/cost-tuition/

ADDITIONAL INFORMATION

Interesting tidbit: Only permanent residents of North Carolina, South Carolina, Virginia, Tennessee, Georgia, and Washington D.C. are eligible to apply to the East Carolina University's PA Program.

Important Updates due to COVID-19: The program accepts online lab experiences acquired during and after spring 2020. The clinical hour requirement is currently waived.

Were tests required? GRE required.

Are tests expected next year? Yes.

What international experiences are available? N/A

What dual degree options exist? N/A

What service-learning opportunities exist? N/A

PANCE First-Time Pass Rate: 97% (2020)

ALABAMA
ARKANSAS
DELAWARE
DISTRICT OF COLUMBIA
FLORIDA
GEORGIA
KENTUCKY
LOUISIANA
MARYLAND
MISSISSIPPI
NORTH CAROLINA
OKLAHOMA
SOUTH CAROLINA
TENNESSEE
TEXAS
VIRGINIA
WEST VIRGINIA

SOUTH

ELON UNIVERSITY

Address: 762 East Haggard Ave., Elon, NC 27244
Website: *https://www.elon.edu/u/academics/health-sciences/physician-assistant/*
Contact: *gradadm@elon.edu*
Phone: 336-278-7600

COST OF ATTENDANCE

Tuition and Fees: $50,789
Additional Expenses: $22,500
Total: $73,289

Financial Aid: https://www.elon.edu/u/academics/health-sciences/physician-assistant/admissions-information/tuition-financial-aid/

ADDITIONAL INFORMATION

Interesting tidbit: The Elon PA program, along with the Elon Doctor of Physical Therapy program, is housed within the School of Health Sciences. Interprofessional learning opportunities are embedded into the curriculum and afford students opportunities to collaborate to provide optimal patient care.

Important Updates due to COVID-19: The admissions committee will accept Pass/Fail coursework for 2020 and 2021. All interviews for 2020-21 are conducted in a virtual setting.

Were tests required? No.

Are tests expected next year? No.

What international experiences are available? International rotations through Global Learning Opportunities. See https://www.elon.edu/u/academics/health-sciences/glo/

What dual degree options exist? N/A

What service-learning opportunities exist? Open Door Clinic of Alamance County. See https://opendoorclinic.net/

PANCE First-Time Pass Rate: 100% (2021)

Other: Accelerated Pathways available for Elon undergraduates. See https://www.elon.edu/u/academics/health-sciences/accelerated-pathways/

GARDNER-WEBB UNIVERSITY

Address: 110 S. Main Street, Boiling Springs, NC 28017
Website: *https://gardner-webb.edu/programs/physician-assistant-studies/*
Contact: *paadmissions@gardner-webb.edu*
Phone: 704-406-2017

COST OF ATTENDANCE

Tuition and Fees: $40,068
Additional Expenses: $36,585
Total: $76,653

Financial Aid: https://gardner-webb.edu/admissions-aid/financial-aid/

ADDITIONAL INFORMATION

Interesting tidbit: Located in a former hospital, the Inter-professional Hub once served as the Emergency room and housed the operating rooms. Today, the integrity of the hospital's original design is preserved in realistic instructional labs. Here students utilize learning spaces including an ER/trauma lab, OR/minor surgery lab, skills lab, eight patient exam rooms, and four debriefing rooms.

Important Updates due to COVID-19: N/A

Were tests required? Altus Suite required.

Are tests expected next year? Yes.

What international experiences are available? N/A

What dual degree options exist? N/A

What service-learning opportunities exist? Monthly health screenings for the homeless and underserved population of Cleveland County.

PANCE First-Time Pass Rate: 94% (2020)

ALABAMA
ARKANSAS
DELAWARE
DISTRICT OF COLUMBIA
FLORIDA
GEORGIA
KENTUCKY
LOUISIANA
MARYLAND
MISSISSIPPI
NORTH CAROLINA
OKLAHOMA
SOUTH CAROLINA
TENNESSEE
TEXAS
VIRGINIA
WEST VIRGINIA

SOUTH

ALABAMA

ARKANSAS

DELAWARE

DISTRICT OF COLUMBIA

FLORIDA

GEORGIA

KENTUCKY

LOUISIANA

MARYLAND

MISSISSIPPI

NORTH CAROLINA

OKLAHOMA

SOUTH CAROLINA

TENNESSEE

TEXAS

VIRGINIA

WEST VIRGINIA

HIGH POINT UNIVERSITY

Address: One University Parkway, High Point, NC 27288
Website: *http://www.highpoint.edu/physicianassistant/*
Contact: *PAprogram@highpoint.edu*
Phone: 336-841-9382

COST OF ATTENDANCE

Tuition and Fees: $44,208
Additional Expenses: $27,000
Total: $71,208

Financial Aid: https://www.highpoint.edu/financialplanning/graduate-financial-assistance-programs/

ADDITIONAL INFORMATION

Interesting tidbit: The 27 month PA Program course of study is divided into a 15-month didactic phase and a 12-month clinical phase. The didactic phase centers around "Clinical Decision Making", a series of courses taught using an organ system approach through the lifespan and illustrating the standards of care across the gamut of health care delivery venues. The clinical phase also includes an evidence-based Master's project.

Important Updates due to COVID-19: For the 2020-21 Admissions Cycle, the program will review and consider Pass/Fail courses obtained in the Spring and Summer 2020 semesters. If the applicant's institution has moved Spring/Summer/Fall 2020 laboratory courses online, the MPAS Program will review these on an individual basis.

Were tests required? GRE required.

Are tests expected next year? Yes.

What international experiences are available? N/A

What dual degree options exist? N/A

What service-learning opportunities exist? N/A

PANCE First-Time Pass Rate: 100% (2020)

METHODIST UNIVERSITY

Address: 5107 College Center Drive, Fayetteville, NC 28311
Website: *http://www.methodist.edu/paprogram*
Contact: *jmish@methodist.edu*
Phone: 910-630-7615

COST OF ATTENDANCE

Tuition and Fees: $43,950
Additional Expenses: $19,985
Total: $63,935

Financial Aid: See "Financing Your Education and Additional Expenses" on https://www.methodist.edu/paprogram/tuition-fees/

ADDITIONAL INFORMATION

Interesting tidbit: The Medical Lecture Hall facility is home to all didactic classes and houses a 161-seat lecture hall, with four breakout classrooms. The human anatomy lab experience is a critical component of the didactic year and lays a strong foundation for the program's curriculum.

Important Updates due to COVID-19: N/A

Were tests required? GRE required.

Are tests expected next year? Yes.

What international experiences are available? N/A

What dual degree options exist? N/A

What service-learning opportunities exist? N/A

PANCE First-Time Pass Rate: 100% (2020)

Other: Early Assurance Program for high school seniors. See https://www.methodist.edu/paprogram/admission-preference/

Other: Reserved seats (2) for Native American students who will graduate from the University of North Carolina at Pembroke (UNCP). See https://www.methodist.edu/paprogram/admission-preference/

Other: Reserved seat (1) for a student who has completed the Meredith College Pre-Health Post-Baccalaureate (Post-Bacc) Certificate Program. See https://www.methodist.edu/paprogram/admission-preference/

ALABAMA
ARKANSAS
DELAWARE
DISTRICT OF COLUMBIA
FLORIDA
GEORGIA
KENTUCKY
LOUISIANA
MARYLAND
MISSISSIPPI
NORTH CAROLINA
OKLAHOMA
SOUTH CAROLINA
TENNESSEE
TEXAS
VIRGINIA
WEST VIRGINIA

SOUTH

PFEIFFER UNIVERSITY

Address: 48380 US Hwy 52, Misenheimer, NC 28109
Website: *https://www.pfeiffer.edu/mspas*
Contact: *pfeifferpa@pfeiffer.edu*
Phone: 704-464-3167

COST OF ATTENDANCE

Tuition and Fees: $40,755
Additional Expenses: $26,613
Total: $67,368

Financial Aid: https://www.pfeiffer.edu/admissions/financial-aid

ADDITIONAL INFORMATION

Interesting tidbit: The Master of Science in Physician Assistant Studies (MS-PAS) program is located in the Pfeiffer University Health Science Center, which features the Center for Advanced Clinical Simulation Education (CACSE). The CACSE includes four simulated ICU rooms, one Surgical Suite, one Emergency Department Trauma Bay and a fully functional clinic with six exam rooms, where physician assistant students alongside our board-certified and licensed physician assistant faculty, will provide much-needed community health services.

Important Updates due to COVID-19: The program will accept pass/fail grades for Psychology, Statistics, and Medical Terminology. Due to the COVID-19 pandemic, all applications will be considered regardless of clinical hours completed at the time of application. Also, the PA-CAT is not required for the 2021-2022 application cycle.

Were tests required? CASPer required.

Are tests expected next year? PA-CAT and CASPer required.

What international experiences are available? N/A

What dual degree options exist? N/A

What service-learning opportunities exist? CACSE clinic.

PANCE First-Time Pass Rate: N/A (will be available after graduation of its first cohort in 2022)

ALABAMA

ARKANSAS

DELAWARE

DISTRICT OF COLUMBIA

FLORIDA

GEORGIA

KENTUCKY

LOUISIANA

MARYLAND

MISSISSIPPI

NORTH CAROLINA

OKLAHOMA

SOUTH CAROLINA

TENNESSEE

TEXAS

VIRGINIA

WEST VIRGINIA

UNIVERSITY OF NORTH CAROLINA - CHAPEL HILL

Address: 321 S Columbia Street, Chapel Hill, NC 27514
Website: *http://www.med.unc.edu/ahs/unc-pa*
Contact: *paprogram@unc.edu*
Phone: 919-962-8008

COST OF ATTENDANCE

In-State Tuition and Fees: $28,359
Additional Expenses: $27,501
Total: $55,860

Out-of-State Tuition and Fees: $50,874
Additional Expenses: $27,501
Total: $78,375

Financial Aid: See "Financial Aid Opportunities" on https://www.med.unc.edu/ahs/unc-pa/admissions/tuition/

ADDITIONAL INFORMATION

Interesting tidbit: The UNC-Chapel Hill Physician Assistant program has drawn much attention for its goal to recruit veterans with military health backgrounds. UNC-CH and the Joint Special Operations Command at Fort Bragg signed a memorandum of agreement to expand educational collaboration to create a physician assistant program. This collaboration envisioned a program that could provide a pathway for U.S. Army Special Forces Medical Sergeants to translate the skills and expertise gained through military service into a civilian career.

Important Updates due to COVID-19: Prerequisite coursework submitted during the Spring and Summer sessions of 2020 receiving Pass/Fail, Satisfactory/Unsatisfactory grading are eligible for prerequisite fulfillment.

Were tests required? GRE required.

Are tests expected next year? Yes.

What international experiences are available? N/A

What dual degree options exist? N/A

What service-learning opportunities exist? N/A

PANCE First-Time Pass Rate: 94% (2020)

ALABAMA
ARKANSAS
DELAWARE
DISTRICT OF COLUMBIA
FLORIDA
GEORGIA
KENTUCKY
LOUISIANA
MARYLAND
MISSISSIPPI
NORTH CAROLINA
OKLAHOMA
SOUTH CAROLINA
TENNESSEE
TEXAS
VIRGINIA
WEST VIRGINIA

SOUTH

ALABAMA

ARKANSAS

DELAWARE

DISTRICT OF COLUMBIA

FLORIDA

GEORGIA

KENTUCKY

LOUISIANA

MARYLAND

MISSISSIPPI

NORTH CAROLINA

OKLAHOMA

SOUTH CAROLINA

TENNESSEE

TEXAS

VIRGINIA

WEST VIRGINIA

WAKE FOREST UNIVERSITY - WINSTON-SALEM

Address: 525 Vine Street, Winston-Salem, NC 27101
Website: *http://www.wakehealth.edu/Physician-Assistant-Program/*
Contact: *paadmit@wakehealth.edu*
Phone: 336-716-4356
Other Locations: Boone, NC

COST OF ATTENDANCE

Tuition and Fees: $42,700
Additional Expenses: $37,210
Total: $79,910

Financial Aid: https://school.wakehealth.edu/Education-and-Training/PA-Program/Costs-and-Financial-Aid

ADDITIONAL INFORMATION

Interesting tidbit: The Wake Forest PA Program features inquiry-based, small-group, self-directed learning centered on real patient medical problems. The inquiry-based learning model is complemented by instruction in basic sciences, pharmacology, and evidence-based medicine with a focus on primary health care delivery.

Important Updates due to COVID-19: The program will consider pass/fail grades for prerequisite courses taken during the spring and summer 2020 terms on a case by case basis. All interviews for the 2021-2022 admissions cycle will be conducted virtually.

Were tests required? GRE and CASPer required.

Are tests expected next year? Yes.

What international experiences are available? N/A

What dual degree options exist? N/A

What service-learning opportunities exist? N/A

PANCE First-Time Pass Rate: 98% (2020)

Other: Emerging Leaders Program offers two separate sequential degree tracks - Business or Law. See https://school.wakehealth.edu/Education-and-Training/PA-Program/Emerging-Leaders-Program

Other: PhD/MMS Sequential Degree program (5- to 7-yr). See https://school.wakehealth.edu/Education-and-Training/PA-Program/Sequential-Degree-Program

WAKE FOREST UNIVERSITY - BOONE

Address: 1179 State Farm Road, Boone, NC 28608
Website: *https://school.wakehealth.edu/Education-and-Training/PA-Program*
Contact: *paadmit@wakehealth.edu*
Phone: 828-262-8145

Other Locations: Winston-Salem, NC

COST OF ATTENDANCE

Tuition and Fees: $47,200
Additional Expenses: $38,222
Total: $80,922

Financial Aid: https://school.wakehealth.edu/Education-and-Training/PA-Program/Costs-and-Financial-Aid

ADDITIONAL INFORMATION

Interesting tidbit: During the preclinical year, 64 study at the campus in Winston-Salem, and 24 study at our Boone campus. The clinical year is centrally coordinated for all 88 students.

Important Updates due to COVID-19: The program will consider pass/fail grades for prerequisite courses taken during the spring and summer 2020 terms on a case by case basis. All interviews for the 2021-2022 admissions cycle will be conducted virtually.

Were tests required? GRE and CASPer required.

Are tests expected next year? Yes.

What international experiences are available? N/A

What dual degree options exist? N/A

What service-learning opportunities exist? N/A

PANCE First-Time Pass Rate: 98% (2020)

Other: Emerging Leaders Program offers two separate sequential degree tracks - Business or Law. See https://school.wakehealth.edu/Education-and-Training/PA-Program/Emerging-Leaders-Program

Other: PhD/MMS Sequential Degree program (5- to 7-yr). See https://school.wakehealth.edu/Education-and-Training/PA-Program/Sequential-Degree-Program

ALABAMA
ARKANSAS
DELAWARE
DISTRICT OF COLUMBIA
FLORIDA
GEORGIA
KENTUCKY
LOUISIANA
MARYLAND
MISSISSIPPI
NORTH CAROLINA
OKLAHOMA
SOUTH CAROLINA
TENNESSEE
TEXAS
VIRGINIA
WEST VIRGINIA

SOUTH

ALABAMA

ARKANSAS

DELAWARE

DISTRICT OF
COLUMBIA

FLORIDA

GEORGIA

KENTUCKY

LOUISIANA

MARYLAND

MISSISSIPPI

NORTH CAROLINA

OKLAHOMA

SOUTH CAROLINA

TENNESSEE

TEXAS

VIRGINIA

WEST VIRGINIA

WINGATE UNIVERSITY

Address: 220 N Camden Rd Wingate, NC 28174
Website: *http://pa.wingate.edu/*
Contact: *pa@wingate.edu*
Phone: 704-233-8993

Other Locations: Hendersonville, NC

COST OF ATTENDANCE

Tuition and Fees: $39,980
Additional Expenses: N/A
Total: $39,980*

*This figure does not include cost of living or other related costs.

Financial Aid: https://www.wingate.edu/admissions/financial-aid

ADDITIONAL INFORMATION

Interesting tidbit: The Wingate University Physician Assistant Studies Program uses synchronous distance learning, wherein faculty interact in real time with students, regardless of which Wingate University location they're attending. Most lectures originate from the Wingate campus.

Important Updates due to COVID-19: N/A

Were tests required? GRE required.

Are tests expected next year? Yes.

What international experiences are available? N/A

What dual degree options exist? N/A

What service-learning opportunities exist? N/A

PANCE First-Time Pass Rate: 100% (2020)

WINGATE UNIVERSITY - HENDERSONVILLE

Address: 805 6th Avenue W, Suite 200, Hendersonville, NC 28739
Website: *https://www.wingate.edu/academics/hendersonville/physician-assistant*
Contact: *hendersonville@wingate.edu*
Phone: 828-697-0105

Other Locations: Wingate, NC

COST OF ATTENDANCE

Tuition and Fees: $39,980
Additional Expenses: N/A
Total: $39,980*

*This figure does not include cost of living or other related costs.

Financial Aid: https://www.wingate.edu/admissions/financial-aid

ADDITIONAL INFORMATION

Interesting tidbit: There are 15 seats on the Hendersonville campus and 40 on the Wingate campus. Applicants must choose a campus when applying through CASPA. An applicant cannot be considered for both campuses.

Important Updates due to COVID-19: N/A

Were tests required? GRE required.

Are tests expected next year? Yes.

What international experiences are available? N/A

What dual degree options exist? N/A

What service-learning opportunities exist? N/A

PANCE First-Time Pass Rate: 100% (2020)

ALABAMA
ARKANSAS
DELAWARE
DISTRICT OF COLUMBIA
FLORIDA
GEORGIA
KENTUCKY
LOUISIANA
MARYLAND
MISSISSIPPI
NORTH CAROLINA
OKLAHOMA
SOUTH CAROLINA
TENNESSEE
TEXAS
VIRGINIA
WEST VIRGINIA

SOUTH

NORTHEASTERN STATE UNIVERSITY

Address: 2400 West Shawnee St., Muskogee, OK 74401
Website: *https://academics.nsuok.edu/healthprofessions/
DegreePrograms/Graduate/PhysicianAssistantStudies/*
Contact: *paprogram@nsuok.edu*
Phone: 918-444-5464

COST OF ATTENDANCE

In-State Tuition and Fees: $19,446
Additional Expenses: $33,965
Total: $53,410

Out-of-State Tuition and Fees: $35,319
Additional Expenses: $33,965
Total: $69,284

Financial Aid: https://academics.nsuok.edu/healthprofessions/
DegreePrograms/Graduate/PhysicianAssistantStudies/Finance.
aspx

ADDITIONAL INFORMATION

Interesting tidbit: Northeastern State University (NSU) is a regional university founded on the rich heritage of the Cherokee Nation. The Physician Assistant Studies Program, housed on NSU's Muskogee Campus is part of a broad university plan for developing and implementing programming that provides direct benefit to the regional needs of northeastern Oklahoma.

Important Updates due to COVID-19: N/A

Were tests required? No.

Are tests expected next year? No.

What international experiences are available? N/A

What dual degree options exist? N/A

What service-learning opportunities exist? N/A

PANCE First-Time Pass Rate: N/A (available after inaugural cohort graduates in 2022)

ALABAMA
ARKANSAS
DELAWARE
DISTRICT OF COLUMBIA
FLORIDA
GEORGIA
KENTUCKY
LOUISIANA
MARYLAND
MISSISSIPPI
NORTH CAROLINA
OKLAHOMA
SOUTH CAROLINA
TENNESSEE
TEXAS
VIRGINIA
WEST VIRGINIA

OKLAHOMA CITY UNIVERSITY

Address: 2501 N Blackwelder Ave., Oklahoma City, OK 73106
Website: *https://www.okcu.edu/physician-assistant/home/*
Contact: *ahicks@okcu.edu*
Phone: 405-208-6260

COST OF ATTENDANCE

Tuition and Fees: $38,946
Additional Expenses: $29,265
Total: $68,211

Financial Aid: https://www.okcu.edu/financialaid/home

ADDITIONAL INFORMATION

Interesting tidbit: A unique aspect of the OCU PA program involves providing a parallel online course of study in business aspects of medicine. This added component provides the OCU PA student a greater understanding of medical practice management which is critical to a successful practice.

Important Updates due to COVID-19: N/A

Were tests required? No.

Are tests expected next year? No.

What international experiences are available? N/A

What dual degree options exist? N/A

What service-learning opportunities exist? N/A

PANCE First-Time Pass Rate: 94% (2020)

ALABAMA

ARKANSAS

DELAWARE

DISTRICT OF COLUMBIA

FLORIDA

GEORGIA

KENTUCKY

LOUISIANA

MARYLAND

MISSISSIPPI

NORTH CAROLINA

OKLAHOMA

SOUTH CAROLINA

TENNESSEE

TEXAS

VIRGINIA

WEST VIRGINIA

SOUTH

OKLAHOMA STATE UNIVERSITY

Address: 1111 W. 17 Street, Tulsa, OK 74107
Website: *https://medicine.okstate.edu/pa/index.html*
Contact: *physician.assistant@okstate.edu*
Phone: 918-561-1145

COST OF ATTENDANCE

In-State Tuition and Fees: $13,500
Additional Expenses: $3,309*
Total: $16,809*

Out-of-State Tuition and Fees: $29,500
Additional Expenses: $3,309*
Total: $32,809*

*This figure does not include cost of living or other related costs.

Financial Aid: N/A

ADDITIONAL INFORMATION

Interesting tidbit: The program embodies the idea of interprofessional education and as a result a significant portion of the courses occur alongside students in other academic programs on campus. This unique aspect to the program helps to foster relationships between health care providers early on which in turn builds a more successful patient-centered health care team.The first cohort begins in July 2021.

Important Updates due to COVID-19: A grade of "pass" is acceptable for courses completed in 2020.

Were tests required? GRE and Altus Suite required.

Are tests expected next year? Yes.

What international experiences are available? N/A

What dual degree options exist? N/A

What service-learning opportunities exist? N/A

PANCE First-Time Pass Rate: N/A (will be available after the first class graduates in 2023)

UNIVERSITY OF OKLAHOMA, OKLAHOMA CITY

Address: 940 Stanton L. Young Blvd., Ste. 357, Oklahoma City, OK 73104
Website: *https://medicine.ouhsc.edu/Prospective-Students/Degree-Programs/Physician-Associate-Program*
Contact: *infookc pa@ouhsc.edu*
Phone: 405-271-2058

COST OF ATTENDANCE

In-State Tuition and Fees: $19,585
Additional Expenses: $35,414
Total: $54,999

Out-of-State Tuition and Fees: $36,471
Additional Expenses: $35,414
Total: $71,885

Financial Aid: https://financialservices.ouhsc.edu/Departments/Student-Financial-Aid

Note: For PA program-specific scholarships, see https://medicine.ouhsc.edu/Current-Learners/Physician-Associate-Program/Student-Scholarships

ADDITIONAL INFORMATION

Interesting tidbit: OU Physician Associate program is one of the original six accredited programs in the United States and has maintained continuous accreditation since 1972. The program takes advantage of its place in an academic medical center to teach the next generation of clinicians.

Important Updates due to COVID-19: N/A

Were tests required? Altus Suite required.

Are tests expected next year? Yes.

What international experiences are available? N/A

What dual degree options exist? N/A

What service-learning opportunities exist? N/A

PANCE First-Time Pass Rate: 96% (2020)

ALABAMA
ARKANSAS
DELAWARE
DISTRICT OF COLUMBIA
FLORIDA
GEORGIA
KENTUCKY
LOUISIANA
MARYLAND
MISSISSIPPI
NORTH CAROLINA
OKLAHOMA
SOUTH CAROLINA
TENNESSEE
TEXAS
VIRGINIA
WEST VIRGINIA

SOUTH

UNIVERSITY OF OKLAHOMA, TULSA

Address: 4502 E. 41st Street, Tulsa, OK 74135
Website: *https://www.ou.edu/tulsa/community_medicine/scm-pa-program*
Contact: *outulsapa@ouhsc.edu*
Phone: 918-660-3842

COST OF ATTENDANCE

In-State Tuition and Fees: $18,303
Additional Expenses: $34,558
Total: $52,861

Out-of-State Tuition and Fees: $35,189
Additional Expenses: $34,558
Total: $69,747

Financial Aid: https://www.ou.edu/tulsa/community_medicine/
scm-pa-program/finances

ADDITIONAL INFORMATION

Interesting tidbit: The OU-TU School of Community Medicine physician assistant program is a joint effort between the University of Oklahoma and The University of Tulsa. Its commitment to primary care and the underserved in Oklahoma manifests in its curriculum. Clinical rotations during the second year include 22 weeks of primary care exposure, a four-week underserved medicine rotation, and a two week Community Impact experience, which includes exposure to various agencies.

Important Updates due to COVID-19: N/A

Were tests required? GRE required.

Are tests expected next year? Yes.

What international experiences are available? N/A

What dual degree options exist? N/A

What service-learning opportunities exist? Summer Institute; Bedlam evening clinic; Physicians Family Medicine Clinic. See https://www.ou.edu/tulsa/community_medicine/scm-pa-program/student-clinics

PANCE First-Time Pass Rate: 95% (2020)

CHARLESTON SOUTHERN UNIVERSITY

Address: 9200 University Blvd., Health Science Bldg., Charleston, SC 29409
Website: *http://www.csuniv.edu/pa*
Contact: *paprogram@csuniv.edu*
Phone: 843-863-7427

COST OF ATTENDANCE

Tuition and Fees: $46,500
Additional Expenses: $46,088
Total: $92,588

Financial Aid: See "PA Student Financial Aid" on https://www.charlestonsouthern.edu/academics/physician-assistant/cost-aid/

ADDITIONAL INFORMATION

Interesting tidbit: The program is dedicated to fostering a healthy and supportive Christian learning environment that prepares students appropriately to transition from student to clinician.

Important Updates due to COVID-19: Courses taken between January 1, 2020 and September 1, 2021 and awarded satisfactory completion (P), to meet prerequisite requirements, will be accepted to accommodate students enrolled in these courses whose universities have moved to a P/F grading scale. Courses taken between January 1, 2020 and September 1, 2021 including those with lab components that were transitioned to an online format will be accepted if completed with a grade of "C" or higher or with a satisfactory completion (P). For the 2020 – 2021 and 2021 – 2022 application cycles only, the minimum of 1,000 hours of direct patient care experience required at the time of application submission will be reduced to 500 hours of direct patient care experience. Also for the 2020 – 2021 and 2021 – 2022 application cycles only, only one of three LORs must be from a healthcare setting. Virtual interviews are utilized.

Were tests required? GRE required.

Are tests expected next year? Yes.

What international experiences are available? Medical mission trip to the Dominican Republic.

What dual degree options exist? N/A

What service-learning opportunities exist? Service project as part of the "Path to Becoming a PA" course series.

PANCE First-Time Pass Rate: 93% (2020)

ALABAMA
ARKANSAS
DELAWARE
DISTRICT OF COLUMBIA
FLORIDA
GEORGIA
KENTUCKY
LOUISIANA
MARYLAND
MISSISSIPPI
NORTH CAROLINA
OKLAHOMA
SOUTH CAROLINA
TENNESSEE
TEXAS
VIRGINIA
WEST VIRGINIA

SOUTH

MEDICAL UNIVERSITY OF SOUTH CAROLINA

Address: 151 Rutledge Ave A., Charleston, SC 29403
Website: *https://education.musc.edu/students/enrollment/bulletin/colleges-and-degrees/health-professions/ms-in-physician-assistant*
Contact: *chpstusv@musc.edu*
Phone: 843-792-3326

COST OF ATTENDANCE

In-State Tuition and Fees: $26,922
Additional Expenses: N/A
Total: $26,922*

Out-of-State Tuition and Fees: $46,461
Additional Expenses: N/A
Total: $46,461*

*This figure does not include cost of living or other related costs.

Financial Aid: https://chp.musc.edu/current-students/financial-aid-and-scholarships

ADDITIONAL INFORMATION

Interesting tidbit: The Medical University of South Carolina (MUSC) is an academic teaching hospital and the PAS program benefits from the vast resources available from the University including access to interprofessional experiences and simulation technology.

Important Updates due to COVID-19: N/A

Were tests required? PA-CAT required.

Are tests expected next year? Yes.

What international experiences are available? International missions trips.

What dual degree options exist? N/A

What service-learning opportunities exist? Free clinics.

PANCE First-Time Pass Rate: 95% (2020)

NORTH GREENVILLE UNIVERSITY

Address: 405 Lancaster Avenue, Greer, SC 29650
Website: *http://www.ngu.edu/pa-medicine.php*
Contact: *paadmissions@ngu.edu*
Phone: 864-663-0266

COST OF ATTENDANCE

Tuition and Fees: $54,495
Additional Expenses: $31,967
Total: $86,462

Financial Aid: See "Financial Aid" on https://ngu.edu/about/
our-colleges/humanities-sciences/health-professionals-school/pa-
tuition-fees/

ADDITIONAL INFORMATION

Interesting tidbit: NGU PA program consists of 131 semester
hours divided into three phases that span 24 consecutive months.
The Didactic Phase represents the preclinical year and spans 12
months. The Clinical Phase represents the clinical year and consists
of 11 months of supervised clinical education and coursework. The
Summative Phase is 1 month in duration and represents the final
stage of training.

Important Updates due to COVID-19: Courses taken during Spring
2020 through Fall 2021 that have a S or P grade instead of a letter
grade will be accepted for prerequisite requirements, if this was an
institutional change secondary to the COVID-19 crisis. Online lab
courses completed during Spring 2020 through Fall 2021 will be
accepted for prerequisite requirements.

Were tests required? GRE required.

Are tests expected next year? Yes.

What international experiences are available? Two opportunities
to participate in an international clerkship in a developing country.
See PA Missions Abroad (https://ngu.edu/about/our-colleges/
humanities-sciences/health-professionals-school/pa-missions-
abroad/)

What dual degree options exist? N/A

What service-learning opportunities exist? Free clinic.

PANCE First-Time Pass Rate: 86% (2020)

ALABAMA
ARKANSAS
DELAWARE
DISTRICT OF COLUMBIA
FLORIDA
GEORGIA
KENTUCKY
LOUISIANA
MARYLAND
MISSISSIPPI
NORTH CAROLINA
OKLAHOMA
SOUTH CAROLINA
TENNESSEE
TEXAS
VIRGINIA
WEST VIRGINIA

SOUTH

ALABAMA

ARKANSAS

DELAWARE

DISTRICT OF
COLUMBIA

FLORIDA

GEORGIA

KENTUCKY

LOUISIANA

MARYLAND

MISSISSIPPI

NORTH CAROLINA

OKLAHOMA

SOUTH CAROLINA

TENNESSEE

TEXAS

VIRGINIA

WEST VIRGINIA

PRESBYTERIAN COLLEGE

Address: 503 South Broad Street, Clinton, SC 29325
Website: *https://www.presby.edu/academics/graduate-professional/physician-assistant-program/*
Contact: *https://www.presby.edu/academics/graduate-professional/physician-assistant-program/contact-us/*
Phone: 864-833-2820

COST OF ATTENDANCE

Tuition and Fees: $53,400
Additional Expenses: $21,880
Total: $75,280

Financial Aid: https://www.presby.edu/academics/graduate-professional/physician-assistant-program/admissions-pa-program/tuition-fees-pa-program/financial-aid-pa-program/

Note: Presbyterian College or the PA program do not offer scholarships.

ADDITIONAL INFORMATION

Interesting tidbit: The compelling purpose of Presbyterian College Physician Assistant Studies Program, as part of a church-related college, is to develop within the framework of Christian faith the medical, mental, moral, physical, and spiritual capacities of each student in preparation for a lifetime of service to our patients and those in need in our society.

Important Updates due to COVID-19: N/A

Were tests required? GRE required.

Are tests expected next year? Yes.

What international experiences are available? N/A

What dual degree options exist? N/A

What service-learning opportunities exist? N/A

PANCE First-Time Pass Rate: N/A (the inaugural cohort will graduate in September 2021)

UNIVERSITY OF SOUTH CAROLINA SCHOOL OF MEDICINE

Address: 6311 Garners Ferry Road, Columbia, SC 29209
Website: *http://pa.med.sc.edu/*
Contact: *paprogram@uscmed.sc.edu*
Phone: 803-216-3950

COST OF ATTENDANCE

In-State Tuition and Fees: $22,635
Additional Expenses: $23,568
Total: $46,203

Out-of-State Tuition and Fees: $39,384
Additional Expenses: $23,568
Total: $63,852

Financial Aid: https://sc.edu/study/colleges_schools/medicine/education/student_career_services/financial_aid/index.php

ADDITIONAL INFORMATION

Interesting tidbit: Through the UofSC SOM PA program's extensive curriculum, students will gain experience through simulations, hands-on training and cadaver-based anatomy instruction. You will also learn the latest ultrasound techniques.

Important Updates due to COVID-19: The UofSC SOM PA Program will accept Pass or Satisfactory grades for courses taken between January 1, 2020 and May 31, 2021 from institutions that moved entirely to a Pass/Fail grading scale. Lab courses or courses taken with a lab component that transitioned to an online format will be accepted. The program is holding virtual interviews.

Were tests required? GRE required.

Are tests expected next year? Yes.

What international experiences are available? N/A

What dual degree options exist? N/A

What service-learning opportunities exist? N/A

PANCE First-Time Pass Rate: 96% (2020)

ALABAMA
ARKANSAS
DELAWARE
DISTRICT OF COLUMBIA
FLORIDA
GEORGIA
KENTUCKY
LOUISIANA
MARYLAND
MISSISSIPPI
NORTH CAROLINA
OKLAHOMA
SOUTH CAROLINA
TENNESSEE
TEXAS
VIRGINIA
WEST VIRGINIA

SOUTH

ALABAMA

ARKANSAS

DELAWARE

DISTRICT OF
COLUMBIA

FLORIDA

GEORGIA

KENTUCKY

LOUISIANA

MARYLAND

MISSISSIPPI

NORTH CAROLINA

OKLAHOMA

SOUTH CAROLINA

TENNESSEE

TEXAS

VIRGINIA

WEST VIRGINIA

BETHEL UNIVERSITY

Address: 302B Tyson Avenue, Paris, TN 38242
Website: *https://www.bethelu.edu/academics/colleges/college-of-health-sciences/physician-assistant-studies*
Contact: *paprogram@bethelu.edu*
Phone: 731-407-7650

COST OF ATTENDANCE

Tuition and Fees: $37,500
Additional Expenses: $3,155*
Total: $40,655

*This figure does not include cost of living or other related costs.

Financial Aid: https://www.bethelu.edu/admissions/tuition-and-fees/graduate-student-tuition/adult-degree-program-financial-aid

ADDITIONAL INFORMATION

Interesting tidbit: the Bethel University Physician Assistant Program (BUPAP) is a 27-month educational program, which consists of 12 months of didactic education and 15 months of clinical experience. It trains future PAs who will practice medicine within an ethical framework grounded in Christian principles.

Important Updates due to COVID-19: N/A

Were tests required? GRE required.

Are tests expected next year? Yes.

What international experiences are available? N/A

What dual degree options exist? N/A

What service-learning opportunities exist? N/A

PANCE First-Time Pass Rate: 96% (2020)

CHRISTIAN BROTHERS UNIVERSITY

Address: 650 East Parkway South, Memphis, TN 38104
Website: *https://www.cbu.edu/pa*
Contact: *pas@cbu.edu*
Phone: 901-321-3388

COST OF ATTENDANCE

Tuition and Fees: $37,050
Additional Expenses: $6,970
Total: $44,020

Financial Aid: https://live-crbu.pantheonsite.io/admissions-aid/financial-aid/

ADDITIONAL INFORMATION

Interesting tidbit: Students are oriented in their first semester to IPEC (Interprofessional Educational Collaborative) competencies. The cohorts have Interprofessional experiences with the Southern College of Optometry students, Union University social work students, and Union pharmacy students. The program is partnered with nationally-renowned medical facilities to offer exceptional clinical experiences during both phases of the program, with an orthopedic thread.

Important Updates due to COVID-19: Online courses and labs can satisfy prerequisite course requirements. Pass grades in a P/F grading system will be accepted.

Were tests required? CASPer required.

Are tests expected next year? Yes.

What international experiences are available? N/A

What dual degree options exist? N/A

What service-learning opportunities exist? N/A

PANCE First-Time Pass Rate: 91% (2020)

ALABAMA
ARKANSAS
DELAWARE
DISTRICT OF COLUMBIA
FLORIDA
GEORGIA
KENTUCKY
LOUISIANA
MARYLAND
MISSISSIPPI
NORTH CAROLINA
OKLAHOMA
SOUTH CAROLINA
TENNESSEE
TEXAS
VIRGINIA
WEST VIRGINIA

SOUTH

LINCOLN MEMORIAL UNIVERSITY

Address: 6965 Cumberland Gap Parkway, Harrogate, TN 37752
Website: *https://www.lmunet.edu/school-of-medical-sciences/pa-harrogate/index.php*
Contact: *paadmissions@lmunet.edu*
Phone: 423-869-6669

Other Locations: Knoxville, TN

COST OF ATTENDANCE

Tuition and Fees: $40,975
Additional Expenses: N/A
Total: $40,975*

*This figure does not include cost of living or other related costs.

Financial Aid: https://www.lmunet.edu/student-financial-services/graduate/index.php

ADDITIONAL INFORMATION

Interesting tidbit: The Physician Assistant (PA) Program at Lincoln Memorial University in Harrogate has a primary care focus. It utilizes dedicated, experienced faculty in academics with clinical and research expertise, and state-of-the-art technology to provide its students first-class, hands-on medical education.

Important Updates due to COVID-19: Online science prerequisites are accepted for Spring 2020 - Spring 2021.

Were tests required? GRE required.

Are tests expected next year? Yes.

What international experiences are available? N/A

What dual degree options exist? N/A

What service-learning opportunities exist? N/A

PANCE First-Time Pass Rate: 93% (2020)

LINCOLN MEMORIAL UNIVERSITY - KNOXVILLE

Address: 421 Park 40 N Blvd., Knoxville, TN 37923
Website: *https://www.lmunet.edu/school-of-medical-sciences/pa-knoxville/index.php*
Contact: *paknox@lmunet.edu*
Phone: 875-338-5685

COST OF ATTENDANCE

Tuition and Fees: $40,950
Additional Expenses: $38,680
Total: $79,630

Financial Aid: https://www.lmunet.edu/school-of-medical-sciences/pa-knoxville/financial-services.php

ADDITIONAL INFORMATION

Interesting tidbit: The LMU-Knoxville PA Program matriculated its first class in October of 2020. With three semesters of human cadaver anatomy and up to 20 weeks of clinical experiences in surgical disciplines, the curriculum prepares graduates to provide safe and effective care of patients in surgical and acute care settings.

Important Updates due to COVID-19: The program waived all health care experience requirements for the 2019-2020 and 2020-2021 application cycles. Also, prerequisite course grades of Pass (P), Satisfactory (S), or equivalent for prerequisite courses completed during the spring and summer 2020 semesters that were converted from a letter grade to Pass/Fail (or Satisfactory/Unsatisfactory) are acceptable.

Were tests required? No.

Are tests expected next year? No.

What international experiences are available? N/A

What dual degree options exist? N/A

What service-learning opportunities exist? N/A

PANCE First-Time Pass Rate: N/A (will be available spring of 2023)

ALABAMA
ARKANSAS
DELAWARE
DISTRICT OF COLUMBIA
FLORIDA
GEORGIA
KENTUCKY
LOUISIANA
MARYLAND
MISSISSIPPI
NORTH CAROLINA
OKLAHOMA
SOUTH CAROLINA
TENNESSEE
TEXAS
VIRGINIA
WEST VIRGINIA

SOUTH

ALABAMA

ARKANSAS

DELAWARE

DISTRICT OF
COLUMBIA

FLORIDA

GEORGIA

KENTUCKY

LOUISIANA

MARYLAND

MISSISSIPPI

NORTH CAROLINA

OKLAHOMA

SOUTH CAROLINA

TENNESSEE

TEXAS

VIRGINIA

WEST VIRGINIA

LIPSCOMB UNIVERSITY

Address: One University Park Drive, Nashville, TN 37204
Website: *https://www.lipscomb.edu/academics/programs/physician-assistant-studies*
Contact: *stephen.heffington@lipscomb.edu*
Phone: 615-966-7247

COST OF ATTENDANCE

Tuition and Fees: $52,027
Additional Expenses: N/A
Total: $52,027*

*This figure does not include cost of living or other related costs.

Financial Aid: See "Financial Aid" on https://www.lipscomb.edu/academics/programs/physician-assistant-studies

ADDITIONAL INFORMATION

Interesting tidbit: Faith is an important infusion to learning at Lipscomb: in ethics, mentoring, the clinical experience or servanthood. Its PA program will serve the students' spiritual and vocational goals, as they train to serve others.

Important Updates due to COVID-19: The program will accept online credit for classes with corresponding labs ONLY if the transition to an online platform was due to COVID-19. If pass/fail grading was used, the admissions committee may require official documentation from your university stating what the letter grade would have been if that option had been chosen.

Were tests required? No.

Are tests expected next year? No.

What international experiences are available? N/A

What dual degree options exist? N/A

What service-learning opportunities exist? N/A

PANCE First-Time Pass Rate: 100% (2020)

MILLIGAN UNIVERSITY

Address: 1 Blowers Boulevard, Milligan, TN 37682
Website: *https://www.milligan.edu/pa/#pa*
Contact: *PA@milligan.edu*
Phone: 423-461-8424

COST OF ATTENDANCE

Tuition and Fees: $46,080
Additional Expenses: $5,200
Total: $51,280

*This figure does not include cost of living or other related costs.

Financial Aid: https://www.milligan.edu/sfs/graduate-professional/#payment-options

ADDITIONAL INFORMATION

Interesting tidbit: Milligan's MSPAS program has received the status of Accreditation-Provisional from the Accreditation Review Commission on Education for the Physician Assistant (ARC-PA) and began its first class in January 2018. The program continues to begin a new class of students in January of each year.

Important Updates due to COVID-19: N/A

Were tests required? GRE required.

Are tests expected next year? Yes.

What international experiences are available? N/A

What dual degree options exist? N/A

What service-learning opportunities exist? Providence Medical Clinic.

PANCE First-Time Pass Rate: 95% (2020)

ALABAMA
ARKANSAS
DELAWARE
DISTRICT OF COLUMBIA
FLORIDA
GEORGIA
KENTUCKY
LOUISIANA
MARYLAND
MISSISSIPPI
NORTH CAROLINA
OKLAHOMA
SOUTH CAROLINA
TENNESSEE
TEXAS
VIRGINIA
WEST VIRGINIA

SOUTH

ALABAMA

ARKANSAS

DELAWARE

DISTRICT OF
COLUMBIA

FLORIDA

GEORGIA

KENTUCKY

LOUISIANA

MARYLAND

MISSISSIPPI

NORTH CAROLINA

OKLAHOMA

SOUTH CAROLINA

TENNESSEE

TEXAS

VIRGINIA

WEST VIRGINIA

SOUTH COLLEGE - KNOXVILLE

Address: 400 Goody's Lane, Parkside Campus, Knoxville, TN 37922
Website: *https://www.south.edu/programs/master-health-science-physician-assistant-studies/knoxville/*
Contact: *dboromei@south.edu*
Phone: 865-329-7801

Other Locations: Atlanta, GA; Nashville, TN

COST OF ATTENDANCE

Tuition and Fees: $47,000
Additional Expenses: $7,124*
Total: $54,124*

*This figure does not include cost of living or other related costs.

Financial Aid: See "Physician Assistant Financial and Resources" on https://www.south.edu/programs/master-health-science-physician-assistant-studies/tuition-and-fees/

ADDITIONAL INFORMATION

Interesting tidbit: The Capstone Research Project requires each student to apply specific knowledge and skills acquired in the structured competency-based PA curriculum to a specific research or practical clinical experience oriented project.

Important Updates due to COVID-19: N/A

Were tests required? GRE required.

Are tests expected next year? Yes.

What international experiences are available? N/A

What dual degree options exist? N/A

What service-learning opportunities exist? N/A

PANCE First-Time Pass Rate: 94% (2020)

SOUTH COLLEGE - NASHVILLE

Address: 616 Marriott Drive, Nashville, TN 37214
Website: *https://www.south.edu/programs/master-health-science-physician-assistant-studies/nashville/*
Contact: *panashville@south.edu*
Phone: 626-802-3000

Other Locations: Atlanta, GA; Knoxville, TN

COST OF ATTENDANCE

Tuition and Fees: $47,000
Additional Expenses: $7,124*
Total: $54,124*

*This figure does not include cost of living or other related costs.

Financial Aid: See "Physician Assistant Financial and Resources" on https://www.south.edu/programs/master-health-science-physician-assistant-studies/tuition-and-fees/

ADDITIONAL INFORMATION

Interesting tidbit: The Nashville program initiated its first cohort in the Fall of 2019, and the third cohort in October 2021. The program grants a Master of Health Science in Physician Assistant Studies (MHScPAS) degree upon completion of a 27-month medical education.

Important Updates due to COVID-19: N/A

Were tests required? GRE required.

Are tests expected next year? Yes.

What international experiences are available? N/A

What dual degree options exist? N/A

What service-learning opportunities exist? N/A

PANCE First-Time Pass Rate: N/A (will be available once Nashville 2021 cohort graduates)

ALABAMA
ARKANSAS
DELAWARE
DISTRICT OF COLUMBIA
FLORIDA
GEORGIA
KENTUCKY
LOUISIANA
MARYLAND
MISSISSIPPI
NORTH CAROLINA
OKLAHOMA
SOUTH CAROLINA
TENNESSEE
TEXAS
VIRGINIA
WEST VIRGINIA

SOUTH

ALABAMA

ARKANSAS

DELAWARE

DISTRICT OF
COLUMBIA

FLORIDA

GEORGIA

KENTUCKY

LOUISIANA

MARYLAND

MISSISSIPPI

NORTH CAROLINA

OKLAHOMA

SOUTH CAROLINA

TENNESSEE

TEXAS

VIRGINIA

WEST VIRGINIA

TREVECCA NAZARENE UNIVERSITY

Address: 333 Murfreesboro Road, Nashville, TN 37210
Website: *https://www.trevecca.edu/programs/physician-assistant*
Contact: *admissions_pa@trevecca.edu*
Phone: 615-248-1225

COST OF ATTENDANCE

Tuition and Fees: $41,600
Additional Expenses: N/A
Total: $41,600*

*This figure does not include cost of living or other related costs.

Financial Aid: https://www.trevecca.edu/financial-aid

ADDITIONAL INFORMATION

Interesting tidbit: Trevecca is proud to be home to the first and longest running Physician Assistant Master of Science in Medicine degree in the state of Tennessee. It aims to integrate faith and learning in every area of our curriculum.

Important Updates due to COVID-19: Online and hybrid science courses will be accepted for the spring and summer semesters of 2021 in addition to spring, summer, and fall semesters of 2020. Applicants may submit their applications before completing 250 (minimum) direct patient care hours and 10 (minimum) shadowing hours but will not be processed for interview selection until all minimum hours are completed and uploaded.

Were tests required? GRE required.

Are tests expected next year? Yes.

What international experiences are available? Foreign mission trips and clinical rotations.

What dual degree options exist? N/A

What service-learning opportunities exist? The Clinic at Mercury Court; Room in The Inn.

PANCE First-Time Pass Rate: 98% (2020)

Other: Early Assurance Process available for Trevecca undergraduates. See https://www.trevecca.edu/programs/pre-physician-assistant

UNIVERSITY OF TENNESSEE HEALTH SCIENCE CENTER

Address: 66 North Pauline, Suite 116, Memphis, TN 38163
Website: *https://www.uthsc.edu/physician-assistant/*
Contact: *paprograminfo@uthsc.edu*
Phone: 901-448-8000

COST OF ATTENDANCE

In-State Tuition and Fees: $22,924
Additional Expenses: $35,572
Total: $58,496

Out-of-State Tuition and Fees: $38,962
Additional Expenses: $35,572
Total: $74,534

Financial Aid: https://www.uthsc.edu/financial-aid/

Note: See Scholarship Opportunities https://www.uthsc.edu/physician-assistant/cost-of-attendance.php

ADDITIONAL INFORMATION

Interesting tidbit: The UTHSC PA program's mission is aligned with that of the University of Tennessee, the University of Tennessee Health Science Center, and the College of Medicine: achieving and maintaining human health.

Important Updates due to COVID-19: For 2020 and 2021, the UTHSC PA program will accept prerequisites as pass/fail courses. It will also accept online labs to meet its requirements. It waives its minimum requirement for shadowing or direct care experience.

Were tests required? No.

Are tests expected next year? No.

What international experiences are available? N/A

What dual degree options exist? N/A

What service-learning opportunities exist? N/A

PANCE First-Time Pass Rate: 93% (2020)

ALABAMA
ARKANSAS
DELAWARE
DISTRICT OF COLUMBIA
FLORIDA
GEORGIA
KENTUCKY
LOUISIANA
MARYLAND
MISSISSIPPI
NORTH CAROLINA
OKLAHOMA
SOUTH CAROLINA
TENNESSEE
TEXAS
VIRGINIA
WEST VIRGINIA

SOUTH

BAYLOR COLLEGE OF MEDICINE

Address: One Baylor Plaza, Houston, TX 77030
Website: *https://www.bcm.edu/education/school-of-health-professions/physician-assistant-program*
Contact: *paprogram@bcm.edu*
Phone: 713-798-3663

COST OF ATTENDANCE

Tuition and Fees: $32,030
Additional Expenses: $13,109*
Total: $45,139*

*This figure does not include cost of living or other related costs.

Financial Aid: https://www.bcm.edu/education/financial-aid

ADDITIONAL INFORMATION

Interesting tidbit: Being housed in the Texas Medical Center, the world's largest medical complex ensures PA students have the opportunity to explore the full range of practice options. Its curriculum leverages all the resources of Baylor College of Medicine, which include one of the largest biomedical research enterprises in the nation and a top-ranked School of Medicine, Graduate School of Biomedical Sciences, and Doctor of Nursing Practice-Nurse Anesthesia program as well as the National School of Tropical Medicine.

Important Updates due to COVID-19: The BCM PA Program will accept online laboratory courses completed in the Spring of 2020, Summer of 2020, Fall of 2020, Spring of 2021, Summer of 2021 and Fall of 2021.

Were tests required? No.

Are tests expected next year? No.

What international experiences are available? Global Outreach. See https://www.bcm.edu/community/global-outreach

What dual degree options exist? N/A

What service-learning opportunities exist? All enrolled students in the PA Program are required to complete a minimum of 12 hours of service learning (SL) within a specified community agency.

PANCE First-Time Pass Rate: 100% (2020)

HARDIN-SIMMONS UNIVERSITY

Address: 2200 Hickory Street, Abilene, TX 79698
Website: *https://www.hsutx.edu/pa*
Contact: *padept@hsutx.edu*
Phone: 325-670-1702

COST OF ATTENDANCE

Tuition and Fees: $29,958
Additional Expenses: $4,279*
Total: $34,237*

*This figure does not include cost of living or other related costs.

Financial Aid: https://www.hsutx.edu/tuition-aid/affording-hsu/

ADDITIONAL INFORMATION

Interesting tidbit: Every HSU PA student is required to complete a minimum of one clinical rotation in a rural or medically underserved area and 50 hours of community service approved by the student advisor.

Important Updates due to COVID-19: Pass/Fail grading will be accepted for prerequisite courses if taken during the 2020-2021 pandemic.

Were tests required? GRE and Altus Suite required.

Are tests expected next year? Yes.

What international experiences are available? Medical trip in collaboration with Bucker International.

What dual degree options exist? N/A

What service-learning opportunities exist? N/A

PANCE First-Time Pass Rate: 100% (2020)

ALABAMA

ARKANSAS

DELAWARE

DISTRICT OF
COLUMBIA

FLORIDA

GEORGIA

KENTUCKY

LOUISIANA

MARYLAND

MISSISSIPPI

NORTH CAROLINA

OKLAHOMA

SOUTH CAROLINA

TENNESSEE

TEXAS

VIRGINIA

WEST VIRGINIA

SOUTH

ALABAMA

ARKANSAS

DELAWARE

DISTRICT OF
COLUMBIA

FLORIDA

GEORGIA

KENTUCKY

LOUISIANA

MARYLAND

MISSISSIPPI

NORTH CAROLINA

OKLAHOMA

SOUTH CAROLINA

TENNESSEE

TEXAS

VIRGINIA

WEST VIRGINIA

TEXAS TECH UNIVERSITY HEALTH SCIENCES CENTER

Address: 3600 N Garfield Street, Midland, TX 79705
Website: *https://www.ttuhsc.edu/health-professions/master-physician-assistant-studies/*
Contact: *health.professions@ttuhsc.edu*
Phone: 432-620-1120

COST OF ATTENDANCE

In-State Tuition and Fees: $15,163
Additional Expenses: $39,180
Total: $54,343

Out-of-State Tuition and Fees: $40,061
Additional Expenses: $38,180
Total: $79,241

Financial Aid: https://www.ttuhsc.edu/financial-aid/

ADDITIONAL INFORMATION

Interesting tidbit: With a focus on primary care and family medicine, the program awards a Master of Physician Assistant Studies degree upon successful completion of a 27-month curriculum. The 15-month academic phase of the program is conducted in a dedicated, state-of-the art facility in Midland, Texas, and the 12-month clinical experience takes place at a variety of sites throughout West Texas.

Important Updates due to COVID-19: N/A

Were tests required? GRE required.

Are tests expected next year? Yes.

What international experiences are available? N/A

What dual degree options exist? N/A

What service-learning opportunities exist? N/A

PANCE First-Time Pass Rate: 91% (2020)

UNIVERSITY OF MARY HARDIN BAYLOR

Address: 900 College Street, Belton, TX 76513
Website: *https://go.umhb.edu/graduate/physician-assistant/home*
Contact: *paprogram@umhb.edu*
Phone: 254-295-5444

COST OF ATTENDANCE

Tuition and Fees: $38,215
Additional Expenses: $15,804
Total: $54,019

Financial Aid: https://go.umhb.edu/graduate/physician-assistant/program-costs#1845

ADDITIONAL INFORMATION

Interesting tidbit: The MSPA program at UMHB began the inaugural cohort in January 2021.

Important Updates due to COVID-19: Beginning January 2020, online prerequisite courses, including those with lab components, will be acceptable options to fulfill its prerequisite requirements. Pass/Fail or Credit/No Credit courses will be accepted.

Were tests required? No.

Are tests expected next year? No.

What international experiences are available? N/A

What dual degree options exist? N/A

What service-learning opportunities exist? N/A

PANCE First-Time Pass Rate: N/A (available after the first cohort graduates in Spring 2023)

ALABAMA
ARKANSAS
DELAWARE
DISTRICT OF COLUMBIA
FLORIDA
GEORGIA
KENTUCKY
LOUISIANA
MARYLAND
MISSISSIPPI
NORTH CAROLINA
OKLAHOMA
SOUTH CAROLINA
TENNESSEE
TEXAS
VIRGINIA
WEST VIRGINIA

SOUTH

UNIVERSITY OF NORTH TEXAS HEALTH SCIENCE CENTER

Address: 3500 Camp Bowie Boulevard, Fort Worth, TX 76107
Website: *https://www.unthsc.edu/school-of-health-professions/physician-assistant-studies/*
Contact: *admissions@unthsc.edu*
Phone: 817-735-2003

COST OF ATTENDANCE

In-State Tuition and Fees: $6,408
Additional Expenses: $36,614
Total: $43,022

Out-of-State Tuition and Fees: $23,136
Additional Expenses: $36,614
Total: $59,906

Financial Aid: https://www.unthsc.edu/financial-aid/

ADDITIONAL INFORMATION

Interesting tidbit: The HSC at Fort Worth PA Program is housed within the School of Health Professions, an optimal environment for interprofessional learning. It provides its students with an environment that is both conducive to learning the art and science of medical practice and to helping our students achieve individual growth as healthcare professionals.

Important Updates due to COVID-19: N/A

Were tests required? CASPer required.

Are tests expected next year? Yes.

What international experiences are available? N/A

What dual degree options exist? MPAS/MPH dual degree. See https://www.unthsc.edu/school-of-public-health/future-students/pa-mph-dual-degree-option/

What service-learning opportunities exist? N/A

PANCE First-Time Pass Rate: 99% (2020)

U.S. ARMY MEDICAL CENTER OF EXCELLENCE INTERSERVICE PHYSICIAN ASSISTANT PROGRAM

Address: 3599 Winfield Scott Road, Academy of Health Sciences, Fort Sam Houston, TX 78234
Website: *https://medcoe.army.mil/ipap/*
Contact: *maria.r.charles.civ@mail.mil*
Phone: 210-221-8004

ADDITIONAL INFORMATION

Interesting tidbit: IPAP is a multi-service program, educating military medicine's frontline healthcare providers for the U.S. Army, U.S. Navy, U.S. Air Force, and U.S. Coast Guard. Successful completion of the IPAP awards the student a Master of Physician Assistant Studies (MPAS) from the University of Nebraska Medical Center. Only Military applicants are accepted.

Important Updates due to COVID-19: N/A

Were tests required? SAT required.

Are tests expected next year? Yes.

What international experiences are available? N/A

What dual degree options exist? N/A

What service-learning opportunities exist? N/A

PANCE First-Time Pass Rate: 98% (2020)

ALABAMA
ARKANSAS
DELAWARE
DISTRICT OF COLUMBIA
FLORIDA
GEORGIA
KENTUCKY
LOUISIANA
MARYLAND
MISSISSIPPI
NORTH CAROLINA
OKLAHOMA
SOUTH CAROLINA
TENNESSEE
TEXAS
VIRGINIA
WEST VIRGINIA

SOUTH

UNIVERSITY OF TEXAS HEALTH SCIENCE CENTER - LAREDO

Address: 1937 Bustamante Street, Laredo, TX 78041
Website: *https://www.uthscsa.edu/academics/health-professions/ programs/physician-assistant-studies-ms/laredo-pa-extension- program*
Contact: *pastudies@uthscsa.edu*
Phone: 210-567-6220

Other Locations: San Antonio, TX

COST OF ATTENDANCE

In-State Tuition and Fees: $18,816
Additional Expenses: $48,320
Total: $67,136

Out-of-State Tuition and Fees: $45,743
Additional Expenses: $48,320
Total: $94,063

Financial Aid: https://students.uthscsa.edu/financialaid/

ADDITIONAL INFORMATION

Interesting tidbit: The PA program will be offered on the main campus at UT Health San Antonio and at the regional campus in Laredo, Texas. Up to 10 qualified students will be admitted to this location.

Important Updates due to COVID-19: The program will accept PASS/FAIL grades and online coursework completed during the Spring, Summer, and Fall semesters of 2020 toward prerequisite coursework for 2020-2021 admissions cycle only.

Were tests required? GRE and Altus Suite required.

Are tests expected next year? Yes.

What international experiences are available? N/A

What dual degree options exist? N/A

What service-learning opportunities exist? N/A

PANCE First-Time Pass Rate: 93% (2020)

UNIVERSITY OF TEXAS HEALTH SCIENCE CENTER - SAN ANTONIO

Address: 7703 Floyd Curl Drive, San Antonio, TX 78229
Website: *https://www.uthscsa.edu/academics/health-professions/
programs/physician-assistant-studies-ms*
Contact: *pastudies@uthscsa.edu*
Phone: 210-567-6220
Other Locations: Laredo, TX

COST OF ATTENDANCE

In-State Tuition and Fees: $18,816
Additional Expenses: $48,320
Total: $67,136

Out-of-State Tuition and Fees: $45,743
Additional Expenses: $48,320
Total: $94,063

Financial Aid: https://students.uthscsa.edu/financialaid/

ADDITIONAL INFORMATION

Interesting tidbit: All applicants are asked to select their campus location preference upon submission of their CASPA application as either "San Antonio", "Laredo", or "either campus". All admitted students will spend a week of mandatory in-residence orientation on the San Antonio campus.

Important Updates due to COVID-19: The program will accept PASS/FAIL grades and online coursework completed during the Spring, Summer, and Fall semesters of 2020 toward prerequisite coursework for 2020-2021 admissions cycle only.

Were tests required? GRE and Altus Suite required.

Are tests expected next year? Yes.

What international experiences are available? N/A

What dual degree options exist? N/A

What service-learning opportunities exist? N/A

PANCE First-Time Pass Rate: 93% (2020)

ALABAMA
ARKANSAS
DELAWARE
DISTRICT OF COLUMBIA
FLORIDA
GEORGIA
KENTUCKY
LOUISIANA
MARYLAND
MISSISSIPPI
NORTH CAROLINA
OKLAHOMA
SOUTH CAROLINA
TENNESSEE
TEXAS
VIRGINIA
WEST VIRGINIA

SOUTH

ALABAMA

ARKANSAS

DELAWARE

DISTRICT OF
COLUMBIA

FLORIDA

GEORGIA

KENTUCKY

LOUISIANA

MARYLAND

MISSISSIPPI

NORTH CAROLINA

OKLAHOMA

SOUTH CAROLINA

TENNESSEE

TEXAS

VIRGINIA

WEST VIRGINIA

UNIVERSITY OF TEXAS MEDICAL BRANCH AT GALVESTON

Address: 301 University Boulevard, Galveston, TX 77555
Website: *https://www.utmb.edu/som/physician-assistant/pas*
Contact: *pasrqinf@utmb.edu*
Phone: 409-772-3048

COST OF ATTENDANCE:

In-State Tuition and Fees: $25,354
Additional Expenses: $26,980
Total: $52,334

Out-of-State Tuition and Fees: $48,050
Additional Expenses: $26,980
Total: $75,030

Financial Aid: https://www.utmb.edu/enrollmentservices/
resources/financial-aid

ADDITIONAL INFORMATION

Interesting tidbit: At UTMB, students will be a part of a Faculty Coached Learning Team (FCLT). FCLTs are a special way UTMB fosters a sense of strong community even though the PA class is large. Students are teamed with their very own faculty mentor and then meet each week in a small group to talk about life, medicine, and career development.

Important Updates due to COVID-19: N/A

Were tests required? GRE and Altus Suite required.

Are tests expected next year? Yes.

What international experiences are available? International rotations.

What dual degree options exist? N/A

What service-learning opportunities exist? N/A

PANCE First-Time Pass Rate: 97% (2020)

UNIVERSITY OF TEXAS RIO GRANDE VALLEY

Address: 1201 West University Drive Edinburgh, TX 78539
Website: *https://www.utrgv.edu/pa/*
Contact: *pad@utrgv.edu*
Phone: 956-665-7049

COST OF ATTENDANCE

In-State Tuition and Fees: $8,586
Additional Expenses: $21,234
Total: $29,820

Out-of-State Tuition and Fees: $21,618
Additional Expenses: $21,234
Total: $42,852

Financial Aid: https://www.utrgv.edu/graduate/funding/financial-assistance/index.htm

ADDITIONAL INFORMATION

Interesting tidbit: The Physician Assistant Department (PAD) is located just 20 minutes from the Texas-Mexican border. The PAD is recognized nationally as a leader in physician assistant student Hispanic enrollment. Also, the UTRGV PA program is the only physician assistant program in Texas that is not located nor affiliated with a medical center.

Important Updates due to COVID-19: The UTRGV Graduate College waived the 2020 – 2021 GRE test score requirement in response to restrictions caused by the COVID-19 outbreak. The requirement is reinstated starting with the 2021-2022 application cycle.

Were tests required? GRE required.

Are tests expected next year? Yes.

What international experiences are available? N/A

What dual degree options exist? N/A

What service-learning opportunities exist? N/A

PANCE First-Time Pass Rate: 85% (2020)

Other: Master in Physician Assistant Studies Bridge Program (MPAS-BP) available for the clinically practicing physician assistant. See https://www.utrgv.edu/pa/graduate-programs/master-physician-assistant-studies-bridge/index.htm

Other: Physician Assistant Career Track (PACT) Early Assurance Program available for qualified South Texas high school students. See https://www.utrgv.edu/pa/pact/index.htm

ALABAMA
ARKANSAS
DELAWARE
DISTRICT OF COLUMBIA
FLORIDA
GEORGIA
KENTUCKY
LOUISIANA
MARYLAND
MISSISSIPPI
NORTH CAROLINA
OKLAHOMA
SOUTH CAROLINA
TENNESSEE
TEXAS
VIRGINIA
WEST VIRGINIA

SOUTH

ALABAMA

ARKANSAS

DELAWARE

DISTRICT OF
COLUMBIA

FLORIDA

GEORGIA

KENTUCKY

LOUISIANA

MARYLAND

MISSISSIPPI

NORTH CAROLINA

OKLAHOMA

SOUTH CAROLINA

TENNESSEE

TEXAS

VIRGINIA

WEST VIRGINIA

UNIVERSITY OF TEXAS SOUTHWESTERN SCHOOL OF HEALTH PROFESSIONS

Address: 6011 Harry Hines Blvd., Dallas, TX 75390
Website: http://www.utsouthwestern.edu/pa
Contact: pa.sshp@utsouthwestern.edu
Phone: 214-648-1702

COST OF ATTENDANCE

In-State Tuition and Fees: $16,017
Additional Expenses: $34,660
Total: $50,677

Out-of-State Tuition and Fees: $33,032
Additional Expenses: $34,660
Total: $67,692

Financial Aid: https://www.utsouthwestern.edu/about-us/administrative-offices/financial-aid/

ADDITIONAL INFORMATION

Interesting tidbit: UT Southwestern Medical Center's Master of Physician Assistant Studies Program offers unmatched resources of UT Southwestern, including Parkland Memorial Hospital. Parkland has earned a place on U.S. News and World Report's list of America's Best Hospitals for more than a decade. Also, William P. Clements Jr. University Hospital, the new clinical facility offers a dynamic learning environment that includes areas for collaborative, team-based education.

Important Updates due to COVID-19: N/A

Were tests required? GRE required.

Are tests expected next year? Yes.

What international experiences are available? N/A

What dual degree options exist? N/A

What service-learning opportunities exist? N/A

PANCE First-Time Pass Rate: 100% (2021)

EASTERN VIRGINIA MEDICAL SCHOOL

Address: 651 Colley Avenue, Norfolk, VA 23501
Website: *http://www.evms.edu/education/masters_programs/
physician_assistant_program/*
Contact: *paprogram@evms.edu*
Phone: 757-446-7158

COST OF ATTENDANCE

In-State Tuition and Fees: $25,246
Additional Expenses: $23,219
Total: $48,465

Out-of-State Tuition and Fees: $31,046
Additional Expenses: $23,219
Total: $54,511

Financial Aid: https://www.evms.edu/education/financial_aid/

ADDITIONAL INFORMATION

Interesting tidbit: EVMS' vision is to be recognized as the most community-oriented school of medicine and health professions in the United States. Its PA curriculum is modeled after school of medicine on the campus of a medical school.

Important Updates due to COVID-19: The program accepts up to two (2) prerequisite courses with a non-traditional letter grade and a minimum GPA of 3.0 to be eligible for admission. It does not discriminate on the basis of where prerequisite courses are taken.

Were tests required? CASPer required.

Are tests expected next year? Yes.

What international experiences are available? N/A

What dual degree options exist? N/A

What service-learning opportunities exist? HOPES Free Clinic. See https://www.evms.edu/education/resources/community-engaged_learning/hopes/

PANCE First-Time Pass Rate: 97% (2020)

Other: Early Assurance Program available for qualified undergraduate students. See https://www.evms.edu/education/masters_programs/physician_assistant_program/admissions_information/early_assurance_program/

ALABAMA

ARKANSAS

DELAWARE

DISTRICT OF COLUMBIA

FLORIDA

GEORGIA

KENTUCKY

LOUISIANA

MARYLAND

MISSISSIPPI

NORTH CAROLINA

OKLAHOMA

SOUTH CAROLINA

TENNESSEE

TEXAS

VIRGINIA

WEST VIRGINIA

SOUTH

ALABAMA

ARKANSAS

DELAWARE

DISTRICT OF COLUMBIA

FLORIDA

GEORGIA

KENTUCKY

LOUISIANA

MARYLAND

MISSISSIPPI

NORTH CAROLINA

OKLAHOMA

SOUTH CAROLINA

TENNESSEE

TEXAS

VIRGINIA

WEST VIRGINIA

EMORY & HENRY COLLEGE

Address: 565 Radio Hill Road, Marion, VA 24354
Website: *https://www.ehc.edu/academics/physician-assistant-studies/*
Contact: srichards@ehc.edu
Phone: 276-944-6342

COST OF ATTENDANCE

Tuition and Fees: $35,832
Additional Expenses: $20,475
Total: $56,307

Financial Aid: https://www.ehc.edu/academics/physician-assistant-studies/admission-tuition-info/tuition-fees/

ADDITIONAL INFORMATION

Interesting tidbit: The program was developed at the request of local communities to assist in meeting the needs of the region. Given this, its training emphasis is on rural primary care for the underserved. Unlike most PA program, E&H PA students do not have to relocate for their clinical rotations as all of rotations can be completed in the area, with an average mileage from campus to clinical site of 33.5 miles

Important Updates due to COVID-19: The program accepts pass/fail grades for mandatory prerequisites in the Spring, Summer, and Fall of 2020 only.

Were tests required? GRE required.

Are tests expected next year? Yes.

What international experiences are available? N/A

What dual degree options exist? N/A

What service-learning opportunities exist? Mel Leaman Free Clinic. See https://www.melleamanfreeclinic.org/

PANCE First-Time Pass Rate: 86% (2020)

JAMES MADISON UNIVERSITY

Address: 235 Martin Luther King Jr. Way, MSC 4315, Harrisonburg, VA 22807
Website: *http://www.healthsci.jmu.edu/PA/*
Contact: *paprogram@jmu.edu*
Phone: 540-568-2395

COST OF ATTENDANCE

In-State Tuition and Fees: $36,575
Additional Expenses: $4,675*
Total: $41,250*

Out-of-State Tuition and Fees: $47,080
Additional Expenses: $4,675*
Total: $51,755*

*This figure does not include cost of living or other related costs.

Financial Aid: https://healthprof.jmu.edu/pa/expenses.html

ADDITIONAL INFORMATION

Interesting tidbit: JMU has a vision to be the national model for the engaged university. The JMU PA program strives to meet this vision through engaged learning, civic engagement, and community engagement.

Important Updates due to COVID-19: N/A

Were tests required? GRE required.

Are tests expected next year? Yes.

What international experiences are available? International elective rotation in Peru. See https://healthprof.chbs.jmu.edu/pa/international.html

What dual degree options exist? N/A

What service-learning opportunities exist? Suitcase Clinic (https://www.iihhs.jmu.edu/suitcaseclinic/); Blue Ridge Free Clinic (https://www.blueridgefreeclinic.org/)

PANCE First-Time Pass Rate: 94% (2020)

ALABAMA
ARKANSAS
DELAWARE
DISTRICT OF COLUMBIA
FLORIDA
GEORGIA
KENTUCKY
LOUISIANA
MARYLAND
MISSISSIPPI
NORTH CAROLINA
OKLAHOMA
SOUTH CAROLINA
TENNESSEE
TEXAS
VIRGINIA
WEST VIRGINIA

SOUTH

ALABAMA

ARKANSAS

DELAWARE

DISTRICT OF
COLUMBIA

FLORIDA

GEORGIA

KENTUCKY

LOUISIANA

MARYLAND

MISSISSIPPI

NORTH CAROLINA

OKLAHOMA

SOUTH CAROLINA

TENNESSEE

TEXAS

VIRGINIA

WEST VIRGINIA

MARY BALDWIN UNIVERSITY

Address: 100 Baldwin Boulevard, Fishersville, VA 22939
Website: *https://go.marybaldwin.edu/health_sciences/pas/*
Contact: *mdchsadmit@marybaldwin.edu*
Phone: 540-887-4110

COST OF ATTENDANCE

Tuition and Fees: $36,400
Additional Expenses: $30,990
Total: $67,390

Financial Aid: https://marybaldwin.edu/financial-aid/graduate/

ADDITIONAL INFORMATION

Interesting tidbit: MBU PA program embraces the team-based, collaborative and interprofessional approach to patient care. Students work together in coursework, special interprofessional case study groups, research and clinical skills scenarios. Collaboration extends, but is not limited, to students from occupational therapy, physical therapy, medicine, nursing, and social work.

Important Updates due to COVID-19: N/A

Were tests required? GRE required.

Are tests expected next year? Yes.

What international experiences are available? N/A

What dual degree options exist? N/A

What service-learning opportunities exist? N/A

PANCE First-Time Pass Rate: 100% (2020)

RADFORD UNIVERSITY CARILION

Address: 101 Elm Avenue SE, CRCH, Roanoke, VA 24013
Website: *https://www.radford.edu/content/grad/home/academics/graduate-programs/pa.html*
Contact: *rhadley1@radford.edu*
Phone: 540-985-4016

COST OF ATTENDANCE

In-State Tuition and Fees: $45,100
Additional Expenses: N/A
Total: $45,100*

Out-of-State Tuition and Fees: $46,145
Additional Expenses: N/A
Total: $46,145*

*This figure does not include cost of living or other related costs.

Financial Aid: https://www.radford.edu/content/financial-aid/home.html

ADDITIONAL INFORMATION

Interesting tidbit: Radford University Carilion (RUC) provides a rigorous real-world learning experience to students pursuing degrees in the health sciences. RUC boasts a faculty of practicing clinicians who, in a clinical setting on the campus of Carilion Medical Center. RUC is born out of collaboration among Carilion Clinic, Jefferson College of Health Sciences and Radford University.

Important Updates due to COVID-19: N/A

Were tests required? GRE required.

Are tests expected next year? Yes.

What international experiences are available? N/A

What dual degree options exist? N/A

What service-learning opportunities exist? N/A

PANCE First-Time Pass Rate: 97% (2020)

ALABAMA
ARKANSAS
DELAWARE
DISTRICT OF
COLUMBIA
FLORIDA
GEORGIA
KENTUCKY
LOUISIANA
MARYLAND
MISSISSIPPI
NORTH CAROLINA
OKLAHOMA
SOUTH CAROLINA
TENNESSEE
TEXAS
VIRGINIA
WEST VIRGINIA

SOUTH

SHENANDOAH UNIVERSITY - LOUDOUN

Address: 44160 Scholar Plaza, Leesburg, VA 20176
Website: *https://www.su.edu/physician-assistant/masters-of-science-in-physician-assistant-studies/*
Contact: *pa@su.edu*
Phone: 540-545-7356

Other Locations: Winchester, VA

COST OF ATTENDANCE

Tuition and Fees: $34,500
Additional Expenses: $4,880*
Total: $39,380*

*This figure does not include cost of living or other related costs.

Financial Aid: https://www.su.edu/financial-aid/incoming-graduate-aid/

ADDITIONAL INFORMATION

Interesting tidbit: Shenandoah University's Physician Assistant (SUPA) program is offered at two locations - Winchester campus and Scholar Plaza campus. Scholar Plaza Loudoun, located in Leesburg, VA, is on the campus of Loudoun Hospital, a nationally recognized hospital.

Important Updates due to COVID-19: The SUPA program will accept P/F grades for prerequisite courses and virtual lab experiences taken from spring 2020 through spring 2021 semesters. Courses including those with laboratory components that were transitioned to an online format during the spring 2020 through the spring 2021 semester will also be accepted.

Were tests required? No.

Are tests expected next year? No.

What international experiences are available? Global Experiential Learning Program. See https://www.su.edu/education-abroad/global-experiential-learning

What dual degree options exist? PA-MPH dual degree. See https://www.su.edu/health/pa-mph-dual-degree/

What service-learning opportunities exist? N/A

PANCE First-Time Pass Rate: 91% (2020)

Other: Early Assurance Pathway (EA-MSPAS) available for high school students. See https://www.su.edu/admissions/future-freshmen/application-information/early-assurance-pathway-application-requirements/physician-assistant-studies-early-assurance-pathway-ea-mspas/

SHENANDOAH UNIVERSITY - WINCHESTER

Address: 1775 North Sector Ct., Winchester, VA 22601
Website: *https://www.su.edu/physician-assistant/masters-of-science-in-physician-assistant-studies/*
Contact: *pa@su.edu*
Phone: 540-542-6208

Other Locations: Leesburg, VA

COST OF ATTENDANCE

Tuition and Fees: $34,500
Additional Expenses: $4,880*
Total: $39,380*

*This figure does not include cost of living or other related costs.

Financial Aid: https://www.su.edu/financial-aid/incoming-graduate-aid/

ADDITIONAL INFORMATION

Interesting tidbit: The SUPA program is housed in the Health Professions Building on the campus of the Winchester Medical Center, a regional referral hospital. The Health & Life Sciences Building provides a state-of-the-art facility for health care education

Important Updates due to COVID-19: The SUPA program will accept P/F grades for prerequisite courses and virtual lab experiences taken from spring 2020 through spring 2021 semesters. Courses including those with laboratory components that were transitioned to an online format during the spring 2020 through the spring 2021 semester will also be accepted.

Were tests required? No.

Are tests expected next year? No.

What international experiences are available? Global Experiential Learning Program. See https://www.su.edu/education-abroad/global-experiential-learning

What dual degree options exist? PA-MPH dual degree. See https://www.su.edu/health/pa-mph-dual-degree/

What service-learning opportunities exist? N/A

PANCE First-Time Pass Rate: 91% (2020)

Other: Early Assurance Pathway (EA-MSPAS) available for high school students. See https://www.su.edu/admissions/future-freshmen/application-information/early-assurance-pathway-application-requirements/physician-assistant-studies-early-assurance-pathway-ea-mspas/

ALABAMA
ARKANSAS
DELAWARE
DISTRICT OF COLUMBIA
FLORIDA
GEORGIA
KENTUCKY
LOUISIANA
MARYLAND
MISSISSIPPI
NORTH CAROLINA
OKLAHOMA
SOUTH CAROLINA
TENNESSEE
TEXAS
VIRGINIA
WEST VIRGINIA

SOUTH

SOUTH UNIVERSITY, RICHMOND

Address: 2151 Old Brick Road, Glen Allen, VA 23060
Website: *https://www.southuniversity.edu/richmond/physician-assistant-ms*
Contact: *richmondpaprogram@southuniversity.edu*
Phone: 804-727-6894

COST OF ATTENDANCE

Tuition and Fees: $40,000
Additional Expenses: $8,410*
Total: $48,410*

*This figure does not include cost of living or other related costs.

Financial Aid: https://www.southuniversity.edu/paying-for-college

ADDITIONAL INFORMATION

Interesting tidbit: The South University PA students rotate in busy clinics, private physician offices, teaching hospitals, large institutions, and military hospitals and clinics. They are offered a wide variety of experiences and locations for their clinical rotations that are designed to round out the application of knowledge and skills to actual patient care.

Important Updates due to COVID-19: The South University PA programs will accept prerequisite courses, including lab work, completed online or on campus from any regionally-accredited U.S. college or university. It will accept "Satisfactory/Unsatisfactory" or "Pass/Fail" grades for courses affected by the COVID-19 pandemic as submitted through CASPA.

Were tests required? GRE required.

Are tests expected next year? Yes.

What international experiences are available?

What dual degree options exist?

What service-learning opportunities exist?

PANCE First-Time Pass Rate: 97% (2020)

UNIVERSITY OF LYNCHBURG

Address: 1501 Lakeside Drive, Lynchburg, VA 24501
Website: *https://www.lynchburg.edu/academics/college-of-health-sciences/physician-assistant-medicine/*
Contact: *pa@lynchburg.edu*
Phone: 434-544-8876

COST OF ATTENDANCE

Tuition and Fees: $38,250
Additional Expenses: $24,304
Total: $62,554

Financial Aid: https://www.lynchburg.edu/graduate-admission/graduate-financial-aid/

ADDITIONAL INFORMATION

Interesting tidbit: UL PA students will benefit from facilities designed specifically to meet the needs of the PA Medicine students. This 26,000 square-foot building features state-of-the-art equipment and technology.

Important Updates due to COVID-19: Applicants who were required to complete a prerequisite course as Pass/Fail or Credit/No Credit between March 1, 2020 and September 1, 2020 may apply for consideration of their coursework with supporting documentation. Courses required to transition to an online format during the spring 2020 semester, including those with laboratory components, will be accepted. Inability to fulfill the requirement a minimum of 500 hours of direct patient care and 8 hours of shadowing a PA due to the Covid-19 pandemic will be considered and evaluated on a case by case basis.

Were tests required? GRE required.

Are tests expected next year? Yes.

What international experiences are available? N/A

What dual degree options exist? N/A

What service-learning opportunities exist? N/A

PANCE First-Time Pass Rate: 93% (2020)

ALABAMA
ARKANSAS
DELAWARE
DISTRICT OF COLUMBIA
FLORIDA
GEORGIA
KENTUCKY
LOUISIANA
MARYLAND
MISSISSIPPI
NORTH CAROLINA
OKLAHOMA
SOUTH CAROLINA
TENNESSEE
TEXAS
VIRGINIA
WEST VIRGINIA

SOUTH

ALDERSON-BROADDUS UNIVERSITY

Address: 101 College Hill Drive, Philippi, WV 26416
Website: *http://ab.edu/academics/master-of-science-in-physician-assistant-studies/*
Contact: *pa@ab.edu*
Phone: 304-457-6283

COST OF ATTENDANCE

Tuition and Fees: $43,500
Additional Expenses: $37,673
Total: $81,173

Financial Aid: https://ab.edu/financial-aid/

ADDITIONAL INFORMATION

Interesting tidbit: Formative assessment strategies are embedded throughout the didactic year to offer critical feedback and early intervention measures prior to students embarking on their clinical rotation year.

Important Updates due to COVID-19: N/A

Were tests required? GRE required.

Are tests expected next year? Yes.

What international experiences are available? N/A

What dual degree options exist? N/A

What service-learning opportunities exist? N/A

PANCE First-Time Pass Rate: 88% (2020)

MARSHALL UNIVERSITY JOAN C. EDWARDS SCHOOL OF MEDICINE

Address: 1542 Spring Valley Drive, Huntington, WV 25704
Website: *https://jcesom.marshall.edu/students/physician-assistant-program/*
Contact: *paprogram@marshall.edu*
Phone: 304-696-6035

COST OF ATTENDANCE

In-State Tuition and Fees: $29,418
Additional Expenses: $30,707
Total: $60,125

Out-of-State Tuition and Fees: $45,918
Additional Expenses: $30,707
Total: $76,625

Financial Aid: https://jcesom.marshall.edu/students/financial-assistance/

ADDITIONAL INFORMATION

Interesting tidbit: Marshall University's PA program is dedicated to training its students to evaluate, diagnose, and manage patients in primary and specialty care across all stages of life as well as patients in culturally diverse and rural settings.

Important Updates due to COVID-19: N/A

Were tests required? GRE/MCAT and CASPer required.

Are tests expected next year? Yes.

What international experiences are available? N/A

What dual degree options exist? N/A

What service-learning opportunities exist? N/A

PANCE First-Time Pass Rate: N/A (available after the inaugural class graduates in May 2023)

ALABAMA
ARKANSAS
DELAWARE
DISTRICT OF COLUMBIA
FLORIDA
GEORGIA
KENTUCKY
LOUISIANA
MARYLAND
MISSISSIPPI
NORTH CAROLINA
OKLAHOMA
SOUTH CAROLINA
TENNESSEE
TEXAS
VIRGINIA
WEST VIRGINIA

SOUTH

UNIVERSITY OF CHARLESTON

Address: 2300 MacCorkle Avenue SE, Charleston, WV 25304
Website: *http://www.ucwv.edu/pa/*
Contact: *jenniferpack@ucwv.edu*
Phone: 304-357-4790

COST OF ATTENDANCE

Tuition and Fees: $36,780
Additional Expenses: $33,106
Total: $69,886

Financial Aid: https://www.ucwv.edu/admissions/financial-aid/

Note: PA specific "Scholarship Opportunities" on https://www.ucwv.edu/academics/school-of-health-sciences/physician-assistant-program/program-costs/

ADDITIONAL INFORMATION

Interesting tidbit: The UC PA program utilizes a pass/fail grading structure to encourage students to work together rather than work to outperform one another.

Important Updates due to COVID-19: The UCPA program will accept pass/fail grades for prerequisite courses completed in Spring and Summer 2020 semesters. It will also waive lab requirements for prerequisites for the Spring and Summer 2020 semesters. Interviews will be conducted via Zoon during the 2021-22 Admissions Cycle. The program strongly recommends that applicants complete CASPA's optional COVID-19 Impact Essay clarifying the reasons for missing requirements.

Were tests required? GRE and CASPer required.

Are tests expected next year? Yes.

What international experiences are available? N/A

What dual degree options exist? N/A

What service-learning opportunities exist? N/A

PANCE First-Time Pass Rate: 97% (2021)

Other: PA Fast Track Admission Pathway available for current full time students at the University of Charleston. See https://www.ucwv.edu/academics/school-of-health-sciences/physician-assistant-program/admissions/pa-fast-track-admission-pathway/

WEST LIBERTY UNIVERSITY

Address: 208 University Drive, West Liberty, WV 26074
Website: *http://www.westliberty.edu/physician-assistant/*
Contact: *paprogram@westliberty.edu*
Phone: 304-336-5098

COST OF ATTENDANCE

In-State Tuition and Fees: $29,106
Additional Expenses: $15,299
Total: $61,014

Out-of-State Tuition and Fees: $45,715
Additional Expenses: $15,299
Total: $61,014

Financial Aid: https://westliberty.edu/physician-assistant/
admissions/financial-aid/

Note: No grants or scholarships are provided by the program.

ADDITIONAL INFORMATION

Interesting tidbit: Because of the close working relationship that PAs have with physicians, PAs are educated in a medical school model. The original concept was to train PAs as primary care providers who could practice with the collaboration and direction but not necessarily in the presence of a physician. Thus, primary care remains the foundation of physician assistant education and training.

Important Updates due to COVID-19: N/A

Were tests required? GRE and Altus Suite required.

Are tests expected next year? Yes.

What international experiences are available? N/A

What dual degree options exist? N/A

What service-learning opportunities exist? N/A

PANCE First-Time Pass Rate: 94% (2020)

ALABAMA
ARKANSAS
DELAWARE
DISTRICT OF COLUMBIA
FLORIDA
GEORGIA
KENTUCKY
LOUISIANA
MARYLAND
MISSISSIPPI
NORTH CAROLINA
OKLAHOMA
SOUTH CAROLINA
TENNESSEE
TEXAS
VIRGINIA
WEST VIRGINIA

SOUTH

ALABAMA

ARKANSAS

DELAWARE

DISTRICT OF
COLUMBIA

FLORIDA

GEORGIA

KENTUCKY

LOUISIANA

MARYLAND

MISSISSIPPI

NORTH CAROLINA

OKLAHOMA

SOUTH CAROLINA

TENNESSEE

TEXAS

VIRGINIA

WEST VIRGINIA

WEST VIRGINIA UNIVERSITY SCHOOL OF MEDICINE

Address: 64 Medical Center Drive, Morgantown, WV 26506
Website: *https://medicine.hsc.wvu.edu/physician-assistant-studies/*
Contact: *jjmomen@hsc.wvu.edu*
Phone: 304-293-1690

COST OF ATTENDANCE

In-State Tuition and Fees: $21,334
Additional Expenses: $17,283
Total: $38,617

Out-of-State Tuition and Fees: $33,332
Additional Expenses: $17,721
Total: $51,053

Financial Aid: https://financialaid.wvu.edu/students/professional-hsc

ADDITIONAL INFORMATION

Interesting tidbit: The Physician Assistant Studies program at the West Virginia University School of Medicine held its inaugural White Coat Ceremony on July 11, 2021. The ceremony for the PA Class of 2022 marks the transition from didactic learning in classrooms and labs to clinical rotations.

Important Updates due to COVID-19: Online courses and courses graded as Pass/Fail which were taken during the spring or summer semesters of 2020 will be accepted to fulfill ALL PA program prerequisites.

Were tests required? GRE required.

Are tests expected next year? Yes.

What international experiences are available? N/A

What dual degree options exist? N/A

What service-learning opportunities exist? N?A

PANCE First-Time Pass Rate: N/A (available after the inaugural class graduates in May 2022)

CHAPTER 5

REGION FOUR
WEST

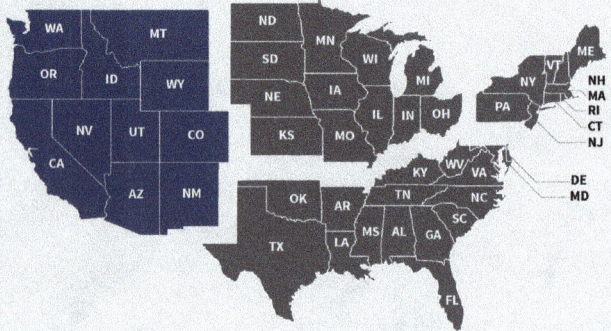

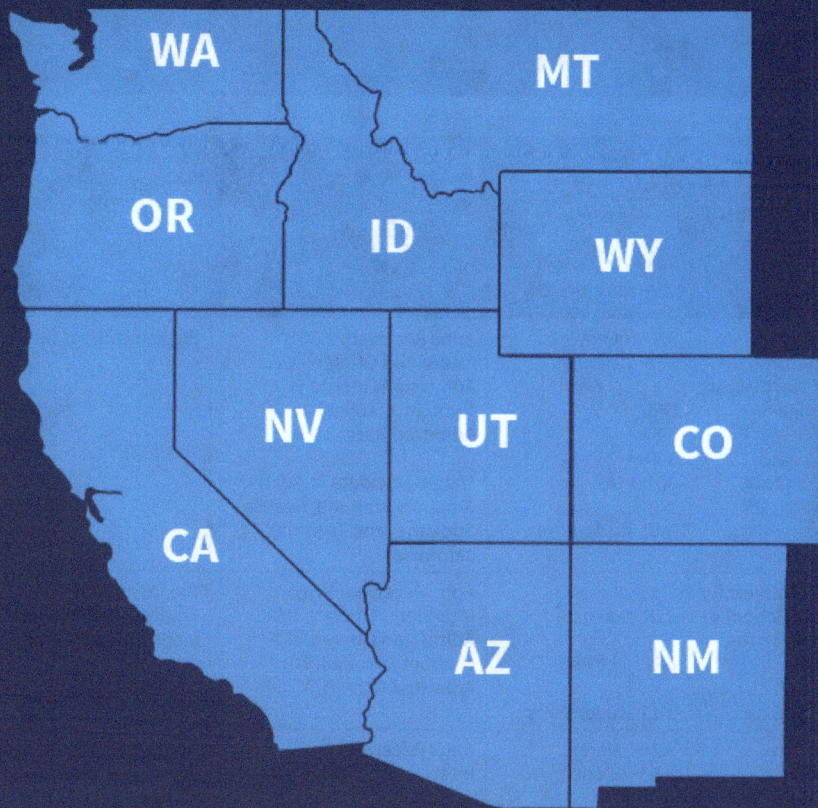

42 Programs | 13 States

PA PROGRAMS

PA School	Ave. GPA & GRE (Verbal, Quantitative, Analy. Writing) Int'l Students: Yes/No	Admission Statistics	Prerequisite Coursework Other than Gen Bio, Gen Chem, Human Anatomy, Human Physiology, Microbiology, Statistics, Psychology
University of Washington - MEDEX Northwest, Anchorage 1901 Bragaw Road, Suite 205, Anchorage, AK 99508	3.0+ (overall) 3.0+ (science) GRE: 30%+ (V) 30%+ (Q) 30%+ (A) Int'l Student: Yes	Apps Received: 1,301* Interviews Offered: N/A Admission Offered: N/A Number Enrolled: 25 Admitted Rate: 1.9% *Aggregate data for all five (Anchorage, Kona, Seattle, Spokane, and Tacoma) campuses.	English courses (2)
A.T. Still University - Arizona School of Health Sciences 5850 E. Still Circle Mesa, AZ 85206	3.55 (overall) 3.51 (science) GRE: Not Req. Int'l Student: Yes	Apps Received: N/A Interviews Offered: N/A Admission Offered: N/A Number Enrolled: 70 Admitted Rate: N/A	Biochemistry; English Composition; Medical Terminology
Midwestern University - Glendale 19555 59th Avenue, Glendale, AZ 85254	3.70 (overall) 3.62 (science) GRE: 70% (V) 61% (Q) 4.3 (A) Int'l Student: Yes	Apps Received: 1,662 Interviews Offered: N/A Admission Offered: N/A Number Enrolled: 90 Admitted Rate: 5.4%	College Algebra or higher; English Composition; OChem
Northern Arizona University 435 N. 5th Street, Phoenix, AZ 85004	3.57 (overall) 3.54 (science) GRE: Not Req. Int'l Student: Yes	Apps Received: 2,000 Interviews Offered: N/A Admission Offered: N/A Number Enrolled: 50 Admitted Rate: 2.5%	Biochemistry or OChem; Upper-level Science courses
California Baptist University 8432 Magnolia Ave., Riverside, CA 92504	3.74 (overall) 3.67 (science) GRE: Not Req. Int'l Student: Yes	Apps Received: N/A Interviews Offered: N/A Admission Offered: N/A Number Enrolled: 30 Admitted Rate: N/A	English Composition; Genetics; Social Sciences/ Humanities (3)
California State University - Monterey Bay 1450 N. Main Street, Salinas, CA 93906	3.35 (overall) 3.29 (science) GRE: Not Req. Int'l Student: Yes	Apps Received: 281 Interviews Offered: 60 Admission Offered: N/A Number Enrolled: 29 Admitted Rate: 10.3%	English Composition; Spanish

PA School	Ave. GPA & GRE (Verbal, Quantitative, Analy. Writing) Int'l Students: Yes/No	Admission Statistics	Prerequisite Coursework Other than Gen Bio, Gen Chem, Human Anatomy, Human Physiology, Microbiology, Statistics, Psychology
Chapman University 9401 Geronimo Road, Irvine, CA 92618	3.56 (overall) 3.47 (science) GRE: N/A Int'l Student: No	Apps Received: N/A Interviews Offered: N/A Admission Offered: N/A Number Enrolled: 50 Admitted Rate: N/A	English Composition; Genetics; Medical Terminology; Pre-Calculus or Calculus; Sociology or Cultural Anthropology;
Charles R. Drew University 1731 E. 120th Street, Los Angeles, CA 90059	3.40 (overall) 3.40 (science) GRE: Not Req. Int'l Student: Yes	Apps Received: 3,853 Interviews Offered: 117 Admission Offered: N/A Number Enrolled: 26 Admitted Rate: 0.7%	College Algebra or higher; English Composition; Medical Terminology
Dominican University of California 50 Acacia Avenue, San Rafael, CA 94901	3.50 (overall) 3.50 (science) GRE: Not Req. Int'l Student: Yes	Apps Received: N/A Interviews Offered: N/A Admission Offered: N/A Number Enrolled: 30 Admitted Rate: N/A	College Algebra or higher
Loma Linda University 24785 Stewart Street, Loma Linda, CA 92350	3.58 (overall) 3.56 (science) GRE: Not Req. Int'l Student: Yes	Apps Received: 2,415 Interviews Offered: 124 Admission Offered: N/A Number Enrolled: 38 Admitted Rate: 1.6%	College Algebra or higher; English Composition; Sociology or Cultural Anthropology
Marshall B. Ketchum University 2575 Yorba Linda Blvd., Fullerton, CA 92831	3.50 (overall) 3.46 (science) GRE: Not Req. Int'l Student: Yes	Apps Received: N/A Interviews Offered: N/A Admission Offered: N/A Number Enrolled: 40 Admitted Rate: N/A	Biochemistry or OChem; Genetics;
Point Loma Nazarene University 3900 Lomaland Drive, San Diego, CA 92106	3.0+ (overall) 3.0+ (science) GRE: Not Req. Int'l Student: Yes	Apps Received: N/A Interviews Offered: N/A Admission Offered: N/A Number Enrolled: 30 Admitted Rate: N/A	Biochemistry; OChem

WEST

PA PROGRAMS

PA School	Ave. GPA & GRE (Verbal, Quantitative, Analy. Writing) Int'l Students: Yes/No	Admission Statistics	Prerequisite Coursework Other than Gen Bio, Gen Chem, Human Anatomy, Human Physiology, Microbiology, Statistics, Psychology
Samuel Merritt University 3100 Telegraph Avenue, Suite 1000, Oakland, CA 94609	3.34 (overall) 3.28 (science) GRE: Not Req. Int'l Student: Yes	Apps Received: N/A Interviews Offered: N/A Admission Offered: N/A Number Enrolled: 44 Admitted Rate: N/A	Biology Elective; OChem
Southern California University of Health Sciences 16200 Amber Valley Drive, Whittier, CA 90604	3.46 (overall) GRE: Not Req. Int'l Student: Yes	Apps Received: N/A Interviews Offered: N/A Admission Offered: N/A Number Enrolled: 50 Admitted Rate: N/A	English Composition; Medical Terminology; Sociology or Anthropology
Stanford University 1265 Welch Rd., Stanford, CA 94305	3.60 (overall) 3.60 (science) GRE: 73% (V) 66% (Q) 79% (A) Int'l Student: Yes	Apps Received: N/A Interviews Offered: N/A Admission Offered: N/A Number Enrolled: 27 Admitted Rate: N/A	N/A
Touro University California* 1310 Club Drive, Vallejo, CA 94592	3.30 (overall) 3.24 (science) GRE: Not Req. Int'l Student: No	Apps Received: N/A Interviews Offered: N/A Admission Offered: N/A Number Enrolled: 48 Admitted Rate: N/A	*PA/MPH dual degree program
University of California, Davis 2570 48th St., Sacramento, CA 95817	3.0+ (overall) 2.7+ (science) GRE: Not Req. Int'l Student: Yes	Apps Received: N/A Interviews Offered: N/A Admission Offered: N/A Number Enrolled: 65 Admitted Rate: N/A	English Composition; Social Sciences (2)
University of La Verne 1950 Third Street, La Verne, CA 91750	3.40 (overall) 3.75 (science) GRE: Not Req. Int'l Student: Yes	Apps Received: 756 Interviews Offered: 65 Admission Offered: N/A Number Enrolled: 30 Admitted Rate: 4.0%	English Composition; Medical Terminology; Philosophy or Religion or Ethics or Critical Thinking; Sociology or Anthropology; Speech Communication

PA School	Ave. GPA & GRE (Verbal, Quantitative, Analy. Writing) Int'l Students: Yes/No	Admission Statistics	Prerequisite Coursework Other than Gen Bio, Gen Chem, Human Anatomy, Human Physiology, Microbiology, Statistics, Psychology
University of Southern California 1000 S. Fremont Avenue, Bldg. A-11, Alhambra, CA 91803	3.46 (overall) 3.35 (science) GRE: 306 (Q&V combined) Int'l Student: Yes	Apps Received: N/A Interviews Offered: N/A Admission Offered: N/A Number Enrolled: 60 Admitted Rate: N/A	N/A
University of the Pacific 3200 5th Avenue, Sacramento, CA 95817	3.74 (overall) 3.72 (science) GRE: Not Req. Int'l Student: Yes	Apps Received: N/A Interviews Offered: N/A Admission Offered: N/A Number Enrolled: 45 Admitted Rate: N/A	English Composition
Western University of Health Sciences 309 E. Second St., Pomona, CA 91766	3.66 (overall) 3.67 (science) GRE: Not Req. Int'l Student: Yes	Apps Received: 2,114 Interviews Offered: 485 Admission Offered: N/A Number Enrolled: 98 Admitted Rate: 4.6%	College Algebra; English Composition; Genetics; Sociology; Humanities
Colorado Mesa University 1100 North Avenue, Grand Junction, CO 81501	3.68 (overall) 3.68 (science) GRE: Not Req. Int'l Student: Yes	Apps Received: N/A Interviews Offered: N/A Admission Offered: N/A Number Enrolled: 16 Admitted Rate: N/A	Genetics
Red Rocks Community College 10280 West 55th Avenue, Arvada, CO 80002	3.50 (overall) 3.43 (science) GRE: Not Req. Int'l Student: Yes	Apps Received: N/A Interviews Offered: N/A Admission Offered: N/A Number Enrolled: 33 Admitted Rate: N/A	College Algebra or higher; Cell Biology; Genetics; OChem; Physics;

WEST

PA PROGRAMS

PA School	Ave. GPA & GRE (Verbal, Quantitative, Analy. Writing) Int'l Students: Yes/No	Admission Statistics	Prerequisite Coursework Other than Gen Bio, Gen Chem, Human Anatomy, Human Physiology, Microbiology, Statistics, Psychology
Rocky Vista University 8401 S. Chambers Road, Parker, CO 80134	3.64 (overall) 3.35 (science) GRE: 50%+ (V) 50%+ (Q) 50%+ (A) Int'l Student: No	Apps Received: N/A Interviews Offered: 110-150 Admission Offered: N/A Number Enrolled: 36 Admitted Rate: N/A	N/A
University of Colorado 1635 Aurora Ct, Aurora, CO 80045	3.80 (overall) 3.76 (science) GRE: Not Req. Int'l Student: Yes	Apps Received: 2,061 Interviews Offered: 143 Admission Offered: N/A Number Enrolled: 44 Admitted Rate: 2.1%	Genetics
University of Washington - MEDEX Northwest, Kona 81-6350 Mamalahoa Hwy, Kealakekua, HI 96750	3.0+ (overall) 3.0+ (science) GRE: 30%+ (V) 30%+ (Q) 30%+ (A) Int'l Student: Yes	Apps Received: 1,301* Interviews Offered: N/A Admission Offered: N/A Number Enrolled: 17 Admitted Rate: 1.3% *Aggregate data for all five (Anchorage, Kona, Seattle, Spokane, and Tacoma) campuses.	English courses (2)
Idaho State University - Caldwell 2112 Cleveland Blvd., Caldwell, ID 83605	3.88 (science) GRE: 78% (V) 58% (Q) Int'l Student: Yes	Apps Received: 857* Interviews Offered: 163* Admission Offered: N/A Number Enrolled: 12 Admitted Rate: 1.4% *Aggregate data for all three (Caldwell, Meridian, and Pocatello) campuses.	Biochemistry
Idaho State University - Meridian 1311 E. Central Dr., Meridian, ID 83642	3.88 (science) GRE: 78% (V) 58% (Q) Int'l Student: Yes	Apps Received: 857* Interviews Offered: 163* Admission Offered: N/A Number Enrolled: 36 Admitted Rate: 4.2% *Aggregate data for all three (Caldwell, Meridian, and Pocatello) campuses.	Biochemistry

PA School	Ave. GPA & GRE (Verbal, Quantitative, Analy. Writing) Int'l Students: Yes/No	Admission Statistics	Prerequisite Coursework Other than Gen Bio, Gen Chem, Human Anatomy, Human Physiology, Microbiology, Statistics, Psychology
Idaho State University - Pocatello 1021 S. Red Hill Road, Red Hill Building #40, Pocatello, ID 83209	3.88 (science) GRE: 78% (V) 58% (Q) Int'l Student: Yes	Apps Received: 857* Interviews Offered: 163* Admission Offered: N/A Number Enrolled: 24 Admitted Rate: 2.8% *Aggregate data for all three (Caldwell, Meridian, and Pocatello) campuses.	Biochemistry
Rocky Mountain College 1511 Poly Drive, BIllings, MT 59102	3.0+ (overall) 3.0+ (science) GRE: 291+ (Q&V combined) Int'l Student: Yes	Apps Received: N/A Interviews Offered: N/A Admission Offered: N/A Number Enrolled: 36 Admitted Rate: N/A	Biochemistry; English Composition; Medical Terminology; OChem; Social Science
Touro University Nevada 874 American Pacific Drive, Henderson, NV 89011	3.46 (overall) 3.41 (science) GRE: N/A Int'l Student: No	Apps Received: N/A Interviews Offered: N/A Admission Offered: N/A Number Enrolled: 80 Admitted Rate: N/A	Biochemistry; OChem
University of Nevada, Reno 18600 Wedge Parkway, Reno, NV 89511	3.50 (overall) 3.54 (science) GRE: Not Req. Int'l Student: No	Apps Received: 1,328 Interviews Offered: 82 Admission Offered: N/A Number Enrolled: 24 Admitted Rate: 1.8%	N/A
University of New Mexico 1 University of New Mexico,, Albuquerque, NM 87131	3.72 (overall) 3.77 (science) GRE: 153 (V) 150 (Q) 3.9 (A) Int'l Student: Yes	Apps Received: 500 Interviews Offered: 60 Admission Offered: N/A Number Enrolled: 22 Admitted Rate: 4.4%	Cellular & Molecular Biology; Writing/Literature/Public Speaking/Linguistics (2)

WEST

PA PROGRAMS

PA School	Ave. GPA & GRE (Verbal, Quantitative, Analy. Writing) Int'l Students: Yes/No	Admission Statistics	Prerequisite Coursework Other than Gen Bio, Gen Chem, Human Anatomy, Human Physiology, Microbiology, Statistics, Psychology
University of St. Francis 1500 N Renaissance Blvd. NE, Suite C, Albuquerque, NM 87107	3.56 (overall) 3.45 (science) GRE: 150 (V) 150 (Q) 4 (A) Int'l Student: Yes	Apps Received: N/A Interviews Offered: N/A Admission Offered: N/A Number Enrolled: 30 Admitted Rate: N/A	Genetics
George Fox University 414 North Meridian Street Newberg, OR 97132	3.69 (overall) 3.76 (science) GRE: N/A Int'l Student: Yes	Apps Received: N/A Interviews Offered: N/A Admission Offered: N/A Number Enrolled: 20 Admitted Rate: N/A	N/A
Oregon Health & Science University 2730 SW Moody Ave., Portland, OR 97201	3.47 (overall) GRE: Not Req. Int'l Student: Yes	Apps Received: 1,230 Interviews Offered: 150 Admission Offered: N/A Number Enrolled: 41 Admitted Rate: 3.3%	N/A
Pacific University 190 SE 8th Avenue, Suite 181, Hillsboro, OR 97123	3.89 (overall) 3.77 (science) GRE: Not Req. Int'l Student: Yes	Apps Received: 2,216 Interviews Offered: 161 Admission Offered: N/A Number Enrolled: 60 Admitted Rate: 2.7%	Biochemistry or OChem
Rocky Mountain University of Health Professions 122 East 1700 South, Provo, UT 84606	3.2+ (overall) 3.0+ (science) GRE: 290+ (Q&V combined) 3.5+ (A) Int'l Student: Yes	Apps Received: N/A Interviews Offered: N/A Admission Offered: N/A Number Enrolled: 50 Admitted Rate: N/A	College Algebra or higher; Medical Terminology
University of Utah 375 Chipeta Way, Salt Lake City, UT 84108	3.57 (overall) 3.53 (science) GRE: Not Req. Int'l Student: Yes	Apps Received: 2,982 Interviews Offered: 161 Admission Offered: N/A Number Enrolled: 68 Admitted Rate: 2.3%	N/A

PA School	Ave. GPA & GRE (Verbal, Quantitative, Analy. Writing) Int'l Students: Yes/No	Admission Statistics	Prerequisite Coursework Other than Gen Bio, Gen Chem, Human Anatomy, Human Physiology, Microbiology, Statistics, Psychology
University of Washington - MEDEX Northwest, Seattle 4311 11th Avenue NE, Suite 200, Seattle, WA 98105	3.49 (overall) GRE: 30%+ (V) 30%+ (Q) 30%+ (A) Int'l Student: Yes	Apps Received: 1,301* Interviews Offered: N/A Admission Offered: N/A Number Enrolled: 46 Admitted Rate: 3.5% *Aggregate data for all five (Anchorage, Kona, Seattle, Spokane, and Tacoma) campuses.	English courses (2)
University of Washington - MEDEX Northwest, Spokane 502 E Boone Ave., Spokane, WA 99258	3.0+ (overall) 3.0+ (science) GRE: 30%+ (V) 30%+ (Q) 30%+ (A) Int'l Student: Yes	Apps Received: 1,301* Interviews Offered: N/A Admission Offered: N/A Number Enrolled: 31 Admitted Rate: 2.4% *Aggregate data for all five (Anchorage, Kona, Seattle, Spokane, and Tacoma) campuses.	English courses (2)
University of Washington - MEDEX Northwest, Tacoma 1900 Commerce Street, Tacoma, WA 98402	3.0+ (overall) 3.0+ (science) GRE: 30%+ (V) 30%+ (Q) 30%+ (A) Int'l Student: Yes	Apps Received: 1,301* Interviews Offered: N/A Admission Offered: N/A Number Enrolled: 21 Admitted Rate: 1.6% *Aggregate data for all five (Anchorage, Kona, Seattle, Spokane, and Tacoma) campuses.	English courses (2)

WEST

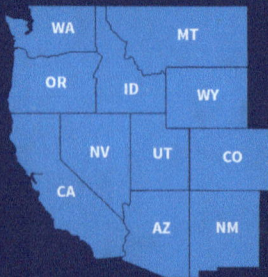

UNIVERSITY OF WASHINGTON - MEDEX NORTHWEST, ANCHORAGE

Address: 1901 Bragaw Road, Suite 205, Anchorage, AK 99508
Website: *https://depts.washington.edu/medex/pa-program/*
Contact: *medex@uw.edu*
Phone: 907-786-5481

Other Locations: Kona, HI; Seattle, WA; Spokane, WA; Tacoma, WA

COST OF ATTENDANCE

Tuition and Fees: $37,940
Additional Expenses: $9,973*
Total: $47,913*

*This figure does not include cost of living or other indirect costs.

Financial Aid: https://depts.washington.edu/medex/pa-program/program-cost/financial-aid/

ADDITIONAL INFORMATION

Interesting tidbit: The MEDEX Anchorage campus opened in 2009. Anchorage students begin their training in Seattle, where they join the rest of their cohort from all sites for the opening summer session. The Anchorage site seeks to train PAs who will serve the communities of Alaska.

Important Updates due to COVID-19: For the 2021-2022 application cycle, the GRE is not required, however it is recommended. Prerequisite courses completed on a pass/no pass grading scale for courses taken between Jan 2020 – August 2021 will be accepted. MEDEX Northwest will accept virtual shadowing.

Were tests required? No.

Are tests expected next year? GRE required.

What international experiences are available? N/A

What dual degree options exist? N/A

What service-learning opportunities exist? N/A

PANCE First-Time Pass Rate: 100% (2020)

Note: Applicants will indicate their first and second campus location preference on their MEDEX Supplemental Application. Applicants will be considered primarily for their first campus location choice. All students are required to be in Seattle for two weeks for New Student Orientation. Students will return to their home campuses for the remainder of the didactic curriculum.

ALASKA

ARIZONA

CALIFORNIA

COLORADO

HAWAII

IDAHO

MONTANA

NEVADA

NEW MEXICO

OREGON

UTAH

WASHINGTON

WYOMING

A.T. STILL UNIVERSITY - ARIZONA SCHOOL OF HEALTH SCIENCES

Address: 5850 E. Still Circle Mesa, AZ 85206
Website: *https://www.atsu.edu/physician-assistant-degree*
Contact: *admissions@atsu.edu*
Phone: 480-219-6000

COST OF ATTENDANCE

Tuition and Fees: $51,306
Additional Expenses: N/A
Total: $51,306*

*This figure does not include cost of living or other indirect costs.

Financial Aid: https://www.atsu.edu/pdf/financial-aid-paying-for-health-professions-school.pdf

ADDITIONAL INFORMATION

Interesting tidbit: Through a partnership with the National Association of Community Health Centers (NACHC), we are training whole-person-care, community-centered practitioners through year-long clinical experience at a CHC for a selected portion of the class. ATSU-ASHS graduates strive to provide culturally and spiritually competent primary care where and to whom healing is needed the most at one of our partner Community Health Centers across the country.

Important Updates due to COVID-19: The ATSU-ASHS PA Program will accept pass/fail for prerequisites but only if letter grades are no longer an option.

Were tests required? No.

Are tests expected next year? No.

What international experiences are available? N/A

What dual degree options exist? N/A

What service-learning opportunities exist? N/A

PANCE First-Time Pass Rate: 94% (2020)

ALASKA

ARIZONA

CALIFORNIA

COLORADO

HAWAII

IDAHO

MONTANA

NEVADA

NEW MEXICO

OREGON

UTAH

WASHINGTON

WYOMING

WEST

ALASKA

ARIZONA

CALIFORNIA

COLORADO

HAWAII

IDAHO

MONTANA

NEVADA

NEW MEXICO

OREGON

UTAH

WASHINGTON

WYOMING

MIDWESTERN UNIVERSITY - GLENDALE

Address: 19555 59th Avenue, Glendale, AZ 85254
Website: *https://www.midwestern.edu/academics/degrees-and-programs/master-of-medical-sciences-in-physician-assistant-studies-az.xml*
Contact: *admissaz@midwestern.edu*
Phone: 623-572-3614

COST OF ATTENDANCE

Tuition and Fees: $60,207
Additional Expenses: $6,887*
Total: $67,094*

*This figure does not include cost of living or other indirect costs.

Financial Aid: https://www.midwestern.edu//admissions/tuition-and-financial-aid.xml

ADDITIONAL INFORMATION

Interesting tidbit: The Midwestern University - Glendale PA program has recently received approval from ARC-PA to transition our curriculum from a 27-month to a 24-month program beginning Summer 2021.

Important Updates due to COVID-19: N/A

Were tests required? GRE and CASPer required.

Are tests expected next year? Yes.

What international experiences are available? n/A

What dual degree options exist? N/A

What service-learning opportunities exist? N/A

PANCE First-Time Pass Rate: 98% (2020)

NORTHERN ARIZONA UNIVERSITY

Address: 435 N. 5th Street, Phoenix, AZ 85004
Website: *http://www.nau.edu/pa*
Contact: *PAProg@nau.edu*
Phone: 602-827-2450

COST OF ATTENDANCE

In-State Tuition and Fees: $19,555
Additional Expenses: $48,975
Total: $40,180

Out-of-State Tuition and Fees: $34,951
Additional Expenses: $48,975
Total: $83,926

Financial Aid: https://nau.edu/office-of-scholarships-and-financial-aid/#

ADDITIONAL INFORMATION

Interesting tidbit: The Northern Arizona University PA Program is Arizona's only public university PA program. The program operates in collaboration with the University of Arizona – Phoenix College of Medicine.

Important Updates due to COVID-19: For March 1, 2020 through September 1, 2020 ONLY, applicants who completed a prerequisite course as Pass/Fail or Credit/No Credit during the approved time period may submit those courses for prerequisite consideration.

Were tests required? No.

Are tests expected next year? No.

What international experiences are available? N/A

What dual degree options exist? N/A

What service-learning opportunities exist? N/A

PANCE First-Time Pass Rate: 94% (2020)

ALASKA

ARIZONA

CALIFORNIA

COLORADO

HAWAII

IDAHO

MONTANA

NEVADA

NEW MEXICO

OREGON

UTAH

WASHINGTON

WYOMING

WEST

ALASKA

ARIZONA

CALIFORNIA

COLORADO

HAWAII

IDAHO

MONTANA

NEVADA

NEW MEXICO

OREGON

UTAH

WASHINGTON

WYOMING

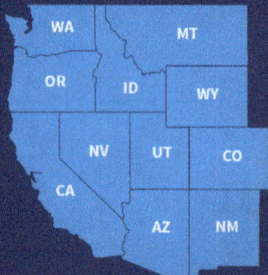

CALIFORNIA BAPTIST UNIVERSITY

Address: 8432 Magnolia Ave., Riverside CA 92504
Website: *https://calbaptist.edu/programs/master-of-science-physician-assistant-studies/*
Contact: *pagrogram@calbaptist.edu*
Phone: 951-552-8515

COST OF ATTENDANCE

Tuition and Fees: $56,670
Additional Expenses: $15,200*
Total: $71,870*

*This figure does not include cost of living or other indirect costs.

Financial Aid: https://calbaptist.edu/financial-aid/graduate/
Note: The physician assistant program does not provide grants or scholarships at this time.

ADDITIONAL INFORMATION

Interesting tidbit: In the first two years of CBU MSPAS program, the students won the CAPA Student Medical Challenge Bowl back-to-back. Since then, CBU has won the first-ever virtual CPAP Student Medical Challenge in 2020, thereby making it three wins in the first four years of the program.

Important Updates due to COVID-19: For courses for Spring 2020, Summer 2020, Fall 2020, Spring 2021 and Summer 2021, CBU will accept online coursework and lab. If letter grades were replaced with Pass/No Pass grades during this period, those grades will also be accepted.

Were tests required? No.

Are tests expected next year? No.

What international experiences are available? N/A

What dual degree options exist? N/A

What service-learning opportunities exist? Global Health Engagement course.

PANCE First-Time Pass Rate: 89% (2020)

CALIFORNIA STATE UNIVERSITY - MONTEREY BAY

Address: 1450 N. Main Street, Salinas, CA 93906
Website: *http://csumb.edu/mspa*
Contact: *mspa@csumb.edu*
Phone: 831-772-7070

COST OF ATTENDANCE

Tuition and Fees: $54,600
Additional Expenses: $29,058
Total: $83,658

Financial Aid: https://csumb.edu/financialaid/

ADDITIONAL INFORMATION

Interesting tidbit: The MSPA curriculum at CSUMB is eparated into didactic, clinical, and hybrid semesters. During the didactic year, students will become familiar with health issues specific to the local community and patient education and evaluation techniques in both English and Spanish. The final hybrid semester includes clinical, didactic, and professional components, and the graduate project.

Important Updates due to COVID-19: Interview may be conducted virtually.

Were tests required? No.

Are tests expected next year? No.

What international experiences are available? N/A

What dual degree options exist? N/A

What service-learning opportunities exist? N/A

PANCE First-Time Pass Rate: N/A (data will be updated for its inaugural class of 2021)

ALASKA

ARIZONA

CALIFORNIA

COLORADO

HAWAII

IDAHO

MONTANA

NEVADA

NEW MEXICO

OREGON

UTAH

WASHINGTON

WYOMING

WEST

ALASKA

ARIZONA

CALIFORNIA

COLORADO

HAWAII

IDAHO

MONTANA

NEVADA

NEW MEXICO

OREGON

UTAH

WASHINGTON

WYOMING

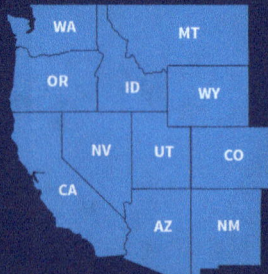

CHAPMAN UNIVERSITY

Address: 9401 Jeronimo Road, Irvine, CA 92618
Website: *https://www.chapman.edu/crean/academic-programs/graduate-programs/physician-assistant/index.aspx*
Contact: *paprogram@chapman.edu*
Phone: 714-744-2190

COST OF ATTENDANCE

Tuition and Fees: $59,365
Additional Expenses: $5,660*
Total: $65,025*

*This figure does not include cost of living or other indirect costs.
Financial Aid: https://www.chapman.edu/students/tuition-and-aid/financial-aid/graduate/index.aspx

Note: Simon Schoar PA Scholarship Program. See https://www.chapman.edu/crean/academic-programs/graduate-programs/physician-assistant/scholarship-simon-scholar-physician-assistant-program.aspx

ADDITIONAL INFORMATION

Interesting tidbit: Chapman University PA Program is a research-based institution that offers a rigorous, interprofessional education. Its emphasis is on best practices to provide optimum patient well-being.

Important Updates due to COVID-19: N/A

Were tests required? GRE required.

Are tests expected next year? Yes.

What international experiences are available? N/A

What dual degree options exist? N/A

What service-learning opportunities exist? Community outreach programs. See https://www.chapman.edu/crean/academic-programs/graduate-programs/physician-assistant/community-outreach.aspx

PANCE First-Time Pass Rate: 100% (2020)

Other: MMS-PA/BS Bridge Program available for highly qualified Health Science majors at Chapman University. See https://www.chapman.edu/crean/academic-programs/bridge-linkage-programs/bs-health-science-ms-physician-assistant.aspx

CHARLES R. DREW UNIVERSITY

Address: 1731 E. 120th Street, Los Angeles, CA 90059
Website: *https://www.cdrewu.edu/cosh/PA*
Contact: *admissionsinfo@cdrewwu.edu*
Phone: 323-563-4800

COST OF ATTENDANCE

Tuition and Fees: $65,582
Additional Expenses: $38,886
Total: $104,468

Financial Aid: https://www.cdrewu.edu/admissions/financial-aid/
LoanRepaymentPrograms/GraduateResources

Note: For Scholarships and Grants, see https://www.cdrewu.edu/
cosh/PA/Scholarship

ADDITIONAL INFORMATION

Interesting tidbit: The Charles R. Drew University PA Program
was the first Physician Assistant program in the state of California.
The Master of Health Sciences-Physician Assistant program was
established in 2016.

Important Updates due to COVID-19: N/A

Were tests required? No.

Are tests expected next year? No.

What international experiences are available? N/A

What dual degree options exist? N/A

What service-learning opportunities exist? N/A

PANCE First-Time Pass Rate: 92% (2020)

ALASKA

ARIZONA

CALIFORNIA

COLORADO

HAWAII

IDAHO

MONTANA

NEVADA

NEW MEXICO

OREGON

UTAH

WASHINGTON

WYOMING

WEST

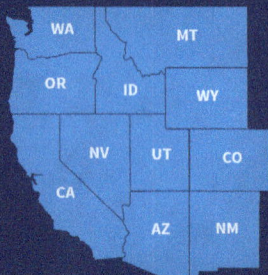

DOMINICAN UNIVERSITY OF CALIFORNIA

Address: 50 Acacia Avenue, San Rafael, CA 94901
Website: *https://www.dominican.edu/directory/physician-assistant-studies*
Contact: *marybeth.culler@dominican.edu*
Phone: 415-482-3571

COST OF ATTENDANCE

Tuition and Fees: $41,481
Additional Expenses: N/A
Total: $41,481*

*This figure does not include cost of living or other indirect costs.

Financial Aid: https://www.dominican.edu/admissions/tuition-and-financial-aid/total-cost-attendance/graduate-tuition-and-aid/physician-assistant-studies-mspas-tuition-and-aid

Note: There are no institutional grants or scholarships for the Master of Science Physician Assistant Studies Program.

ADDITIONAL INFORMATION

Interesting tidbit: Dominican's Master in Physician Assistant Studies is a 28-month program. Students complete 16 months of didactic education in medicine, followed by a 12-month clinical education.

Important Updates due to COVID-19: N/A

Were tests required? No.

Are tests expected next year? No.

What international experiences are available? N/A

What dual degree options exist? N/A

What service-learning opportunities exist? N/A

PANCE First-Time Pass Rate: 100% (2020)

LOMA LINDA UNIVERSITY

Address: 24785 Stewart Street, Evans Hall 201, Loma Linda, CA 92350
Website: *http://www.llu.edu/allied-health/sahp/pa*
Contact: *pa@llu.edu*
Phone: 909-558-7295

COST OF ATTENDANCE

Tuition and Fees: $54,796
Additional Expenses: $33,086
Total: $87,882

Financial Aid: https://home.llu.edu/campus-and-spiritual-life/
student-services/financial-life/financial-aid

ADDITIONAL INFORMATION

Interesting tidbit: LLU MPA Program was established in 2000 to train physician assistants with an emphasis on primary care. The curriculum is divided into a 12-month didactic education and a 12-month clinical education. During the clinical year, students take the PA Professional Issues course as well as complete their Capstone project.

Important Updates due to COVID-19: For the 2021-2022 CASPA Application Cycle, Loma Linda University PA Sciences will allow for three total outstanding prerequisite courses at the time of application, with a maximum of 2 science courses outstanding at the time of application. It will not be accepting prerequisite courses which were changed to Pass/Fail (P/F) due to closure of an academic institution during the COVID-19 pandemic. All pre-requisite courses must contain a letter grade to be accepted for our admissions process. Interviews are conducted virtually using the Zoom platform.

Were tests required? No.

Are tests expected next year? No.

What international experiences are available? International elective rotations.

What dual degree options exist? N/A

What service-learning opportunities exist? N/A

PANCE First-Time Pass Rate: 94% (2020)

ALASKA

ARIZONA

CALIFORNIA

COLORADO

HAWAII

IDAHO

MONTANA

NEVADA

NEW MEXICO

OREGON

UTAH

WASHINGTON

WYOMING

WEST

ALASKA

ARIZONA

CALIFORNIA

COLORADO

HAWAII

IDAHO

MONTANA

NEVADA

NEW MEXICO

OREGON

UTAH

WASHINGTON

WYOMING

MARSHALL B. KETCHUM UNIVERSITY

Address: 2575 Yorba Linda Boulevard, Fullerton, CA 92831
Website: *https://www.ketchum.edu/pa-studies*
Contact: *PAadmissions@ketchum.edu*
Phone: 714-992-7808

COST OF ATTENDANCE

Tuition and Fees: $38,235
Additional Expenses: $27,168
Total: $65,403

Financial Aid: https://www.ketchum.edu/pa-studies/cost-aid

ADDITIONAL INFORMATION

Interesting tidbit: Founded in 1904, MBKU is a private, non-profit institution with a legacy of clinical and academic excellence and a pioneering reputation in the emerging field of interprofessional education. MBKU PA Studies program was the first accredited PA program in Orange County and boasts one of the most desirable student-to-faculty ratios in the United States (8:1).

Important Updates due to COVID-19: N/A

Were tests required? No.

Are tests expected next year? No.

What international experiences are available? N/A

What dual degree options exist? N/A

What service-learning opportunities exist? N/A

PANCE First-Time Pass Rate: 90% (2020)

POINT LOMA NAZARENE UNIVERSITY

Address: 3900 Lomaland Drive, San Diego, CA 92106
Website: *https://www.pointloma.edu/graduate-studies/programs/physician-assistant-msm*
Contact: *gradinfo@pointloma.edu*
Phone: 619-329-6799

COST OF ATTENDANCE

Tuition and Fees: $51,455
Additional Expenses: N/A
Total: $51,455*

*This figure does not include cost of living or other indirect costs.

Financial Aid: https://www.pointloma.edu/graduate-studies/programs/financial-aid/types-aid

ADDITIONAL INFORMATION

Interesting tidbit: The Physician Assistant program at Point Loma Nazarene University blends service experiences into the curriculum throughout both the didactic and clinical phases, including a dedicated month each year allowing domestic, national, or international medical exposures through the extensive networks and local connections in Southern California.

Important Updates due to COVID-19: N/A

Were tests required? CASPer required.

Are tests expected next year? Yes.

What international experiences are available? The Program claims there will be international medical exposures but no further details are provided.

What dual degree options exist? N/A

What service-learning opportunities exist? The Program claims service experiences but no further details are provided.

PANCE First-Time Pass Rate: N/A (Performance data of the first class, Class of 2023 will be available in early 2024)

ALASKA

ARIZONA

CALIFORNIA

COLORADO

HAWAII

IDAHO

MONTANA

NEVADA

NEW MEXICO

OREGON

UTAH

WASHINGTON

WYOMING

WEST

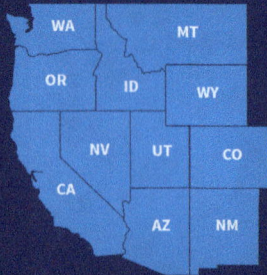

SAMUEL MERRITT UNIVERSITY

Address: 3100 Telegraph Avenue, Suite 1000, Oakland, CA 94609
Website: *http://www.samuelmerritt.edu/physician_assistant*
Contact: *admission@samuelmerritt.edu*
Phone: 510-869-6576

COST OF ATTENDANCE

Tuition and Fees: $59,352
Additional Expenses: N/A
Total: $59,352*

*This figure does not include cost of living or other indirect costs.

Financial Aid: https://www.samuelmerritt.edu/admission/
affording-smu/financial-aid-and-scholarships

ADDITIONAL INFORMATION

Interesting tidbit: In 2019, the SMU PA Program also experienced its worst PANCE performance in its more than 20-year history (78%). In response, the program implemented a PANCE success plan that includes student-specific PANCE study plans based on test preparation, literature, and individualized coaching. Since then, graduating classes have achieved 98% and 100% first-time pass rate.

Important Updates due to COVID-19: The program will accept all prerequisite coursework (including labs) completed online from an accredited institution. It will accept prerequisite courses completed on a Pass/Fail basis, beginning with Spring 2020 and continuing until further notice. It will virtual shadowing experience for the 2020-21 admission cycle and conduct admissions interviews online.

Were tests required? No.

Are tests expected next year? No.

What international experiences are available? N/A

What dual degree options exist? N/A

What service-learning opportunities exist? N/A

PANCE First-Time Pass Rate: 100% (2020)

ALASKA

ARIZONA

CALIFORNIA

COLORADO

HAWAII

IDAHO

MONTANA

NEVADA

NEW MEXICO

OREGON

UTAH

WASHINGTON

WYOMING

SOUTHERN CALIFORNIA UNIVERSITY OF HEALTH SCIENCES

Address: 16200 Amber Valley Drive, Whittier, CA 90604
Website: *https://www.scuhs.edu/academics/csih/master-of-science-physician-assistant-program/*
Contact: *physicianassistant@scuhs.edu*
Phone: 562-947-8755

COST OF ATTENDANCE

Tuition and Fees: $48,926
Additional Expenses: N/A
Total: $48,926*

*This figure does not include cost of living or other indirect costs.

Financial Aid: https://www.scuhs.edu/financial-aid/

ADDITIONAL INFORMATION

Interesting tidbit: This innovative program at Southern California University of Health Sciences (SCU) is the first and only PA program to immerse students in integrative healthcare. Students learn to use science and evidence-based research to provide patient care alongside other disciplines, including SCU's Chiropractic and Acupuncture and Chinese Medicine programs.

Important Updates due to COVID-19: N/A

Were tests required? No.

Are tests expected next year? No.

What international experiences are available? N/A

What dual degree options exist? N/A

What service-learning opportunities exist? N/A

PANCE First-Time Pass Rate: 91% (2020)

ALASKA

ARIZONA

CALIFORNIA

COLORADO

HAWAII

IDAHO

MONTANA

NEVADA

NEW MEXICO

OREGON

UTAH

WASHINGTON

WYOMING

WEST

ALASKA

ARIZONA

CALIFORNIA

COLORADO

HAWAII

IDAHO

MONTANA

NEVADA

NEW MEXICO

OREGON

UTAH

WASHINGTON

WYOMING

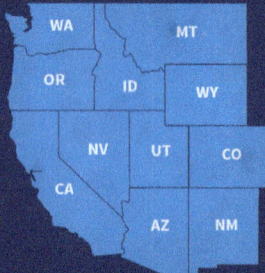

STANFORD UNIVERSITY

Address: 1265 Welch Rd., Stanford, CA 94305
Website: *https://med.stanford.edu/pa*
Contact: *paadmission@stanford.edu*
Phone: 650-725-6959

COST OF ATTENDANCE

Tuition and Fees: $54,315
Additional Expenses: $46,714
Total: $101,027

Financial Aid: https://med.stanford.edu/pa/financial-aid.html

ADDITIONAL INFORMATION

Interesting tidbit: During the didactic work, PA students will be located at the medical school and benefit from an educational model known as the "flipped classroom", which moves traditional lecture content to online video, thereby freeing classroom time for interactive learning among peers and faculty. Students will be required to select a leadership track and complete a Capstone Project. The leadership tracks include: Community Health, Health Services and Policy Research, Clinical Research, Medical Education, and Healthcare Administration.

Important Updates due to COVID-19: N/A

Were tests required? CASPer required.

Are tests expected next year? Yes.

What international experiences are available? N/A

What dual degree options exist? N/A

What service-learning opportunities exist? N/A

PANCE First-Time Pass Rate: 100% (2020)

TOURO UNIVERSITY - CALIFORNIA

Address: 1310 Club Drive, Vallejo, CA 94592
Website: *http://cehs.tu.edu/paprogram/*
Contact: *admit@tu.edu*
Phone: 707-638-5200

COST OF ATTENDANCE

Tuition and Fees: $35,380
Additional Expenses: $36,654
Total: $72,034

Financial Aid: http://studentservices.tu.edu/financialaid/#

ADDITIONAL INFORMATION

Interesting tidbit: The program at TUC is a Joint MSPAS/MPH Program. In 33 months, students earn two master's degrees - a Master of Science in Physician Assistant Studies, and a Master of Public Health. The PH and PA curricula are integrated - credits from the PA Program are applied towards your PH degree, and vice versa.

Important Updates due to COVID-19: Changes to the admissions requirements for the cycle of 2020-2021 are (1) Cumulative and Science GPA requirements lower from 3.0 to 2.9, (2) Experience requirement of 1000 hours now includes both patient care and healthcare, instead of patient care only, and (3) Courses that switched to Pass/Fail or an online format are accepted.

Were tests required? No.

Are tests expected next year? No.

What international experiences are available? N/A

What dual degree options exist? N/A

What service-learning opportunities exist? N/A

PANCE First-Time Pass Rate: 96% (2020)

ALASKA

ARIZONA

CALIFORNIA

COLORADO

HAWAII

IDAHO

MONTANA

NEVADA

NEW MEXICO

OREGON

UTAH

WASHINGTON

WYOMING

WEST

ALASKA

ARIZONA

CALIFORNIA

COLORADO

HAWAII

IDAHO

MONTANA

NEVADA

NEW MEXICO

OREGON

UTAH

WASHINGTON

WYOMING

UNIVERSITY OF CALIFORNIA, DAVIS

Address: 2570 48th St., Sacramento, CA 95817
Website: *https://health.ucdavis.edu/nursing/admissions/programs/mhs-pa.html*
Contact: *hs-bettyirenemooreson@ucdavis.edu*
Phone: 916-734-2145

COST OF ATTENDANCE

Tuition and Fees: $63,480
Additional Expenses: N/A
Total: $63,480*

*This figure does not include cost of living or other indirect costs.

Financial Aid: See "Financial Support" on https://health.ucdavis.edu/nursing/admissions/programs/mhs-pa.html

Note: The physician assistant program is a self-supporting degree program. Students are not eligible for California-state-supported fellowships.

ADDITIONAL INFORMATION

Interesting tidbit: The interprofessional PA program at the School of Nursing is led by the Nursing Science and Health-Care Leadership Graduate Group, an interprofessional team of more than 55 faculty from disciplines such as nursing, medicine, health informatics, nutrition, biostatistics, pharmacy, sociology and public health. A mandatory Leadership Immersion Experience, full-time, three-day experience runs the week prior to the first summer quarter.

Important Updates due to COVID-19: N/A

Were tests required? No.

Are tests expected next year? No.

What international experiences are available? N/A

What dual degree options exist? N/A

What service-learning opportunities exist? N/A

PANCE First-Time Pass Rate: 71% (2020)

UNIVERSITY OF LA VERNE

Address: 1950 Third Street, La Verne, CA 91750
Website: *https://artsci.laverne.edu/physician-assistant/*
Contact: *paprogram@laverne.edu*
Phone: 909-448-1475

COST OF ATTENDANCE

Tuition and Fees: $46,481
Additional Expenses: $12.497*
Total: $58,978*

*This figure does not include cost of living or other indirect costs.

Financial Aid: https://laverne.edu/financial-aid/graduates/

ADDITIONAL INFORMATION

Interesting tidbit: At La Verne University, a Master's in Physician Assistant Practice is a graduate program in the College of Arts and Sciences. Thus, the Program provides students with the foundation of a liberal arts education.

Important Updates due to COVID-19: N/A

Were tests required? No.

Are tests expected next year? No.

What international experiences are available? N/A

What dual degree options exist? N/A

What service-learning opportunities exist? N/A

PANCE First-Time Pass Rate: 75% (2020)

ALASKA

ARIZONA

CALIFORNIA

COLORADO

HAWAII

IDAHO

MONTANA

NEVADA

NEW MEXICO

OREGON

UTAH

WASHINGTON

WYOMING

WEST

ALASKA

ARIZONA

CALIFORNIA

COLORADO

HAWAII

IDAHO

MONTANA

NEVADA

NEW MEXICO

OREGON

UTAH

WASHINGTON

WYOMING

UNIVERSITY OF SOUTHERN CALIFORNIA

Address: 1000 S. Fremont Avenue, Bldg. A-11, Alhambra, CA 91803
Website: *https://keck.usc.edu/physician-assistant-program/*
Contact: *uscpa@usc.edu*
Phone: 626-457-4240

COST OF ATTENDANCE

Tuition and Fees: $66,702
Additional Expenses: N/A
Total: $66,702*

*This figure does not include cost of living or other indirect costs.

Financial Aid: https://keck.usc.edu/physician-assistant-program/
courses/financial-aid/

ADDITIONAL INFORMATION

Interesting tidbit: The program begins each year by having incoming PA students volunteer alongside faculty and staff for a day of service. During the sixth semester, students complete an average of 240 hours of additional training in a clinical specialty of interest, where students are provided more opportunities to learn and develop their skills before graduation.

Important Updates due to COVID-19: The program will accept prerequisite courses completed on a pass/no pass grading scale for Spring 2020 through Summer 2021. The GRE requirement is temporarily suspended for the 2021-2022 admissions cycle. The program will accept virtual PA shadowing experience for the 2020-2021 admissions cycle.

Were tests required? No.

Are tests expected next year? GRE or MCAT required.

What international experiences are available? N/A

What dual degree options exist? N/A

What service-learning opportunities exist? Service Orientation; Student-Run-Clinics; service projects.

PANCE First-Time Pass Rate: 88% (2020)

WA
MT
OR
ID
WY
NV
UT
CO
CA
AZ
NM

UNIVERSITY OF THE PACIFIC

Address: 3200 5th Avenue, Sacramento, CA 95817
Website: *http://pacific.edu/PAprogram*
Contact: *paprogram@pacific.edu*
Phone: 916-739-7365

COST OF ATTENDANCE

Tuition and Fees: $62,559
Additional Expenses: N/A
Total: $62,559*

*This figure does not include cost of living or other indirect costs.

Financial Aid: https://grad.pacific.edu/admission/graduate/financial-aid

ADDITIONAL INFORMATION

Interesting tidbit: Pacific's PA program provides numerous opportunities for interprofessional education through involvement with Pacific's other health-related schools, such as the Arthur A. Dugoni School of Dentistry, the Thomas J. Long School of Pharmacy, and the School of Health Sciences.

Important Updates due to COVID-19: N/A

Were tests required? No.

Are tests expected next year? No.

What international experiences are available? N/A

What dual degree options exist? N/A

What service-learning opportunities exist? N/A

PANCE First-Time Pass Rate: 100% (2020)

ALASKA

ARIZONA

CALIFORNIA

COLORADO

HAWAII

IDAHO

MONTANA

NEVADA

NEW MEXICO

OREGON

UTAH

WASHINGTON

WYOMING

WEST

ALASKA

ARIZONA

CALIFORNIA

COLORADO

HAWAII

IDAHO

MONTANA

NEVADA

NEW MEXICO

OREGON

UTAH

WASHINGTON

WYOMING

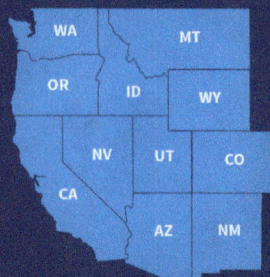

WESTERN UNIVERSITY OF HEALTH SCIENCES

Address: 309 E. Second St. Pomona, CA 91766
Website: *http://prospective.westernu.edu/physician-assistant/welcome-14/*
Contact: *admissions@westernu.edu*
Phone: 909-469-5335

COST OF ATTENDANCE

Tuition and Fees: $46,645
Additional Expenses: $28,402
Total: $75,047

Financial Aid: https://prospective.westernu.edu/health-sciences/mspa/tuition-scholarships/

ADDITIONAL INFORMATION

Interesting tidbit: During the first year of the program, students will meet with nine fellow students and one faculty facilitator for several case studies. Each case study consists of a diverse mix of students from eight of WesternU's professional programs in Pomona, CA - Osteopathic Medicine (DO), Physical Therapy (DPT), Pharmacy (PharmD), Nursing (MSN), Veterinary Medicine (DVM), Optometry (OD), and Dental Medicine (DMD). The IPE curriculum continues in the second year, where PA students will have the opportunity to work with their fellow students across all disciplines in an online setting.

Important Updates due to COVID-19: Online prerequisite labs will be accepted for all labs completed in 2020, Spring 2021, and Summer 2021 if the on-campus lab they were enrolled in was converted to an online format. Pass credit will be accepted for those courses taken in Spring 2020, Summer 2020, and Fall 2020. They will be counted as a "B" when calculating GPA. Outside the terms aforementioned, pass credit will not be accepted for prerequisites and counted as a "C" for non-prerequisite coursework when calculating GPAs.

Were tests required? No.

Are tests expected next year? No.

What international experiences are available? N/A

What dual degree options exist? N/A

What service-learning opportunities exist? N/A

PANCE First-Time Pass Rate: 90% (2020)

COLORADO MESA UNIVERSITY

Address: 1100 North Avenue, Grand Junction, CO 81501
Website: *https://www.coloradomesa.edu/kinesiology/graduate/pa-program/index.html*
Contact: *paprogram@coloradomesa.edu*
Phone: 970-248-1482

COST OF ATTENDANCE

In-State Tuition and Fees: $39,250
Additional Expenses: $39,700
Total: $78,950

Out-of-State Tuition and Fees: $65,250
Additional Expenses: $39,700
Total: $104,950

Financial Aid: https://www.coloradomesa.edu/financial-aid/graduate-students.html

ADDITIONAL INFORMATION

Interesting tidbit: CMU PA Program holds its admission interviews during the summer and fall of the year prior to matriculation. Interviewees are evaluated on their performance on such interview activities as individual interview, group activity, writing sample and video biography. The program matriculates a new class every January.

Important Updates due to COVID-19: Due to the COVID-19 pandemic, all interviews will be conducted online for the 2021-2022 admission cycle.

Were tests required? CASPer required.

Are tests expected next year? Yes.

What international experiences are available? N/A

What dual degree options exist? N/A

What service-learning opportunities exist? N/A

PANCE First-Time Pass Rate: N/A (PANCE result for its first graduating class of 2021 has not been updated.)

ALASKA

ARIZONA

CALIFORNIA

COLORADO

HAWAII

IDAHO

MONTANA

NEVADA

NEW MEXICO

OREGON

UTAH

WASHINGTON

WYOMING

WEST

ALASKA

ARIZONA

CALIFORNIA

COLORADO

HAWAII

IDAHO

MONTANA

NEVADA

NEW MEXICO

OREGON

UTAH

WASHINGTON

WYOMING

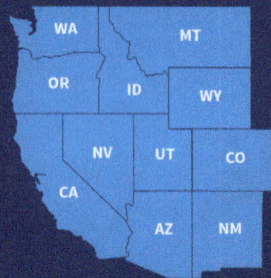

RED ROCKS COMMUNITY COLLEGE

Address: 10280 West 55th Avenue, Arvada, CO 80002
Website: *https://www.rrcc.edu/physician-assistant*
Contact: *pa.program@rrcc.edu*
Phone: 303-914-6048

COST OF ATTENDANCE

In-State Tuition and Fees: $43,204
Additional Expenses: $28,192
Total: $71,396

Out-of-State Tuition and Fees: $49,718
Additional Expenses: $28,192
Total: $77,910

Financial Aid: https://www.rrcc.edu/financial-aid/masters-physician-assistant

ADDITIONAL INFORMATION

Interesting tidbit: The Red Rocks Physician Assistant Program is a rigorous 27-month, state-sponsored, nationally accredited program. The program was established in 1998 and has maintained accreditation since inception. The RRCC PA program became the first community college in the US to confer its own master's degree.

Important Updates due to COVID-19: The healthcare-relevant experience requirement has been reduced to 1800 paid hours (from minimum 2,000 paid hours) for the 2021 application cycle.

Were tests required? No.

Are tests expected next year? No.

What international experiences are available? N/A

What dual degree options exist? N/A

What service-learning opportunities exist? 9Health Fair; Patterson Elementary; Edgewater Plaza Wellness Clinic.

PANCE First-Time Pass Rate: 97% (2020)

ROCKY VISTA UNIVERSITY

Address: 8401 S. Chambers Road, Parker, CO 80134
Website: *https://www.rvu.edu/admissions/mpas/*
Contact: *admissions@rvu.edu*
Phone: 303-373-2008

COST OF ATTENDANCE

Tuition and Fees: $52,428
Additional Expenses: $32,961
Total: $85,389

Financial Aid: https://www.rvu.edu/admissions/financial-aid/

Note: For MPAS Scholarships, https://www.rvu.edu/admissions/financial-aid/scholarships/mpas/

ADDITIONAL INFORMATION

Interesting tidbit: The RVU MPAS curriculum is divided into Didactic Phase (two semesters) and Clinical Phase (five semesters). In the Didactic Phase, students will move from foundational concepts to clinically oriented content. In the Clinical Phase, students advance and achieve competency through supervised clinical practice experiences and clinical seminars.

Important Updates due to COVID-19: N/A

Were tests required? GRE required.

Are tests expected next year? Yes.

What international experiences are available? N/A

What dual degree options exist? N/A

What service-learning opportunities exist? N/A

PANCE First-Time Pass Rate: 80% (2020)

ALASKA

ARIZONA

CALIFORNIA

COLORADO

HAWAII

IDAHO

MONTANA

NEVADA

NEW MEXICO

OREGON

UTAH

WASHINGTON

WYOMING

WEST

ALASKA

ARIZONA

CALIFORNIA

COLORADO

HAWAII

IDAHO

MONTANA

NEVADA

NEW MEXICO

OREGON

UTAH

WASHINGTON

WYOMING

UNIVERSITY OF COLORADO

Address: 1635 Aurora Ct, Aurora, CO 80045
Website: *https://medschool.cuanschutz.edu/physician-assistant-program*
Contact: *pa-info@ucdenver.edu*
Phone: 303-724-7963

COST OF ATTENDANCE

In-State Tuition and Fees: $18,033
Additional Expenses: $34,827
Total: $52,860

Out-of-State Tuition and Fees: $39,043
Additional Expenses: $34,827
Total: $73,870

Financial Aid: https://medschool.cuanschutz.edu/physician-assistant-program/prospective-students/tuition-financial-aid-and-expenses

Note: For PA program-specific scholarships, https://medschool.cuanschutz.edu/physician-assistant-program/current-students/scholarship-opportunities

ADDITIONAL INFORMATION

Interesting tidbit: the University of Colorado PA program adopted what is known as the Colorado Curriculum in 2018 and applies to students graduating in 2021 and beyond. The Colorado Curriculum consists of two didactic years, with clinical experiences integrated across both years. The third year of the program consists of 10 one-month rotations.

Important Updates due to COVID-19: The Program will accept Pass/Fail grades for Spring 2020 and Summer 2020 courses only.

Were tests required? CASPer required.

Are tests expected next year? Yes.

What international experiences are available? N/A

What dual degree options exist? N/A

What service-learning opportunities exist? N/A

PANCE First-Time Pass Rate: 95% (2020)

UNIVERSITY OF WASHINGTON - MEDEX NORTHWEST, KONA

Address: 81-6350 Mamalahoa Hwy, Kealakekua, HI 96750
Website: *https://depts.washington.edu/medex/pa-program/*
Contact: *mxhawaii@uw.edu*
Phone: 206-473-2369

COST OF ATTENDANCE

Tuition and Fees: $37,940
Additional Expenses: $9,973*
Total: $47,913*

*This figure does not include cost of living or other indirect costs.

Financial Aid: https://depts.washington.edu/medex/pa-program/program-cost/financial-aid/

ADDITIONAL INFORMATION

Interesting tidbit: The Kona campus on the Island of Hawaii is the newest campus for MEDEX Northwest PA education. The Big Island has a population of over 200,000; this population is medically underserved with the greatest shortage of healthcare workers in Hawaii. On-site classroom instruction for the 17 students in the inaugural cohort of the new MEDEX Kailua-Kona campus began September 2020.

Important Updates due to COVID-19: For the 2021-2022 application cycle, the Graduate Record Examination (GRE) is not required, however it is recommended. Prerequisite courses completed on a pass/no pass grading scale for courses taken between Jan 2020 – August 2021 will be accepted. MEDEX Northwest will accept virtual shadowing.

Were tests required? No.

Are tests expected next year? GRE required.

What international experiences are available? N/A

What dual degree options exist? N/A

What service-learning opportunities exist? N/A

PANCE First-Time Pass Rate: N/A (the inaugural class of 2021 has not taken the test)

Note: Applicants will indicate their first and second campus location preference on their MEDEX Supplemental Application. Applicants will be considered primarily for their first campus location choice. All students are required to be in Seattle for two weeks for New Student Orientation. Students will return to their home campuses for the remainder of the didactic curriculum.

ALASKA

ARIZONA

CALIFORNIA

COLORADO

HAWAII

IDAHO

MONTANA

NEVADA

NEW MEXICO

OREGON

UTAH

WASHINGTON

WYOMING

WEST

ALASKA

ARIZONA

CALIFORNIA

COLORADO

HAWAII

IDAHO

MONTANA

NEVADA

NEW MEXICO

OREGON

UTAH

WASHINGTON

WYOMING

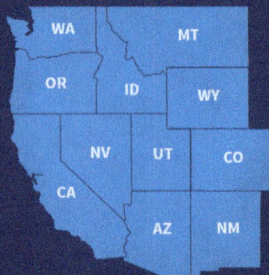

IDAHO STATE UNIVERSITY - CALDWELL

Address: 2112 Cleveland Blvd., Caldwell, ID 83605
Website: *https://www.isu.edu/pa/*
Contact: *pa@isu.edu*
Phone: 208-459-5126

Other Locations: Meridian, ID; Pocatello, ID

COST OF ATTENDANCE

Tuition and Fees: $68,884
Additional Expenses: N/A
Total: $68,884*

*This figure does not include cost of living or other indirect costs.

Financial Aid: https://www.isu.edu/pa/tuition-and-fees/

ADDITIONAL INFORMATION

Interesting tidbit: The ISU PA program is run on three different campuses. In 2009, the program expanded to the ISU-Meridian Health Science Center. In 2013, the program entered into a partnership with the College of Idaho and opened a new location at the West Hall Center for PA Studies in Caldwell, ID. The Caldwell campus is a public-private partnership between ISU and The College of Idaho.

Important Updates due to COVID-19: Up to one P/F or S/U grade awarded during affected semesters will be forgiven, with credit given toward prerequisite progression but no grade utilized in the applicant's prerequisite GPA calculation. Additional P/F or S/U grades awarded during affected semesters will either be substituted with the applicant's science GPA or a course grade of B in calculations, with consideration for which provides the best file score for the applicant. Also, at this time, all interviews will take place digitally through Zoom.

Were tests required? GRE required.

Are tests expected next year? Yes.

What international experiences are available? Two medical missions to Dominican Republic and Peru; international clinical rotation in Belize.

What dual degree options exist? N/A

What service-learning opportunities exist? Two medical missions to Dominican Republic and Peru.

PANCE First-Time Pass Rate: 99% (2020)

Other: Grit Early Assurance Program available for juniors and seniors at Idaho State University. See https://www.isu.edu/grit/

IDAHO STATE UNIVERSITY - MERIDIAN

Address: 1311 E. Central Dr., Meridian, ID 83642
Website: *https://www.isu.edu/pa/*
Contact: *pa@isu.edu*
Phone: 208-373-1804

COST OF ATTENDANCE

In-State Tuition and Fees: $43,232
Additional Expenses: N/A
Total: $43,232*

Out-of-State Tuition and Fees: $69,677
Additional Expenses: N/A
Total: $69,677*

*This figure does not include cost of living or other indirect costs.

Financial Aid: https://www.isu.edu/pa/tuition-and-fees/

ADDITIONAL INFORMATION

Interesting tidbit: The ISU PA program is run on three different campuses. In 2009, the program expanded to the ISU-Meridian Health Science Center. In 2013, the program entered into a partnership with the College of Idaho and opened a new location at the West Hall Center for PA Studies in Caldwell, ID. A class of 72 students is enrolled each fall semester with 24 seats located at the Pocatello campus, 36 seats located at the Meridian campus, and 12 seats located at the College of Idaho campus in Caldwell.

Important Updates due to COVID-19: Up to one P/F or S/U grade awarded during affected semesters will be forgiven, with credit given toward prerequisite progression but no grade utilized in the applicant's prerequisite GPA calculation. Additional P/F or S/U grades awarded during affected semesters will either be substituted with the applicant's science GPA or a course grade of B in calculations, with consideration for which provides the best file score for the applicant. Also, at this time, all interviews will take place digitally through Zoom.

Were tests required? GRE required.

Are tests expected next year? Yes.

What international experiences are available? Two medical missions to Dominican Republic and Peru; international clinical rotation in Belize.

What dual degree options exist? N/A

What service-learning opportunities exist? Two medical missions to Dominican Republic and Peru.

PANCE First-Time Pass Rate: 99% (2020)

Other: Grit Early Assurance Program available for juniors and seniors at Idaho State University. See https://www.isu.edu/grit/

ALASKA

ARIZONA

CALIFORNIA

COLORADO

HAWAII

IDAHO

MONTANA

NEVADA

NEW MEXICO

OREGON

UTAH

WASHINGTON

WYOMING

WEST

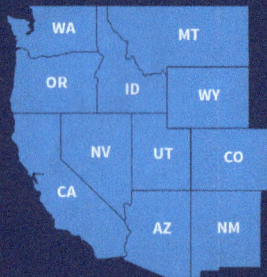

IDAHO STATE UNIVERSITY - POCATELLO

Address: 1021 S. Red Hill Road, Red Hill Building #40, Pocatello, ID 83209
Website: *https://www.isu.edu/pa/*
Contact: *pa@isu.edu*
Phone: 208-282-4726

COST OF ATTENDANCE

In-State Tuition and Fees: $43,232
Additional Expenses: N/A
Total: $43,232*

Out-of-State Tuition and Fees: $69,677
Additional Expenses: N/A
Total: $69,677*

*This figure does not include cost of living or other indirect costs.

Financial Aid: https://www.isu.edu/pa/tuition-and-fees/

ADDITIONAL INFORMATION

Interesting tidbit: The ISU PA program is run on three different campuses. In 2009, the program expanded to the ISU-Meridian Health Science Center. In 2013, the program entered into a partnership with the College of Idaho and opened a new location at the West Hall Center for PA Studies in Caldwell, ID. A class of 72 students is enrolled each fall semester with 24 seats located at the Pocatello campus, 36 seats located at the Meridian campus, and 12 seats located at the College of Idaho campus in Caldwell.

Important Updates due to COVID-19: Up to one P/F or S/U grade awarded during affected semesters will be forgiven, with credit given toward prerequisite progression but no grade utilized in the applicant's prerequisite GPA calculation. Additional P/F or S/U grades awarded during affected semesters will either be substituted with the applicant's science GPA or a course grade of B in calculations, with consideration for which provides the best file score for the applicant. Also, at this time, all interviews will take place digitally through Zoom.

Were tests required? GRE required.

Are tests expected next year? Yes.

What international experiences are available? Two medical missions to Dominican Republic and Peru; international clinical rotation in Belize.

What dual degree options exist? N/A

What service-learning opportunities exist? Two medical missions to Dominican Republic and Peru.

PANCE First-Time Pass Rate: 99% (2020)

Other: Grit Early Assurance Program available for juniors and seniors at Idaho State University. See https://www.isu.edu/grit/

ROCKY MOUNTAIN COLLEGE

Address: 1511 Poly Drive, Billings, MT 59102
Website: *http://pa.rocky.edu/*
Contact: *halversonc@rocky.edu*
Phone: 406-657-1198

COST OF ATTENDANCE

Tuition and Fees: $39,745
Additional Expenses: $21,610
Total: $61,355

Financial Aid: https://www.rocky.edu/admissions-aid/financial-aid

ADDITIONAL INFORMATION

Interesting tidbit: RMC PA curriculum places emphasis on clinical skills through workshops (faculty-to-student ratio for workshops is 1:6). The program offers broad training opportunities ranging from rural primary care to technically challenging specialties such as cardiovascular surgery.

Important Updates due to COVID-19: N/A

Were tests required? GRE required.

Are tests expected next year? Yes.

What international experiences are available? N/A

What dual degree options exist? N/A

What service-learning opportunities exist? N/A

PANCE First-Time Pass Rate: 94% (2020)

ALASKA

ARIZONA

CALIFORNIA

COLORADO

HAWAII

IDAHO

MONTANA

NEVADA

NEW MEXICO

OREGON

UTAH

WASHINGTON

WYOMING

WEST

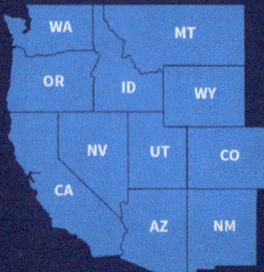

TOURO UNIVERSITY - NEVADA

Address: 874 American Pacific Drive, Henderson, NV 89011
Website: *https://tun.touro.edu/programs/physician-assistant-studies/*
Contact: *mcastill13@touro.edu*
Phone: 702-777-1750

COST OF ATTENDANCE

Tuition and Fees: $44,100
Additional Expenses: $42,310
Total: $86,410

Financial Aid: See "Potential Aid" on https://tun.touro.edu/admissions--aid/cost-of-attendance/

ADDITIONAL INFORMATION

Interesting tidbit: TUN PA program works on multiple philanthropic initiatives in our local community including our mobile health clinic that provides care to homeless, seniors and veterans and our collaboration with the women's shelter clinic. Even as first-year PA students, students will work with real patients from the neediest people in underserved areas of Nevada and be a part of real change.

Important Updates due to COVID-19: For the 2020-2021 and 2021-2022 admissions cycles, Touro Nevada will accept Pass/Fail grades and online coursework for the duration that institutions remain closed and are unable to offer in-person classes due to the pandemic. Due to COVID-19, only virtual interviews will be conducted until further notice.

Were tests required? GRE required.

Are tests expected next year? Yes.

What international experiences are available? N/A

What dual degree options exist? N/A

What service-learning opportunities exist? Mobile health clinic; Women's Shelter clinic.

PANCE First-Time Pass Rate: 90% (2020)

ALASKA

ARIZONA

CALIFORNIA

COLORADO

HAWAII

IDAHO

MONTANA

NEVADA

NEW MEXICO

OREGON

UTAH

WASHINGTON

WYOMING

UNIVERSITY OF NEVADA, RENO

Address: 18600 Wedge Parkway, Reno, NV 89511
Website: *https://med.unr.edu/physician-assistant*
Contact: *paprogram@med.unr.edu*
Phone: 775-784-4843

COST OF ATTENDANCE

Tuition and Fees: $44,510
Additional Expenses: $26,870
Total: $71,380

Financial Aid: https://med.unr.edu/physician-assistant/financial-planning

ADDITIONAL INFORMATION

Interesting tidbit: The program was developed to become a signature academic program of the University of Nevada, Reno School of Medicine and is located at the University of Nevada, Reno Redfield Campus.

Important Updates due to COVID-19: During COVID, a minimum of 1500 paid direct-hands on clinical patient care will be acceptable.

Were tests required? No.

Are tests expected next year? No.

What international experiences are available? N/A

What dual degree options exist? N/A

What service-learning opportunities exist? N/A

PANCE First-Time Pass Rate: 79% (2020)

ALASKA

ARIZONA

CALIFORNIA

COLORADO

HAWAII

IDAHO

MONTANA

NEVADA

NEW MEXICO

OREGON

UTAH

WASHINGTON

WYOMING

WEST

ALASKA

ARIZONA

CALIFORNIA

COLORADO

HAWAII

IDAHO

MONTANA

NEVADA

NEW MEXICO

OREGON

UTAH

WASHINGTON

WYOMING

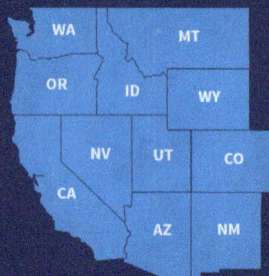

UNIVERSITY OF NEW MEXICO

Address: 1 University of New Mexico, Albuquerque, NM 87131
Website: *http://goto.unm.edu/pa*
Contact: *paprogram@salud.unm.edu*
Phone: 505-272-9864

COST OF ATTENDANCE

In-State Tuition and Fees: $31,979
Additional Expenses: N/A
Total: $31,979*

Out-of-State Tuition and Fees: $43,435
Additional Expenses: N/A
Total: $43,435*

*This figure does not include cost of living or other indirect costs.

Financial Aid: https://unm-student.custhelp.com/
app/answers/detail/a_id/3865/kw/3865/session/
L3Nuby8xL3RpbWUvMTQxMDk3MjgxOS9zaWQvQ1dOVpEMm0%3D

ADDITIONAL INFORMATION

Interesting tidbit: In keeping with the program's mission, much of the curriculum is devoted to preparing the student for eventual service in the underserved and rural areas of New Mexico. Many of the clinical clerkships are in rural communities and require students to be away from metropolitan areas for as much as half of their clinical time.

Important Updates due to COVID-19: Prerequisite lab courses taking for P/F in calendar year 2020 and 2021will be accepted. All lecture prerequisite courses must continue to be taken for a letter grade. Prerequisite courses taken online during calendar year 2020 and 2021 will be accepted without limitations.

Were tests required? Altus Suite required.

Are tests expected next year? Yes.

What international experiences are available? N/A

What dual degree options exist? N/A

What service-learning opportunities exist? N/A

PANCE First-Time Pass Rate: 88% (2019)

UNIVERSITY OF ST. FRANCIS

Address: 1500 N Renaissance Blvd. NE, Suite C, Albuquerque, NM 87107
Website: *http://www.stfrancis.edu/academics/physician-assistant-studies*
Contact: *tdiesel@stfrancis.edu*
Phone: 505-266-5565

COST OF ATTENDANCE

Tuition and Fees: $43,375
Additional Expenses: N/A
Total: $43,475*

*This figure does not include cost of living or other indirect costs.

Financial Aid: https://www.stfrancis.edu/admissions-aid/financial-aid-services/graduate-financial-assistance/

ADDITIONAL INFORMATION

Interesting tidbit: University of St. Francis (Joliet, IL) opened a satellite campus in 2006 in Albuquerque, New Mexico to create a site for a graduate program in Physician Assistant Studies. The primary on-site program offered in Albuquerque is the Physician Assistant Studies (M.S.) program, and several other programs are offered via online delivery.

Important Updates due to COVID-19: N/A

Were tests required? GRE required.

Are tests expected next year? Yes.

What international experiences are available? N/A

What dual degree options exist? N/A

What service-learning opportunities exist? N/A

PANCE First-Time Pass Rate: 97% (2020)

ALASKA

ARIZONA

CALIFORNIA

COLORADO

HAWAII

IDAHO

MONTANA

NEVADA

NEW MEXICO

OREGON

UTAH

WASHINGTON

WYOMING

WEST

GEORGE FOX UNIVERSITY

Address: 414 North Meridian Street, Newberg, Oregon 97132
Website: *https://www.georgefox.edu/pa/index.html*
Contact: *cschmitt@georgefox.edu*
Phone: 503-554-6097

COST OF ATTENDANCE

Tuition and Fees: $58,800
Additional Expenses: $14,309*
Total: $73,109*

*This figure does not include cost of living or other indirect costs.

Financial Aid: https://www.georgefox.edu/offices/student-accounts/grad/tuition/policies.html

ADDITIONAL INFORMATION

Interesting tidbit: George Fox MMSc PA program takes the problem-based learning (PBL) teaching approach. In problem-based learning, students work in collaborative small groups to solve complex real-world medical problems while building communication skills at the same time. In the George Fox MMSc PA program, new cases are introduced each week while other classes support and supplement the learning that takes place, filling in any gaps the students might not have explored or discovered in the PBL class.

Important Updates due to COVID-19: The GRE is waived during the 2020 and 2021 application cycles. In response to academic changes related to Covid-19, GFU will accept classes, both lectures and labs, that were completed online during the 2019-20 and 2020-21 school years. GFU will also accept classes taken winter/spring of 2020 resulting in a PASS/FAIL grade.

Were tests required? No.

Are tests expected next year? GRE required.

What international experiences are available? N/A

What dual degree options exist? N/A

What service-learning opportunities exist? N/A

PANCE First-Time Pass Rate: N/A (the first cohort will take PANCE in the winter of 2022-2023)

ALASKA

ARIZONA

CALIFORNIA

COLORADO

HAWAII

IDAHO

MONTANA

NEVADA

NEW MEXICO

OREGON

UTAH

WASHINGTON

WYOMING

OREGON HEALTH & SCIENCE UNIVERSITY

Address: 2730 SW Moody Avenue, Portland, OR 97201
Website: *https://www.ohsu.edu/school-of-medicine/physician-assistant*
Contact: *paprgm@ohsu.edu*
Phone: 503-494-3633

COST OF ATTENDANCE

Tuition and Fees: $40,824
Additional Expenses: $9,758*
Total: $50,582*

*This figure does not include cost of living or other indirect costs.

Financial Aid: https://www.ohsu.edu/education/financial-aid

Note: For PA scholarships, see https://www.ohsu.edu/school-of-medicine/physician-assistant/scholarships

ADDITIONAL INFORMATION

Interesting tidbit: In the spring of 2001, the OHSU PA Program became a free-standing Division within the School of Medicine. As Oregon's only public academic health center, OHSU is devoted to health sciences education, patient care, research and outreach services.

Important Updates due to COVID-19: The program will accept pass/no pass grading (only passes are acceptable to meet prerequisites) for courses/labs taken beginning spring 2020 term until further notice. The program will accept courses and labs taken beginning spring 2020 term and until further notice that are delivered via online or distance learning.

Were tests required? No.

Are tests expected next year? No.

What international experiences are available? N/A

What dual degree options exist? N/A

What service-learning opportunities exist? N/A

PANCE First-Time Pass Rate: 93% (2020)

ALASKA

ARIZONA

CALIFORNIA

COLORADO

HAWAII

IDAHO

MONTANA

NEVADA

NEW MEXICO

OREGON

UTAH

WASHINGTON

WYOMING

WEST

ALASKA

ARIZONA

CALIFORNIA

COLORADO

HAWAII

IDAHO

MONTANA

NEVADA

NEW MEXICO

OREGON

UTAH

WASHINGTON

WYOMING

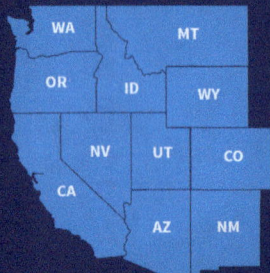

PACIFIC UNIVERSITY

Address: 190 SE 8th Avenue, Suite 181, Hillsboro, OR 97123
Website: *http://www.pacificu.edu/pa*
Contact: *admissions@pacificu.edu*
Phone: 503-352-7224

COST OF ATTENDANCE

Tuition and Fees: $47,394
Additional Expenses: $27,039
Total: $74,433

Financial Aid: https://www.pacificu.edu/physician-assistant-studies/cost-financial-aid

ADDITIONAL INFORMATION

Interesting tidbit: The didactic phase at Pacific University PA program is taught in a modular curriculum. The didactic curriculum is organized into blocks to allow for a comprehensive and integrated approach to learning medicine across the lifespan by organ system. Each clinical medicine module contains anatomy, physiology, pathophysiology, clinical skills, laboratory studies, study of disease states, pharmacology, behavioral medicine, preventive medicine, and evidence based healthcare (EBHC).

Important Updates due to COVID-19: The program will accept Pass/No Pass grades for our science prerequisites that were taken in 2020 as well. However, it will not accept science pass/no pass courses taken prior to 2020.

Were tests required? No.

Are tests expected next year? No.

What international experiences are available? International community medicine rotation.

What dual degree options exist? N/A

What service-learning opportunities exist? Low-cost clinic.

PANCE First-Time Pass Rate: 95% (2020)

ROCKY MOUNTAIN UNIVERSITY OF HEALTH PROFESSIONS

Address: 122 East 1700 South, Provo, UT 84606
Website: *https://rm.edu/academics/master-of-physician-assistant-studies/*
Contact: *admissions@rmuohp.edu*
Phone: 801-375-5125

COST OF ATTENDANCE

Tuition and Fees: $51,844
Additional Expenses: $31,577
Total: $83,421

Financial Aid: https://rm.edu/financial-aid/

ADDITIONAL INFORMATION

Interesting tidbit: Each year during the summer semester break, students have the opportunity to travel with faculty and university administration to provide humanitarian work and gain exposure in third-world clinical environments. Current service expeditions include Africa and Guatemala, where students spend time in the local clinics, hospitals, and villages.

Important Updates due to COVID-19: Applicants may have a total of 12 outstanding credits when applying to the program. These courses must be completed and grades received before May 2, 2022.

Were tests required? GRE required.

Are tests expected next year? Yes.

What international experiences are available? International service-learning opportunities.

What dual degree options exist? N/A

What service-learning opportunities exist? International service-learning opportunities.

PANCE First-Time Pass Rate: 96% (2020)

ALASKA

ARIZONA

CALIFORNIA

COLORADO

HAWAII

IDAHO

MONTANA

NEVADA

NEW MEXICO

OREGON

UTAH

WASHINGTON

WYOMING

WEST

ALASKA

ARIZONA

CALIFORNIA

COLORADO

HAWAII

IDAHO

MONTANA

NEVADA

NEW MEXICO

OREGON

UTAH

WASHINGTON

WYOMING

UNIVERSITY OF UTAH

Address: 375 Chipeta Way, Suite A, Salt Lake City, UT 84108
Website: *https://medicine.utah.edu/dfpm/physician-assistant-studies/program/*
Contact: *admissions@upap.utah.edu*
Phone: *801-581-7766*

Other Locations: St. George, UT

COST OF ATTENDANCE

In-State Tuition and Fees: $33,480
Additional Expenses: N/A
Total: $33,480*

Out-of-State Tuition and Fees: $62,125
Additional Expenses: N/A
Total: $62,125*

*This figure does not include cost of living or other indirect costs.

Financial Aid: https://financialaid.utah.edu/

ADDITIONAL INFORMATION

Interesting tidbit: The Utah Physician Assistant Program (UPAP) at the University of Utah, School of Medicine is one of the oldest PA programs in the country, and has held continued accreditation since 1971. The program was created from the medical education (MEDEX) model.

Important Updates due to COVID-19: The program will accept "pass" or "credit" marked on transcripts to meet prerequisites. It also temporarily reduced our minimum healthcare experience requirement to apply to 1500 hours. It expects to return to the minimum requirement of 2000 hours in the 2022 application cycle.

Were tests required? Altus Suite required.

Are tests expected next year? Yes.

What international experiences are available? Thailand Elective; Nepal Elective; Guatemala Elective. See https://medicine.utah.edu/dfpm/physician-assistant-studies/program/international.php

What dual degree options exist? N/A

What service-learning opportunities exist? Friday clinic; Student-run free clinics at Maliheh; Doctors Volunteer Clinic of St. George

PANCE First-Time Pass Rate: 83% (2020)

UNIVERSITY OF WASHINGTON - MEDEX NORTHWEST, SEATTLE

Address: 4311 11th Avenue NE, Suite 200, Seattle, WA 98105
Website: *https://depts.washington.edu/medex/pa-program/*
Contact: *medex@uw.edu*
Phone: 206-616-4001
Other Locations: Anchorage, AK; Kona, HI; Spokane, WA; Tacoma, WA

COST OF ATTENDANCE

Tuition and Fees: $37,940
Additional Expenses: $32,017
Total: $69,957

Financial Aid: https://depts.washington.edu/medex/pa-program/program-cost/financial-aid/

ADDITIONAL INFORMATION

Interesting tidbit: MEDEX Northwest currently operates five campus locations - Seattle, WA, Spokane, WA, Tacoma, WA, Anchorage, AK and Kona, HI. The Seattle campus, housed in the University of Washington School of Medicine, is the founding site of MEDEX and the home of MEDEX operations. Seattle hosts the largest MEDEX class with 40 to 50 seats accepted annually.

Important Updates due to COVID-19: For the 2021-2022 application cycle, the Graduate Record Examination (GRE) is not required, however it is recommended. Prerequisite courses completed on a pass/no pass grading scale for courses taken between Jan 2020 – August 2021 will be accepted. MEDEX Northwest will accept virtual shadowing.

Were tests required? No.

Are tests expected next year? GRE required.

What international experiences are available? N/A

What dual degree options exist? N/A

What service-learning opportunities exist? N/A

PANCE First-Time Pass Rate: 95% (2020)

Note: Applicants will indicate their first and second campus location preference on their MEDEX Supplemental Application. Applicants will be considered primarily for their first campus location choice. All students are required to be in Seattle for two weeks for New Student Orientation. Students will return to their home campuses for the remainder of the didactic curriculum.

ALASKA

ARIZONA

CALIFORNIA

COLORADO

HAWAII

IDAHO

MONTANA

NEVADA

NEW MEXICO

OREGON

UTAH

WASHINGTON

WYOMING

WEST

UNIVERSITY OF WASHINGTON - MEDEX NORTHWEST, SPOKANE

Address: 502 E Boone Ave., Spokane, WA 99258
Website: *https://depts.washington.edu/medex/pa-program/*
Contact: *medex@uw.edu*
Phone: 509-313-7936

Other Locations: Anchorage, AK; Kona, HI; Seattle, WA; Tacoma, WA

COST OF ATTENDANCE

Tuition and Fees: $37,940
Additional Expenses: $9,973*
Total: $47,913*

*This figure does not include cost of living or other indirect costs.

Financial Aid: https://depts.washington.edu/medex/pa-program/program-cost/financial-aid/

ADDITIONAL INFORMATION

Interesting tidbit: MEDEX Northwest is housed in the Schoenberg Center on the Gonzaga University campus. The Spokane campus has a smaller classroom size (average size 25) and provides students with many opportunities for interaction with medical, pharmacy, dental and other allied health professions students. The program has three full-time faculty and one support person.

Important Updates due to COVID-19: For the 2021-2022 application cycle, the Graduate Record Examination (GRE) is not required, however it is recommended. Prerequisite courses completed on a pass/no pass grading scale for courses taken between Jan 2020 – August 2021 will be accepted. MEDEX Northwest will accept virtual shadowing.

Were tests required? No.

Are tests expected next year? GRE required.

What international experiences are available? N/A

What dual degree options exist? N/A

What service-learning opportunities exist? House of Charity Clinic.

PANCE First-Time Pass Rate: 94% (2020)

Note: Applicants will indicate their first and second campus location preference on their MEDEX Supplemental Application. Applicants will be considered primarily for their first campus location choice. All students are required to be in Seattle for two weeks for New Student Orientation. Students will return to their home campuses for the remainder of the didactic curriculum.

ALASKA

ARIZONA

CALIFORNIA

COLORADO

HAWAII

IDAHO

MONTANA

NEVADA

NEW MEXICO

OREGON

UTAH

WASHINGTON

WYOMING

UNIVERSITY OF WASHINGTON - MEDEX NORTHWEST, TACOMA

Address: 1900 Commerce Street, Tacoma, Washington 98402
Website: *https://depts.washington.edu/medex/pa-program/*
Contact: *medex@uw.edu*
Phone: 253-692-5950

Other Locations: Anchorage, AK; Kona, HI; Seattle, WA; Spokane, WA

COST OF ATTENDANCE

Tuition and Fees: $37,940
Additional Expenses: $30,484
Total: $68,424

Financial Aid: https://depts.washington.edu/medex/pa-program/program-cost/financial-aid/

ADDITIONAL INFORMATION

Interesting tidbit: Neighboring Joint Base Lewis-McChord (at historic Ft. Lewis) and Naval Base Kitsap (Bremerton, WA) bring a substantial veteran population to the Tacoma MEDEX campus. MEDEX Tacoma makes an active effort to reach out to active duty military and veterans. The Tacoma campus hosts a small class size (averaging 30).

Important Updates due to COVID-19: For the 2021-2022 application cycle, the Graduate Record Examination (GRE) is not required, however it is recommended. Prerequisite courses completed on a pass/no pass grading scale for courses taken between Jan 2020 – August 2021 will be accepted. MEDEX Northwest will accept virtual shadowing.

Were tests required? No.

Are tests expected next year? GRE required.

What international experiences are available? N/A

What dual degree options exist? N/A

What service-learning opportunities exist? N/A

PANCE First-Time Pass Rate: 93% (2020)

Note: Applicants will indicate their first and second campus location preference on their MEDEX Supplemental Application. Applicants will be considered primarily for their first campus location choice. All students are required to be in Seattle for two weeks for New Student Orientation. Students will return to their home campuses for the remainder of the didactic curriculum.

ALASKA

ARIZONA

CALIFORNIA

COLORADO

HAWAII

IDAHO

MONTANA

NEVADA

NEW MEXICO

OREGON

UTAH

WASHINGTON

WYOMING

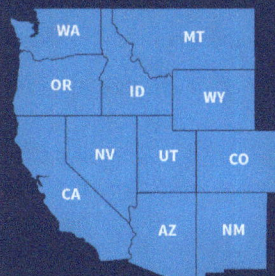

WEST

CHAPTER 6

REGION FIVE
U.S TERRITORIES

PA School	GPA & GRE (Verbal, Quantitative, Analy. Writing) Int'l Students: Yes/No	Admissions Statistics	Prerequisite Coursework Other than Gen Bio, Gen Chem, Human Anatomy, Human Physiology, Microbiology, Statistics, Psychology
San Juan Bautista School of Medicine Autopista Luis A. Ferré, Caguas, 00727, Puerto Rico	3.0+ (overall) 3.0+ (science) GRE: Not Req. Int'l Student: Yes	Apps Received: N/A Interviews Offered: N/A Admission Offered: N/A Number Enrolled: 35 Admitted Rate: N/A	English Composition; Humanities; OChem; Pre-calculus or higher

SAN JUAN BAUTISTA SCHOOL OF MEDICINE

Address: Autopista Luis A. Ferré, Caguas, 00727, Puerto Rico
Website: *https://www.sanjuanbautista.edu/education/programs/pa-program.html*
Contact: *PAadmissions@sanjuanbautista.edu*
Phone: 787-743-3038

COST OF ATTENDANCE

In-State Tuition and Fees: $35,000
Additional Expenses: $8,597*
Total: $43,597*

Out-of-State Tuition and Fees: $43,400
Additional Expenses: $ 8,597*
Total: $51,997*

*This figure does not include cost of living or other indirect costs.

Financial Aid: https://www.sanjuanbautista.edu/financial-aid.html

ADDITIONAL INFORMATION

Interesting tidbit: All textbooks, lectures, and exams (including the national boards called the PANCE) are delivered in English while the clinical experiences will be in Spanish and English and language proficiency is integral.

Important Updates due to COVID-19: The SJB PA Program accepts pass/fail coursework ONLY if it was mandated by the applicants' institutions because of COVID-19 and for the 2020-2021 cycle only. Applicants must submit additional documentation from their institution on school letterhead or authorized registrar email. Applications will be accepted and processed without completed Direct Patient Care experience hours with the understanding that these hours will be completed as soon as permissible and may be required in the event of acceptance if circumstances allow. We will accept virtual shadowing hours.

Were tests required? No.

Are tests expected next year? No.

What international experiences are available? N/A

What dual degree options exist? N/A

What service-learning opportunities exist? N/A

PANCE First-Time Pass Rate: N/A (the inaugural class of 2023 has not taken the test)

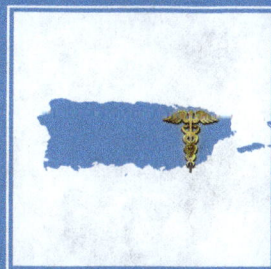

PUERTO RICO

PUERTO RICO

PHYSICIAN
ASSISTANT
SCHOOL LISTS

CHAPTER 7

PHYSICIAN ASSISTANT SCHOOLS BY CITY/STATE

PA School	City	State	Website
University of Washington - MEDEX Northwest, Anchorage	Anchorage	AK	https://depts.washington.edu/medex/pa-program/
University of Alabama at Birmingham	Birmingham	AL	http://www.uab.edu/shp/cds/physician-assistant
Samford University	Homewood	AL	https://www.samford.edu/healthprofessions/master-of-science-in-physician-assistant-studies
University of South Alabama	Mobile	AL	https://www.southalabama.edu/colleges/alliedhealth/pa/
Faulkner University	Montgomery	AL	https://www.faulkner.edu/graduate/graduate-degrees/physican-assistant-studies-ms-pas/
University of Arkansas	Little Rock	AR	http://healthprofessions.uams.edu/programs/physicianassistant/
Harding University	Searcy	AR	http://www.harding.edu/PAprogram/
Midwestern University - Glendale	Glendale	AZ	https://www.midwestern.edu/academics/degrees-and-programs/master-of-medical-sciences-in-physician-assistant-studies-az.xml
A.T. Still University - Arizona School of Health Sciences	Mesa	AZ	https://www.atsu.edu/physician-assistant-degree
Northern Arizona University	Phoenix	AZ	http://www.nau.edu/pa
University of Southern California	Alhambra	CA	https://keck.usc.edu/physician-assistant-program/
Marshall B. Ketchum University	Fullerton	CA	https://www.ketchum.edu/pa-studies
Chapman University	Irvine	CA	https://www.chapman.edu/crean/academic-programs/graduate-programs/physician-assistant/index.aspx

PA School	City	State	Website
University of La Verne	La Verne	CA	https://artsci.laverne.edu/physician-assistant/
Loma Linda University	Loma Linda	CA	http://www.llu.edu/allied-health/sahp/pa
Charles R. Drew University	Los Angeles	CA	https://www.cdrewu.edu/cosh/PA
Samuel Merritt University	Oakland	CA	http://www.samuelmerritt.edu/physician_assistant
Western University of Health Sciences	Pomona	CA	http://prospective.westernu.edu/physician-assistant/welcome-14/
California Baptist University	Riverside	CA	https://calbaptist.edu/programs/master-of-science-physician-assistant-studies/
University of California, Davis	Sacramento	CA	https://health.ucdavis.edu/nursing/admissions/programs/mhs-pa.html
University of the Pacific	Sacramento	CA	http://pacific.edu/PAprogram
California State University, Monterey Bay	Salinas	CA	http://csumb.edu/mspa
Point Loma Nazarene University	San Diego	CA	https://www.pointloma.edu/graduate-studies/programs/physician-assistant-ms-m#applicationinformation
Dominican University of California	San Rafael	CA	https://www.dominican.edu/directory/physician-assistant-studies
Stanford University	Stanford	CA	https://med.stanford.edu/pa
Touro University California	Vallejo	CA	http://cehs.tu.edu/paprogram/
Southern California University of Health Sciences	Whittier	CA	https://www.scuhs.edu/academics/csih/master-of-science-physician-assistant-program/
Red Rocks Community College	Arvada	CO	https://www.rrcc.edu/physician-assistant

PA School	City	State	Website
University of Colorado	Aurora	CO	http://www.ucdenver.edu/academics/colleges/medicalschool/education/degree_programs/PAProgram/Pages/Home.aspx
Colorado Mesa University	Grand Junction	CO	https://www.coloradomesa.edu/kinesiology/graduate/pa-program/index.html
Rocky Vista University	Parker	CO	https://www.rvu.edu/admissions/mpas/
Yale University	New Haven	CT	http://www.paprogram.yale.edu/
University of Bridgeport	Bridgeport	CT	http://www.bridgeport.edu/academics/schools-colleges/physician-assistant-institute/physician-assistant-ms
Sacred Heart University	Fairfield	CT	https://www.sacredheart.edu/majors--programs/physician-assistant-studies---mpas/
Quinnipiac University	Hamden	CT	http://www.quinnipiac.edu/gradphysicianasst
University of Saint Joseph	West Hartford	CT	https://www.usj.edu/academics/academic-schools/sppas/physician-assistant-studies/admissions/
George Washington University	Washington	DC	https://smhs.gwu.edu/physician-assistant/
Keiser University	Fort Lauderdale	FL	https://www.keiseruniversity.edu/master-of-science-in-physician-assistant/
Nova Southeastern University - Fort Lauderdale	Fort Lauderdale	FL	http://www.nova.edu/chcs/pa/fortlauderdale/index.html
Nova Southeastern University - Orlando	Fort Lauderdale	FL	https://healthsciences.nova.edu/pa/orlando/index.html
Florida Gulf Coast University	Fort Myers	FL	https://www2.fgcu.edu/mariebcollege/HS/MPAS/index.html

PA School	City	State	Website
Nova Southeastern University - Fort Myers	Fort Myers	FL	https://healthsciences.nova.edu/pa/fort-myers/index.html
University of Florida	Gainesville	FL	https://pap.med.ufl.edu/
Nova Southeastern University - Jacksonville	Jacksonville	FL	https://healthsciences.nova.edu/pa/jacksonville/index.html
Barry University - Miami	Miami	FL	http://www.barry.edu/physician-assistant/
Barry University - St. Petersburg	Miami	FL	http://www.barry.edu/physician-assistant/
Florida International University Herbert Wertheim College of Medicine	Miami	FL	https://medicine.fiu.edu/academics/degrees-and-programs/master-in-physician-studies/index.html
Miami Dade College	Miami	FL	http://www.mdc.edu/physicianassistantas/
AdventHealth University	Orlando	FL	https://www.ahu.edu/academics/ms-physician-assistant
South University, West Palm Beach	Royal Palm Beach	FL	https://www.southuniversity.edu/west-palm-beach/physician-assistant-ms
Gannon University - Ruskin	Ruskin	FL	https://www.gannon.edu/academic-offerings/health-professions-and-sciences/graduate/master-of-physician-assistant-science/admission-requirements/
Florida State University	Tallahassee	FL	https://med.fsu.edu/index.cfm?page=pa.home
South University, Tampa	Tampa	FL	http://www.southuniversity.edu/tampa/areas-of-study/physician-assistant/physician-assistant-master-of-science-ms
University of South Florida	Tampa	FL	https://health.usf.edu/medicine/pa/
University of Tampa	Tampa	FL	https://www.ut.edu/graduate-degrees/physician-assistant-medicine-program
Emory University	Atlanta	GA	http://med.emory.edu/pa/

PA School	City	State	Website
Mercer University	Atlanta	GA	http://chp.mercer.edu/academics-departments/physician-assistant-studies/
Morehouse School of Medicine	Atlanta	GA	http://www.msm.edu//physicianassistantprogram/index.php
South College - Atlanta	Atlanta	GA	https://www.south.edu/programs/master-health-science-physician-assistant-studies/atlanta/
Augusta University	Augusta	GA	https://www.augusta.edu/alliedhealth/pa/
Brenau University	Gainesville	GA	https://www.brenau.edu/healthsciences/physician-assistant-studies/
South University, Savannah	Savannah	GA	https://www.southuniversity.edu/savannah/areas-of-study/physician-assistant/physician-assistant-master-of-science-ms
PCOM - Georgia	Suwanee	GA	https://www.pcom.edu/academics/programs-and-degrees/physician-assistant-studies/georgia.html
University of Washington - MEDEX Northwest, Kona	Kealakekua	HI	https://depts.washington.edu/medex/pa-program/
St. Ambrose University	Davenport	IA	http://www.sau.edu/master-of-physician-assistant-studies
Des Moines University	Des Moines	IA	https://www.dmu.edu/pa/
University of Dubuque	Dubuque	IA	http://www.dbq.edu/Academics/OfficeofAcademicAffairs/GraduatePrograms/MasterofScienceinPhysician-AssistantStudies/
University of Iowa	Iowa City	IA	http://www.medicine.uiowa.edu/pa/
Northwestern College	Orange City	IA	https://www.nwciowa.edu/graduate/physician-assistant
Idaho State University - Caldwell	Caldwell	ID	https://www.isu.edu/pa/

PA School	City	State	Website
Idaho State University - Meridian	Meridian	ID	https://www.isu.edu/pa/
Idaho State University - Pocatello	Meridian	ID	https://www.isu.edu/pa/
Southern Illinois University	Carbondale	IL	https://www.siumed.edu/paprogram
Northwestern University	Chicago	IL	http://www.feinberg.northwestern.edu/sites/pa/
Rush University	Chicago	IL	http://www.rushu.rush.edu/pa-program
Midwestern University - Downers Grove	Downers Grove	IL	https://www.midwestern.edu/admissions/apply/master-of-medical-sciences-in-physician-assistant-studies-in-downers-grove.xml
Rosalind Franklin University of Medicine	North Chicago	IL	https://www.rosalindfranklin.edu/academics/college-of-health-professions/degree-programs/physician-assistant-practice-ms/
Dominican University of Illinois	River Forest	IL	https://www.dom.edu/admission/graduate/health-sciences-programs/mmspas
Trine University	Angola	IN	http://www.trine.edu/academics/majors-and-minors/graduate/master-physician-assistant-studies/index.aspx
University of Evansville	Evansville	IN	https://www.evansville.edu/majors/physicianassistant/
University of Saint Francis	Fort Wayne	IN	http://pa.sf.edu/
Franklin College	Franklin	IN	https://franklincollege.edu/academics/graduate-programs/master-science-physician-assistant/
Butler University	Indianapolis	IN	http://www.butler.edu/physician-assistant/

PA School	City	State	Website
Indiana University School of Health and Human Sciences	Indianapolis	IN	https://shhs.iupui.edu/admissions/graduate-professional/master-physician-assistant-studies.html
Indiana State University	Terre Haute	IN	https://www.indstate.edu/health/program/pa
Valparaiso University	Valparaiso	IN	https://www.valpo.edu/physician-assistant-program/programs/admission/
Wichita State University	Wichita	KS	http://www.wichita.edu/thisis/home/?u=pa
University of Kentucky - Lexington	Lexington	KY	http://www.uky.edu/chs/academic-programs/physician-assistant-studies
Sullivan University	Louisville	KY	https://www.sullivan.edu/programs/master-of-science-in-physician-assistant
University of Kentucky - Morehead	Morehead	KY	https://www.uky.edu/chs/academic-programs/physician-assistant-studies
University of the Cumberlands	Williamsburg	KY	http://gradweb.ucumberlands.edu/medicine/mpas/overview
University of the Cumberlands, Northern Kentucky Campus	Williamsburg	KY	https://www.ucumberlands.edu/academics/graduate/programs/master-science-physician-assistant-studies
Franciscan Missionaries of Our Lady University	Baton Rouge	LA	https://www.franu.edu/academics/academic-programs/physician-assistant-studies
Lousiana State University - New Orleans	New Orleans	LA	http://alliedhealth.lsuhsc.edu/pa/
Xavier University of Louisiana	New Orleans	LA	https://www.xula.edu/physician-assistant-program-about
Louisiana State University Health Sciences Center Shreveport	Shreveport	LA	https://lsuhscshreveportedu.finalsite.com/departments/allied-health-professions-departments/physician-assistant

PA School	City	State	Website
Boston University School of Medicine	Boston	MA	http://bu.edu/paprogram
MCPHS - Boston	Boston	MA	https://www.mcphs.edu/academics/school-of-physician-assistant-studies/physician-assistant/physician-assistant-studies-mpas
MGH Institute of Health Professions	Boston	MA	http://www.mghihp.edu/academics/school-of-health-and-rehabilitation-sciences/physician-assistant-studies/default.aspx
Northeastern University	Boston	MA	https://bouve.northeastern.edu/physician-assistant/ms/
Tufts University	Boston	MA	https://medicine.tufts.edu/education/physician-assistant
Bay Path University	East Longmeadow	MA	https://www.baypath.edu/academics/graduate-programs/physician-assistant-studies-ms/
Springfield College	Springfield	MA	https://springfield.edu/programs/physician-assistant-studies
Westfield State University	Westfield	MA	https://www.westfield.ma.edu/academics/master-of-science-in-physician-assistant-studies/
MCPHS - Worcester	Worcester	MA	https://www.mcphs.edu/academics/school-of-physician-assistant-studies/physician-assistant/physican-assistant-studies-mpas-accelerated
University of Maryland Baltimore/ Ann Arundel Community College	Arnold	MD	https://graduate.umaryland.edu/mshs-pa-umb/
Towson University CCBC - Essex	Baltimore	MD	https://www.towson.edu/chp/departments/health-sciences/grad/physician-assistant/

PA School	City	State	Website
Frostburg State University	Hagerstown	MD	https://www.frostburg.edu/ academics/majorminors/ graduate/ms-physician-assistant/index.php
University of Maryland Eastern Shore	Princess Anne	MD	http://www.umes.edu/pa
University of New England	Portland	ME	http://www.une.edu/wchp/ pa
Concordia University Ann Arbor	Ann Arbor	MI	https://www.cuaa.edu/ academics/programs/ physician-assistant-masters/ index.html#overview
University of Detroit Mercy	Detroit	MI	http://healthprofessions. udmercy.edu/academics/pa/ grad.php
Wayne State Unversity	Detroit	MI	http://www.pa.cphs.wayne. edu/
University of Michigan - Flint	Flint	MI	https://www.umflint.edu/ physician-assistant-ms/
Grand Valley State University - Grand Rapids	Grand Rapids	MI	http://www.gvsu.edu/pas
Western Michigan University	Kalamazoo	MI	http://www.wmich.edu/pa
Central Michigan University	Mount Pleasant	MI	https://www.cmich.edu/ colleges/CHP/hp_academics/ srms/physician_assistant/ Pages/PA-Program-at-CMU. aspx
Grand Valley State University - Traverse City	Traverse City	MI	https://www.gvsu.edu/pas/ traverse-city-campus-89.htm
Eastern Michigan University	Ypsilanti	MI	http://www.emich.edu/pa
College of St. Scholastica	Duluth	MN	http://www.css.edu/ graduate/masters-doctoral-and-professional-programs/ areas-of-study/ms-physician-assistant.html
Augsburg University	Minneapolis	MN	http://www.augsburg.edu/ pa/

PA School	City	State	Website
Mayo Clinic School of Health Sciences	Rochester	MN	https://college.mayo.edu/academics/health-sciences-education/physician-assistant-program-minnesota/
Saint Catherine University	Saint Paul	MN	https://www.stkate.edu/academic-programs/gc/physician-assistant-studies-mpas
Bethel University	St. Paul	MN	https://www.bethel.edu/graduate/academics/physician-assistant/
Stephens College	Columbia	MO	https://www.stephens.edu/academics/graduate-programs/master-in-physician-assistant-studies/
University of Missouri-Kansas City	Kansas City	MO	http://med.umkc.edu/pa/
Saint Louis University	Saint Louis	MO	https://www.slu.edu/doisy/degrees/graduate/physician-assistant-mms.php
Missouri State University	Springfield	MO	http://www.missouristate.edu/pas
Mississippi College	Clinton	MS	http://www.mc.edu/academics/departments/pa/
Mississippi State University - Meridian	Meridian	MS	https://www.meridian.msstate.edu/academics/physician-assistant/
Rocky Mountain College	Billings	MT	http://pa.rocky.edu/
Gardner-Webb University	Boiling Springs	NC	https://gardner-webb.edu/academic-programs-and-resources/colleges-and-schools/health-sciences/schools-and-departments/physician-assistant-studies/index
Wake Forest University - Boone	Boone	NC	http://www.wakehealth.edu/Physician-Assistant-Program/
Campbell University	Buies Creek	NC	https://cphs.campbell.edu/academic-programs/physician-assistant/master-physician-assistant-practice/

PA School	City	State	Website
UNC-Chapel Hill	Chapel Hill	NC	http://www.med.unc.edu/ahs/unc-pa
Duke University	Durham	NC	http://pa.duke.edu/
Elon University	Elon	NC	https://www.elon.edu/u/academics/health-sciences/physician-assistant/
Methodist University	Fayetteville	NC	http://www.methodist.edu/paprogram
East Carolina University	Greenville	NC	http://www.ecu.edu/pa
Wingate University - Hendersonville	Hendersonville	NC	https://www.wingate.edu/academics/hendersonville/physician-assistant
High Point University	High Point	NC	http://www.highpoint.edu/physicianassistant/
Pfeiffer University	Misenheimer	NC	https://www.pfeiffer.edu/mspas
Wingate University	Wingate	NC	http://pa.wingate.edu/
Wake Forest University - Winston Salem	Winston-Salem	NC	http://www.wakehealth.edu/Physician-Assistant-Program/
University of North Dakota	Grand Forks	ND	http://med.und.edu/physician-assistant/index.cfm
University of Nebraska Medical Center - Kearney	Kearney	NE	https://www.unmc.edu/alliedhealth/education/pa/
Union College	Lincoln	NE	http://www.ucollege.edu/pa
College of Saint Mary	Omaha	NE	http://www.csm.edu/academics/health-human-services/master-science-degree-physician-assistant-studies
Creighton University	Omaha	NE	https://medschool.creighton.edu/program/physician-assistant-mpas
University of Nebraska Medical Center - Omaha	Omaha	NE	https://www.unmc.edu/alliedhealth/education/pa/

PA School	City	State	Website
MCPHS - Manchester	Manchester	NH	https://www.mcphs.edu/academics/school-of-physician-assistant-studies/physician-assistant/physican-assistant-studies-mpas-accelerated
Franklin Pierce University	West Lebanon	NH	http://www.franklinpierce.edu/academics/gradstudies/programs_of_study/mpas/index.htm
Saint Elizabeth University	Morristown	NJ	https://cse.smartcatalogiq.com/en/2019-2020/academic-catalog/academic-programs/physician-assistant/ms-in-physician-assistant
Seton Hall University	Nutley	NJ	https://www.shu.edu/academics/ms-physician-assistant.cfm
Kean University	Union	NJ	https://www.kean.edu/academics/programs/physician-assistant-studies-ms
Thomas Jefferson University - New Jersey	Voorhees	NJ	https://www.jefferson.edu/university/health-professions/departments/physician-assistant-studies/degrees-programs/graduate/ms-new-jersery.html
Monmouth University	West Long Branch	NJ	https://www.monmouth.edu/graduate/ms-physician-assistant/
Rutgers University	West Piscataway	NJ	https://shp.rutgers.edu/physician-assistant/master-of-science-physician-assistant-program/
University of New Mexico	Albuquerque	NM	http://goto.unm.edu/pa
University of St. Francis	Albuquerque	NM	http://www.stfrancis.edu/academics/physician-assistant-studies
Touro University Nevada	Henderson	NV	https://tun.touro.edu/programs/physician-assistant-studies/

PA School	City	State	Website
University of Nevada, Reno	Reno	NV	https://med.unr.edu/physician-assistant
Albany Medical College	Albany	NY	https://www.amc.edu/academic/PhysicianAssistant/index.cfm
Daemen College	Amherst	NY	https://www.daemen.edu/academics/areas-study/physician-assistant/physician-assistant-studies-ms
Mercy College	Bronx	NY	https://www.mercy.edu/degrees-programs/ms-physician-assistant
Long Island University	Brooklyn	NY	https://www.liu.edu/Brooklyn/Academics/Schools/School-of-Health-Professions/Dept/Physician-Assistant/MS-PAS
SUNY Downstate Medical Center	Brooklyn	NY	https://sls.downstate.edu/admissions/chrp/pa/index.html
Canisius College	Buffalo	NY	https://www.canisius.edu/academics/programs/physician-assistant
D'Youville College	Buffalo	NY	http://www.dyc.edu/academics/pa/
Touro College - Long Island	Central Islip	NY	https://shs.touro.edu/programs/physician-assistant/physician-assistant-long-island/
Touro College - NUMC	East Meadow	NY	https://shs.touro.edu/programs/physician-assistant/physician-assistant-long-island/
Hofstra University	Hempstead	NY	https://www.hofstra.edu/academics/colleges/nursing-physician-assistant/physician-assistant/
Ithaca College	Ithaca	NY	https://www.ithaca.edu/academics/school-health-sciences-and-human-performance/graduate-programs/physician-assistant-studies

PA School	City	State	Website
CUNY York College	Jamaica	NY	http://www.york.cuny.edu/academics/departments/health-professions/physician-assistant
Pace University - Lenox Hill Hospital, NYC	New York	NY	http://www.pace.edu/college-health-professions/explore-programs/physician-assistant-program
The CUNY School of Medicine	New York	NY	https://www.ccny.cuny.edu/csom/
Touro College Manhattan	New York	NY	https://shs.touro.edu/programs/physician-assistant/physician-assistant-manhattan/
Weil Cornell Graduate School of Medical Sciences	New York	NY	https://gradschool.weill.cornell.edu/programs/health-sciences-physician-assistants
Yeshiva University, Katz School of Science and Health	New York	NY	https://www.yu.edu/katz/programs/graduate/physician-assistant
New York Institute of Technology	Old Westbury	NY	http://www.nyit.edu/pa
Pace University - Pleasantville	Pleasantville	NY	https://www.pace.edu/college-health-professions/graduate-degree-programs/physician-assistant-program-pleasantville
Clarkson University	Potsdam	NY	http://www.clarkson.edu/pa
Marist College	Poughkeepsie	NY	http://www.marist.edu/science/physassist/
St. John's University	Queens	NY	https://www.stjohns.edu/academics/programs/physician-assistant-master-science
Rochester Institute of Technology	Rochester	NY	http://www.rit.edu/healthsciences/graduate-programs/physician-assistant
Stony Brook University Southhampton	Southampton	NY	https://healthtechnology.stonybrookmedicine.edu/programs/pa/elpa

PA School	City	State	Website
St. Bonaventure University	St. Bonaventure	NY	https://www.sbu.edu/academics/physician-assistant-studies
Wagner College	Staten Island	NY	http://wagner.edu/physician-assistant/
Stony Brook University Health Science Center	Stony Brook	NY	https://healthtechnology.stonybrookmedicine.edu/programs/pa/elpa
Le Moyne College	Syracuse	NY	https://www.lemoyne.edu/pa
SUNY Upstate Medical Center	Syracuse	NY	http://www.upstate.edu/chp/programs/pa/index.php
University of Mount Union	Alliance	OH	https://www.mountunion.edu/physician-assistant-studies
Ashland University	Ashland	OH	https://www.ashland.edu/conhs/majors/master-science-physician-assistant-studies
Baldwin Wallace University	Berea	OH	https://www.bw.edu/graduate/physician-assistant/
Mount St. Joseph University	Cincinnati	OH	http://www.msj.edu/PA
Case Western Reserve University	Cleveland	OH	http://case.edu/medicine/physician-assistant/
Ohio Dominican University	Columbus	OH	http://www.ohiodominican.edu/academics/graduate/physician-assistant-program
University of Dayton	Dayton	OH	https://udayton.edu/education/departments_and_programs/pa/index.php
Ohio University	Dublin	OH	https://www.ohio.edu/chsp/rcs/pa/
University of Findlay	Findlay	OH	https://www.findlay.edu/healthprofessions/physicianassistant-ma/
Kettering College	Kettering	OH	http://kc.edu/academics/physician-assistant/
Marietta College	Marietta	OH	https://www.marietta.edu/pa-program
Lake Erie College	Painesville	OH	http://www.lec.edu/pa

PA School	City	State	Website
Mercy College of Ohio	Toledo	OH	https://mercycollege.edu/academics/programs/graduate/physician-assistant-studies
University of Toledo	Toledo	OH	http://www.utoledo.edu/med/grad/pa/
Northeastern State University	Muskogee	OK	https://academics.nsuok.edu/healthprofessions/Degree-Programs/Graduate/Physician-Assistant-Studie
Oklahoma City University	Oklahoma City	OK	https://www.okcu.edu/physician-assistant/home
University of Oklahoma - Oklahoma City	Oklahoma City	OK	https://medicine.ouhsc.edu/Prospective-Students/Degree-Programs/Physician-Associate-Program
Oklahoma State University Center for Health Sciences	Tulsa	OK	https://medicine.okstate.edu/pa/index.html
University of Oklahoma - Tulsa	Tulsa	OK	http://www.ou.edu/tulsa/community_medicine/scm-pa-program
Pacific University	Hillsboro	OR	http://www.pacificu.edu/pa
George Fox University	Newberg	OR	https://www.georgefox.edu/pa/index.html
Oregon Health & Science University	Portland	OR	https://www.ohsu.edu/school-of-medicine/physician-assistant
DeSales University	Center Valley	PA	https://www.desales.edu/academics/graduate-studies/master-of-science-in-physician-assistant-studies-(mspas)
Misericordia University	Dallas	PA	https://www.misericordia.edu/page.cfm?p=655
Salus University	Elkins Park	PA	http://www.salus.edu/Colleges/Health-Sciences/Physician-Assistant.aspx
Gannon University - Erie, PA	Erie	PA	http://www.gannon.edu/academic-departments/physician-assistant-department/

PA School	City	State	Website
Mercyhurst University	Erie	PA	https://www.mercyhurst.edu/academics/physician-assistant-studies-program
Arcadia University	Glenside	PA	https://www.arcadia.edu/academics/programs/physician-assistant
Seton Hill University	Greensburg	PA	https://www.setonhill.edu/academics/graduate-programs/physician-assistant-ms/
Thiel College	Greenville	PA	https://www.thiel.edu/graduate-degrees/physician-assistant
Penn State University	Hershey	PA	https://med.psu.edu/physician-assistant
Lock Haven University	Lock Haven	PA	https://paportal.lhup.edu/PA/
Saint Francis University	Loretto	PA	https://www.francis.edu/Physician-Assistant-Science/
Drexel University	Philadelphia	PA	http://drexel.edu/cnhp/academics/departments/Physician-Assistant/
Philadelphia College of Osteopathic Medicine (PCOM)	Philadelphia	PA	https://www.pcom.edu/academics/programs-and-degrees/physician-assistant-studies/
Temple University Lewis Katz School of Medicine	Philadelphia	PA	https://medicine.temple.edu/education/physician-assistant-program
Thomas Jefferson University - City Center	Philadelphia	PA	https://www.jefferson.edu/university/health-professions/departments/physician-assistant-studies/degrees-programs/graduate/ms-center-city.html
Thomas Jefferson University - East Falls	Philadelphia	PA	https://www.jefferson.edu/university/health-professions/departments/physician-assistant-studies/degrees-programs/graduate/ms-east-falls/applying.html

PA School	City	State	Website
University of the Sciences	Philadelphia	PA	https://www.usciences.edu/samson-college-of-health-sciences/physician-assistant-studies/index.html
Chatham University	Pittsburgh	PA	http://www.chatham.edu/mpas/
Duquesne University	Pittsburgh	PA	http://www.duq.edu/academics/schools/health-sciences/academic-programs/physician-assistant
University of Pittsburgh	Pittsburgh	PA	https://www.shrs.pitt.edu/PAProgram
Marywood University	Scranton	PA	http://www.marywood.edu/pa-program
Slippery Rock University	Slippery Rock	PA	http://www.sru.edu/academics/graduate-programs/physician-assistant-studies-master-of-science
West Chester University	West Chester	PA	https://www.wcupa.edu/healthSciences/physicianAssistant/default.aspx?gclid=EAIaIQobChMInYy7kYO36wIVAeWzCh-2qzAkbEAAYASAAEgItF-vD_BwE
King's College	Wilkes-Barre	PA	https://www.kings.edu/academics/undergraduate_majors/physicianassistant
Pennsylvania College of Technology	Williamsport	PA	https://www.pct.edu/academics/nhs/physician-assistant/physician-assistant-studies
San Juan Bautista School of Medicine	Caguas	PR	https://www.sanjuanbautista.edu/education/programs/pa-program.html
Johnson & Wales University	Providence	RI	http://www.jwu.edu/PA
Bryant University	Smithfield	RI	http://gradschool.bryant.edu/health-sciences.htm
Charleston Southern University	Charleston	SC	http://www.csuniv.edu/pa

PA School	City	State	Website
Medical University of South Carolina	Charleston	SC	https://education.musc.edu/students/enrollment/bulletin/colleges-and-degrees/health-professions/ms-in-physician-assistant
Presbyterian College	Clinton	SC	https://www.presby.edu/academics/graduate-professional/physician-assistant-program/
University of South Carolina SOM	Columbia	SC	http://www.southalabama.edu/alliedhealth/pa
North Greenville University	Greer	SC	http://www.ngu.edu/pa-medicine.php
University of South Dakota	Vemillion	SD	http://www.usd.edu/pa
Lincoln Memorial University	Harrogate	TN	https://www.lmunet.edu/school-of-medical-sciences/pa-harrogate/index.php
Lincoln Memorial University - Knoxville	Knoxville	TN	https://www.lmunet.edu/school-of-medical-sciences/pa-knoxville/index.php
South College - Knoxville	Knoxville	TN	https://www.south.edu/programs/master-health-science-physician-assistant-studies/knoxville/
Christian Brothers University	Memphis	TN	https://www.cbu.edu/pa
University of Tennessee Health Science Center	Memphis	TN	http://www.uthsc.edu/allied/pa
Milligan University	Milligan	TN	http://www.milligan.edu/pa
Lipscomb University	Nashville	TN	https://www.lipscomb.edu
South College - Nashville	Nashville	TN	https://www.south.edu/programs/master-health-science-physician-assistant-studies/nashville/
Trevecca Nazarene University	Nashville	TN	https://www.trevecca.edu/programs/physician-assistant
Bethel University (TN)	Paris	TN	https://www.bethelu.edu/academics/degrees-and-programs/physician-assistant-studies

PA School	City	State	Website
Hardin-Simmons University	Abilene	TX	https://www.hsutx.edu/pa
University of Mary Hardin-Baylor	Belton	TX	https://go.umhb.edu/graduate/physician-assistant/home
University of Texas Southwestern Medical Center	Dallas	TX	http://www.utsouthwestern.edu/pa
University of Texas Rio Grande Valley	Edinburgh	TX	https://www.utrgv.edu/pa/
U.S. Army Medical Center of Excellence IPAP	Fort Sam Houston	TX	https://medcoe.army.mil/ipap
University of North Texas HS Center Fort Worth	Fort Worth	TX	https://www.unthsc.edu/school-of-health-professions/physician-assistant-studies/
University of Texas Medical Branch at Galveston	Galveston	TX	http://shp.utmb.edu/PhysicianAssistantStudies/
Baylor College of Medicine	Houston	TX	https://www.bcm.edu/education/school-of-health-professions/physician-assistant-program
University of Texas Health Science Center - Laredo	Laredo	TX	https://www.uthscsa.edu/academics/health-professions/programs/physician-assistant-studies-ms/laredo-pa-extension-program
Texas Tech University Health Sciences Center	Midland	TX	https://www.ttuhsc.edu/health-professions/master-physician-assistant-studies/
University of Texas Health Science Center - San Antonio	San Antonio	TX	http://www.uthscsa.edu/shp/pa/
University of Utah	Salt Lake City	UT	https://medicine.utah.edu/dfpm/physician-assistant-studies/program/
Rocky Mountain University of Health Professions	South Provo	UT	https://rm.edu/academics/master-of-physician-assistant-studies/

PA School	City	State	Website
South University, Richmond	Glen Allen	VA	https://www.southuniversity.edu/richmond/physician-assistant-ms
James Madison University	Harrisonburg	VA	http://www.healthsci.jmu.edu/PA/
Shenandoah University - Loudoun	Leesburg	VA	https://www.su.edu/physician-assistant/masters-of-science-in-physician-assistant-studies/
University of Lynchburg	Lynchburg	VA	http://www.lynchburg.edu/graduate/physician-assistant-medicine/
Emory & Henry College	Marion	VA	http://www.ehc.edu/academics/programs/school-health-sciences/shs-programs/school-health-sciences-graduate-programs/physician-assistant-pa/
Eastern Virginia Medical School (early assurance, too)	Norfolk	VA	http://www.evms.edu/education/masters_programs/physician_assistant_program/
Mary Baldwin University	Roanoke	VA	https://go.marybaldwin.edu/health_sciences/pas/
Radford University Carilion	Roanoke	VA	https://www.radford.edu/content/grad/home/academics/graduate-programs/pa.html
Shenandoah Universityn - Winchester	Winchester	VA	https://www.su.edu/physician-assistant/masters-of-science-in-physician-assistant-studies/
University of Washington - MEDEX Northwest, Seattle	Seattle	WA	https://depts.washington.edu/medex/pa-program/
University of Washington - MEDEX Northwest, Spokane	Spokane	WA	https://depts.washington.edu/medex/pa-program/
University of Washington - MEDEX Northwest, Tacoma	Tacoma	WA	https://depts.washington.edu/medex/pa-program/
University of Wisconsin - La Crosse	La Crosse	WI	https://www.uwlax.edu/grad/physician-assistant-studies/

PA School	City	State	Website
University of Wisconsin-Madison	Madison	WI	https://www.med.wisc.edu/education/physician-assistant-pa-program/
Concordia University - Wisconsin	Mequon	WI	https://www.cuw.edu/academics/programs/physician-assistant-masters/
Marquette University	Milwaukee	WI	http://www.marquette.edu/physician-assistant
Caroll University	Waukesha	WI	http://www.carrollu.edu/gradprograms/physasst/admission.asp
University of Charleston	Charleston	WV	http://www.ucwv.edu/pa/
Marshall University Joan C. Edwards School of Medicine	Huntington	WV	https://jcesom.marshall.edu/students/physician-assistant-program/
West Virginia University	Morgantown	WV	https://medicine.hsc.wvu.edu/physician-assistant-studies/
Alderson-Broaddus University	Philippi	WV	http://ab.edu/academics/master-of-science-in-physician-assistant-studies/
West Liberty University	West Liberty	WV	http://www.westliberty.edu/physician-assistant/

CHAPTER 8

TOP 10 PHYSICIAN ASSISTANT SCHOOLS

Ranking	PA School	Website
#1	Duke University	http://pa.duke.edu/
#1	University of Iowa	http://www.medicine.uiowa.edu/pa/
#3	Baylor College of Medicine	https://www.bcm.edu/education/school-of-health-professions/physician-assistant-program
#4	University of Utah	https://medicine.utah.edu/dfpm/physician-assistant-studies/program/
#5	Emory University	http://med.emory.edu/pa/
#6	George Washington University	https://smhs.gwu.edu/physician-assistant/
#7	University of Colorado	http://www.ucdenver.edu/academics/colleges/medicalschool/education/degree_programs/PAProgram/Pages/Home.aspx
#8	University of Texas Southwestern Medical Center	http://www.utsouthwestern.edu/pa
#9	Wake Forest University - Winston Salem	http://www.wakehealth.edu/Physician-Assistant-Program/
10	Drexel University	http://drexel.edu/cnhp/academics/departments/Physician-Assistant/

CHAPTER 9

PHYSICIAN ASSISTANT SCHOOLS BY COST OF ATTENDANCE

PA School	In-State Tuition	Out-of-State Tuition	COA (O)
U.S. Army Medical Center of Excellence IPAP	$0.00	$0.00	$0.00
Oklahoma State University Center for Health Sciences	$13,500.00	$29,500.00	$32,809.22
Weil Cornell Graduate School of Medical Sciences	$32,822.00	$32,822.00	$32,822.00
Yeshiva University, Katz School of Science and Health	$30,720.00	$30,720.00	$32,978.00
University of Dubuque	$30,666.67	$30,666.67	$33,862.67
University of North Dakota	$21,220.35	$31,830.54	$34,218.09
Hardin-Simmons University	$29,958.00	$29,958.00	$34,236.52
Barry University - Miami	$33,795.00	$33,795.00	$34,395.00
Barry University - St. Petersburg	$33,795.00	$33,795.00	$34,395.00
Daemen College	$30,907.00	$30,907.00	$34,830.00
University of the Cumberlands	$33,999.00	$33,999.00	$34,950.00
University of the Cumberlands, Northern Kentucky Campus	$33,999.00	$33,999.00	$34,950.00
The CUNY School of Medicine	$16,635.00	$34,200.00	$36,111.90
University of Missouri-Kansas City	$30,316.50	$36,381.30	$37,239.30
Arcadia University	$32,268.00	$32,268.00	$37,313.00
Eastern Michigan University	$10,260.00	$18,240.00	$37,790.00
CUNY York College	$16,130.00	$39,960.00	$38,092.67
Missouri State University	$23,000.00	$36,311.00	$38,533.00
Grand Valley State University - Grand Rapids	$36,995.00	$36,995.00	$38,775.00
Grand Valley State University - Traverse City	$36,995.00	$36,995.00	$38,930.00
St. Ambrose University	$38,583.00	$38,583.00	$39,003.00
Samford University	$25,018.00	$25,018.00	$39,024.00
Shenandoah University - Loudoun	$34,500.00	$34,500.00	$39,380.00
Shenandoah University - Winchester	$34,500.00	$34,500.00	$39,380.00
Wingate University	$39,750.00	$39,750.00	$39,980.00
Wingate University - Hendersonville	$39,750.00	$39,750.00	$39,980.00
MCPHS - Boston	$34,700.00	$34,700.00	$40,051.00
SUNY Downstate Medical Center	$21,628.00	$39,972.00	$40,306.00
Bethel University (TN)	$37,500.00	$37,500.00	$40,655.00

PA School	In-State Tuition	Out-of-State Tuition	COA (O)
University of Dayton	$36,765.00	$36,765.00	$40,924.00
Lincoln Memorial University	$39,780.00	$39,780.00	$40,975.00
Touro College Manhattan	$37,460.00	$37,460.00	$41,060.00
Faulkner University	$25,500.00	$25,500.00	$41,160.00
University of Detroit Mercy	$34,418.00	$34,418.00	$41,183.00
Dominican University of California	$39,510.00	$39,510.00	$41,481.00
Trevecca Nazarene University	$41,600.00	$41,600.00	$41,600.00
University of Arkansas	$20,001.00	$31,500.00	$41,731.00
Kettering College	$38,334.00	$38,334.00	$41,761.25
St. John's University	$41,850.00	$41,850.00	$41,850.00
Touro College - Long Island	$38,580.00	$38,580.00	$42,280.00
Touro College - NUMC	$38,580.00	$38,580.00	$42,280.00
University of Wisconsin - La Crosse	$17,991.00	$36,644.00	$42,737.91
University of Texas Rio Grande Valley	$8,585.50	$21,617.50	$42,851.22
University of New Mexico	$26,978.67	$38,435.11	$43,435.11
University of St. Francis	$38,000.00	$38,000.00	$43,475.00
DeSales University	$28,000.00	$28,000.00	$43,662.00
Baldwin Wallace University	$43,750.00	$43,750.00	$43,750.00
Mount St. Joseph University	$39,600.00	$39,600.00	$43,862.00
Christian Brothers University	$37,050.00	$37,050.00	$44,020.00
East Carolina University	$17,985.51	$37,706.01	$44,063.01
New York Institute of Technology	$36,960.00	$36,960.00	$44,163.67
Canisius College	$41,250.00	$41,250.00	$44,210.00
Temple University Lewis Kats School of Medicine	$39,798.00	$41,742.00	$44,662.00
Concordia University - Wisconsin	$41,250.00	$41,250.00	$44,868.00
Baylor College of Medicine	$32,030.00	$32,030.00	$45,139.00
Franciscan Missionaries of Our Lady University	$40,300.47	$40,300.47	$45,288.42
Seton Hall University	$43,200.00	$43,200.00	$45,742.00
Radford University Carilion	$45,100.00	$46,145.00	$46,145.00
Long Island University	$40,269.00	$40,269.00	$46,363.00
Medical University of South Carolina	$24,822.00	$44,361.00	$46,461.00
University of Mount Union	$37,500.00	$37,500.00	$46,500.00
Seton Hill University	$46,510.00	$46,510.00	$46,510.00

PA School	In-State Tuition	Out-of-State Tuition	COA (O)
Trine University	$45,600.00	$45,600.00	$46,541.00
Mercy College of Ohio	$41,700.00	$41,700.00	$46,720.00
University of Toledo	$29,118.23	$46,870.43	$46,870.43
AdventHealth University	$40,500.00	$40,500.00	$46,975.00
Mayo Clinic School of Health Sciences	$40,920.00	$40,920.00	$47,170.00
University of Michigan - Flint	$30,720.00	$47,312.00	$47,312.00
Saint Elizabeth University	$39,039.00	$39,039.00	$47,624.00
Kean University	$32,799.00	$42,069.00	$47,901.11
University of Washington - MEDEX Northwest, Anchorage	$37,940.00	$37,940.00	$47,913.00
University of Washington - MEDEX Northwest, Kona	$37,940.00	$37,940.00	$47,913.00
University of Washington - MEDEX Northwest, Spokane	$37,940.00	$37,940.00	$47,913.00
Indiana University School of Health and Human Sciences	$30,810.00	$44,440.00	$48,246.00
St. Bonaventure University	$41,500.00	$41,500.00	$48,310.00
South University, Tampa	$40,000.00	$40,000.00	$48,410.00
South University, West Palm Beach	$40,000.00	$40,000.00	$48,410.00
South University, Savannah	$40,000.00	$40,000.00	$48,410.00
South University, Richmond	$40,000.00	$40,000.00	$48,410.00
University of Wisconsin-Madison	$19,378.91	$39,319.35	$48,444.35
Marywood University	$45,835.00	$45,835.00	$48,540.00
George Washington University	$48,480.00	$48,480.00	$48,615.00
University of Evansville	$42,450.00	$42,450.00	$48,650.00
Salus University	$45,670.00	$45,670.00	$48,766.00
University of Bridgeport	$43,995.00	$43,995.00	$48,835.00
Keiser University	$42,336.00	$42,336.00	$48,924.82
Southern California University of Health Sciences	$46,713.00	$46,713.00	$48,926.00
Clarkson University	$46,323.00	$46,323.00	$48,948.00
Marquette University	$44,970.00	$44,970.00	$48,955.00
Thomas Jefferson University - City Center	$47,638.00	$47,638.00	$49,034.00
Thomas Jefferson University - East Falls	$47,638.00	$47,638.00	$49,034.00

PA School	In-State Tuition	Out-of-State Tuition	COA (O)
Thomas Jefferson University - New Jersey	$47,638.00	$47,638.00	$49,034.00
South College - Atlanta	$45,000.00	$45,000.00	$49,274.00
D'Youville College	$29,812.00	$29,812.00	$49,362.99
Wichita State University	$15,400.00	$37,819.00	$49,460.00
Concordia University Ann Arbor	$41,250.00	$41,250.00	$49,637.00
Louisiana State University - New Orleans	$21,022.00	$42,868.00	$49,677.50
Ohio University	$30,056.00	$31,444.00	$49,744.00
Ohio Dominican University	$46,440.00	$46,440.00	$49,840.00
Oregon Health & Science University	$40,824.00	$40,824.00	$50,582.00
Westfield State University	$44,160.00	$44,160.00	$50,660.00
Augusta University	$20,925.00	$41,850.00	$50,770.00
Sacred Heart University	$43,500.00	$43,500.00	$50,910.00
University of Findlay	$41,668.00	$41,668.00	$50,983.00
West Virginia University	$21,334.00	$33,332.00	$51,053.00
Milligan University	$46,080.00	$46,080.00	$51,280.00
University of Saint Joseph	$49,041.00	$49,041.00	$51,291.00
A.T. Still University - Arizona School of Health Sciences	$48,268.00	$48,268.00	$51,306.00
Point Loma Nazarene University	$49,650.00	$49,650.00	$51,455.00
James Madison University	$36,575.00	$47,080.00	$51,755.00
Florida State University	$27,999.00	$38,001.00	$51,944.00
San Juan Bautista School of Medicine	$35,000.00	$43,400.00	$51,997.00
Lipscomb University	$45,750.00	$45,750.00	$52,027.00
Union College	$34,800.00	$34,800.00	$52,172.00
Albany Medical College	$28,818.00	$28,818.00	$52,409.00
Bryant University	$46,985.33	$46,985.33	$52,637.33
University of Kentucky - Morehead	$20,926.00	$49,262.00	$53,291.00
Western Michigan University	$29,311.81	$49,247.03	$53,521.85
Hofstra University	$50,890.00	$50,890.00	$53,611.50
University of Kentucky - Lexington	$20,926.00	$49,262.00	$53,835.00
University of Mary Hardin-Baylor	$38,215.00	$38,215.00	$54,019.00
South College - Knoxville	$47,000.00	$47,000.00	$54,124.00
South College - Nashville	$47,000.00	$47,000.00	$54,124.00
Bay Path University	$51,885.00	$51,885.00	$54,385.00

PA School	In-State Tuition	Out-of-State Tuition	COA (O)
Thiel College	$47,150.00	$47,150.00	$54,388.00
University of Maryland Eastern Shore	$25,881.90	$46,028.40	$54,123.40
Eastern Virginia Medical School	$25,246.00	$31,046.00	$54,511.00
King's College	$46,341.00	$46,341.00	$54,898.00
Creighton University	$25,500.00	$25,500.00	$55,094.00
Northeastern University	$48,525.00	$48,525.00	$55,278.00
Stony Brook University Health Science Center	$20,952.00	$38,723.00	$55,657.06
Stony Brook University Southampton	$20,952.00	$38,723.00	$55,657.06
Mercy College	$46,350.00	$46,350.00	$55,753.00
Emory & Henry College	$35,832.00	$35,832.00	$56,307.00
MCPHS - Worcester	$51,090.00	$51,090.00	$56,441.00
MCPHS - Manchester	$51,090.00	$51,090.00	$56,441.00
Tufts University	$34,608.00	$34,608.00	$56,843.00
Campbell University	$47,880.00	$47,880.00	$56,906.00
Emory University	$45,201.00	$45,201.00	$57,321.00
Monmouth University	$54,558.00	$54,558.00	$57,570.00
Drexel University	$49,898.00	$49,898.00	$57,798.00
West Chester University	$42,866.00	$55,572.40	$58,116.40
College of St. Scholastica	$49,419.00	$49,419.00	$58,311.00
Boston University School of Medicine	$47,782.00	$47,782.00	$58,581.00
Augsburg University	$53,692.00	$53,692.00	$58,692.00
Penn State University	$39,033.00	$39,033.00	$58,973.00
University of La Verne	$46,481.33	$46,481.33	$58,978.33
Midwestern University - Downers Grove	$51,638.00	$51,638.00	$59,287.00
University of Pittsburgh	$44,420.00	$53,123.00	$59,289.00
Samuel Merritt University	$54,592.00	$54,592.00	$59,352.00
Slippery Rock University	$36,718.94	$53,852.33	$59,673.84
Misericordia University	$38,175.00	$38,175.00	$59,840.00
University of North Texas HS Center Fort Worth	$6,408.00	$23,136.00	$59,906.00
Mercyhurst University	$52,205.00	$52,205.00	$59,990.00
Chatham University	$49,953.00	$49,953.00	$60,399.50

PA School	In-State Tuition	Out-of-State Tuition	COA (O)
Saint Catherine University	$49,680.00	$49,680.00	$60,410.00
Wayne State University	$25,727.10	$49,463.10	$60,570.90
Franklin Pierce University	$35,100.00	$35,100.00	$60,930.00
West Liberty University	$29,106.00	$45,715.00	$61,014.00
Xavier University of Louisiana	$36,900.00	$36,900.00	$61,058.00
Gannon University - Ruskin	$54,900.00	$54,900.00	$61,281.00
Rocky Mountain College	$39,745.00	$39,745.00	$61,355.00
University of Utah	$31,699.20	$60,344.37	$62,125.47
University of Lynchburg	$38,250.00	$38,250.00	$62,554.00
University of the Pacific	$53,958.00	$53,958.00	$62,559.00
University of Maryland Baltimore/ Ann Arundel Community College	$39,799.20	$54,359.20	$63,040.20
University of California, Davis	$63,480.00	$63,480.00	$63,480.00
University of South Carolina SOM	$22,635.00	$39,384.00	$63,852.00
Methodist University	$43,950.00	$43,950.00	$63,935.00
University of Saint Francis	$43,095.00	$43,095.00	$63,945.00
Valparaiso University	$56,000.00	$56,000.00	$64,213.00
Pennsylvania College of Technology	$33,459.00	$47,823.00	$64,325.00
Lake Erie College	$37,200.00	$37,200.00	$64,575.00
Chapman University	$59,365.00	$59,365.00	$65,025.00
Carroll University	$45,201.00	$45,201.00	$65,295.00
Marietta College	$42,500.00	$42,500.00	$65,300.00
Marshall B. Ketchum University	$38,235.00	$38,235.00	$65,403.00
University of Alabama at Birmingham	$27,456.00	$65,424.00	$65,624.00
University of Tampa	$43,911.00	$43,911.00	$65,792.11
Franklin College	$52,027.00	$52,027.00	$66,112.00
Mississippi College	$33,900.00	$33,900.00	$66,153.00
University of Southern California	$60,446.00	$60,446.00	$66,702.00
Butler University	$47,050.00	$47,050.00	$66,772.00
Brenau University	$40,500.00	$40,500.00	$67,032.00
Midwestern University - Glendale	$60,207.00	$60,207.00	$67,094.00
Pfeiffer University	$40,755.00	$40,755.00	$67,368.00
Mary Baldwin University	$36,400.00	$36,400.00	$67,390.00
Dominican University of Illinois	$52,510.00	$52,510.00	$67,460.00

PA School	In-State Tuition	Out-of-State Tuition	COA (O)
University of Texas Southwestern Medical Center	$16,017.00	$33,032.00	$67,692.00
Oklahoma City University	$38,946.00	$38,946.00	$68,211.00
Rush University	$25,590.00	$25,590.00	$68,336.00
University of Washington - MEDEX Northwest, Tacoma	$37,940.00	$37,940.00	$68,424.00
Lock Haven University	$38,656.00	$53,342.00	$68,467.00
Rochester Institute of Technology	$50,136.00	$50,136.00	$68,533.00
Ashland University	$46,250.00	$46,250.00	$68,809.00
Idaho State University - Caldwell	$63,623.94	$63,623.94	$68,883.94
Northeastern State University	$19,445.70	$35,319.20	$69,283.95
College of Saint Mary	$42,150.00	$42,150.00	$69,653.80
Idaho State University - Meridian	$37,931.94	$64,376.94	$69,676.94
Idaho State University - Pocatello	$43,232.00	$69,677.00	$69,677.00
University of Oklahoma - Tulsa	$18,303.00	$35,189.00	$69,747.00
University of Charleston	$36,780.00	$36,780.00	$69,886.43
University of Washington - MEDEX Northwest, Seattle	$37,940.00	$37,940.00	$69,957.00
High Point University	$44,208.00	$44,208.00	$71,208.00
University of Nevada, Reno	$44,510.40	$44,510.40	$71,380.40
Des Moines University	$41,382.00	$41,382.00	$71,647.00
Ithaca College	$50,580.00	$50,580.00	$71,672.00
University of Iowa	$22,725.12	$44,660.12	$71,858.12
California Baptist University	$56,670.00	$56,670.00	$71,870.00
University of Oklahoma - Oklahoma City	$19,585.00	$36,471.00	$71,885.00
Touro University California	$35,380.00	$35,380.00	$72,034.00
Morehouse School of Medicine	$45,006.00	$45,006.00	$72,385.00
Johnson & Wales University	$49,083.00	$49,083.00	$72,432.00
SUNY Upstate Medical Center	$24,330.00	$44,970.00	$72,452.00
Bethel University	$49,147.00	$49,147.00	$72,473.00
Saint Francis University	$59,032.00	$59,032.00	$72,656.00
Saint Louis University	$48,900.00	$48,900.00	$72,786.00
George Fox University	$58,800.00	$58,800.00	$73,109.00
Sullivan University	$52,347.50	$52,347.50	$73,228.50
Wagner College	$54,920.00	$54,920.00	$73,266.00
Elon University	$50,789.00	$50,789.00	$73,289.00

PA School	In-State Tuition	Out-of-State Tuition	COA (O)
University of the Sciences	$50,000.00	$50,000.00	$73,382.00
Pace University - Pleasantville	$70,000.00	$70,000.00	$73,586.00
Case Western Reserve University	$40,020.00	$40,020.00	$73,733.00
University of South Dakota	$20,019.20	$39,717.70	$73,760.91
Springfield College	$59,670.00	$59,670.00	$73,823.50
University of Colorado	$18,033.00	$39,043.00	$73,870.00
Pacific University	$47,394.00	$47,394.00	$74,433.00
University of Tennessee Health Science Center	$22,924.00	$38,962.00	$74,534.00
Le Moyne College	$46,268.00	$46,268.00	$74,663.00
University of Texas Medical Branch at Galveston	$25,354.40	$48,049.90	$75,029.90
Western University of Health Sciences	$45,345.00	$45,345.00	$75,047.00
Presbyterian College	$53,400.00	$53,400.00	$75,280.00
Gannon University - Erie, PA	$53,385.00	$53,385.00	$75,732.00
Mississippi State University - Meridian	$30,000.00	$55,000.00	$76,065.00
Marshall University Joan C. Edwards School of Medicine	$29,418.00	$45,918.00	$76,624.60
Gardner-Webb University	$40,068.00	$40,068.00	$76,652.75
Florida Gulf Coast University	$24,455.11	$61,546.22	$76,712.89
Pace University - Lenox Hill Hospital, NYC	$70,000.00	$70,000.00	$76,942.00
Towson University CCBC - Essex	$33,102.00	$59,670.00	$77,702.00
Rosalind Franklin University of Medicine	$48,709.00	$48,709.00	$77,857.00
Red Rocks Community College	$43,204.00	$49,718.00	$77,910.00
UNC-Chapel Hill	$28,359.00	$50,874.00	$78,375.00
Central Michigan University	$52,234.00	$52,234.00	$78,703.00
Duke University	$45,259.00	$45,259.00	$78,706.00
Harding University	$45,471.00	$45,471.00	$79,071.00
Texas Tech University Health Sciences Center	$15,163.00	$40,061.00	$79,241.00
Nova Southeastern University - Fort Lauderdale	$36,923.01	$36,923.01	$79,486.01
Nova Southeastern University - Fort Myers	$36,923.01	$36,923.01	$79,486.01

PA School	In-State Tuition	Out-of-State Tuition	COA (O)
Nova Southeastern University - Jacksonville	$36,923.01	$36,923.01	$79,486.01
Nova Southeastern University - Orlando	$36,923.01	$36,923.01	$79,486.01
Lincoln Memorial University - Knoxville	$40,950.00	$40,950.00	$79,630.00
Wake Forest University - Winston Salem	$42,700.00	$42,700.00	$79,910.00
Marist College	$50,850.00	$50,850.00	$80,496.00
Miami Dade College	$35,786.85	$56,076.58	$80,602.08
Yale University	$46,708.00	$46,708.00	$80,881.00
Wake Forest University - Boone	$42,700.00	$42,700.00	$80,922.00
Alderson-Broaddus University	$43,500.00	$43,500.00	$81,173.00
Frostburg State University	$35,905.00	$52,360.00	$82,164.00
University of New England	$46,530.00	$46,530.00	$82,399.00
Rocky Mountain University of Health Professions	$51,844.00	$51,844.00	$83,421.00
Indiana State University	$39,618.00	$77,841.00	$83,601.00
California State University, Monterey Bay	$54,600.00	$54,600.00	$83,658.00
University of Nebraska Medical Center - Kearney	$18,950.00	$49,260.00	$83,805.00
University of Nebraska Medical Center - Omaha	$18,950.00	$49,260.00	$83,805.00
University of South Alabama	$25,575.00	$59,620.00	$83,862.00
Northern Arizona University	$19,555.00	$34,951.00	$83,926.00
PCOM - Georgia	$51,312.00	$51,312.00	$84,490.00
Philadelphia College of Osteopathic Medicine (PCOM)	$51,312.00	$51,312.00	$84,706.00
Rocky Vista University	$52,428.00	$52,428.00	$85,389.00
Florida International University Herbert Wertheim College of Medicine	$45,478.00	$46,675.00	$85,906.00
Touro University Nevada	$44,100.00	$44,100.00	$86,410.00
North Greenville University	$54,495.00	$54,495.00	$86,462.00
University of Florida	$27,940.00	$61,276.84	$86,841.84
Quinnipiac University	$72,050.00	$72,050.00	$87,170.00
Mercer University	$46,414.00	$46,414.00	$87,754.00

PA School	In-State Tuition	Out-of-State Tuition	COA (O)
Loma Linda University	$54,796.00	$54,796.00	$87,882.00
MGH Institute of Health Professions	$53,100.00	$53,100.00	$87,895.00
Duquesne University	$69,430.00	$69,430.00	$88,442.00
Northwestern University	$49,629.00	$49,629.00	$88,558.00
Rutgers University	$31,000.00	$42,400.00	$88,650.00
Northwestern College	$54,000.00	$54,000.00	$89,395.00
Stephens College	$45,750.00	$45,750.00	$91,710.00
Charleston Southern University	$46,500.00	$46,500.00	$92,588.00
University of South Florida	$34,083.00	$64,533.00	$93,115.00
University of Texas Health Science Center - Laredo	$18,816.00	$45,743.00	$94,063.00
University of Texas Health Science Center - San Antonio	$18,816.00	$45,743.00	$94,063.00
Louisiana State University Health Sciences Center Shreveport	$30,816.00	$43,122.00	$98,190.00
Stanford University	$54,315.00	$54,315.00	$101,027.00
Charles R. Drew University	$65,582.00	$65,582.00	$104,468.00
Colorado Mesa University	$39,250.00	$65,250.00	$104,950.00
Southern Illinois University	$42,026.00	$81,820.50	$107,128.50

CHAPTER 10

PHYSICIAN ASSISTANT SCHOOLS BY NUMBER OF INCOMING STUDENTS

PA School	# enrolled in 2020
University of Texas Health Science Center - Laredo	10
Grand Valley State University - Traverse City	12
Idaho State University - Caldwell	12
University of Nebraska Medical Center - Kearney	15
Wingate University - Hendersonville	15
University of Kentucky - Morehead	16
Colorado Mesa University	16
University of Maryland Eastern Shore	17
University of Washington - MEDEX Northwest, Kona	17
Shenandoah University - Loudoun	18
West Liberty University	18
Kean University	20
Misericordia University	20
University of Missouri-Kansas City	20
Mercy College of Ohio	20
Carroll University	20
Florida Gulf Coast University	20
Mississippi State University - Meridian	20
UNC-Chapel Hill	20
Northeastern State University	20
George Fox University	20
University of Washington - MEDEX Northwest, Tacoma	21
University of Findlay	22
University of New Mexico	22
Franklin Pierce University	24
Franklin College	24
Mayo Clinic School of Health Sciences	24
Wake Forest University - Boone	24
University of Oklahoma - Tulsa	24
West Virginia University	24
Idaho State University - Pocatello	24
University of Nevada, Reno	24
St. Bonaventure University	25
Stony Brook University Southampton	25
University of Saint Francis	25
University of Dubuque	25

PA School	# enrolled in 2020
University of Iowa	25
University of South Dakota	25
Frostburg State University	25
Charleston Southern University	25
Marshall University Joan C. Edwards School of Medicine	25
University of Washington - MEDEX Northwest, Anchorage	25
Boston University School of Medicine	26
Lake Erie College	26
Oklahoma State University Center for Health Sciences	26
Milligan University	26
Charles R. Drew University	26
West Chester University	27
Stanford University	27
University of La Verne	27
Creighton University	28
University of Wisconsin - La Crosse	28
California State University, Monterey Bay	29
Bay Path University	30
Westfield State University	30
Monmouth University	30
Canisius College	30
Clarkson University	30
CUNY York College	30
Ithaca College	30
Yeshiva University, Katz School of Science and Health	30
Mercyhurst University	30
Penn State University	30
Temple University Lewis Kats School of Medicine	30
Dominican University of Illinois	30
Rush University	30
Indiana State University	30
St. Ambrose University	30
Eastern Michigan University	30
College of St. Scholastica	30
Missouri State University	30
Stephens College	30

PA School	# enrolled in 2020
Union College	30
Ashland University	30
Concordia University - Wisconsin	30
AdventHealth University	30
Gannon University - Ruskin	30
University of the Cumberlands	30
University of the Cumberlands, Northern Kentucky Campus	30
Franciscan Missionaries of Our Lady University	30
Mississippi College	30
North Greenville University	30
University of South Carolina SOM	30
University of Tennessee Health Science Center	30
Hardin-Simmons University	30
Mary Baldwin University	30
University of Charleston	30
California Baptist University	30
Dominican University of California	30
Point Loma Nazarene University	30
University of St. Francis	30
University of Washington - MEDEX Northwest, Spokane	31
Touro College - NUMC	32
Northwestern College	32
Concordia University Ann Arbor	32
Bethel University	32
Saint Catherine University	32
Mount St. Joseph University	32
PCOM - Georgia	32
Christian Brothers University	32
James Madison University	32
Red Rocks Community College	32
Augsburg University	33
Brenau University	33
Presbyterian College	34
Emory & Henry College	34
Springfield College	35
Pace University - Pleasantville	35

PA School	# enrolled in 2020
SUNY Upstate Medical Center	35
The CUNY School of Medicine	35
University of North Dakota	35
Baldwin Wallace University	35
Faulkner University	35
Louisiana State University - New Orleans	35
High Point University	35
San Juan Bautista School of Medicine	35
Rochester Institute of Technology	36
Johnson & Wales University	36
Northwestern University	36
Trine University	36
Grand Valley State University - Grand Rapids	36
Case Western Reserve University	36
Marietta College	36
Harding University	36
Towson University CCBC - Essex	36
East Carolina University	36
Gardner-Webb University	36
Pfeiffer University	36
Oklahoma City University	36
South University, Richmond	36
Alderson-Broaddus University	36
Rocky Vista University	36
Idaho State University - Meridian	36
Rocky Mountain College	36
Elon University	38
Loma Linda University	38
University of Bridgeport	40
Yale University	40
Saint Elizabeth University	40
Wagner College	40
Duquesne University	40
Thiel College	40
Southern Illinois University	40
University of Evansville	40

PA School	# enrolled in 2020
Central Michigan University	40
Western Michigan University	40
College of Saint Mary	40
University of Dayton	40
University of Mount Union	40
University of Toledo	40
University of South Alabama	40
University of Arkansas	40
Keiser University	40
South University, West Palm Beach	40
Morehouse School of Medicine	40
South College - Atlanta	40
University of Kentucky - Lexington	40
Xavier University of Louisiana	40
University of Maryland Baltimore/Ann Arundel Community College	40
Methodist University	40
Wingate University	40
Baylor College of Medicine	40
University of Mary Hardin-Baylor	40
University of Lynchburg	40
Marshall B. Ketchum University	40
Oregon Health & Science University	41
Sacred Heart University	42
Albany Medical College	42
Long Island University	42
Weil Cornell Graduate School of Medical Sciences	42
Radford University Carilion	42
Shenandoah University - Winchester	42
MGH Institute of Health Professions	44
Stony Brook University Health Science Center	44
Indiana University School of Health and Human Sciences	44
Augusta University	44
Samuel Merritt University	44
University of Colorado	44
SUNY Downstate Medical Center	45

PA School	# enrolled in 2020
University of the Sciences	45
Valparaiso University	45
Ohio University	45
Florida International University Herbert Wertheim College of Medicine	45
University of Texas Health Science Center - San Antonio	45
University of the Pacific	45
Saint Louis University	46
University of Washington - MEDEX Northwest, Seattle	46
University of Saint Joseph	47
Marist College	48
Chatham University	48
University of Pittsburgh	48
Bryant University	48
Wichita State University	48
South University, Tampa	48
University of Tampa	48
Sullivan University	48
Touro University California	48
Salus University	49
University of New England	50
Tufts University	50
Rutgers University	50
Seton Hill University	50
Thomas Jefferson University - City Center	50
Des Moines University	50
University of Michigan - Flint	50
Wayne State University	50
University of Nebraska Medical Center - Omaha	50
Ohio Dominican University	50
University of South Florida	50
University of Oklahoma - Oklahoma City	50
Bethel University (TN)	50
Trevecca Nazarene University	50
Northern Arizona University	50
Chapman University	50

PA School	# enrolled in 2020
Southern California University of Health Sciences	50
Rocky Mountain University of Health Professions	50
Northeastern University	52
Slippery Rock University	52
University of Wisconsin-Madison	52
Nova Southeastern University - Fort Myers	53
Quinnipiac University	54
Emory University	54
Campbell University	54
D'Youville College	55
Saint Francis University	55
Miami Dade College	55
New York Institute of Technology	56
Texas Tech University Health Sciences Center	57
Gannon University - Erie, PA	58
Philadelphia College of Osteopathic Medicine (PCOM)	59
Seton Hall University	60
Marywood University	60
University of Detroit Mercy	60
Kettering College	60
Florida State University	60
Nova Southeastern University - Jacksonville	60
University of Florida	60
Medical University of South Carolina	60
Lincoln Memorial University - Knoxville	60
South College - Nashville	60
University of Texas Southwestern Medical Center	60
University of Southern California	60
Pacific University	60
Nova Southeastern University - Orlando	64
Wake Forest University - Winston Salem	64
Daemen College	65
Mercy College	65
Touro College - Long Island	65
Touro College Manhattan	65
University of California, Davis	65

PA School	# enrolled in 2020
Rosalind Franklin University of Medicine	67
George Washington University	68
University of Utah	68
Mercer University	70
A.T. Still University - Arizona School of Health Sciences	70
University of Alabama at Birmingham	71
Lock Haven University	72
Pace University - Lenox Hill Hospital, NYC	73
Hofstra University	75
Le Moyne College	75
St. John's University	75
King's College	75
Butler University	75
Marquette University	75
Nova Southeastern University - Fort Lauderdale	75
University of North Texas HS Center Fort Worth	75
Drexel University	77
DeSales University	80
Eastern Virginia Medical School	80
Touro University Nevada	80
South College - Knoxville	85
Midwestern University - Downers Grove	86
Duke University	90
University of Texas Medical Branch at Galveston	90
Midwestern University - Glendale	90
Lincoln Memorial University	96
Western University of Health Sciences	98
MCPHS - Boston	100
Barry University - Miami	100
Barry University - St. Petersburg	100
University of Texas Rio Grande Valley	100
Arcadia University	105
Thomas Jefferson University - East Falls	109
Thomas Jefferson University - New Jersey	109
MCPHS - Worcester	125
MCPHS - Manchester	125

PA School	# enrolled in 2020
U.S. Army Medical Center of Excellence IPAP	N/A
Pennsylvania College of Technology	N/A
Samford University	N/A
South University, Savannah	N/A
Louisiana State University Health Sciences Center Shreveport	N/A
Lipscomb University	N/A

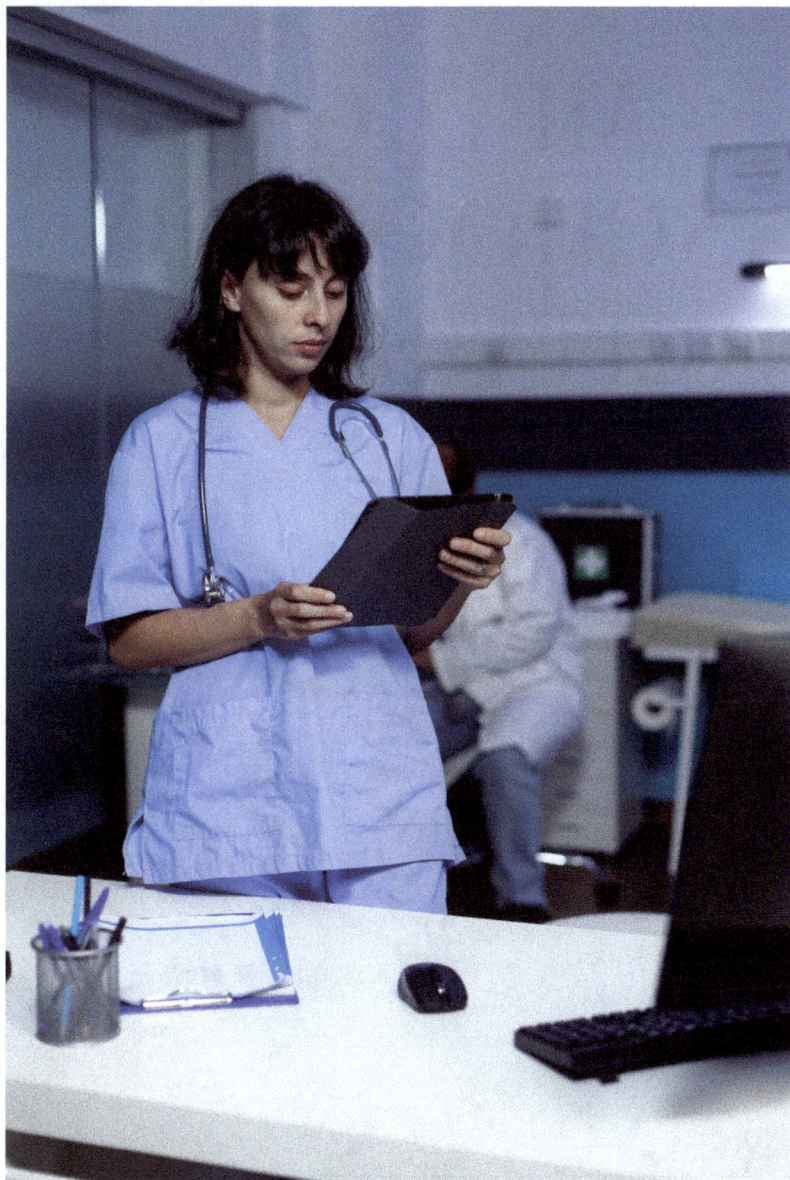

CHAPTER 11

MEDICAL SCHOOLS BY CITY/STATE

MD Schools	City	State	Website
University of Alabama School of Medicine	Birmingham	AL	https://www.uab.edu/medicine/home/
University of South Alabama College of Medicine	Mobile	AL	https://www.southalabama.edu/colleges/com/
University of Arkansas for Medical Sciences College of Medicine	Little Rock	AR	https://medicine.uams.edu/
The University of Arizona College of Medicine – Phoenix	Phoenix	AZ	https://phoenixmed.arizona.edu/
The University of Arizona College of Medicine – Tucson	Tucson	AZ	https://medicine.arizona.edu/
California University of Science and Medicine – School of Medicine	Colton	CA	https://www.cusm.org/
California Northstate University College of Medicine	Elk Grove	CA	https://medicine.cnsu.edu/
University of California, Irvine School of Medicine	Irvine	CA	https://www.som.uci.edu/
University of California, San Diego School of Medicine	La Jolla	CA	https://medschool.ucsd.edu/Pages/default.aspx
Loma Linda University School of Medicine	Loma Linda	CA	https://medicine.llu.edu/
David Geffen School of Medicine at UCLA	Los Angeles	CA	https://medschool.ucla.edu/
Keck School of Medicine of the University of Southern California	Los Angeles	CA	https://keck.usc.edu/
Kaiser Permanente School of Medicine	Pasadena	CA	https://medschool.kp.org/
University of California, Riverside School of Medicine	Riverside	CA	https://medschool.ucr.edu/
University of California, Davis School of Medicine	Sacramento	CA	https://health.ucdavis.edu/medschool/
University of California, San Francisco School of Medicine	San Francisco	CA	https://medschool.ucsf.edu/
Stanford University School of Medicine	Stanford	CA	http://med.stanford.edu/
University of Colorado School of Medicine	Aurora	CO	https://medschool.cuanschutz.edu/
University of Connecticut School of Medicine	Farmington	CT	https://medicine.uconn.edu/

MD Schools	City	State	Website
Frank H. Netter MD School of Medicine at Quinnipiac University	Hamden	CT	https://www.qu.edu/schools/medicine.html
Yale School of Medicine	New Haven	CT	https://medicine.yale.edu/
Georgetown University School of Medicine	Washington	DC	https://som.georgetown.edu/
Howard University College of Medicine	Washington	DC	https://medicine.howard.edu/
The George Washington University School of Medicine and Health Sciences	Washington	DC	https://smhs.gwu.edu/
Charles E. Schmidt College of Medicine at Florida Atlantic University	Boca Raton	FL	http://med.fau.edu/
Nova Southeastern University Dr. Kiran C. Patel College of Allopathic Medicine	Davie	FL	https://md.nova.edu/index.html
University of Florida College of Medicine	Gainesville	FL	https://med.ufl.edu/
Florida International University Herbert Wertheim College of Medicine	Miami	FL	https://medicine.fiu.edu/
University of Miami Leonard M. Miller School of Medicine	Miami	FL	https://med.miami.edu/
University of Central Florida College of Medicine	Orlando	FL	https://med.ucf.edu/
The Florida State University College of Medicine	Tallahassee	FL	https://med.fsu.edu/
USF Health Morsani College of Medicine	Tampa	FL	https://health.usf.edu/medicine
Emory University School of Medicine	Atlanta	GA	https://www.med.emory.edu/
Morehouse School of Medicine	Atlanta	GA	https://www.msm.edu/
Medical College of Georgia at Augusta University	Augusta	GA	https://www.augusta.edu/mcg/
Mercer University School of Medicine	Macon	GA	https://medicine.mercer.edu/
John A. Burns School of Medicine University of Hawaii at Manoa	Honolulu	HI	https://jabsom.hawaii.edu/

MD Schools	City	State	Website
University of Iowa Roy J. and Lucille A. Carver College of Medicine	Iowa City	IA	https://medicine.uiowa.edu/
Carle Illinois College of Medicine	Champaign	IL	https://medicine.illinois.edu/
Northwestern University Feinberg School of Medicine	Chicago	IL	https://www.feinberg.northwestern.edu/
Rush Medical College of Rush University Medical Center	Chicago	IL	https://www.rushu.rush.edu/rush-medical-college
University of Chicago Division of the Biological Sciences, The Pritzker School of Medicine	Chicago	IL	https://pritzker.uchicago.edu/
University of Illinois College of Medicine	Chicago	IL	https://medicine.uic.edu/
Loyola University Chicago Stritch School of Medicine	Maywood	IL	https://ssom.luc.edu/
Chicago Medical School at Rosalind Franklin University of Medicine and Science	North Chicago	IL	https://www.rosalindfranklin.edu/academics/chicago-medical-school/
Southern Illinois University School of Medicine	Springfield	IL	https://www.siumed.edu/
Indiana University School of Medicine	Indianapolis	IN	https://medicine.iu.edu/
University of Kansas School of Medicine	Kansas City	KS	http://www.kumc.edu/school-of-medicine.html
University of Kentucky College of Medicine	Lexington	KY	https://med.uky.edu/
University of Louisville School of Medicine	Louisville	KY	http://louisville.edu/medicine
LSU Health Sciences Center School of Medicine in New Orleans	New Orleans	LA	https://www.medschool.lsuhsc.edu/
Tulane University School of Medicine	New Orleans	LA	https://medicine.tulane.edu/
Louisiana State University School of Medicine in Shreveport	Shreveport	LA	https://www.lsuhs.edu/our-schools/school-of-medicine
Boston University School of Medicine	Boston	MA	https://www.bumc.bu.edu/busm/
Harvard Medical School	Boston	MA	https://hms.harvard.edu/

MD Schools	City	State	Website
Tufts University School of Medicine	Boston	MA	https://medicine.tufts.edu/
University of Massachusetts Medical School	North Worcester	MA	https://www.umassmed.edu/
Johns Hopkins University School of Medicine	Baltimore	MD	https://www.hopkinsmedicine.org/som/
University of Maryland School of Medicine	Baltimore	MD	https://www.medschool.umaryland.edu/
Uniformed Services University of the Health Sciences, F. Edward Hébert School of Medicine	Bethesda	MD	https://www.usuhs.edu/medschool
University of Michigan Medical School	Ann Arbor	MI	https://medicine.umich.edu/medschool/home
Wayne State University School of Medicine	Detroit	MI	https://www.med.wayne.edu/
Michigan State University College of Human Medicine	East Lansing	MI	http://humanmedicine.msu.edu/
Western Michigan University Homer Stryker M.D. School of Medicine	Kalamazoo	MI	https://med.wmich.edu/
Central Michigan University College of Medicine	Mt Pleasant	MI	https://www.cmich.edu/colleges/med/Pages/default.aspx
Oakland University William Beaumont School of Medicine	Rochester	MI	https://oakland.edu/medicine/
University of Minnesota Medical School	Minneapolis	MN	https://med.umn.edu/
Mayo Clinic Alix School of Medicine	Rochester	MN	https://college.mayo.edu/academics/school-of-medicine/
University of Missouri-Columbia School of Medicine	Columbia	MO	https://medicine.missouri.edu/
University of Missouri-Kansas City School of Medicine	Kansas City	MO	https://med.umkc.edu/
Saint Louis University School of Medicine	St. Louis	MO	https://www.slu.edu/medicine/index.php
Washington University in St. Louis School of Medicine	St. Louis	MO	https://medicine.wustl.edu/
University of Mississippi School of Medicine	Jackson	MS	https://www.umc.edu/som/SOM_Home.html

MD Schools	City	State	Website
University of North Carolina School of Medicine	Chapel Hill	NC	https://www.med.unc.edu/
Duke University School of Medicine	Durham	NC	https://medschool.duke.edu/
The Brody School of Medicine at East Carolina University	Greenville	NC	https://medicine.ecu.edu/
Wake Forest School of Medicine of Wake Forest Baptist Medical Center	Winston-Salem	NC	https://school.wakehealth.edu/
University of North Dakota School of Medicine and Health Sciences	Grand Forks	ND	https://med.und.edu/
Creighton University School of Medicine	Omaha	NE	https://medschool.creighton.edu/
University of Nebraska College of Medicine	Omaha	NE	https://www.unmc.edu/com/
Geisel School of Medicine at Dartmouth	Hanover	NH	https://geiselmed.dartmouth.edu/
Cooper Medical School of Rowan University	Camden	NJ	https://cmsru.rowan.edu/
Rutgers, Robert Wood Johnson Medical School	New Brunswick	NJ	http://rwjms.rutgers.edu/
Rutgers New Jersey Medical School	Newark	NJ	http://njms.rutgers.edu/
Hackensack-Meridian School of Medicine at Seton Hall University	Nutley	NJ	https://www.shu.edu/medicine/
University of New Mexico School of Medicine	Albuquerque	NM	https://hsc.unm.edu/school-of-medicine/
University of Nevada, Las Vegas School of Medicine	Las Vegas	NV	https://www.unlv.edu/medicine
University of Nevada, Reno School of Medicine	Reno	NV	https://med.unr.edu/
Albany Medical College	Albany	NY	https://www.amc.edu/Academic/index.cfm
Albert Einstein College of Medicine	Bronx	NY	https://www.einstein.yu.edu/
State University of New York Downstate Medical Center College of Medicine	Brooklyn	NY	https://www.downstate.edu/college-of-medicine/

MD Schools	City	State	Website
Jacobs School of Medicine and Biomedical Sciences at the University at Buffalo	Buffalo	NY	http://medicine.buffalo.edu/
New York University Long Island School of Medicine	Mineola	NY	https://medli.nyu.edu/
Columbia University Vagelos College of Physicians and Surgeons	New York	NY	https://www.ps.columbia.edu/
CUNY School of Medicine	New York	NY	https://www.ccny.cuny.edu/csom
Donald and Barbara Zucker School of Medicine at Hofstra/Northwell	New York	NY	https://medicine.hofstra.edu/
Icahn School of Medicine at Mount Sinai	New York	NY	https://icahn.mssm.edu/
New York University Grossman School of Medicine	New York	NY	https://med.nyu.edu/our-community/about-us
Weill Cornell Medicine	New York	NY	https://weill.cornell.edu/
University of Rochester School of Medicine and Dentistry	Rochester	NY	https://www.urmc.rochester.edu/smd.aspx
Renaissance School of Medicine at Stony Brook University	Stony Brook	NY	https://renaissance.stonybrookmedicine.edu/
State University of New York Upstate Medical University College of Medicine	Syracuse	NY	https://www.upstate.edu/com/
New York Medical College	Valhalla	NY	https://www.nymc.edu/
University of Cincinnati College of Medicine	Cincinnati	OH	https://www.med.uc.edu/
Case Western Reserve University School of Medicine	Cleveland	OH	https://case.edu/medicine/
The Ohio State University College of Medicine	Columbus	OH	https://medicine.osu.edu/
Boonshoft School of Medicine Wright State University	Dayton	OH	https://medicine.wright.edu/
Northeast Ohio Medical University College of Medicine	Rootstown	OH	https://www.neomed.edu/
The University of Toledo College of Medicine and Life Sciences	Toledo	OH	https://www.utoledo.edu/med/
University of Oklahoma College of Medicine	Oklahoma City	OK	https://medicine.ouhsc.edu/

MD Schools	City	State	Website
Oregon Health & Science University School of Medicine	Portland	OR	https://www.ohsu.edu/school-of-medicine
Penn State College of Medicine	Hershey	PA	https://med.psu.edu/
Drexel University College of Medicine	Philadelphia	PA	https://drexel.edu/medicine/
Lewis Katz School of Medicine at Temple University	Philadelphia	PA	https://medicine.temple.edu/
Sidney Kimmel Medical College at Thomas Jefferson University	Philadelphia	PA	https://www.jefferson.edu/university/skmc.html
The Raymond and Ruth Perelman School of Medicine at the University of Pennsylvania	Philadelphia	PA	https://www.med.upenn.edu/
University of Pittsburgh School of Medicine	Pittsburgh	PA	https://www.medschool.pitt.edu/
Geisinger Commonwealth School of Medicine	Scranton	PA	https://www.geisinger.edu/education
Universidad Central del Caribe School of Medicine	Bayamon	PR	http://www.uccaribe.edu/medicine/
San Juan Bautista School of Medicine	Caguas	PR	https://www.sanjuanbautista.edu/
Ponce Health Sciences University School of Medicine	Ponce	PR	https://www.psm.edu/school-of-medicine/
University of Puerto Rico School of Medicine	San Juan	PR	https://md.rcm.upr.edu/md-program/
The Warren Alpert Medical School of Brown University	Providence	RI	https://medical.brown.edu/
Medical University of South Carolina College of Medicine	Charleston	SC	https://medicine.musc.edu/
University of South Carolina School of Medicine, Columbia	Columbia	SC	https://www.sc.edu/study/colleges_schools/medicine/index.php
University of South Carolina School of Medicine, Greenville	Greenville	SC	https://www.sc.edu/study/colleges_schools/medicine_greenville/index.php
University of South Dakota Sanford School of Medicine	Sioux Falls	SD	https://www.usd.edu/medicine
East Tennessee State University James H. Quillen College of Medicine	Johnson City	TN	https://www.etsu.edu/com/

MD Schools	City	State	Website
University of Tennessee Health Science Center College of Medicine	Memphis	TN	https://www.uthsc.edu/medicine/
Meharry Medical College School of Medicine	Nashville	TN	https://home.mmc.edu/
Vanderbilt University School of Medicine	Nashville	TN	https://medschool.vanderbilt.edu/
The University of Texas at Austin Dell Medical School	Austin	TX	https://dellmed.utexas.edu/
Texas A&M University Health Science Center College of Medicine	Bryan	TX	https://medicine.tamu.edu/
The University of Texas Southwestern Medical School	Dallas	TX	https://www.utsouthwestern.edu/education/medical-school/
The University of Texas Rio Grande Valley School of Medicine	Edinburg	TX	https://www.utrgv.edu/school-of-medicine/
Paul L. Foster School of Medicine Texas Tech University Health Sciences Center	El Paso	TX	https://elpaso.ttuhsc.edu/som/
TCU and UNTHSC School of Medicine	Fort Worth	TX	https://mdschool.tcu.edu/
The University of Texas Medical Branch at Galveston School of Medicine	Galveston	TX	https://som.utmb.edu/
Baylor College of Medicine	Houston	TX	https://www.bcm.edu/
McGovern Medical School at The University of Texas Health Science Center at Houston	Houston	TX	https://med.uth.edu/
University of Houston College of Medicine	Houston	TX	https://www.uh.edu/medicine/
Texas Tech University Health Sciences Center School of Medicine	Lubbock	TX	https://www.ttuhsc.edu/medicine/default.aspx
The University of Texas Health Science Center at San Antonio Joe R. and Teresa Lozano Long School of Medicine	San Antonio	TX	http://som.uthscsa.edu/
University of Utah School of Medicine	Salt Lake City	UT	https://medicine.utah.edu/

MD Schools	City	State	Website
University of Virginia School of Medicine	Charlottesville	VA	https://med.virginia.edu/
Eastern Virginia Medical School	Norfolk	VA	https://www.evms.edu/
Virginia Commonwealth University School of Medicine	Richmond	VA	https://medschool.vcu.edu/
Virginia Tech Carilion School of Medicine	Roanoke	VA	https://medicine.vtc.vt.edu/
The Robert Larner, M.D. College of Medicine at the University of Vermont	Burlington	VT	http://www.med.uvm.edu/
University of Washington School of Medicine	Seattle	WA	https://www.uwmedicine.org/school-of-medicine
Washington State University Elson S. Floyd College of Medicine	Spokane	WA	https://medicine.wsu.edu/
University of Wisconsin School of Medicine and Public Health	Madison	WI	https://www.med.wisc.edu/
Medical College of Wisconsin	Milwaukee	WI	https://www.mcw.edu/
Marshall University Joan C. Edwards School of Medicine	Huntington	WV	https://jcesom.marshall.edu/
West Virginia University School of Medicine	Morgantown	WV	https://medicine.hsc.wvu.edu/

CHAPTER 12

DENTAL SCHOOLS BY CITY/STATE

Dental Schools	City	State	Website
University of Alabama at Birmingham School of Dentistry	Birmingham	AL	https://www.uab.edu/dentistry/home/
Midwestern University College of Dental Medicine-Arizona	Glendale	AZ	https://www.midwestern.edu/academics/our-colleges/college-of-dental-medicine%E2%80%93arizona.xml
Arizona School of Dentistry & Oral Health	Mesa	AZ	https://www.atsu.edu/arizona-school-of-dentistry-and-oral-health
California North State College of Dental Medicine	Elk Grove	CA	http://dentalmedicine.cnsu.edu/
Loma Linda University School of Dentistry	Loma Linda	CA	https://dentistry.llu.edu/
Herman Ostrow School of Dentistry of USC	Los Angeles	CA	https://dentistry.usc.edu/
University of California, Los Angeles, School of Dentistry	Los Angeles	CA	https://www.dentistry.ucla.edu/
Western University of Health Sciences College of Dental Medicine	Pomona	CA	https://www.westernu.edu/dentistry/
University of California, San Francisco, School of Dentistry	San Francisco	CA	https://dentistry.ucsf.edu/
University of the Pacific Arthur A. Dugoni School of Dentistry	San Francisco	CA	https://www.dental.pacific.edu/
University of Colorado School of Dental Medicine	Aurora	CO	http://www.ucdenver.edu/academics/colleges/dentalmedicine/Pages/DentalMedicine.aspx
University of Connecticut School of Dental Medicine	Farmington	CT	https://dentalmedicine.uconn.edu/
Howard University College of Dentistry	Washington	DC	http://healthsciences.howard.edu/education/colleges/dentistry
Lake Erie College of Osteopathic Medicine School of Dental Medicine	Bradenton	FL	https://lecom.edu/academics/school-of-dental-medicine/
Nova Southeastern University College of Dental Medicine	Davie	FL	https://dental.nova.edu/index.html

Dental Schools	City	State	Website
University of Florida College of Dentistry	Gainesville	FL	https://dental.ufl.edu/
Dental College of Georgia at Augusta University	Augusta	GA	https://www.augusta.edu/dentalmedicine/
The University of Iowa College of Dentistry & Dental Clinics	Iowa City	IA	https://www.dentistry.uiowa.edu/
Southern Illinois University School of Dental Medicine	Alton	IL	http://www.siue.edu/dental/
University of Illinois at Chicago College of Dentistry	Chicago	IL	https://dentistry.uic.edu/
Midwestern University College of Dental Medicine-Illinois	Downers Grove	IL	https://www.midwestern.edu/academics/our-colleges/college-of-dental-medicine%E2%80%93illinois.xml
Indiana University School of Dentistry	Indianapolis	IN	https://dentistry.iu.edu/
University of Kentucky College of Dentistry	Lexington	KY	https://dentistry.uky.edu/
University of Louisville School of Dentistry	Louisville	KY	https://louisville.edu/dentistry
Louisiana State University Health New Orleans School of Dentistry	New Orleans	LA	https://www.lsusd.lsuhsc.edu/
Boston University Henry M. Goldman School of Dental Medicine	Boston	MA	http://www.bu.edu/dental/
Harvard School of Dental Medicine	Boston	MA	https://hsdm.harvard.edu/
Tufts University School of Dental Medicine	Boston	MA	https://dental.tufts.edu/
University of Maryland School of Dentistry	Baltimore	MD	https://www.dental.umaryland.edu/
University of New England College of Dental Medicine	Portland	ME	https://www.une.edu/dentalmedicine
University of Michigan School of Dentistry	Ann Arbor	MI	https://www.dent.umich.edu/
University of Detroit Mercy School of Dentistry	Detroit	MI	https://dental.udmercy.edu/
University of Minnesota School of Dentistry	Minneapolis	MN	https://www.dentistry.umn.edu/

Dental Schools	City	State	Website
University of Missouri-Kansas City School of Dentistry	Kansas City	MO	https://dentistry.umkc.edu/
Missouri School of Dentistry & Oral Health	Kirksville	MO	https://www.atsu.edu/missouri-school-of-dentistry-and-oral-health
University of Mississippi Medical Center School of Dentistry	Jackson	MS	https://www.umc.edu/sod/SOD_Home.html
University of North Carolina at Chapel Hill Adams School of Dentistry	Chapel Hill	NC	https://www.dentistry.unc.edu/
East Carolina University School of Dental Medicine	Greenville	NC	https://www.ecu.edu/cs-dhs/dental/
University of Nebraska Medical Center College of Dentistry	Lincoln	NE	https://www.unmc.edu/dentistry/
Creighton University School of Dentistry	Omaha	NE	https://dentistry.creighton.edu/
Rutgers, The State University of New Jersey, School of Dental Medicine	Newark	NJ	http://sdm.rutgers.edu/
University of Nevada, Las Vegas, School of Dental Medicine	Las Vegas	NV	https://www.unlv.edu/dental
University at Buffalo School of Dental Medicine	Buffalo	NY	http://dental.buffalo.edu/
Touro College of Dental Medicine at New York Medical College	Hawthorne	NY	https://dental.touro.edu/
Columbia University College of Dental Medicine	New York	NY	https://www.dental.columbia.edu/
NYU College of Dentistry	New York	NY	https://dental.nyu.edu/
Stony Brook University School of Dental Medicine	Stony Brook	NY	https://dentistry.stonybrookmedicine.edu/
Case Western Reserve University School of Dental Medicine	Cleveland	OH	https://case.edu/dental/
The Ohio State University College of Dentistry	Columbus	OH	https://dentistry.osu.edu/
University of Oklahoma College of Dentistry	Oklahoma City	OK	https://dentistry.ouhsc.edu/

Dental Schools	City	State	Website
Oregon Health & Science University School of Dentistry	Portland	OR	https://www.ohsu.edu/school-of-dentistry
The Maurice H. Kornberg School of Dentistry, Temple University	Philadelphia	PA	https://dentistry.temple.edu/
University of Pennsylvania School of Dental Medicine	Philadelphia	PA	https://www.dental.upenn.edu/
University of Pittsburgh School of Dental Medicine	Pittsburgh	PA	https://www.dental.pitt.edu/
University of Puerto Rico School of Dental Medicine	San Juan	PR	https://dental.rcm.upr.edu/
Medical University of South Carolina James B. Edwards College of Dental Medicine	Charleston	SC	https://dentistry.musc.edu/
University of Tennessee Health Science Center College of Dentistry	Memphis	TN	https://www.uthsc.edu/dentistry/
Meharry Medical College School of Dentistry	Nashville	TN	https://home.mmc.edu/school-of-dentistry/
Texas A&M College of Dentistry	Dallas	TX	https://dentistry.tamu.edu/
Texas Tech University Health Sciences Center El Paso Woody L. Hunt School of Dental Medicine	El Paso	TX	https://elpaso.ttuhsc.edu/sdm/
The University of Texas School of Dentistry at Houston	Houston	TX	https://dentistry.uth.edu/
UT Health San Antonio School of Dentistry	San Antonio	TX	https://www.uthscsa.edu/academics/dental
University of Utah School of Dentistry	Salt Lake City	UT	https://dentistry.utah.edu/
Roseman University of Health Sciences College of Dental Medicine – South Jordan, Utah	South Jordan	UT	https://dental.roseman.edu/
Virginia Commonwealth University School of Dentistry	Richmond	VA	https://dentistry.vcu.edu/
University of Washington School of Dentistry	Seattle	WA	https://dental.washington.edu/

Dental Schools	City	State	Website
Marquette University School of Dentistry	Milwaukee	WI	https://www.marquette.edu/dentistry/
West Virginia University School of Dentistry	Morgantown	WV	https://dentistry.wvu.edu/

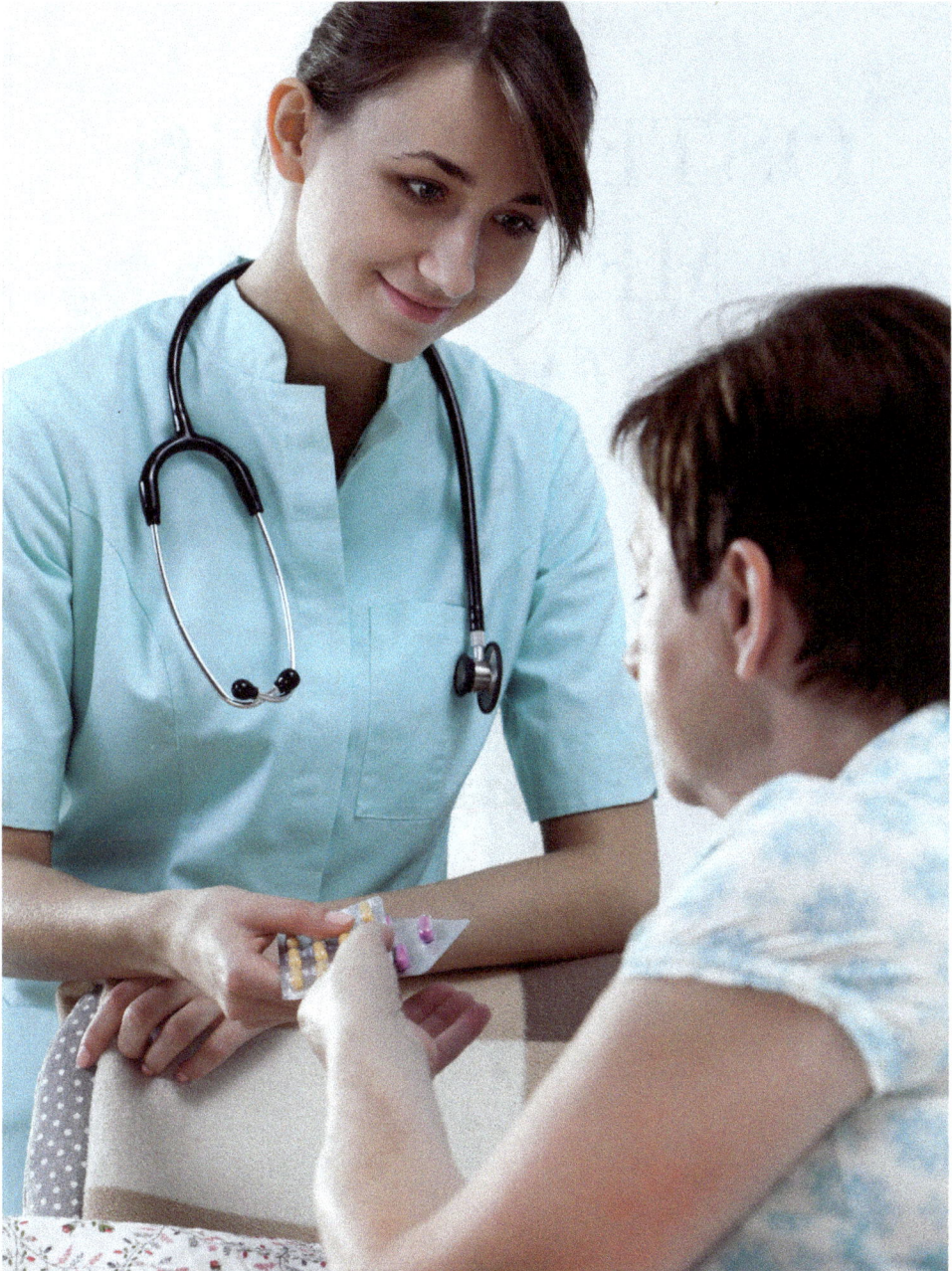

CHAPTER 13

OSTEOPATHIC MEDICAL SCHOOLS BY CITY/STATE

DO Schools	City	State	Website
Edward Via College of Osteopathic Medicine (VCOM - Auburn Campus)	Auburn	AL	https://www.vcom.edu/
Alabama College of Osteopathic Medicine (ACOM)	Dothan	AL	https://www.acom.edu/
Arkansas College of Osteopathic Medicine (ARCOM)	Fort Smith	AR	https://acheedu.org/arcom/
New York Institute of Technology College of Osteopathic Medicine at Arkansas State (NYITCOM)	Jonesboro	AR	https://www.nyit.edu/arkansas
Midwestern University Arizona College of Osteopathic Medicine (MWU/AZCOM)	Glendale	AZ	https://www.midwestern.edu/academics/our-colleges/arizona-college-of-osteopathic-medicine.xml
A.T. Still University, School of Osteopathic Medicine in Arizona (ATSU-SOMA)	Mesa	AZ	https://www.atsu.edu/school-of-osteopathic-medicine-arizona
California Health Sciences University College of Osteopathic Medicine (CHSU-COM)	Clovis	CA	https://osteopathic.chsu.edu/
Western University of Health Sciences College of Osteopathic Medicine of the Pacific (WesternU/COMP)	Pomona	CA	https://www.westernu.edu/osteopathic/
Touro University College of Osteopathic Medicine-California (TUCOM)	Vallejo	CA	http://com.tu.edu/
Rocky Vista University College of Osteopathic Medicine (RVUCOM)	Parker	CO	http://www.rvu.edu/rvu-su/college-of-osteopathic-medicine/
Lake Erie College of Osteopathic Medicine-Bradenton (LECOM-Bradenton)	Bradenton	FL	https://lecom.edu/
Nova Southeastern University Dr. Kiran C. Patel College of Osteopathic Medicine (NSU-KPCOM-Clearwater)	Clearwater	FL	https://osteopathic.nova.edu/index.html
Nova Southeastern University Dr. Kiran C. Patel College of Osteopathic Medicine (NSU-KPCOM)	Fort Lauderdale	FL	https://osteopathic.nova.edu/index.html
Philadelphia College of Osteopathic Medicine South Georgia (PCOM South Georgia)	Moultrie	GA	https://www.pcom.edu/south-georgia/

DO Schools	City	State	Website
Philadelphia College of Osteopathic Medicine Georgia (PCOM Georgia)	Suwanee	GA	https://www.pcom.edu/campuses/georgia-campus/
Des Moines University College of Osteopathic Medicine (DMU-COM)	Des Moines	IA	https://www.dmu.edu/do/
Idaho College of Osteopathic Medicine (ICOM)	Meridian	ID	https://www.idahocom.org/
Midwestern University Chicago College of Osteopathic Medicine (MWU/CCOM)	Downers Grove	IL	https://www.midwestern.edu/academics/degrees-and-programs/doctor-of-osteopathic-medicine-il.xml
Marian University College of Osteopathic Medicine (MU-COM)	Indianapolis	IN	https://www.marian.edu/osteopathic-medical-school
University of Pikeville Kentucky College of Osteopathic Medicine (UP-KYCOM)	Pikeville	KY	https://www.upike.edu/osteopathic-medicine/
Edward Via College of Osteopathic Medicine-Monroe Campus (VCOM - Monroe Campus)	Monroe	LA	https://www.vcom.edu/louisiana
University of New England College of Osteopathic Medicine (UNECOM)	Biddeford	ME	https://www.une.edu/com
Michigan State University College of Osteopathic Medicine (MSUCOM-MUC)	Clinton Twp	MI	https://com.msu.edu/
Michigan State University College of Osteopathic Medicine (MSUCOM-DMC)	Detroit	MI	https://com.msu.edu/
Michigan State University College of Osteopathic Medicine (MSUCOM)	East Lansing	MI	https://com.msu.edu/
Minnesota College of Osteopathic Medicine	Gaylord	MN	N/A
Kansas City University of Medicine and Biosciences College of Osteopathic Medicine (KCU-COM)	Kansas City	MO	http://www.kcumb.edu/programs/college-of-osteopathic-medicine
A. T. Still University Kirksville College of Osteopathic Medicine (ATSU-KCOM)	Kirksville	MO	https://www.atsu.edu/kirksville-college-of-osteopathic-medicine

DO Schools	City	State	Website
William Carey University College of Osteopathic Medicine (WCUCOM)	Hattiesburg	MS	https://www.wmcarey.edu/College/Osteopathic-Medicine
Campbell University Jerry M. Wallace School of Osteopathic Medicine (CUSOM)	Lillington	NC	https://medicine.campbell.edu/
Rowan University School of Osteopathic Medicine (RowanSOM)	Stratford	NJ	https://som.rowan.edu/
Burrell College of Osteopathic Medicine (BCOM)	Las Cruces	NM	https://bcomnm.org/
Kansas City University of Medicine and Biosciences College of Osteopathic Medicine (KCU-COM-Joplin)	Joplin	NO	http://www.kcumb.edu/programs/college-of-osteopathic-medicine
Touro University Nevada College of Osteopathic Medicine (TUNCOM)	Henderson	NV	https://tun.touro.edu/programs/osteopathic-medicine/
Lake Erie College of Osteopathic Medicine - Elmira (LECOM-Elmira)	Elmira	NY	https://lecom.edu/
Touro College of Osteopathic Medicine (TouroCOM-Middletown)	Middletown	NY	https://tourocom.touro.edu/
Touro College of Osteopathic Medicine (TouroCOM-Harlem)	New York	NY	https://tourocom.touro.edu/
New York Institute of Technology College of Osteopathic Medicine (NYITCOM)	Old Westbury	NY	https://www.nyit.edu/medicine
Ohio University Heritage College of Osteopathic Medicine (OU-HCOM)	Athens	OH	https://www.ohio.edu/medicine/
Ohio University Heritage College of Osteopathic Medicine in Dublin (OU-HCOM-Dublin)	Dublin	OH	https://www.ohio.edu/medicine/
Ohio University Heritage College of Osteopathic Medicine in Cleveland (OU-HCOM-Cleveland)	Warrensville Heights	OH	https://www.ohio.edu/medicine/
Oklahoma State University Center for Health Sciences College of Osteopathic Medicine - Tahlequah (OSU-COM Tahlequah)	Tahlequah	OK	https://health.okstate.edu/com/index.html

DO Schools	City	State	Website
Oklahoma State University Center for Health Sciences College of Osteopathic Medicine (OSU-COM)	Tulsa	OK	https://health.okstate.edu/com/index.html
Western University of Health Sciences College of Osteopathic Medicine of the Pacific-Northwest (WesternU/COMP-Northwest)	Lebanon	OR	https://www.westernu.edu/northwest/
Lake Erie College of Osteopathic Medicine-Erie (LECOM)	Erie	PA	https://lecom.edu/
Lake Erie College of Osteopathic Medicine - Seton Hill (LECOM-Seton Hill)	Greensburg	PA	https://lecom.edu/
Philadelphia College of Osteopathic Medicine (PCOM)	Philadelphia	PA	https://www.pcom.edu/
Edward Via College of Osteopathic Medicine-Carolinas Campus (VCOM - Carolinas Campus)	Spartanburg	SC	https://www.vcom.edu/carolinas
Lincoln Memorial University DeBusk College of Osteopathic Medicine (LMU-DCOM)	Harrogate	TN	https://www.lmunet.edu/debusk-college-of-osteopathic-medicine/index.php
Lincoln Memorial University DeBusk College of Osteopathic Medicine - Knoxville (LMU-DCOM Knoxville)	Knoxville	TN	https://www.lmunet.edu/debusk-college-of-osteopathic-medicine/index.php
University of North Texas Health Science Center Texas College of Osteopathic Medicine (UNTHSC/TCOM)	Fort Worth	TX	https://www.unthsc.edu/texas-college-of-osteopathic-medicine/
Sam Houston State University College of Osteopathic Medicine	Huntsville	TX	https://www.shsu.edu/academics/osteopathic-medicine/
University of the Incarnate Word School of Osteopathic Medicine (UIWSOM)	San Antonio	TX	https://osteopathic-medicine.uiw.edu/
Rocky Vista University College of Osteopathic Medicine (RVUCOM-SU Campus)	Ivins	UT	http://www.rvu.edu/rvu-su/college-of-osteopathic-medicine/
Noorda College of Osteopathic Medicine	Provo	UT	https://noordacom.org/

DO Schools	City	State	Website
Edward Via College of Osteopathic Medicine (VCOM-Virginia Campus)	Blacksburg	VA	https://www.vcom.edu/virginia
Liberty University College of Osteopathic Medicine (LUCOM)	Lynchburg	VA	https://www.liberty.edu/lucom/
Pacific Northwest University of Health Sciences College of Osteopathic Medicine (PNWU-COM)	Yakima	WA	https://www.pnwu.edu/
West Virginia School of Osteopathic Medicine (WVSOM)	Lewisburg	WV	https://www.wvsom.edu/

CHAPTER 14

PHARMACY SCHOOLS BY CITY/STATE

PharmD Schools	City	State	Website
Auburn University Harrison School of Pharmacy	Auburn	AL	https://pharmacy.auburn.edu/
Samford University McWhorter School of Pharmacy	Birmingham	AL	https://www.samford.edu/pharmacy/
University of Arkansas for Medical Sciences College of Pharmacy	Little Rock	AR	https://pharmacy.uams.edu/
Harding University College of Pharmacy	Searcy	AR	https://www.harding.edu/academics/colleges-departments/pharmacy
Midwestern University College of Pharmacy-Glendale	Glendale	AZ	https://www.midwestern.edu/academics/our-col-leges/college-of-pharma-cy%E2%80%93glendale.xml
University of Arizona College of Pharmacy	Tucson	AZ	https://www.pharmacy.arizona.edu/
Keck Graduate Institute (KGI) School of Pharmacy and Health Sciences	Claremont	CA	https://www.kgi.edu/academics/school-of-pharmacy-and-health-sciences/overview/
California Health Sciences University College of Pharmacy	Clovis	CA	https://pharmacy.chsu.edu/
California Northstate University College of Pharmacy	Elk Grove	CA	https://pharmacy.cnsu.edu/
Marshall B. Ketchum University College of Pharmacy	Fullerton	CA	https://www.ketchum.edu/pharmacy
Chapman University School of Pharmacy	Irvine	CA	https://www.chapman.edu/pharmacy/index.aspx
University of California, San Diego Skaggs School of Pharmacy & Pharmaceutical Sciences	La Jolla	CA	https://pharmacy.ucsd.edu/
Loma Linda University School of Pharmacy	Loma Linda	CA	https://pharmacy.llu.edu/
West Coast University School of Pharmacy	Los Angeles	CA	https://westcoastuniversity.edu/programs/doctor-pharmacy.html
University of Southern California School of Pharmacy	Los Angeles	CA	https://pharmacyschool.usc.edu/
Western University of Health Sciences College of Pharmacy	Pomona	CA	https://www.westernu.edu/pharmacy/
University of California, San Francisco School of Pharmacy	San Francisco	CA	https://pharmacy.ucsf.edu/

PharmD Schools	City	State	Website
American University of Health Sciences School of Pharmacy	Signal Hill	CA	https://www.auhs.edu/academics/pharmacy/
University of the Pacific Thomas J. Long School of Pharmacy	Stockton	CA	https://www.pacific.edu/academics/schools-and-colleges/thomas-j-long-school-of-pharmacy.html
Touro University - California College of Pharmacy	Vallejo	CA	http://cop.tu.edu/
University of California, Irvine*	Irvine	CA	https://pharmsci.uci.edu/pharm-d/
University of Colorado Anschutz Medical Campus Skaggs School of Pharmacy and Pharmaceutical Sciences	Aurora	CO	http://www.ucdenver.edu/academics/colleges/pharmacy/Pages/SchoolofPharmacy.aspx
Regis University Rueckert-Hartman College for Health Professions School of Pharmacy	Denver	CO	https://www.regis.edu/academics/colleges-and-schools/rueckert-hartman/pharmacy/index
University of Connecticut School of Pharmacy	Storrs	CT	https://pharmacy.uconn.edu/
University of Saint Joseph School of Pharmacy and Physician Assistant Studies	West Hartford	CT	https://www.usj.edu/academics/academic-schools/sppas/
Howard University College of Pharmacy	Washington	DC	http://pharmacy.howard.edu/
Nova Southeastern University College of Pharmacy	Fort Lauderdale	FL	https://pharmacy.nova.edu/index.html
University of Florida College of Pharmacy	Gainesville	FL	https://pharmacy.ufl.edu/
Larkin University College of Pharmacy	Miami	FL	https://ularkin.org/pharmacy/
Florida Agricultural & Mechanical University College of Pharmacy and Pharmaceutical Sciences	Tallahassee	FL	https://pharmacy.famu.edu/
University of South Florida Health Taneja College of Pharmacy	Tampa	FL	https://health.usf.edu/pharmacy
Palm Beach Atlantic University Lloyd L. Gregory School of Pharmacy	West Palm Beach	FL	https://www.pba.edu/academics/schools/gregory-pharmacy/index.html
University of Georgia College of Pharmacy	Athens	GA	https://rx.uga.edu/

PharmD Schools	City	State	Website
Mercer University College of Pharmacy	Atlanta	GA	https://pharmacy.mercer.edu/
South University School of Pharmacy	Savannah	GA	https://www.southuniversity.edu/degree-programs/pharmacy
Philadelphia College of Osteopathic Medicine - Georgia School of Pharmacy	Suwanee	GA	https://www.pcom.edu/academics/programs-and-degrees/doctor-of-pharmacy/
University of Hawaii at Hilo Daniel K. Inouye College of Pharmacy	Hilo	HI	https://pharmacy.uhh.hawaii.edu/
Drake University College of Pharmacy and Health Sciences	Des Moines	IA	https://www.drake.edu/cphs/
University of Iowa College of Pharmacy	Iowa 52242	IA	https://pharmacy.uiowa.edu/
Idaho State University College of Pharmacy	Pocatello	ID	https://www.isu.edu/pharmacy/
University of Illinois at Chicago College of Pharmacy	Chicago	IL	https://pharmacy.uic.edu/
Chicago State University College of Pharmacy	Chicago	IL	https://www.csu.edu/collegeofpharmacy/
Southern Illinois University Edwardsville School of Pharmacy	Edwardsville	IL	https://www.siue.edu/pharmacy/
Midwestern University Chicago College of Pharmacy	IL 60515	IL	https://www.midwestern.edu/academics/degrees-and-programs/doctor-of-pharmacy-il.xml
Rosalind Franklin University of Medicine and Science College of Pharmacy	North Chicago	IL	https://www.rosalindfranklin.edu/academics/college-of-pharmacy/
Roosevelt University College of Pharmacy	Schaumburg	IL	https://www.roosevelt.edu/colleges/pharmacy
Butler University College of Pharmacy and Health Sciences	Indianapolis	IN	https://www.butler.edu/cophs
Manchester University College of Pharmacy, Natural and Health Sciences	North Manchester	IN	https://www.manchester.edu/academics/colleges/college-of-pharmacy-natural-health-sciences
Purdue University College of Pharmacy	West Lafayette	IN	https://www.pharmacy.purdue.edu/

PharmD Schools	City	State	Website
University of Kansas School of Pharmacy	Lawrence	KS	https://pharmacy.ku.edu/
University of Kentucky College of Pharmacy	Lexington	KY	https://pharmacy.uky.edu/
Sullivan University College of Pharmacy	Louisville	KY	https://www.sullivan.edu/colleges/college-of-pharmacy-and-health-sciences
University of Louisiana at Monroe College of Pharmacy	Monroe	LA	https://www.ulm.edu/pharmacy/
Xavier University of Louisiana College of Pharmacy	New Orleans	LA	https://www.xula.edu/collegeofpharmacy
MCPHS University School of Pharmacy - Boston	Boston	MA	https://www.mcphs.edu/
Northeastern University Bouvé College of Health Sciences School of Pharmacy	Boston	MA	https://bouve.northeastern.edu/pharmacy/
Western New England University College of Pharmacy	Springfield	MA	https://www1.wne.edu/pharmacy-and-health-sciences/
MCPHS University School of Pharmacy - Worcester	Worcester	MA	https://www.mcphs.edu/
University of Maryland School of Pharmacy	Baltimore	MD	https://www.pharmacy.umaryland.edu/
Notre Dame of Maryland University School of Pharmacy	Baltimore	MD	https://www.ndm.edu/colleges-schools/school-pharmacy
University of Maryland Eastern Shore School of Pharmacy and Health Professions	Princess Anne	MD	https://www.umes.edu/pharmacy/
Husson University School of Pharmacy	Bangor	ME	https://www.husson.edu/pharmacy/
University of New England College of Pharmacy	Portland	ME	https://www.une.edu/pharmacy
University of Michigan College of Pharmacy	Ann Arbor	MI	https://pharmacy.umich.edu/
Ferris State University College of Pharmacy	Big Rapids	MI	https://www.ferris.edu/pharmacy/
Wayne State University Eugene Applebaum College of Pharmacy and Health Sciences	Detroit	MI	https://cphs.wayne.edu/
University of Minnesota College of Pharmacy	Duluth	MN	https://www.pharmacy.umn.edu/

PharmD Schools	City	State	Website
University of Missouri-Kansas City School of Pharmacy	Kansas City	MO	https://pharmacy.umkc.edu/
St. Louis College of Pharmacy	St. Louis	MO	https://www.uhsp.edu/
William Carey University School of Pharmacy	Biloxi	MS	https://www.wmcarey.edu/School/Pharmacy
University of Mississippi School of Pharmacy	University	MS	https://pharmacy.olemiss.edu/
University of Montana College of Health Professions and Biomedical Sciences Skaggs School of Pharmacy	Missoula	MT	http://health.umt.edu/pharmacy/
Campbell University College of Pharmacy and Health Sciences	Buies Creek	NC	https://cphs.campbell.edu/
University of North Carolina Eshelman School of Pharmacy	Chapel Hill	NC	https://pharmacy.unc.edu/
High Point University Fred Wilson School of Pharmacy	High Point	NC	http://www.highpoint.edu/pharmacy/
Wingate University School of Pharmacy	Wingate	NC	https://www.wingate.edu/academics/graduate/pharmacy
North Dakota State University College of Health Professions School of Pharmacy	Fargo	ND	https://www.ndsu.edu/pharmacy/
University of Nebraska Medical Center College of Pharmacy	Omaha	NE	https://www.unmc.edu/pharmacy/
Creighton University School of Pharmacy and Health Professions	Omaha	NE	https://spahp.creighton.edu/
Fairleigh Dickinson University School of Pharmacy	Florham Park	NJ	https://view2.fdu.edu/academics/pharmacy/
Rutgers, the State University of New Jersey Ernest Mario School of Pharmacy	Piscataway	NJ	https://pharmacy.rutgers.edu/
University of New Mexico College of Pharmacy	Albuquerque	NM	https://hsc.unm.edu/college-of-pharmacy/
Roseman University of Health Sciences College of Pharmacy	Henderson	NV	https://pharmacy.roseman.edu/
Albany College of Pharmacy and Health Sciences School of Pharmacy and Pharmaceutical Sciences	Albany	NY	https://www.acphs.edu/

PharmD Schools	City	State	Website
Long Island University Arnold and Marie Schwartz College of Pharmacy and Health Sciences	Brooklyn	NY	https://liu.edu/Pharmacy
D'Youville College School of Pharmacy	Buffalo	NY	http://www.dyc.edu/academics/schools-and-departments/pharmacy/
University at Buffalo The State University of New York School of Pharmacy & Pharmaceutical Sciences	Buffalo	NY	http://pharmacy.buffalo.edu/
Binghamton University State University of New York School of Pharmacy and Pharmaceutical Sciences	Johnson City	NY	https://www.binghamton.edu/pharmacy-and-pharmaceutical-sciences/
Touro New York College of Pharmacy	New York	NY	https://tcop.touro.edu/
St. John's University College of Pharmacy and Health Sciences	Queens	NY	https://www.stjohns.edu/academics/programs/doctor-pharmacy
St. John Fisher College Wegmans School of Pharmacy	Rochester	NY	https://www.sjfc.edu/schools/school-of-pharmacy/
Ohio Northern University Raabe College of Pharmacy	Ada	OH	https://www.onu.edu/college-pharmacy
Cedarville University School of Pharmacy	Cedarville	OH	https://www.cedarville.edu/Academic-Schools-and-Departments/Pharmacy.aspx
University of Cincinnati James L. Winkle College of Pharmacy	Cincinnati	OH	https://pharmacy.uc.edu/
Ohio State University College of Pharmacy	Columbus	OH	https://pharmacy.osu.edu/
University of Findlay College of Pharmacy	Findlay	OH	https://www.findlay.edu/pharmacy/
Northeast Ohio Medical University College of Pharmacy	Rootstown	OH	https://www.neomed.edu/pharmacy/
University of Toledo College of Pharmacy and Pharmaceutical Sciences	Toledo	OH	https://www.utoledo.edu/pharmacy/
University of Oklahoma College of Pharmacy	Oklahoma City	OK	https://pharmacy.ouhsc.edu/

PharmD Schools	City	State	Website
Southwestern Oklahoma State University College of Pharmacy	Weatherford	OK	https://www.swosu.edu/academics/pharmacy/index.aspx
Oregon State University College of Pharmacy	Corvallis	OR	https://pharmacy.oregonstate.edu/
Pacific University School of Pharmacy	Hillsboro	OR	https://www.pacificu.edu/academics/colleges/college-health-professions/school-pharmacy
Lake Erie College of Osteopathic Medicine School of Pharmacy	Erie	PA	https://lecom.edu/academics/school-of-pharmacy/
Temple University School of Pharmacy	Philadelphia	PA	https://pharmacy.temple.edu/
Thomas Jefferson University Jefferson College of Pharmacy	Philadelphia	PA	https://www.jefferson.edu/university/pharmacy.html
University of the Sciences Philadelphia College of Pharmacy	Philadelphia	PA	https://www.usciences.edu/philadelphia-college-of-pharmacy/
Duquesne University School of Pharmacy	Pittsburgh	PA	https://www.duq.edu/academics/schools/pharmacy
University of Pittsburgh School of Pharmacy	Pittsburgh	PA	https://www.pharmacy.pitt.edu/
Wilkes University Nesbitt School of Pharmacy	Wilkes-Barre	PA	https://www.wilkes.edu/academics/colleges/nesbitt-school-of-pharmacy/index.aspx
University of Puerto Rico Medical Sciences Campus School of Pharmacy	San Juan	PR	https://farmacia.rcm.upr.edu/academic-programs/doctor-of-pharmacy-program/
University of Rhode Island College of Pharmacy	Kingston	RI	https://web.uri.edu/pharmacy/
Medical University of South Carolina College of Pharmacy	Charleston	SC	https://pharmacy.musc.edu/
Presbyterian College School of Pharmacy	Clinton	SC	https://pharmacy.presby.edu/
University of South Carolina College of Pharmacy	Columbia	SC	https://www.sc.edu/study/colleges_schools/pharmacy/index.php

PharmD Schools	City	State	Website
South Dakota State University College of Pharmacy and Allied Health Professions	Brookings	SD	https://www.sdstate.edu/pharmacy-allied-health-professions
Union University College of Pharmacy	Jackson	TN	https://www.uu.edu/programs/pharmacy/
East Tennessee State University Bill Gatton College of Pharmacy	Johnson City	TN	https://www.etsu.edu/pharmacy/
South College School of Pharmacy	Knoxville	TN	https://www.south.edu/programs/doctor-pharmacy/
University of Tennessee Health Science Center College of Pharmacy	Memphis	TN	https://www.uthsc.edu/pharmacy/
Lipscomb University College of Pharmacy and Health Sciences	Nashville	TN	https://www.lipscomb.edu/pharmacy
Belmont University College of Pharmacy	Nashville	TN	http://www.belmont.edu/pharmacy/index.html
University of Texas at Austin College of Pharmacy	Austin	TX	https://pharmacy.utexas.edu/
University of Texas at El Paso School of Pharmacy	El Paso	TX	https://www.utep.edu/pharmacy/
University of North Texas Health Science Center UNT System College of Pharmacy	Fort Worth	tx	https://www.unthsc.edu/college-of-pharmacy/
University of Houston College of Pharmacy	Houston	TX	https://www.uh.edu/pharmacy/
Texas Southern University College of Pharmacy and Health Sciences	Houston	TX	http://www.tsu.edu/academics/colleges-and-schools/college-of-pharmacy-and-health-sciences/
Texas A & M University Health Science Center Irma Lerma Rangel College of Pharmacy	Kingsville	TX	https://pharmacy.tamu.edu/
Texas Tech University Health Sciences Center Jerry H. Hodge School of Pharmacy	Lubbock	TX	https://www.ttuhsc.edu/pharmacy/default.aspx
University of the Incarnate Word Feik School of Pharmacy	San Antonio	TX	https://pharmacy.uiw.edu/
University of Texas at Tyler Ben and Maytee Fisch College of Pharmacy	Tyler	TX	https://www.uttyler.edu/pharmacy/
University of Utah College of Pharmacy	Salt Lake City	UT	https://pharmacy.utah.edu/

PharmD Schools	City	State	Website
Hampton University School of Pharmacy	Hampton	VA	http://wp.hamptonu.edu/pharmacy/
Appalachian College of Pharmacy	Oakwood	VA	https://www.acp.edu/
Virginia Commonwealth University at the Medical College of Virginia Campus School of Pharmacy	Richmond	VA	https://pharmacy.vcu.edu/
Shenandoah University Bernard J. Dunn School of Pharmacy	Winchester	VA	https://www.su.edu/pharmacy/
University of Washington School of Pharmacy	Seattle	WA	https://sop.washington.edu/
Washington State University College of Pharmacy and Pharmaceutical Sciences	Spokane	WA	https://pharmacy.wsu.edu/
University of Wisconsin-Madison School of Pharmacy	Madison	WI	https://pharmacy.wisc.edu/
Concordia University Wisconsin School of Pharmacy	Mequon	WI	https://www.cuw.edu/academics/schools/pharmacy/index.html
Medical College of Wisconsin School of Pharmacy	Milwaukee	WI	https://www.mcw.edu/education/pharmacy-school
University of Charleston School of Pharmacy	Charleston	WV	https://www.ucwv.edu/academics/schools/school-of-pharmacy/
Marshall University School of Pharmacy	Huntington	WV	https://www.marshall.edu/pharmacy/
West Virginia University School of Pharmacy	Morgantown	WV	https://pharmacy.wvu.edu/
University of Wyoming School of Pharmacy	Laramie	WY	http://www.uwyo.edu/pharmacy/

CHAPTER 15

VETERINARY MEDICAL SCHOOLS BY CITY/STATE

Vet Schools	City	State	Website
Auburn University College of Veterinary Medicine	Auburn	AL	https://www.vetmed.auburn.edu/
Tuskegee University School of Veterinary Medicine	Tuskegee	AL	https://www.tuskegee.edu/programs-courses/colleges-schools/cvm
Midwestern University College of Veterinary Medicine	Glendale	AZ	https://www.midwestern.edu/academics/our-colleges/college-of-veterinary-medicine.xml
University of Arizona College of Veterinary Medicine	Oro Valley	AZ	https://vetmed.arizona.edu/
University of California, Davis School of Veterinary Medicine	Davis	CA	https://www.vetmed.ucdavis.edu/
Western University of Health Sciences College of Veterinary Medicine	Pomona	CA	https://www.westernu.edu/veterinary/
Colorado State University College of Veterinary Medicine and Biomedical Sciences	Fort Collins	CO	https://vetmedbiosci.colostate.edu/dvm/
University of Florida College of Veterinary Medicine	Gainesville	FL	https://education.vetmed.ufl.edu/
University of Georgia College of Veterinary Medicine	Athens	GA	https://vet.uga.edu/
Iowa State University College of Veterinary Medicine	Ames	IA	https://vetmed.iastate.edu/
University of Illinois College of Veterinary Medicine	Urbana	IL	https://vetmed.illinois.edu/
Purdue University College of Veterinary Medicine	West Lafayette	IN	https://www.purdue.edu/vet/
Kansas State University College of Veterinary Medicine	Manhattan	KS	https://www.vet.k-state.edu/
Louisiana State University School of Veterinary Medicine	Baton Rouge	LA	https://www.lsu.edu/vetmed/
Tufts University School of Veterinary Medicine	North Grafton	MA	https://vet.tufts.edu/
Michigan State University College of Veterinary Medicine	East Lansing	MI	https://cvm.msu.edu/
University of Minnesota College of Veterinary Medicine	St. Paul	MN	https://vetmed.umn.edu/
University of Missouri - Columbia College of Veterinary Medicine	Columbia	MO	https://cvm.missouri.edu/

Vet Schools	City	State	Website
Mississippi State University College of Veterinary Medicine	Mississippi State	MS	https://www.vetmed.msstate.edu/
North Carolina State University College of Veterinary Medicine	Raleigh	NC	https://cvm.ncsu.edu/
Cornell University College of Veterinary Medicine	Ithica	NY	https://www.vet.cornell.edu/
Long Island University School of Veterinary Medicine	Brookville	NY	https://liu.edu/vetmed
Ohio State University College of Veterinary Medicine	Columbus	OH	https://vet.osu.edu/
Oklahoma State University College of Veterinary Medicine	Stillwater	OK	https://vetmed.okstate.edu/
Oregon State University College of Veterinary Medicine	Corvallis	OR	https://vetmed.oregonstate.edu/
University of Pennsylvania School of Veterinary Medicine	Philadelphia	PA	https://www.vet.upenn.edu/
Lincoln Memorial University College of Veterinary Medicine	Harrogate	TN	https://www.lmunet.edu/college-of-veterinary-medicine/index.php
University of Tennessee College of Veterinary Medicine	Knoxville	TN	https://vetmed.tennessee.edu/
Texas A&M University College of Veterinary Medicine & Biomedical Sciences	College Station	TX	https://vetmed.tamu.edu/
Texas Tech University School of Veterinary Medicine	Amarillo	TX	https://www.depts.ttu.edu/vetschool/
Virginia Tech Virginia-Maryland College of Veterinary Medicine	Blacksburg	VA	http://www.vetmed.vt.edu/
Washington State University College of Veterinary Medicine	Pullman	WA	https://www.vetmed.wsu.edu/
University of Wisconsin-Madison School of Veterinary Medicine	Madison	WI	https://www.vetmed.wisc.edu/

456

COMPREHENSIVE HEALTH CARE SERIES

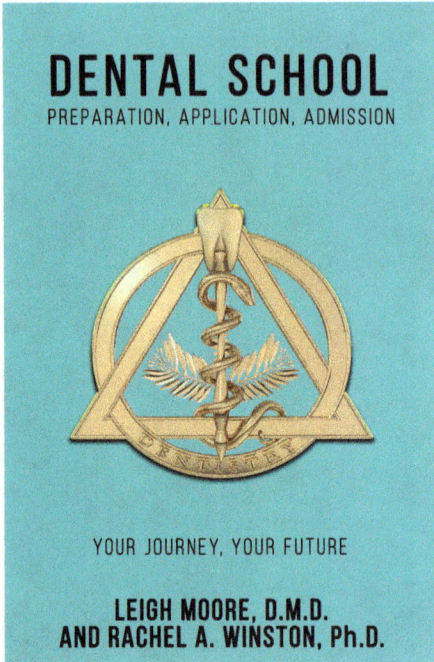

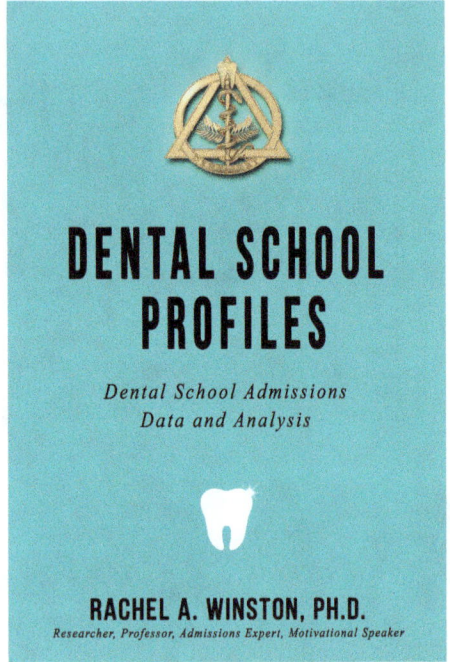

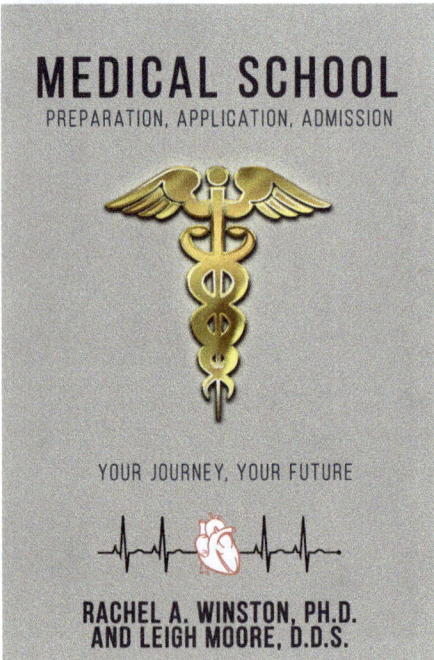

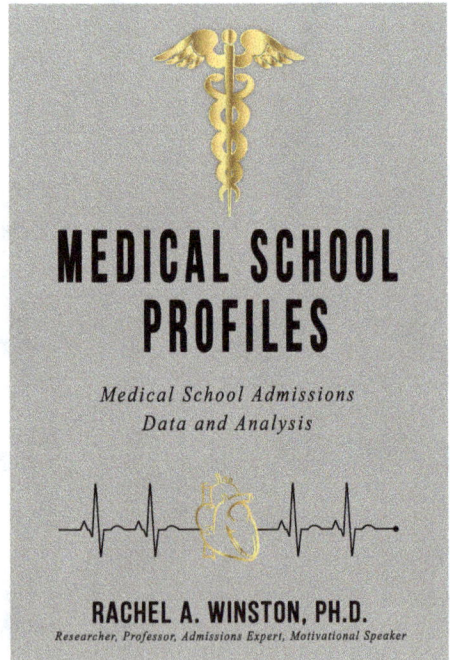

DENTAL SCHOOL
PREPARATION, APPLICATION, ADMISSION

YOUR JOURNEY, YOUR FUTURE

LEIGH MOORE, D.M.D.
AND RACHEL A. WINSTON, Ph.D.

DENTAL SCHOOL PROFILES

*Dental School Admissions
Data and Analysis*

RACHEL A. WINSTON, PH.D.
Researcher, Professor, Admissions Expert, Motivational Speaker

MEDICAL SCHOOL
PREPARATION, APPLICATION, ADMISSION

YOUR JOURNEY, YOUR FUTURE

RACHEL A. WINSTON, PH.D.
AND LEIGH MOORE, D.D.S.

MEDICAL SCHOOL PROFILES

*Medical School Admissions
Data and Analysis*

RACHEL A. WINSTON, PH.D.
Researcher, Professor, Admissions Expert, Motivational Speaker

VET SCHOOL
PREPARATION, APPLICATION, ADMISSION

YOUR JOURNEY, YOUR FUTURE

RACHEL A. WINSTON, PH.D.
Researcher, Professor, Admissions Expert, Motivational Speaker

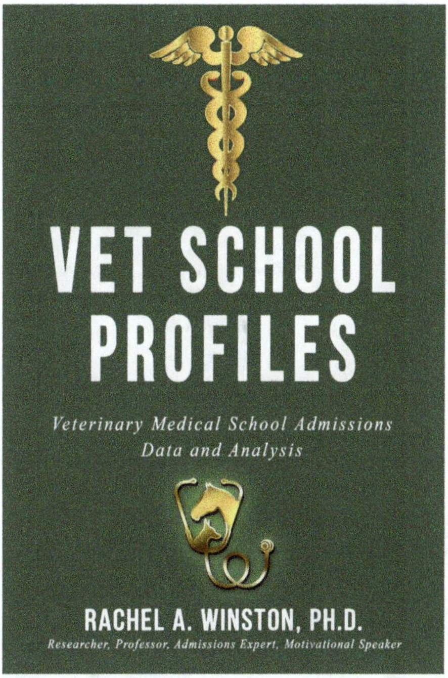

VET SCHOOL PROFILES

Veterinary Medical School Admissions Data and Analysis

RACHEL A. WINSTON, PH.D.
Researcher, Professor, Admissions Expert, Motivational Speaker

PHYSICIAN ASST. (PA) SCHOOL
PREPARATION, APPLICATION, ADMISSION

YOUR JOURNEY, YOUR FUTURE

RACHEL A. WINSTON, PH.D.
Researcher, Professor, Admissions Expert, Motivational Speaker

PHYSICIAN ASST. SCHOOL PROFILES

P.A. School Admissions Data and Analysis

RACHEL A. WINSTON, PH.D.
Researcher, Professor, Admissions Expert, Motivational Speaker

PHARM.D. SCHOOL
PREPARATION, APPLICATION, ADMISSION

YOUR JOURNEY, YOUR FUTURE

RACHEL A. WINSTON, PH.D.
Researcher, Professor, Admissions Expert, Motivational Speaker

PHARM.D.
SCHOOL PROFILES

*Pharmacy School Admissions
Data and Analysis*

RACHEL A. WINSTON, PH.D.
Researcher, Professor, Admissions Expert, Motivational Speaker

OSTEOPATHIC
MEDICAL SCHOOL
PREPARATION, APPLICATION, ADMISSION

YOUR JOURNEY, YOUR FUTURE

RACHEL A. WINSTON, PH.D.
Researcher, Professor, Admissions Expert, Motivational Speaker

OSTEO SCHOOL
PROFILES

*Osteopathic Medical School Admissions
Data and Analysis*

RACHEL A. WINSTON, PH.D.
Researcher, Professor, Admissions Expert, Motivational Speaker

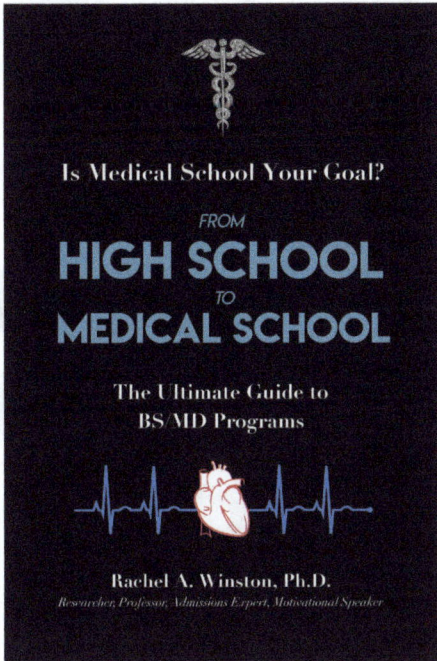

INDEX

A

B

C

D

E

F

G

H

I

J

N

O

P

Q

R

S

T

U

V

W

X

Y

www.ingramcontent.com/pod-product-compliance
Lightning Source LLC
Chambersburg PA
CBHW071959260326
41914CB00004B/863